An Introduction to Survey Research, Polling, and Data Analysis

Third Edition

An Introduction to Survey Research, Polling, and Data Analysis
Third Edition

Herbert F. Weisberg
Jon A. Krosnick
Bruce D. Bowen

SAGE Publications
International Educational and Professional Publisher
Thousand Oaks London New Delhi

For information address:

SAGE Publications, Inc.
2455 Teller Road
Thousand Oaks, California 91320
E-mail: order@sagepub.com

SAGE Publications Ltd.
6 Bonhill Street
London EC2A 4PU
United Kingdom

SAGE Publications India Pvt. Ltd.
M-32 Market
Greater Kailash I
New Delhi 110 048 India

Printed in the United States of America

Library of Congress Cataloging-in-Publication Data

Weisberg, Herbert F.
    An introduction to survey research, polling, and data analysis /
authors, Herbert F. Weisberg, Jon A. Krosnick, Bruce D. Bowen. —
3rd ed.
        p. cm.
    Rev. ed. of: An introduction to survey research and data analysis
/ Herbert F. Weisberg, Jon A. Krosnick, Bruce D. Bowen. 2nd ed.
c1989.
    Includes bibliographical references and index.
    ISBN 0-8039-7401-9 (cloth: acid-free paper). — ISBN
0-8039-7402-7 (pbk.: acid-free paper)
    1. Social surveys. 2. Social sciences—Statistical methods.
I. Krosnick, Jon A. II. Bowen, Bruce D. III. Weisberg, Herbert F.
Introduction to survey research and data analysis. IV. Title.
HN29.W3994 1996
300'.723—dc20   96-4524

96 97 98 99 10 9 8 7 6 5 4 3 2 1

This book is printed on acid-free paper.

Sage Production Editor: Diana E. Axelsen

Sage Typesetter: Danielle Dillahunt

 Brief Table
of Contents

Contents

PART 3: SURVEY GUIDELINES

 Preface

As survey results and statistical analysis are used increasingly in social science courses, beginning students inevitably ask three questions: (a) Why should we believe the results of surveys based on relatively few interviews? (b) How do we make sense of the statistical results? and (c) What are the appropriate cautions in interpreting survey reports? This book is designed to answer those questions. Part 1 describes how surveys are conducted in such a way that they can be believed. Part 2 explains how to read statistical reports and analyze data. Part 3 gives further guidelines that are useful in evaluating polls. This book was written because we consider survey research and data analysis to be essential parts of social science research and because we believe that these topics can and must be communicated to nonspecialists.

Additionally, we regard training in analytical thinking to be an important part of a liberal education. Such training, with its emphasis on explanation, causal processes, and empirical evidence, is critically important in social science research. It is also a welcome departure, for many students, from shallow stereotypes of the attitudes of social groups and from glib generalizations about the impact of public policy on popular attitudes.

Furthermore, job openings in polling and market research have increased rapidly. The material in this book should serve as a useful introduction to those thinking of careers in these areas.

Admittedly, there are differences of opinion within the field about the emphasis to be given to three matters treated here: (a) interval statistics versus ordinal statistics, (b) the role of statistical inference, and (c) the importance of hypothesis testing. We have our own positions on these issues in our research, but we emphasize here the approach we consider to be most useful pedagogically: (a) understanding tables thoroughly before moving to interval statistics, (b) downplaying statistical inference, especially for large surveys, and (c) emphasizing relationships more than hypothesis testing. Because these issues are controversial, we explain both sides when possible. As practice has changed on these matters over the years, our positions have relaxed with each edition of this book.

The practice of survey research has changed considerably over the years since the first edition of this book was written. Telephone interviewing has become more prevalent than face-to-face interviewing. Experiments have changed some of the conventional wisdom about how to word survey questions. The computer card technology described in the original edition has disappeared. The importance of statistical inference procedures and regression analysis in survey analysis has increased. There is more self-conscious concern about ethical problems inherent in survey research. We have shifted our emphasis on several topics to incorporate these changes in this edition.

We would like to express our appreciation to several people and organizations that have affected our thinking and work on this project. Our approaches to survey research and data analysis have been strongly influenced by the Political Behavior Program, the Center for Political Studies, and the Survey Research Center of the University of Michigan's Institute for Social Research. The Survey Research Unit of the Polimetrics Laboratory for Political and Social Research at Ohio State University, headed by Dr. Kathleen Carr, has provided practical information about the functioning of a telephone interviewing operation. Additionally, the National Election Study data used in this book were provided by the Inter-University Consortium for Political and Social Research, which bears no responsibility for the interpretations.

Richard Niemi, George Rabinowitz, Robert Bates, Gerald Finch, Larry Bartels, Edward Carmines, Michael Margolis, and Steven Seitz gave us valuable comments on earlier editions, and Margolis and Seitz also gave us comments on this edition. D. K. and N. A. constantly reminded us of the frailties of survey data. We owe a special debt to the editors who have given us encouragement in this book in its several incarnations: C. Deborah Laughton at Sage; John Covell at Little, Brown; and Dick Lamb at W. H. Freeman. Finally, we would like to thank the several institutions that have provided us with atmospheres in which we could work on this project: the University of Michigan, Ohio State University and its Polimetrics Laboratory for Political and Social Research, Arizona State University, the Inter-University Consortium for Political and Social Research summer program, and Kaiser Foundation Health Plan, Inc.

 Introduction

Every day, we are all constantly bombarded by surveys:

- The morning paper headline says the president's public approval rating is at its high for the year.
- The sports page reports which team was voted number one in the nation in this week's United Press International poll of coaches.
- On the bottom of its editorial page, *USA Today* has the pictures of five "average" Americans, along with quotes from them on its topic of the day.
- On the way to work, you hear on the radio that, according to government statistics, the unemployment rate fell 0.3% last month.
- Walking by a newsstand, you notice a magazine whose cover trumpets a story: "What Features Americans Want in Their Homes."
- At lunch, you debate with a friend how to vote this year for the baseball All Stars team.
- On the way home from work, you hear last week's top 40 countdown of songs on the radio.
- The radio news headline on the hour is that government statistics show an increase in the robbery rate of 3% last month.
- The day's mail includes a questionnaire from your U.S. Representative, asking you to express your opinion on a variety of national issues.
- As you decide where to go for dinner, you look back at last month's *Wichita Monthly* magazine, which included a report of readers' votes for the best and worst restaurants of Wichita.

■ The television evening news begins with a preliminary poll showing that the president's veto of an important bill will be overridden in the Senate tomorrow.

■ The television news devotes 3 minutes to a congressional committee hearing on a bill to ban the reporting of election exit polls before polling places close.

■ You sit down after dinner to watch your favorite television show, and when you find it is not on, you remember that it was canceled because of low ratings.

■ You switch channels and watch the People's Choice Awards to see whom the public voted as their favorite movie, actor, and actress of last year.

■ Just as you get comfortable, the telephone rings and someone asks you a series of questions about your favorite brands of sweaters.

All of the above examples are based on surveys—some of high quality, some not. As surveys and polls increasingly dominate society, it becomes important to be able to differentiate the good polls, the bad polls, and the ugly ones.

In this book, we describe how surveys are conducted and analyzed. We hope this book will be useful to three types of readers:

The person who plans to design and conduct a survey

The person who wants to analyze survey data that someone else has collected

The citizen who reads or hears poll results and wants to decide which to take seriously

The book is divided into three parts. The first part introduces the design of surveys, describing the steps from sampling and question writing through interviewing and coding. The second part explains the analysis of surveys, from simple procedures, such as frequency distributions and cross-tabulations, through more complicated techniques, such as control tables and correlation/regression. The final part of the book presents summaries of the material presented in the first two parts of the book, discusses how to read and write reports of survey results, and considers the ethics of survey research.

PART

1

SURVEY DESIGN

1 ☐☑ The Nature of
☑☐ Survey Research

☑ What are surveys used for? What can they measure? What kinds of questions can they be used to answer? We address these preliminary topics in this chapter to describe the modern polling industry.

It is impossible to determine when the first survey was conducted. Several accounts are given in the Bible, beginning with a census taken after Moses ascended Mount Sinai. Later, the Romans took censuses to prepare for taxation. Other early censuses included the Domesday Book listing of all landowners in England in 1086. During the late 19th century, **social surveys** were conducted by independent individuals and government agencies in England and the United States to study social conditions and the nature of poverty. Shortly thereafter, newspapers and political parties began conducting straw polls in America, and market opinion research also started.[1]

By the beginning of the 20th century, researchers were beginning to employ surveys as we all know them today. The years up through 1950 proved to be a shakedown period for polling.[2] The magazine *Literary Digest* conducted surveys to predict the outcomes of many early 20th-century presidential elections. These polls predicted the outcomes of

the elections from 1916 through 1932 correctly, but in 1936 they predicted victory for the candidate who ultimately lost. Meanwhile, George
Gallup began his political polling in the mid-1930s, as did several university researchers. Many of them worked for the federal government
during World War II, measuring public attitudes on food rationing, price
controls, and foreign policy, as well as studying the attitudes of soldiers.
After the war, these researchers returned to universities to establish some
of the major academic social science research organizations. Meanwhile,
polling specialists formed a national organization, the American Association for Public Opinion Research (AAPOR), in 1946. Even though
surveys were becoming more professional, poll predictions for the first
postwar presidential election—the 1948 election—were again incorrect.

The polling field matured through the 1950s and 1960s. The polling
debacles of 1936 and 1948 led to the adoption of more scientific surveying procedures for personal interviews, as is explained in detail in
Chapter 3. Public confidence in polls was gradually restored. One reflection of this confidence was that Presidents John Kennedy, Lyndon
Johnson, and Richard Nixon paid more attention to polls than had
Harry Truman or Dwight Eisenhower. Surveys also became more important throughout American society, and several major universities established ongoing surveys.

Modern polling technology developed in the 1970s and 1980s, with
the shift to telephone interviewing. Today, survey research is a booming
business. Many thousands of surveys are conducted yearly. Surveys are
sponsored by a wide variety of individuals and organizations. Some are
sponsored by government agencies, such as the Census Bureau. Others
are funded by the media: newspapers, magazines, and television stations.
Still others are conducted for political candidates running for public
office. Companies that manufacture and distribute consumer products
or services—including airlines, dog food manufacturers, and health
insurance companies—also sponsor surveys. And finally, many surveys
are sponsored by researchers at colleges and universities across the
country. Several of these organizations spend more than $10 million a
year on surveys, with the largest market research companies approaching
$500 million of revenue annually. In total, market researchers are esti-
mated to spend more than $1 billion each year surveying the American
public.

Surveys are conducted by hundreds of organizations throughout the
world. Some are conducted by private research firms that are in business
solely to conduct surveys for their clients. You have probably heard of
some of these companies, including the Gallup Organization (which

conducts surveys for the Cable News Network [CNN] and *USA Today*), Roper, and Louis Harris and Associates. Others are conducted by research organizations that are parts of firms (including the major television networks, Procter & Gamble Co., and Quaker Oats), advertising agencies (e.g., Ted Bates and Associates, the Leo Burnett Company), and private consulting companies (e.g., Mathematica, Response Analysis, Westat). These companies employ many thousands of people across the country in one phase or another of survey research.

As a result of the work that these people do, surveys are prominent aspects of contemporary life. Most people see the results of surveys in newspapers or magazines or hear about them on radio or television. Most often, these surveys gauge public attitudes on social and political issues. Surveys conducted by advertising agencies usually measure purchasing behavior, purchasing intentions for the near future, attitudes toward consumer products, and people's reasons for liking or disliking particular products. People who work in marketing departments of large manufacturing and distribution companies make extensive use of surveys when deciding which products to make and sell and which ideas for products not to pursue. Consulting companies that are hired by large corporations measure employees' attitudes about their jobs and workplaces, their communication patterns, and their usual ways of doing their work in order to advise these firms on how to improve employee satisfaction and productivity.

Figure 1.1 is an example of a typical newspaper report of a poll. The poll was conducted by Media General, along with the Associated Press, and the article is a summary of the results from questions relating to fear of crime. This article illustrates how the news media conduct polls to report, an increasingly common practice. The headline also inadvertently illustrates a problem in reporting survey research: the tendency of the media to go beyond the data, here interpreting the poll results in terms of whether getting a gun makes people feel safer, whereas no data were collected on that topic.

Uses of Surveys

Why have surveys become so important? Increasingly, modern society requires information, and information that is useful for answering many important questions can be gathered by interviewing people. Surveys have been put to use in a number of contexts.

GUNS DON'T HELP PEOPLE FEEL SAFER

NEW YORK (AP)—People who keep guns for protection are no more likely to feel safe at home than those who don't have guns, according to a Media General-Associated Press poll.

In fact, gun owners are slightly less likely to feel secure from crime.

But whether they keep guns or not, 70 percent of Americans think people should have the right to shoot intruders, even if they're unsure the person is armed, according to the poll.

Three in 10 Americans keep guns in their homes for security reasons, according to the nationwide telephone poll of 1,251 adult Americans.

Asked whether they generally feel their home is secure from crime, 70 percent of the gun owners and 75 percent of those who don't have guns said yes.

OVERALL, 73 percent of respondents said they felt their homes were safe.

Black and white respondents had significantly different feelings of security. Among blacks, 57 percent felt their homes were secure against crime, and 64 percent felt safe on their streets at night. Among whites, three-quarters felt their homes were secure against crime, and 80 percent felt safe on their streets at night.

Blacks also had less confidence than whites in the protection they received from local police. A total of 39 percent of black respondents thought the police in their communities did a good job against crime, compared with 61 percent of white respondents who said police did a good job.

GUN OWNERS also were less likely to have confidence in the ability of local police to protect them, the poll said. While 54 percent of gun owners thought local police were doing a good job, 61 percent of those who don't have guns felt that way.

Overall, 59 percent said police were doing a good job, 31 percent said they were doing a fair job, 8 percent said police were doing a poor job, and 2 percent didn't know or didn't answer.

The vast majority of gun owners believed they have the right to shoot intruders, even if they're unsure an intruder is armed. Although fewer people who don't keep guns felt that way, a majority also thought people should have the right to shoot intruders.

PEOPLE WHO live in rural areas are far more likely to keep guns for security than those who live in suburbs or cities. Forty-one percent of those from rural areas had guns, compared with about one-quarter of suburban and urban dwellers.

Rural residents were not more likely to feel secure against crime at home than urban or suburban respondents. However, rural and suburban respondents were more likely to feel their communities were safe than urban respondents.

Suburban respondents also had more confidence in local police than either rural or urban respondents.

Figure 1.1. Typical Newspaper Report of a Poll

SOURCE: *Columbus Dispatch,* Feb. 2, 1987. Reprinted with permission of The Associated Press.

Political Polls

We are all familiar with polls conducted to predict who will win an upcoming election. A generation ago, newspaper articles about who was ahead in a political race relied on speculation by political experts. A political reporter, a political scientist, or a politician would have been asked to say which candidate was leading in the race. The experts were rarely identified, so readers were not able to evaluate the credibility of the predictions. As polling techniques were refined, it became clear that the best way to gauge public sentiment about an election was to ask people directly, and so polls have largely replaced political experts as the means for predicting election outcomes.

Surveys now have tremendous impact on political candidates' planning of campaign strategy. In the current age of candidate-centered politics, many political candidates hire polling companies to track public opinion about them and about their opponents. These data are used in determining whether to make certain public appearances, whom to associate with publicly, what to say, what not to say, and so on. For example, in 1994 the Republicans won control of the U.S. House of Representatives after their candidates endorsed a "Contract With America," which was a series of promises chosen by Republican leaders on the basis of which policy changes were most favored in national opinion polls.

Pollsters are also now accepted members of a president's team of advisers. Just as ancient kings kept court magicians around in case they needed special assistance, modern presidents retain pollsters. Thus, George Bush's key advisers included pollster Robert Teeter, and Bill Clinton's presidential advisers included pollster Stanley Greenberg. These pollsters are consulted on a variety of matters as diverse as content of presidential speeches and policy decisions. In general, they advise the president on how to sell his ideas to the public.

Surveys in Court

In addition to their political uses, surveys have often been used as evidence in courts of law. Take, for example, trademark infringement lawsuits. If one company has a trademark on its product and another company produces a similar product, the first company may sue the second for infringing on its trademark. One question the courts want to answer in such cases is whether the public is confusing the second product with the first. That question can best be answered through surveys. An example involved the Dallas Cap and Emblem Company, which put National Football League (NFL) emblems on products they sold. The NFL sued, claiming trademark violation. The league used a survey to show that 80% of the public associated the emblems with the NFL and that 64% thought the items were official NFL products.

The courts were slow to admit survey evidence. In the 1930s, courts viewed such evidence as hearsay and hence inadmissible, particularly because those interviewed could not be cross-examined in court. By the 1950s, some courts held that surveys were not hearsay because they were not being used to prove the truth of what the respondents said. Meanwhile, other courts were accepting surveys as evidence of "present state of mind, attitude, or belief," which is a recognized exception to the hearsay rule. Survey evidence in trademark cases is still often challenged on the basis of the quality of the survey, but surveys are now recognized as appropriate means of testing trademark violation.

Surveys have been admitted in court in many areas beyond trademark cases. For example, in 1963 the Zippo® lighter company accused the Rogers lighter company of unfair competition. Rogers had been manufacturing a cigarette lighter that looked almost identical to the Zippo cigarette lighter, and Zippo claimed that consumers were confused about which lighter was which. The company commissioned surveys in which national samples of American adults were asked to name the company that manufactured various lighters shown during the interview. Many respondents incorrectly identified the Rogers lighter as a Zippo lighter even though the Rogers brand name was stamped on the bottom. The survey evidence was ruled admissible by the judge, although he ultimately found the Rogers company to be not guilty of unfair competition.

Surveys have also been admitted as evidence in cases of misleading advertising. When federal regulatory commissions have charged that advertising creates a false impression in consumers' minds, surveys have been used to show the actual effects of the ads. For example, when the Federal Trade Commission (FTC) charged that Hi-C® fruit drink ads led consumers to believe that Hi-C contained more vitamin C than orange juice, the manufacturer of Hi-C won its case by submitting a survey showing that consumers did not draw that conclusion.

Lawyers sometimes use surveys to prepare for a trial even when the results will not be used as evidence. For example, defendants in some criminal cases seek to move their trial from one community to another because extensive pretrial publicity makes it impossible to impanel a jury that has not heard about the case. Defense lawyers frequently submit survey evidence documenting the extent of public knowledge about the case in the community. Lawyers have also used surveys to find which types of potential jurors will be most sympathetic to the arguments they are planning to make in a case. The lawyers then use their preemptory challenges in such a way as to get jurors with the demographics and other characteristics that are found to be most favorable to their side. Focus groups, as described later in this chapter, are also used in this way. In some cases, such as the 1995 O. J. Simpson case in California, the judge has the prosecution and the defense submit questions for a "jury survey" to be given to prospective jurors to obtain standardized information from them on matters that might be relevant to their jury service. As another example, surveys are used in pornography cases to gain evidence about community standards regarding obscenity.

A specialized legal use of surveys is **contingent valuation (CV).** Assessing fines in lawsuits often requires estimation of what damages are. In the contingent valuation method, a sample of people are asked how much they were injured by an action, and these values are summed to obtain the total damages. For example, after an oil spill from the *Exxon Valdez* in Prince William Sound, Alaska, caused considerable environmental damage, surveys were taken to estimate the value of the damage; the case was settled before trial, so the court did not have the opportunity to rule on the validity of this type of evidence. CV has also been used to measure the value of public goods. A question of this type asked people about the most extra taxes they would be willing to pay to save 50,000 birds from being killed by oil spills (Green, Kahneman, & Kunreuther, 1994). Contingent valuation is used extensively in research on natural resources, energy, and the environment.

Government Surveys

The government also often uses surveys to compile statistics. The most famous government survey is the one taken every 10 years by the Census Bureau to determine the population of the United States. Interviewers fan out across the country and knock on doors to find out how many people live in each house and apartment. That information is used to determine the population of each city, county, and state; several important political decisions are made on that basis. For example, some states gain seats and other states lose seats in the House of Representatives every decade on the basis of the census's determination of their populations. Similarly, census results are used in dividing each state into districts

of equal population for election of representatives to Congress. Alloca-
tion of federal funds to cities is based on their population, so the
population census affects the revenue of cities as well.

The U.S. government's use of surveys goes far beyond the decennial
census. Many government agencies are charged with gathering statistics,
and surveys are used as part of their effort. For example, the 1965 Voting
Rights Act was designed to remove barriers to voting by blacks and other
minorities. As part of the administration of that act, the Census Bureau
conducts a survey after each presidential election, asking people whether
they were registered and whether they voted. Statistics are compiled by
state, race, ethnicity, gender, and other demographics to monitor compliance with the Voting Rights Act.

The Census Bureau also conducts a major monthly survey, the Current Population Survey (CPS). It is conducted in more than 400 areas of
the country, with more than 50,000 housing units sampled each month;
this amounts to more than 100,000 persons age 16 and over being
represented. Because of its government sponsorship, the cooperation
level with this survey is 95% or above. The large sample size makes its
results accurate to 1%. The CPS is actually regarded as more accurate than
the decennial census because highly experienced interviewers collect the
data, although it cannot provide the detailed information about small
geographic areas that the decennial census gives. The cost of this survey
is in excess of $20 million a year. It is the major survey conducted by the
government on the status of the economy and also provides interim data
about population growth between decennial censuses.

Every month, the Labor Department publishes statistics about the
level of unemployment in the United States. The department might
report that the unemployment rate is 7.2%, up 0.3% since the previous
month. Have you ever wondered about the basis of those statistics? The
CPS described above asks people whether they were employed during
the past month. If they were employed, they are asked further questions
about how many hours they worked per week. If they were not employed,
they are asked whether they sought employment—because the people
who do not want a job are not counted as unemployed. It would be
difficult to gauge unemployment accurately without such surveys.

As another example of government use of surveys, consider reports
of the crime rate. There are many ways to determine the level of crime
in the United States. One could collect information from police departments about the numbers of crimes, and the National Institute of Justice
(NIJ) does just that. Not all crime is reported to the authorities, however.
As a result, the NIJ conducts regular surveys of crime victimization,

asking a sample of the public whether they were victimized by crime in the past month. These surveys find much higher rates of certain crimes, such as robbery, than police data show. "Victimless crimes," such as prostitution and drug use, are understated in the surveys, as is murder (the victim is not available to be interviewed).

State and local governments, as well as the federal government, now commonly commission surveys. For example, state and local government agencies routinely conduct surveys to measure public satisfaction with the services they provide. A state department of parks might measure use of state parks, and a local bus company or trash collection service might check the effectiveness of its service. School boards often conduct surveys to determine whether citizens are satisfied with local schools, as well as to gauge public support for school bond issues. Many agencies commission yearly polls so that they can track trends in public views of their services.

Consumer Research

Many commercial firms conduct polls, often as part of regular market opinion research. Companies use surveys to determine what new products to manufacture so that they can gain market share and to determine what features are most desired for those products. Companies planning advertising campaigns often conduct surveys to determine what type of spin to put on advertising pitches to maximize effectiveness. Also, corporations use surveys to determine why a product is not selling well and use what they learn to redesign their product or marketing strategy. Customer satisfaction surveys are now a major type of polling and include monitoring patient satisfaction with hospital care and doctor performance.

The Nielsen ratings of television viewing are especially well-known consumer surveys. Advertisers buy time on television on the basis of the number of viewers of each program as measured by these surveys. The most popular ways to determine this number are by telephoning people to find out what program they are currently watching, having households keep weekly diaries of their television viewing, and attaching a device to televisions in a sample of homes to keep track of when they are on. Networks use this information to determine how much to charge advertisers for each time block. When a program has too low a viewership, the network cannot charge enough for the advertising time and usually cancels the show. Thus, these surveys affect the content of television programming.

Researchers at universities also regularly conduct surveys. For example, the University of Michigan's Survey Research Center surveys about 600 American adults every month to learn about their current family financial situation; their intentions to purchase houses, cars, and major household appliances; and their savings and investment behavior. This survey also measures people's beliefs about the future of the nation's economy. Economists and businesspeople use the results of this survey extensively to forecast future purchasing, saving, and other financial behavior, as well as to plan manufacturing and distribution strategies.

Scholars at the University of Chicago and at the University of Michigan conduct large-scale surveys every year to measure public attitudes on controversial social and political issues. The General Social Survey, conducted by the National Opinion Research Corporation (NORC) at the University of Chicago, has monitored changing social trends since the early 1970s. The National Election Studies, surveys conducted by the Institute for Social Research at the University of Michigan, have tracked national political attitudes since the early 1950s. In addition to these national surveys, university researchers conduct countless state and local polls each year.

The major news media in the United States frequently conduct polls. Because of the expense involved in polling, many of these polls are joint operations of several media. Collaborators pool their questions and use the results differently, according to their differing needs. Television networks generally focus more on a quick summary of public opinion that they can add to a major story, whereas newspapers may print two or three stories about the same poll. For example, the *New York Times* and CBS News have polled together for several years, with the *New York Times* running the interviewing operation and CBS News performing the computer analysis. The Media General-Associated Press poll in the article reprinted in Figure 1.1 is another example of a media poll. In recent years, *Newsweek* and *Time* magazines have also regularly contracted for polls. The Gallup Organization currently conducts polls sponsored jointly by CNN and *USA Today*.

The media use polls to obtain novel news stories. One example is a *New York Times*/CBS News poll before Christmas 1985, in which children were asked whether they believed in Santa Claus—not exactly hard news, but wonderful material for a feature story. The Media General-Associated Press poll on fear of crime similarly provided newspapers with an article on a topic that interests many readers. Before elections, media polls are used in predicting the results. Also, monthly media surveys can be used to trace changing support for political parties and the president over several years. Finally, exit polls conducted during elections measure the demographics, motivations, and behavior of voters.

What Surveys Can Measure

This review illustrates how polls are a prominent part of everyday life and that they have tremendous effects; it also shows that surveys are used to measure many things. Although it is difficult to fit everything a survey can measure into a few categories, most things that surveys are used to measure can be regarded as attitudes (or preferences), beliefs (including predictions and assessments of importance), or facts (including past behavioral experiences). Not all of these can be measured with the same degree of accuracy.

Attitudes and Preferences

Attitudes are likes and dislikes. In more technical terms, an attitude is a positive or negative orientation toward an object, and it can be strong or weak. For example, many children have strong negative attitudes toward spinach, and most Americans have strong positive attitudes toward the American flag. Most attitudes measured in surveys are toward people (e.g., people running for public office) or toward government policies (e.g., legalized abortion, laws to limit who can purchase handguns). Many techniques have been developed to measure how positively or negatively people feel toward attitude objects of all kinds, and they are often used in surveys.

Preferences are based on comparisons of attitudes toward different objects. For example, if people are asked whether they prefer hamburgers or hot dogs, they presumably compare their attitudes toward those two foods and state which they like more. Surveys are frequently used to obtain such preference data, whether preferences about presidential candidates or makes of automobile.

The Media General-Associated Press poll summarized in the article in Figure 1.1 includes many attitude questions. For example, it reports that 70% of the public think "people should have the right to shoot intruders, even if they're unsure the person is armed." That is an attitude toward a policy. Later, the article reports that 59% of the public thought police were doing a good job. Again, that is an attitude, this time toward a group.

Beliefs and Predictions

Beliefs are opinions about the objective state of the world. For example, you might claim that the sky is blue today. This is a statement of a belief. Still another is "the Republican party favors lowering taxes." An example of a belief in the Media General-Associated Press poll report is that 73% of the public thought their homes were safe from crime. Beliefs may be true or untrue; what is important is that the person who holds a belief thinks it is true. When survey researchers measure beliefs, they are not usually interested in finding out the truth; that is, they do not conduct surveys to determine whether the Republican Party actually favors lowering taxes. If they wanted to learn that, there are better ways to do so. Rather, researchers usually measure beliefs in surveys because they are interested in what people *think* is true.

Surveys are also good at measuring **predictions** of the future—which are really the respondents' beliefs about what the future will be like. People might be asked to agree or disagree with such statements as "The national unemployment rate will decrease during the next 12 months" or "I expect to find a job during the next week." These questions are not used to predict the future, but researchers do use them as measures of public confidence in the economy. Other examples are asking people whether they agree that "a Republican will win the next presidential election" or "the president will be reelected." Like beliefs, predictions need not be true, but it can be useful to know what the public believes about the future.

Surveys are often used to measure people's beliefs about how *important* various things are. For examples, surveys often ask the public what they believe is the most important problem facing the United States today. Surveys have also been used to measure how important parents think it is for their children to have various characteristics such as intelligence and honesty. Again, the public's assessments of importance may not be "correct," but they are nevertheless useful in their own right.

Facts and Past Behavioral Experiences

Finally, surveys are often used to measure **facts.** For example, people are often asked how many years they attended school, how many bedrooms are in their home, how many television sets their family owns, and so on. The Media General-Associated Press poll reports the fact that 3 out of 10 Americans keep guns in their homes. The interest here is in learning the truth about these matters, so it is important that what people tell interviewers is actually true.

One of the most common uses of surveys is to measure people's **past behavioral experiences.** The National Health Survey, conducted by the Census Bureau, asks people how many times they visited a doctor during the past 6 months, how many times they were hospitalized, and so on. In the National Crime Survey, respondents are asked to report how many times they were victims of crimes during the previous month. In many political surveys, respondents are asked for whom they voted in the previous presidential election.

The distinction between beliefs and facts is not always clear-cut. Many questions about facts actually turn out to be questions about beliefs. For example, the answer to how often a person was a victim of crime in the past month depends on the person's views about what a crime is. Even when people are asked about their ethnicity, the answers often depend on what ethnic background the people consider themselves—and that is especially the case for people of mixed ethnic heritage (Smith, 1984). The problems involved in asking about beliefs and facts are somewhat different, but the differences are not as large as one might expect.

Goals of Surveys

What kinds of questions can be answered with surveys? Surveys are used to address four broad classes of questions: (a) the prevalence of attitudes, beliefs, and behavior; (b) changes in them over time; (c) differences between groups of people in their attitudes, beliefs, and behavior; and (d) causal propositions about these attitudes, beliefs, and behavior.

Surveys are most often used to measure the frequency of certain attitudes, beliefs, and behavior. Thus, surveys are used to see what proportion of the public approves of the president's performance in office (an attitude), what proportion of the public believes that the Democratic Party is the party best able to deal with the economy (a belief), and what proportion of the public has been unemployed and looked for a job during the previous month (a behavior).

If a researcher wants to ascertain the prevalence of such matters, surveys are an excellent way of measuring their occurrence. In fact, many researchers believe that the best way to find out what people like and believe is to ask them. There might be other ways to find out about behavior, but it is often difficult to determine the frequency of a behavior without asking people whether it is something they have done. As already pointed out, the Media General-Associated Press poll in the article in Figure 1.1 includes questions allowing assessment of the prevalence of attitudes, beliefs, and behavior.

Changes Over Time

Measuring the prevalence of attitudes, beliefs, or behavior is generally only of limited interest. The proportions often mean little by themselves. To say, for example, that 53% of the public approve of the president's performance in office does not in itself tell us much. We know that a bare majority approve of his performance, but is that an improvement over last year's ratings, or is it a decline? Is it better than other presidents have achieved, or is it worse? These are *change* questions, and they are important. Thus, attitude changes are often more interesting than frequencies themselves.

Of course, the same holds for beliefs and behavior. If 33% of the public view the president as a conservative, an interesting question is whether that is higher or lower than it used to be—whether he is seen as moving to the right or to the left. If 22% of high school students have used drugs in the past month, it is useful to know whether that is higher or lower than in previous years—whether there is an increase in drug use or whether it is tapering off. Repeated surveys are good ways for measuring change, as is discussed in Chapter 7.

Differences Between Groups

Another way in which frequencies gain meaning is by comparing the attitudes, beliefs, and behavior for different *groups* of people. It is often interesting to know whether one group is more likely to hold an attitude, have a belief, or perform a behavior than another group. Are men more likely than women to approve of the president's handling of foreign affairs? Are blacks more likely than whites to believe that the president is supportive of a strong federal government? Did men vote at a higher rate than women in the previous election?

There are several possible reasons to look at group differences. Sometimes, researchers are interested in the attitudes, beliefs, and behavior of one group—for example, the political behavior of women. Looking at a single group by itself is not very informative because the researcher cannot tell whether that group differs from the rest of the public. As a result, people interested in one group generally perform their research by comparing groups—for example, by comparing the political behavior of women with that of men.

At other times, researchers are interested in describing the demographics of an attitude, belief, or behavior. When political pollsters examine who supports the president, they are trying to discover the groups to which he appeals in order to understand the bases of his appeals. The article on the Media General-Associated Press poll draws several group comparisons, such as whites feeling more secure against crimes in their homes than blacks, gun owners having less confidence in the local police than those who do not own guns, and rural residents being more likely than urban residents to keep guns for security.

Causal Propositions

Surveys are also used to test causal propositions. Academic researchers are particularly interested in identifying the *causes* of social behavior. Why do some people approve of the president's performance more than others? To what extent is it because of the person's party ties, and to what extent is it because of other factors? Why do some people view the president as more conservative than do others? Why do some people vote in elections and others do not? Is it because of their reactions to the candidates in the particular election, or is it because of their early childhood learning about politics? These types of causal questions can be addressed through surveys.

The Media General-Associated Press poll on crime considers a causal question in its opening paragraphs. The author of the article was interested in what makes people feel safe from crime in their homes, and he or she thought that owning a gun might be a factor in making people feel secure. The poll found that 70% of gun owners felt secure in their homes, compared with 75% of people who did not have guns. With that finding, the author rejected a plausible causal hypothesis. The article does not probe further as to the causes of feeling safe at home; instead, it turns at that point to the presentation of overall frequencies and group differences. The headline notwithstanding, the article, in fact, offers no evidence on the causal link between purchasing/owning a gun and the feeling of safety.

Measuring frequencies, changes, and differences in attitudes, beliefs, and behavior is fairly straightforward, but as you will see, testing causal hypotheses is more complicated. The researcher has to include in the survey a variety of questions that tap alternative causal logics and then analyze the data to determine which causal explanation fits better.

Choosing the Best
Research Design

Surveys are one way to collect information about attitudes, beliefs, and behavior, but they are not the only way. Whenever surveys are considered, it is important to realize their limitations and to consider the alternatives.

Experiments

One alternative is the experiment. **Experiments** permit researchers to control events in a way not possible in a survey. Typically, the experimenter manipulates a causal variable and sees whether the group receiving the treatment then differs from an equivalent control group. For example, if the effects of a political speech are to be studied, it might be appropriate (a) to ask some questions before the speech to gauge prior attitudes, (b) to vary systematically the content of the speech that the experimental subjects hear, and then (c) to observe differences in their subsequent attitudes. Causal propositions about changes in attitudes, beliefs, or behavior can sometimes be tested more definitively in experiments than in surveys.

Experiments in the social sciences, however, often involve artificial conditions. Communications may have different effects in a contrived experimental setting than they would have in more natural settings. It is often unclear what results generalize from an experimental setting with volunteer subjects to the more general population under natural conditions. As a result, surveys might be better able to monitor phenomena such as the effects of campaign communications and attitude change over long periods of time as they naturally occur.

Aggregate Data

Another important alternative to surveys is using **aggregate data,** such as election totals or census data, which measure variables at the level of a state, a county, a city, a ward in a city, a precinct, or a census tract. Aggregate data are widely available and are useful for certain purposes. For example, following a presidential election, vote counts reveal the actual number of votes cast for each candidate and the actual turnout figures. A survey can only estimate these figures.

Aggregate data cannot substitute for survey data for all purposes, however, because aggregate data are not individual-level data. Suppose we were interested in studying the voting behavior of blacks. If we examined the election returns from black precincts, we might find that 90% of the votes cast in those precincts were Democratic. But we still would not know exactly how blacks voted. The black precincts are probably about 90% black, so this may mean that all the blacks in the black precincts voted Democratic, whereas all the whites in those precincts voted Republican. Or it may mean that all the whites in those precincts voted Democratic along with 89% of the blacks, whereas 11% of the blacks voted Republican. If blacks and whites turned out to vote at different rates, then these figures could be wrong. Perhaps all whites voted Democratic, all blacks voted Republican, but very few blacks voted. Furthermore, we have no way of knowing how blacks who did not live in black precincts voted. There is always the strong possibility of failing to notice an **ecological fallacy** when trying to deduce individual behavior (e.g., the voting behavior of individual blacks) from the behavior of aggregates (e.g., precinct election returns).

When only aggregate election data are available, such as when one wants to analyze the 1832 presidential election, one must make the most of it. If one is interested in individual attitudes, however, it is usually better to use survey data.

The explanation of mass behavior often requires mass attitude data that can only be obtained by a **survey.** You cannot assume that people think in certain ways without asking them what they think. You cannot regard aggregate data as equivalent to individual data, nor can you use experiments as alternatives to the collection of data in the natural environment. If it is possible to ask people questions, you can gain much information about what they are thinking—and why they do things. When public attitudes and mass behavior are of interest, surveys play important roles in social science.

Of course, surveys also have their limitations. They are expensive, particularly if sophisticated procedures are implemented. Many surveys are run on a shoestring, but a large-scale national study can cost more than $250,000. Also, people sometimes do not give truthful answers to questions. For example, more white people say they will vote for black candidates than actually do. Thus, surveys are less accurate sources of some sensitive information than are aggregate data.

Actually, surveys are often used in concert with experimental and aggregate data. In evaluation research, for example, a survey might be used to measure the crime rate and fear of crime before a new police program is instituted to fight burglary, and then another survey would be taken a few months later. The surveys help in the evaluation of the experimental program. Analysis of survey data also often makes use of aggregate data. For example, to compare attitudes of people who live in high-status areas and low-status areas, one could add to the survey data some information on the demographic characteristics of each respondent's neighborhood.

Related Data Collection Methods

Some new methods of collecting data are receiving considerable attention. These methods are related to survey research but differ from conventional polls.

In **focus group** research, the investigator invites 10 to 18 people to meet and discuss a particular topic. Participants are generally chosen through a telephone interview, with quotas for particular types of people. Sometimes, the investigator tries to put together a cross section of different types of people; at other times, the group consists of only one type of person because the similarity of participants might foster communication. Even though people are usually paid to attend these sessions, fewer people attend these sessions than say they will. As a result, it is usual practice to call around until more people agree to attend than are actually needed.

The focus group leader, termed a **facilitator** or **moderator,** asks questions and directs the conversation. A formal questionnaire is not used, but the facilitator is usually supposed to cover a series of issues from a list or outline. Different perspectives on the topic are often tested on the participants to determine what arguments might be most effective.

As in survey research, an attempt is made to obtain everyone's views on the chosen topic. The group setting, however, allows a group dynamic to develop, a dynamic that differentiates focus group research from surveys. The argument supporting this approach is that people get to discuss their views with others in formulating their own opinions in the real world, so the group setting adds realism to the research effort. The difficulty is that one or two strong personalities can dominate a session, although a good facilitator can keep the session on target regardless of problem participants. Multiple focus groups are also used sometimes as a means of countering the effects of the personalities in any single group.

Focus group results are not analyzed quantitatively. Instead, the investigator examines the session transcript from a qualitative standpoint, seeing what arguments help sway a group or pulling good quotes from the sessions. Often, the sponsor is also provided with an edited videotape of the session. Focus groups can tell researchers how people think about the topic, what terms they use in discussing it, and what frames of reference they employ; these groups are not well suited to measuring the distribution of opinions on the topic.

Political candidates are increasingly using focus groups to try out particular issues or arguments; for example, before the Alliance attack on Iraq in 1991 to force Saddam Hussein to remove his troops from Kuwait, focus groups were used to find out which arguments for the use of the military would be most persuasive with the American public. They are also used by strategists for candidates who want to test the likely effectiveness of different negative attacks on their opponents. For example, the 1988 Bush presidential campaign found from focus groups that they could effectively attack Democratic nominee Governor Michael Dukakis on his veto of a bill requiring schoolchildren to recite the pledge of allegiance and on a furlough to convicted murderer Willie Horton, who terrorized a family during his time out of prison.

One of the authors has been a participant in two unrelated focus groups. One pertained to a local school bond issue. The session showed considerable participant suspicion of the school board and was dominated by one person who came to deliver a message to the board that it had to cut its spending. Different ways to structure the bond issue were shown to the focus group, and even the most negative participant was willing to indicate conditions under which he could support some versions of the proposal. The results led the school board to put three separate issues on the ballot, rather than a single combined issue; only one issue passed, but that was a better outcome for the board than the defeat of all three.

The other focus group pertained to an idea of some city businesspeople to open a new fish restaurant downtown. The focus group was fairly negative about the original proposal and was instead satisfied with their ability to purchase fresh fish at local grocery chains. The focus group was reconvened a few months later to look at a revised proposal, but its reaction was still tepid. As a result, this restaurant was never opened. This is a good example of the use of focus groups by businesses interested in how to appeal better to consumers.

Focus groups are often used to supplement conventional surveys. The research sponsor might want the topic discussed with a focus group before a final set of survey questions is formulated. Focus groups are also used in pretesting questions for surveys (see Chapter 4) and in developing response categories for questions. And focus groups are sometimes used to provide rich quotes to supplement closed-ended questions in surveys.

Focus groups have become very popular. They are quick and inexpensive to conduct; all it takes is an empty room, a skilled facilitator (sometimes accompanied by other researchers who observe through a one-way mirror), someone to telephone people and ask them to participate, audiotaping or videotaping mechanisms, and some refreshments for the participants. Furthermore, they can be conducted without publicity, so potential competitors do not know that research is being undertaken.

Many major business firms spend large amounts of money on focus group research. Survey research firms often supplement their regular interviewing with focus groups because these are so profitable. They use their telephone interviewers to solicit participants for the focus groups, with one person (often the head of the organization) serving as facilitator. The small number of cases, however, makes it more difficult to generalize safely from focus group research than from surveys.

***

The Deliberative Poll

Another innovative technique is the **deliberative poll,** as suggested by Fishkin (1991). The deliberative poll attempts to find out what people would think about an issue if they could consider it more fully. A random sample of people are brought together to be briefed about the issue, to question experts about the issue, and to discuss it. Ideally, these are several-day discussions of issues by people who are brought in from all around the country.

The first large-scale test of a deliberative poll was in April 1994 in England. Interviews on crime were initially conducted with a random sample of 869 people, of whom 302 accepted the invitation to attend a televised deliberative poll for a weekend in Manchester. Views changed considerably over the weekend, with half the participants changing their minds on some issues. For example, people remained tough on crime but became more sensitive to the rights of defendants and more sensitive to the limitations of prisons for fighting crime. The more educated changed their opinions more, perhaps because they were more able to integrate competing arguments (Fishkin, 1994).

The deliberative poll has been proposed as an alternative to presidential primaries because it can be more representative of the nation than primaries in single states, and it would permit more careful consideration of candidates and issues. Also, televising the proceedings would serve an educational role for the public. The difficulty with this approach is the expense, along with the need to ensure that the participants are representative. The first use of this procedure in the United States was the televised National Issues Convention (NIC) in which 459 delegates were brought together in Austin, Texas in January, 1996 to launch the primary season.

***

Audience Reaction Research

In **audience reaction** research, the investigators invite a larger number of people (usually from 25 to 250) to watch a filmed presentation. Each person is given a dial to turn to show reactions to the film, turning it in one direction to show positive reactions and the other direction to show negative reactions. Strength of reaction is measured by how much the person turns the dial. A rheostat is connected by electric current to a board that keeps track of the reactions. Sometimes, a digital button apparatus is used instead of the dials, or galvanic skin responses may be measured. In any case, the system allows a calculation of the average reaction to each part of the film.

This methodology is used in both the advertising world and the political world. Advertisers use it to test the effectiveness of television commercials, seeing which ads are effective, as well as which parts of ads require editing. Political strategists use it to test reactions to their candidates' speeches, seeing which lines are the most effective and which are counterproductive. The candidate can then repeat the effective lines in subsequent speeches, tailoring the appeal to what sells best.

Some people see this methodology as a cynical manipulation of the public, selling political candidates as advertised products with a greater concern for how to generate an effective appeal than for the content of that appeal. Other analysts argue that this is just another means of helping candidates present themselves effectively to the public. In any case, it is a fairly inexpensive procedure that can help structure advertising and political campaigns. Still, audience reaction research is a special-purpose research technique that is not as broadly useful as survey research.

Secondary Analysis of Survey Data

Often, researchers decide that a survey is the best way to achieve research goals but that collecting a new set of survey data is impractical. In such situations, researchers may decide to analyze survey data that someone else has already collected. This procedure is termed **secondary analysis,** to distinguish it from analysis by the primary investigators, who collected the data.

It is becoming common for those who design a survey to make their data available to other researchers. The expense of surveys makes this availability important because few investigators can afford to collect their own survey data. Making data available to other researchers means that secondary analysts can test their own hypotheses and can check the findings of the original researchers. Even researchers planning to conduct their own surveys benefit from this development. They can learn from other studies on similar topics before they conduct their own projects.

Several major archives now store data released by primary investigators. For example, the Inter-University Consortium for Political and Social Research, based at the University of Michigan, has an extensive archive of thousands of major national surveys from the United States and many other countries. In addition to survey data, the consortium also stores data on national attributes, U.S. census data, and data on world-event interactions. Often within a year of a survey, universities that belong to the consortium can obtain the survey data free, and nonmember universities can purchase individual sets of data for a fee. The National Network of State Polls (NNSP), at the University of North Carolina, maintains a similar archive of state polls. The Gallup, Harris, and Roper polls also have services that permit their surveys to be acquired by interested researchers. Because these archives contain data from surveys conducted over several decades, they permit researchers to evaluate attitude and demographic changes over long periods. The National Science Foundation's (NSF) Division of Social and Economic Science now requires data collected with its funds to be placed into an archive for the general use of the larger scientific community.

Table 1.1 lists some of the continuing surveys in the consortium's holdings. In addition to the ongoing American National Election Studies and the General Social Survey described earlier in this chapter, some continuing studies focus on consumer attitudes, health, nutrition, crime, employment, income, and political socialization. The Euro-Barometers have surveyed since 1970 in several West European nations, focusing on political variables and values. In addition are many state polls and some local polls, including the Detroit Area Study, which has conducted surveys on different sociological and political topics in Detroit since the 1950s.

As a result of the development of such archives, secondary analysis is now very common—probably even more common than primary analysis. Most large universities have large collections of survey and other data available for secondary analysis by faculty and students.

SUMMARY

Survey research is a popular research method. It permits researchers to measure the prevalence of attitudes, beliefs, and behavior; to study change in them over time; to examine group differences; and to test

TABLE 1.1 Some Continuing Surveys Archived by the Inter-University
Consortium for Political and Social Research

Poll	Year(s)
ABC News/*Washington Post* Polls	1981-
American National Election Studies (CPS)	1948-
Americans' Use of Time (SRC)	1965-66, 1975-76, 1985
Annual Housing Surveys (Census Bureau)	1973-
Annual Surveys of Governments (Census Bureau)	1973-
British National Election Studies	1969-
Census of Governments (Census Bureau)	1962-
Census of Population and Housing (Census Bureau)	1790-
Chicago Council on Foreign Relations	1975-
Consumer Attitudes and Behavior (SRC)	1953-
Consumer Expenditure Surveys (Bureau of Labor Statistics)	1888-
Current Population Surveys (Census Bureau)	1968-
Detroit Area Studies	1953-
Euro-Barometers	1970-
General Social Survey (NORC)	1972-
German Election Studies	1961-
Health and Nutrition Examination Surveys (HANES; National Center for Health Statistics)	1959-
Monitoring the Future (SRC)	1976-
National Crime Surveys (Bureau of Justice Statistics)	1972-
National Health Interview Surveys	1970-
National Jail Census	1970-
National Longitudinal Surveys of Labor Market Experience	1966-
National Nursing Home Surveys (National Center for Health Statistics)	1973-
National Surveys of Family Growth (National Center for Health Statistics)	1973-
National Surveys of Jails	1985-
New York Times/CBS News Polls	1976-
Panel Study of Income Dynamics (SRC)	1968-
Survey of Income and Program Participation (Census Bureau)	1984-
Surveys of Inmates of Local Jails (Bureau of Justice Statistics)	1972-
Women in Development (Census Bureau)	1979-83
Youth Socialization Panel Survey	1965-82

NOTE: CPS: Center for Political Studies (University of Michigan); NORC: National Opinion
Research Center (University of Chicago); SRC: Survey Research Center (University of Michigan).

causal propositions about the sources of attitudes, beliefs, and behavior. Surveys are frequently an appropriate and useful means of collecting information, although experiments and aggregate data often provide alternative data sources. Secondary analysis of existing surveys can sometimes substitute for collecting one's own survey data. In any case, surveys can have important advantages over other research methods and are therefore a useful tool for social scientific investigations.

Further Readings

Polling History

Converse, J. M. (1987). *Survey research in the United States.* Berkeley: University of California Press.
Herbst, S. (1993). *Numbered voices.* Chicago: University of Chicago Press.
Moore, D. W. (1992). *The superpollsters.* New York: Four Walls Eight Windows.

Other Research Methods

Krueger, R. A. (1994). *Focus groups.* Thousand Oaks, CA: Sage.

Research Design

Campbell, D. T., & Stanley, J. C. (1963). *Experimental and quasi-experimental designs for research.* Chicago: Rand McNally.
Webb, E. J., Campbell, D. T., Schwartz, R. D., Sechrest, L., & Grove, J. B. (1981). *Nonreactive measures in the social sciences* (2nd ed.). Boston: Houghton Mifflin.

Notes

1. Converse (1987) provides an excellent history of survey research from the early polls of the 19th century through the academic surveys of the 1950s.

2. We use the terms *surveys* and *polls* fairly interchangeably, but *polling* is sometimes used to describe research that ascertains whether there is majority support for a policy position or candidate among citizens.

☑ EXERCISES

1. Look back at Figure 1.1, the reprint of the Media General-Associated Press article on attitudes toward handguns. Newspaper headlines

are usually not written by the reporters who write the stories, so sometimes the headlines do not accurately capture the content of an article. Is the headline of this article accurate, or has the headline writer made an error in summarizing the article?

2. For the next 2 days, keep track of all reports of polls that you read or hear. Be especially sensitive to reports that do not mention polls but that do contain information that could only be obtained through a survey.

3. Find a recent news story that reports a poll. Who sponsored the poll? Does it report attitudes, beliefs, behavior, or some combination of the three? What were the purposes of the poll?

2 □☑ □☑ The Survey Process

☑ Many steps are involved in survey research. Before a survey
is conducted, important decisions must be made about the
objectives of the study and the design of the survey. We
describe each of them in this chapter.

A Statement of Objectives

Any research study must begin with a statement of its objectives. What
does the researcher want to study? On what subject is information
desired? If the goal is to test a certain proposition, the statement of
objectives should state the proposition clearly and should also state how
an appropriate test of the proposition could be constructed. This statement of objectives will guide the selection of respondents (the persons
who are interviewed) and the writing of questions so as to guarantee that
the survey design meshes with the study's objectives. The more complete
the statement of objectives, the more ensurance that the survey design
can be shaped to satisfy them.

Construction of Hypotheses

In scientific research, the specific propositions to be tested are called
hypotheses. The social sciences are most interested in testing **causal**

29

hypotheses, propositions about the causes of phenomena. For example, researchers studying voting might expect that economic conditions influence voting behavior. They might hypothesize that a person's vote will be affected by whether that person's real income has increased or decreased during the preceding year. They might hypothesize further that people whose real income has increased will be more likely to vote for the incumbent party than will people whose real income has decreased.

Operationalization of Concepts

If hypotheses are to be stated so that they can be tested, it is necessary to understand a fundamental idea: concept operationalization. How concepts are to be **operationalized** (defined in such a way that they can be measured) must always be considered carefully. As an example, we might be interested in understanding public opinions on abortion. **Cognitive dissonance theory,** a theory developed by social psychologists, states that members of a group will tend to accept that group's issue positions rather than undergo the stress of disagreeing with their own group. On the basis of this theory, we might hypothesize that Catholics might oppose abortion in order to avoid conflicts with their other religious beliefs. The hypothesis specifies a relation between a person's religion and his or her views on abortion. These concepts may seem straightforward, but they require further precision before they can be tested. Who is a Catholic? A person who answers "Catholic" when asked his or her religion? A person who regularly attends mass? A person who believes in the teachings of the Catholic Church? What do we mean by "opposition to abortion"—opposition to all abortions or only to those for reasons other than medical ones? The concepts could be defined in many ways, and a survey researcher must select the operational definition that provides the most meaningful test of the hypothesis.

Taking Alternative Views Into Account

When testing a hypothesis, it is important to think of alternative explanations. Religion is not the only possible cause of a person's opinion on abortion. We would want to spell out in our statement of objectives other relationships to examine. In this example, we might want to test the impact of gender, education, marital status, and age on a person's opinions about abortion. If we found that older people, regardless of their religion, tend to oppose abortion more than do younger people, then age rather than religion may be the more powerful determinant of views on abortion. The statement of objectives must be framed broadly enough to permit competing explanations to be tested.

The Importance of Theory

Social scientists disagree about how much emphasis should be placed on theory and formal methodology when designing a research project. Some favor a **deductive** approach to advance social science, arguing that all research should derive hypotheses from theories about behavior and then should formally test those hypotheses. By contrast, **inductive** social scientists see no necessity to place such an emphasis on theory and formal methodology. They place their emphasis on discovering relationships in the data and generalizing from those observed relationships. Many other social scientists take the middle ground between the two positions and seek to build theory from relationships found in the data. They see the importance of relating their research to preexisting theory but allow for the discovery of relationships in the data, rather than limit their studies solely to the testing of preestablished hypotheses. Although we favor the middle ground, most of the material in this book is compatible with all three approaches.

Market Opinion Polls

Companies that conduct market opinion polls are less concerned with developing and testing theory than are researchers who conduct scientific surveys. Instead, such companies are concerned with determining the appeal of their products, the perceived advantages of their products as opposed to those of their competitors, and ways they can pitch their advertising campaigns to attract different segments of the market. Market opinion polls still require clear statements of objectives, however. The more clearly the researcher can state the objectives of the polling, the more certain it is that the results can answer the needs of the client companies.

The Survey Design Stage

Once the objectives of the survey are determined, the design of the survey must be chosen. In doing so, it is essential to keep the study objectives in mind so that the data will address those objectives. It is also important to anticipate the data analysis because a desired analysis can be performed only if appropriate design decisions are made. We introduce several basic design questions in this section and discuss them in more detail in later chapters.

What Population Should Be Studied?

In designing a survey, the first basic design question is, What population should be described? Whose attitudes do we want to describe or make generalizations about? In some studies, a researcher may be interested in the entire population of a country (or, for that matter, the entire population of a state or city). Most surveys focus only on part of that population, however—those who are at least 18 years old, who are citizens of that country (or residents of that state or city), and who are not institutionalized in mental hospitals or prisons. Special populations are surveyed in some surveys. For example, if a researcher wanted to study the thinking of those entering the U.S. electorate in the next 2 years, the relevant population might be 16- and 17-year-olds. A study of the attitudes of college students would have the set of college students as its relevant population. The important point is that researchers must describe or define very carefully the population they want to study.

Obviously, one should not choose a population that makes the basic hypotheses impossible to test. We hypothesized above that Catholics might oppose abortion to avoid conflict with their other religious beliefs. One might believe that only Catholics need to be interviewed to test this hypothesis. However, the effect of religion on abortion opinions can only be tested by interviewing Catholics and non-Catholics. If members of other religions are as strongly opposed to abortion as are Catholics, then religion seems not to be an important factor in views on abortion. Researchers usually want to compare the views of different groups, so the population to be studied must include the various groups of interest.

Who Should Be Interviewed?

Once the **target population** is selected, the next study design question is, Who should be interviewed? Is the target population so small and geographically concentrated that it is possible to interview everyone? Is the research so exploratory that a few in-depth interviews with an unsystematic sample would suffice? Or is a large, representative sample required?

How Many Interviews Are Necessary?

If sampling is employed, enough interviews must be taken to permit generalizing to the population of interest. Also, enough interviews are needed to allow the researchers to study subgroups of interest. Financial limits are always present, and more interviews always cost money. Consequently, a balance must be struck between the number of interviews desired and the limits imposed by available funds.

This is a good example of the importance of planning for data analysis when designing a survey. What if a researcher finds, after conducting a survey, that too few interviews were conducted with an important type of respondent? At that point, it is too late to take more interviews. It is essential to anticipate what groups will be of interest and to select a sample that will ensure their adequate coverage.

For example, you will see in the next chapter that a sample comprising 1,500 people is sufficient for studying the voting of the American public. If the total sample is 1,500, however, one would expect to obtain only about 150 interviews with blacks. That number may be enough to permit comparisons of whites with blacks, but it is not adequate if the researcher wants to compare older blacks born in the South with younger blacks born in the North. These categories would not contain enough people to sustain a meaningful analysis. If such comparisons are desired, then either the total sample size must be increased or additional interviews with blacks must be conducted. It is common to **oversample** a group in a survey so that the group can be studied in detail, although those extra interviews are dropped (or counted only partially) when the entire population is being described. Such an approach is possible only if the researcher anticipates such needs at the study design stage.

How Should the Data Be Collected?

Survey data may be collected by three methods. The first method is to send interviewers to the homes of respondents so that they may be interviewed face to face. Second, interviews may be conducted over the telephone. Third, questionnaires may be given (or mailed) to respondents to fill out. Each of these data collection methods has advantages and disadvantages, and some are better suited to particular topics of study.

Are Follow-Up Surveys Necessary?

Another study design question is whether the focus of the study is on change. If so, it makes sense to interview the same people more than once to see whether their attitudes, beliefs, or behavior change. In a typical **cross-section** survey, people are interviewed just once. By contrast, in a **panel** study, the same people are interviewed repeatedly. For example, the same people could be interviewed at successive presidential elections to assess changes in attitude and vote. Long-term panel studies are complicated by the expense and difficulty of finding respondents who have moved in intervening years, but these studies give the best evidence of the extent of attitude change.

Overview of the Survey Process

Answering the study design questions—whether to conduct a survey, what the target population should be, whom to interview, how many interviews to take, how to collect the data, and whether to adopt a panel approach—sets the framework for the study. The full set of steps involved in conducting a survey is listed in Table 2.1.

Each step in Table 2.1 has numerous potential errors associated with it, so each must be performed with care. It is easy to focus on minimizing error in one or two of these steps, such as paying attention to error in sampling and coding, while ignoring more subtle potential sources of error. Survey quality, however, depends on minimizing error throughout the process. Just as a chain is only as strong as its weakest link, so a survey is only as good as its weakest step. As a result, the literature on surveys in the 1980s and 1990s has given much attention to "total survey design"

TABLE 2.1 Stages of the Survey Process (keyed to chapters in this book)	
Stage	*See Chapter*
Survey Design and Data Collection	
Statement of study objectives	2
Preparation of study design	2
Sampling—choosing people to interview	3
Questionnaire construction and pretesting	4
Interviewing—data collection	5
Coding—categorizing the responses	6
Entering the data into the computer	6
Data Analysis	
Specification of hypotheses	8
Tabulation of responses	9
Building new measures	9
Hypothesis testing	10
Analysis of two-variable relationships	11, 12, 14
Use of control variables	13, 14
Reporting Results	
Writing research reports	15
Reading survey reports	16

(Fowler, 1993, pp. 6-8), stressing the need to consider every aspect of a survey in building a quality product. Each chapter of this book will include some discussion of relevant errors in surveys, after which Chapter 16 provides a summary of issues involved in assessing the accuracy of a survey.

The survey design process is the subject of the first part of this book. In this chapter, we have traced through the early stages of the survey process: the study objectives and the study design. In Chapter 3, we describe how the **sample** of people being interviewed is selected so that it is representative of a larger population. It is critical that the sample be selected so that it does not bias the results of the study. In Chapter 4, we discuss how survey questions are carefully written and tested prior to the actual interviews. A questionnaire is put together after the researcher has decided on the exact question wording and the order of the questions. In Chapter 5, we present rules that the interview process must follow to obtain the most complete and most accurate information.

Personal interviews, telephone polls, and self-administered questionnaires can all be used in surveying the public, and each has its own
advantages and disadvantages. In Chapter 6, we show how the verbal
responses of people are then translated into numbers—called **codes**—so
that a computer can be used to analyze the data.

The second part of this book turns to the analysis of data. In this phase,
specific hypotheses are tested. The responses to individual questions are
tabulated and summarized. Then, the relationships between answers to
different questions are analyzed statistically.

The third part of this book provides guidelines on the conduct and
reporting of survey research. The reading and writing of research reports
is discussed. The final chapter focuses on the ethics of survey research.

SUMMARY

A good researcher has clear objectives and keeps those objectives in
mind when deciding how to collect the data. Hypotheses must be
constructed, and the concepts must be operationalized to test between
alternative explanations. If a survey is to be conducted, the researcher
must decide on the population to be studied, who should be interviewed,
how many interviews to take, how the data should be collected, and
whether to take follow-up surveys. Overall, a variety of survey designs can
be used to accommodate different substantive needs and problems—if
those problems are anticipated in the planning of the survey.

Further Readings

Survey Methods

Babbie, E. R. (1990). *Survey research methods* (2nd ed.). Belmont, CA:
    Wadsworth.
Backstrom, C. H., & Hursh-Cesar, G. (1981). *Survey research* (2nd ed.). New
    York: John Wiley.
Fowler, F. J., Jr. (1993). *Survey research methods* (2nd ed.). Newbury Park, CA:
    Sage.
Warwick, D. P., & Lininger, C. A. (1975). *The sample survey: Theory and practice.*
    New York: McGraw-Hill.

☑ EXERCISES

1. Suppose you were concerned with the extent of violence in America and chose to study why some people approve of violence. Further, suppose that interracial violence was of particular concern to you and that you wanted to determine why some people approve of interracial violence whereas others disapprove. Construct a set of hypotheses regarding alternative causes of attitudes toward violence in general and interracial violence in particular. How would you define violence?

2. What research designs would be suited to testing your hypotheses in Question 1? Would experiments be useful in studying attitudes toward violence? How could surveys be used? How would you define your target population for a survey? Would it be valid to interview only those who have participated in violent acts? What about interviewing only men or only city dwellers? Would you use only questions on interracial violence, or would you want to see whether attitudes on interracial violence differed from attitudes on other types of violence?

3 □☑ □□ ☑ Sampling Procedures

☑ Many researchers who conduct surveys do so to understand the attitudes, beliefs, or behavior of a large group of people, such as the entire U.S. population. It would be prohibitively expensive, however, for every researcher to interview each of the 185 million residents age 18 and over in this country. Fortunately, accurate estimates of the nation's attitudes may be obtained by interviewing a sample of a few thousand carefully selected respondents. The technique by which survey researchers choose respondents is called **sampling.** As you will see in this chapter, sampling procedures vary widely; some are easy but sloppy, some are excellent but impractical (e.g., taking a simple random sample in which each citizen of the United States is listed and then given an equal chance of being selected), and some are both sound and practical.

Sampling is widely used in the sciences, and an extensive body of statistical theory has been developed to guide its application. Many sampling procedures can be used to generate samples that are representative of a population. Implementing them correctly requires strict adherence to certain logical principles. In this chapter, we describe some of the sampling procedures that are frequently used in the social sciences.

Sampling Methods

As described in Chapter 2, the first step is to define the relevant population. If the population we are interested in is so small that we can easily interview the entire population, we need not sample at all. For example, we could easily interview everyone on an 11-person city council. But let's assume that the population comprises many thousands or millions of people and that sampling is essential. How can we obtain a representative sample?

Once the population of interest is defined, it is necessary to determine the **sampling frame**—the list of units from which the sample will be drawn. Ideally, the sampling frame would be identical to the population of interest, but often that is not possible. For example, a researcher might want to take a sample of all eligible voters (the population of interest), but doing so from the voter registration list (the sampling frame) would lead to some problems because the voter registration list might be old and incomplete. Similarly, a researcher might want to take a sample of all residents of a city (the population of interest), but doing so by interviewing people who walk by a particular corner (the sampling frame) inadvertently modifies the nature of the sample. Strictly speaking, sampling can just generalize to the sampling frame from which the sample was drawn, rather than to the full population, so the researcher should try to use a sampling frame that corresponds as close as possible to the population.

Nonprobability Sampling Methods

One important distinction to be made is between nonprobability sampling procedures and probability sampling procedures. We begin by describing some **nonprobability sampling** procedures so that the advantages of probability sampling can be shown.

Typical People. We could seek people who seem to be *typical* of the population according to census statistics regarding its social and economic composition. There is no guarantee, however, that people with

typical social and economic characteristics have attitudes that are representative of the entire population. Indeed, such people may actually have
very distinctive attitudes that are not at all like those of sizable groups in
the population, so such a sample would not be representative.

This is where **probability sampling** procedures come to our aid. They
permit us to select a group that is similar to the population in its
composition, although of a much smaller and more manageable size.
The classical procedure used for this purpose is known as **randomization.**
As you will see below, randomization is a procedure that gives everyone
in the population an equal chance of being part of the sample. Randomization thus eliminates the possibility that any portion of the population
will be overrepresented or underrepresented in the sample.

Purposive Samples. Another nonprobability approach is to choose some
cases to study purposively. In studying the elite decision makers in a
community, a researcher might get advice about who the major decision
makers are and then seek to interview them. At best, the success of this
procedure depends on how carefully the people are selected. Even if the
people are carefully selected, however, the possibility remains that some
key decision makers were omitted. Purposive sampling often works well,
but it can be tricky, and it is hard to prove that the researcher has sampled
appropriately.

Volunteer Subjects. Another way of choosing people for a study is to ask
for volunteers. Some people will volunteer to participate, and the researcher can ascertain their attitudes, beliefs, and behavior. The problem
is that people who volunteer may not be typical. Volunteers generally are
more interested in the topic of the study than are other people, so they
are not representative of the larger population.

The most famous example of an interview study using volunteer
subjects is the research in the 1950s by the Kinsey Institute at Indiana
University on the sexual behavior of the American public. The researchers asked their respondents how many times they had engaged in
a long list of sexual activities. The *Kinsey Report* showed that Americans
were much more sexually active than had previously been thought. The
use of volunteers in the study, however, made this conclusion questionable: People who volunteered to participate in a study on their sexual
practices were likely to have been more sexually liberated and more
sexually active than people who were unwilling to participate in such a
study. Thus, the use of volunteer subjects probably biased the results.

A few decades later, Shere Hite asked female volunteer subjects to report on their sexual satisfaction and found that women were surprisingly dissatisfied with their partners. Again, the use of volunteer subjects probably biased her results because women who were more dissatisfied sexually were more likely to be interested in filling out her questionnaires (Moore, 1992). More generally, volunteers are often likely to differ from the rest of the population, so the use of volunteers can bias a study. Early surveys on these topics used volunteer subjects because it was thought that large parts of a representative cross section would be unwilling to discuss their sexual behavior and feelings. The University of Chicago's National Opinion Research Center, however, has shown that carefully trained interviewers can interview people in their homes about these topics (Laumann, Gagnon, Michael, & Michaels, 1994; cf. Lewontin, 1995).

Another example of volunteer subjects is the call-in poll on radio and television that asks people to call one telephone number if they want to vote yes on the issue of the day (e.g., whether prayer should be allowed in schools) and a different number if they want to vote no on that issue. The sample obtained from such a poll consists of volunteer subjects, and as such it measures the views of people who feel strongly enough to call, rather than of the entire audience of the station. The telephone numbers that are to be called in such polls often require a toll charge, which means that only people who are willing to pay to record their views will participate. Furthermore, it is easy for an organized group to rig call-in polls by having their supporters telephone one of the numbers repeatedly so that it looks like their side commands a majority. All in all, call-in polls should not be taken seriously.

Surveys are also now showing up on the Internet. They are sometimes placed on a server or a Web page, with notices of them circulated to relevant groups. Alternatively, surveys are sometimes sent on the Internet to target mailing lists or Usenet groups. In addition to the problems of volunteer subjects as discussed above is the question of whether such mass mailings violate the usual network etiquette rules.

Haphazard Sampling. Another simple sampling procedure is the **haphazard sample,** in which the researcher surveys people who can be contacted easily. For example, a professor might use a questionnaire to measure the attitudes of a college class, but the students' attitudes may not be identical to those of the American public. Haphazard samples can sometimes generate results that are representative of the larger population of interest if there is no source of bias. For example, the now defunct *Literary Digest* conducted some of the earliest election polls in the 1920s and 1930s. It sampled large numbers of people from telephone books and automobile registrations, and it was quite accurate in predicting the winner of presidential elections.

However, haphazard samples can also generate results that are not representative of the population. In the Great Depression, a *Digest* poll with more than 2 million responses predicted a victory by Alf Landon in the 1936 election and lost its credibility when Franklin Roosevelt won in a landslide. The *Digest* poll had missed the large Democratic vote of poor people who lacked telephones and cars during the Depression and who had not been voting in previous elections.[1] Unfortunately, haphazard sampling almost always yields unrepresentative samples. Consequently, this approach is rarely used today in voting studies, though during presidential election campaigns, we still hear of polls based on whether popcorn buyers in movie theaters choose boxes with pictures of elephants or donkeys on them. Haphazard polls remain common in research using school classes, as well as in mall intercept research in which interviewers ask questions of people at shopping malls. These samples are so haphazard, however, that much caution is required in interpreting their results.

Haphazard samples are also used when polls are taken through computer bulletin boards and interactive cable television. The advocates of such technology often justify their procedures in terms of permitting instantaneous polling on matters of public importance. There are clear biases about what types of people have access to this technology, however, as well as about what types of people are likely to respond to these polls. For example, a 1995 poll by Princeton Survey Research Associates for *Newsweek* (1995, p. 32) found that people who were online were more Republican in their party identification than the public as a whole by 15%. Changing technology provides exciting new opportunities for conducting surveys, but the results will clearly be biased toward the views of a technological elite. Indeed, it is not always possible to tell who is answering questions on such systems—whether adults are giving serious answers or whether children are just punching buttons. For all the talk of electronic town meetings, the new technology does not provide a panacea for the problems of democracy in the modern era.

Quota Sampling. Another inexpensive sampling approach is **quota sampling.** If the census indicates that 50% of the U.S. population is female and that 10% is black, then interviewers are told to obtain 50% of their interviews with women and 10% with blacks. The drawback of this approach is that the interviewers will tend to select the people they want to interview. They will tend to choose people they can find easily, people who are particularly willing to be interviewed, and people whom they do not find to be hostile or intimidating. These people usually are similar to the interviewers themselves. Because most interviewers are middle class, the result is typically a middle-class bias, with insufficient interviews with working-class people. Although more complex quotas could be imposed, the bias problem cannot be eliminated unless interviewers make none of the decisions regarding whom to interview.

After the *Literary Digest* debacle, the polls switched to face-to-face interviews. Then, in 1948, the polls declared Thomas Dewey the president-elect, only to be embarrassed when the American public did not concur. One reason why this happened is that the commercial pollsters of that era used a quota-sampling procedure. Harry Truman's victory that year was correctly forecasted only by academic polls using more accurate sampling procedures. Today, pure quota samples are rarely used by academics, although some commercial pollsters such as Roper continue to use them. Quota samples are still used in preelection polls in Great Britain because the short 3-week campaign period does not allow enough time to draw a better sample; this use of quota samples may explain the frequent inaccuracy of British pollsters' election predictions.

In our discussion of volunteer, haphazard, and quota samples, we touched on one of the most important points in sampling: A sampling procedure must avoid bias. Clearly, all the subgroups, classes, and races in a population must have a chance to be included in the sample. If any group is excluded from the sample, then the sample is biased, and generalizations from the sample to the population as a whole may be very inaccurate.

Probability Sampling Methods

Today, most high-quality surveys employ **probability sampling,** in which the sample is drawn before the survey so that each person in the population has a known (but not necessarily equal) probability of being included in the sample. This technique eliminates the bias inherent in the other sampling procedures. A distinction to keep in mind is between probability sampling off a list of people to interview (e.g., from a list of registered voters, from a list of members of a professional association) versus random sampling in the absence of a list.

The Simple Random Sample. One form of probability sampling is done by taking a list of the people in a population and randomly selecting individuals to be surveyed. In principle, this could be done by writing each person's name on a piece of paper, putting all the names into a hat, mixing up the names, and drawing the sample. For larger populations, the random selection is performed with a computer. The result is called a **simple random sample.** This is an excellent sampling procedure. Most probability samples, however, do not use a straight simple random sample because it is not practical; variants of the technique are used instead.

The Systematic Selection Procedure. One convenient variant of the simple random sample is the **systematic selection** procedure. This procedure requires a list of all the people in the population. A random number is selected to choose the first person to be interviewed, and then a specified number of names on the list are skipped to choose the next person, and so on. Suppose, for example, that you were taking a sample of students from a university with 20,000 students and that you wanted a sample of 400 (a 1-in-50 sampling ratio). You could take the student directory and randomly choose 1 of the first 50 students by using a published table of random numbers. If you picked the number 37, you would interview the 37th person and every 50th person following on the list: the 37th, the 87th, the 137th, the 187th, and so on. Through this procedure, you would obtain a sample of 400 people.

One problem with this procedure is that it makes sample selection very easy but only as long as the list corresponds exactly to the population. One potential problem is that available lists may not correspond to the population. We would not want to sample from a student directory that lists only students who live on campus if we wanted to develop a sample of all students at a college. A second problem with this procedure is that the list could contain some periodicity. For example, if your list was of houses, and if you chose the first house and every 15th house down the street, you might accidentally obtain a sample containing only houses on corners, which are sometimes more expensive than houses in the middle of blocks. Fortunately, periodicity is rarely a problem, but when using systematic selection, it is important to be sure that the list has no periodicity.

A third problem with systematic selection is that elements adjacent on the list cannot be included in the same sample. Thus, if you had been selecting a sample of United Nations delegations to interview during the Cold War, systematic sampling using an alphabetical list of member nations would have precluded having interviews with all of the major powers because the Soviet Union (officially the Union of Soviet Socialist Republics), Britain (the United Kingdom), and the United States would all have been in the same part of the alphabet. Similarly, systematic sampling from alphabetic lists of people can encounter problems because several ethnic groups tend to have the same or similar last names; the alphabetic concentration of their last names might prevent a sufficient number of respondents from those groups being selected in a systematic sample. How serious this problem is depends on how the list is organized. Systematic sampling can actually be a powerful sampling procedure if the list is appropriately ordered. For example, if a list of communities is ordered from the largest to the smallest, with each weighted by its size, then systematic sampling guarantees proper coverage of places of different sizes.

Despite their advantages, simple random sampling and systematic sampling share two significant disadvantages. First, they require a listing of the entire population of interest so that random or systematic selection can be made. This is impossible for a national survey in the United States; there are no lists of all residents, citizens, or voters in this country, and no one could afford to construct such a list. Second, it is too expensive to interview a national face-to-face sample based on such sampling procedures. Most survey budgets do not allow for an interviewer to fly to Snowflake, Arizona, for only one interview and then to Casper, Wyoming, for the next interview; transportation costs for interviewers require that several interviews be physically clustered near one another.

Stratifying the Sample. Several approaches are used to solve these problems. One is **stratifying**—dividing the population into small, manageable chunks and randomly sampling from each chunk. If you are interested in sampling the population of the United States and know the proportion of the population living in each region, it makes sense to stratify your sample by region so that the proper proportion of interviews can be taken independently within each region. In that way, you can make sure that 25% of the interviews are taken in the Midwest, that 30% of those are taken in small towns, and so on. Stratifying helps maximize accuracy in a sample because it ensures that certain known population proportions are matched in the sample.

Stratifying is especially useful in increasing accuracy when two groups differ widely on the topic being studied, yet members within each group are very similar. For example, if we were interested in contrasting freshmen with seniors in terms of their views on some issue, we could obtain more accurate estimates of each group's views by sampling from them separately than if we sampled the entire college and then compared the lower-division and upper-division students in the sample. Stratifying is useful if the researcher knows what variables are worth stratifying on.

Unfortunately, stratification is often not possible. Stratification requires knowing all population members' status on the stratifying variable prior to the sampling. This is easy to do with region of the country, for example, but would be much harder to do with religion. There is no easy way to create separate samples of Protestants and Catholics because there are no separate lists of all members of each religion in the nation and no residential segregation by religion. Incidentally, notice that stratifying is not the same as quota sampling because the interviewer is not choosing whom to interview; the selection of exact respondents is still random.

The Cluster Sample. Another approach is to use a **cluster sample.** Because it is too expensive to take each interview in a different neighborhood, the researcher clusters by taking several interviews in one neighborhood. This tactic reduces interviewing costs because the expenses of paying for interviewers' time and transportation decrease.

Regrettably, accuracy declines in cluster sampling. People who live in the same area tend to be similar, so taking several interviews in the same area yields less information than would be gained by spreading the same number of interviews across a wider area. Most survey organizations believe that some loss of accuracy is acceptable if it permits greatly decreased costs. The extent of differences expected within clusters versus between clusters is important to consider in deciding how many interviews to take in each cluster. Only a few interviews per cluster are necessary if clusters are expected to be relatively homogenous internally, whereas several interviews should be taken in each cluster if clusters are expected to be heterogeneous.

Paradoxically, if a cluster sample and a simple random sample *of equal cost* were taken of the same large, geographically dispersed population, the cluster sample would probably be more accurate. The reason is that the reduced cost per interview of the cluster sample allows the sample size to be increased sufficiently to offset the increased error from clustering. Of course, one should certainly not go to the extreme of drawing an entire sample from only one or two clusters; as long as there enough clusters, the error will be within reasonable bounds.

Multistage Area Sampling. Another permutation of probability sampling, **multistage area sampling** first requires sampling a set of geographic regions. Next, a subset of geographic area is sampled within each of those regions, and so on. The chance of an area being included increases with the number of people living in it.

Let's say you begin by randomly selecting 100 towns in the United States. If a particular town is selected, you would next randomly choose neighborhoods—maybe one area in the northeast corner, another on the near south side, and a third in a western suburb. At the next stage, a sample of blocks would be chosen within each neighborhood, and then a sample of houses would be chosen on each block. The advantage of multistage area probability sampling is that a complete listing of the population is now unnecessary. All that is required is a list of towns, a list of neighborhoods within the towns selected, a list of blocks within the neighborhoods chosen, and a list of houses on the blocks that are chosen. The clustering inherent in this scheme means that it yields a higher error rate than simple random samples, but this is offset by the ability to sample without a complete listing of the population and by lower costs per interview.

Multistage area sampling often follows a rule known as "probability proportionate to size" (PPS), which keeps the selection probability equal for each element in the population. For example, suppose you were sampling 600 students at a university of 30,000 students, which is a 2% sampling rate. Suppose the university consists of 45 colleges (including several undergraduate colleges), with their sizes ranging from 60 students in the optometry college to 6,000 students in the largest undergraduate college. Instead of selecting students randomly from the whole university, you might sample colleges to study, which is equivalent here to clustering.

Under PPS sampling, each college would be given a probability of being selected proportional to its size, from .02 for the optometry college to .20 for the largest undergraduate college. You could select 15 clusters by randomly using those probabilities and then interview 40 students per college to get up to the sample of 600 cases. The probability of interviewing an optometry student would then be $15 \times (60/30,000) \times (40/60) = 1/50 = .02$, whereas the probability of interviewing a student from the large undergraduate college would likewise be $15 \times (600/30,000) \times (40/600) = 1/50 = .02$. This is considered to be a very efficient sampling procedure in that full student lists are needed only for the 15 selected colleges, and you might also be able to use the data to describe those colleges. PPS sampling can be adjusted to handle very large clusters (e.g., by putting the largest undergraduate college into the sample with probability 1.00 and then interviewing 2% of its students) or very small clusters (e.g., by combining the smallest colleges into a single cluster).

Hybrid Sampling Situations. In some situations, samplers have resorted to various hybrid sampling procedures. When there is no single good way to sample a particular population, some researchers use **multiple frame designs.** For example, they might supplement a purchased list of telephone numbers with some interviews based on pure random-digit-dialing. A related sampling situation called **parallel samples** occurs when a sample is taken to serve as a comparison group with another sample, as when a cross section of the public is sampled to permit comparisons with a sample from a list of labor union members. As these examples illustrate, experienced samplers often depart from conventional sampling techniques when they must deal with difficult sampling situations.

Summary. Typically, sampling for face-to-face interviews combines the several procedures we mentioned above, which are listed in Table 3.1 along with their advantages and disadvantages. Using only volunteers, taking a haphazard sample, and interviewing through quota techniques are relatively inexpensive, but accuracy suffers. Probability sampling is required if estimates of the survey's accuracy are desired. The simple random sample is the textbook ideal, but it is expensive; its accuracy requires a listing of all elements in the population, as well as interviews in widely scattered locations. Systematic sampling simplifies the sample selection, but it also requires a listing of the population and widely scattered interviews. Multistage area sampling permits the listings to be made only in small areas. Clustering cuts transportation costs, though with some increase in error. Stratification guarantees matching some population proportions to safeguard accuracy. All in all, the accuracy of a survey is significantly affected by its sampling procedures, and the choice of the proper sampling technique is crucial to the success of the survey.

Examples of Samples

To illustrate how samples are actually drawn, we give examples of different strategies you could use to draw a sample from a series of different populations.

TABLE 3.1 Types of Samples

Sampling Method	Advantages	Disadvantages
Nonprobability		
Purposive sample	Inexpensive	No estimates of accuracy
	Uses best available information	May miss important elements
Volunteer subjects	Cooperative respondents	Not representative of population
Haphazard sample	Available sample	No necessary relation to population
Quota sample	Willing respondents	Middle-class and other biases
Probability		
Simple random sample	Accuracy can be estimated	Expensive
	Sampling error can be estimated	Interviews too dispersed and full list required
Systematic selection procedure	Convenience	Periodicity in list
Stratified sample	Guarantees adequate representation of groups	Sometimes requires weighting
	Usually decreased error	
Cluster sample	Decreased cost	Increased error
Multistage area sample	Lower cost than simple random sample for large populations	Higher error than simple random sample
	Lower error than cluster	Higher cost than cluster

A National Sample for Face-to-Face Interviewing

How are national samples for face-to-face interviewing drawn? Simple random sampling cannot be used because of the size and geographic dispersion of the population, so multistage area samples with clustering and stratifying are used instead. For purposes of illustration, we describe the sampling procedures used by the University of Michigan's Survey Research Center (SRC).

Choosing Where to Interview. The SRC sample is a representative sample of occupied housing units. It is a multistage stratified area probability sample with three stages to choose the household.

The first stage consists of sampling a number of **primary sampling units (psu's).** A psu is an area, a Metropolitan Statistical Area (MSA; the Census Bureau's designation for the largest cities, along with the rest of their county and linked adjacent counties), a county, or a set of adjacent small counties. The psu's are stratified by region, as well as by the size of their largest cities. Stratification is essential in national household surveys to ensure proper regional coverage, as well as proper coverage of large cities versus more rural areas. The resulting sample of psu's might include the Syracuse area, a farm area in eastern Kansas, and so on. The largest metropolitan areas are typically represented in every sample, so interviews are always taken in New York City, Los Angeles, Chicago, Philadelphia, and other big cities. SRC chooses a sample of about 100 psu's after each census (Figure 3.1); it uses those psu's for as many of its surveys as possible during the next 10 years. People who live in those psu's are hired as interviewers for that decade to ensure stable, experienced field staffs.

For a national survey, the researcher must first decide how many interviews are to be conducted. This is usually determined by the amount of money available because the bigger the sample, the better. The number of interviews to be assigned in each region of the country is determined by the percentage of the population living in each region. A similar logic is used to determine the number of interviews to take in each psu.

Next, smaller areas are chosen within each psu. Detailed maps and data from the Census Bureau are obtained for the psu for this second-stage sample selection. The areas selected at this stage are called "blocks"; census blocks correspond to conventional blocks in cities but may contain many square miles in rural areas. The sampling of these blocks includes stratification by household income (as listed by the census data) and geography (e.g., central city, suburbs, and remaining counties in MSAs). If the Syracuse area is a psu, for example, then the population of the city, the suburbs, other towns in the county, and rural townships are determined from the Census Bureau's data. Because it contains most of the population in the psu, several blocks in the city of Syracuse would be randomly selected, along with some block equivalents in the rural part of the county.

The third stage of the sampling requires the interviewer to go to the selected blocks and make a detailed list of housing units on those blocks. Houses or apartments on the blocks or areas in the sample are listed,

Figure 3.1. Survey Research Center Primary Sampling Units
SOURCE: Heeringa, Connor, Haeussler, Redmond, and Samunte (1994).

and random samples of the housing units are drawn. Interviewers are then told which houses and apartments to visit. An advantage of this multistage sampling procedure is that detailed housing unit lists are required only at this third stage (Figure 3.2).

Choosing Whom to Interview. Rather than let the interviewer make a subjective choice of respondents, objective procedures have been developed for choosing the resident at each dwelling unit to be interviewed. Table 3.2 shows part of the **cover sheet** given to the interviewer. The interviewer checks to see whether there is more than one housing unit at the address (as when a two-story house contains two apartments). If so, extra housing units are added to the sample.

For each dwelling unit, the interviewer records the name, gender, and age of each person living in the household. The interviewer then numbers these people sequentially, using 1 for the oldest male, 2 for the next oldest male, and so on until all the males have been numbered; the oldest female is given the next number, the next oldest female the next number, and so on. The interviewer then looks at a selection table (or **Kish table**) to see which person to interview. In the example shown on page 55, if one or two people over age 18 are in the household, then Person 1 (the

Stage 1: Sampling of primary sampling units within the United States. Stratification at this stage by region and size of largest city in the psu, with automatic inclusion of largest MSAs. About 100 psu's are selected, from about 2,400 psu's in 1990.

Stage 2: Sampling of blocks within the psu's selected in Stage 1. Stratification at this stage by household income and geography. Blocks are chosen in cities and block equivalents in rural areas. About 1,500 blocks are selected at this stage, with a minimum of 12 in each psu and a high of 52 in the New York MSA.

Stage 3: Sampling of housing units within the blocks selected in Stage 2. Number of housing units expected per block is 48 for non-MSAs and 72 for MSAs. Households chosen randomly at this stage.

Stage 4: Sampling of residents within housing units selected in Stage 3. Intended respondent selected randomly by using a selection table that takes household composition into account.

Figure 3.2. Stages of the University of Michigan Survey Research Center Sampling Method

oldest male if there is one) is interviewed; if three or four people over age 18 are in the household, then Person 2 is interviewed; and if five or more people over age 18 are in the household, then Person 3 is interviewed. Different selection tables are used in different households to randomize the selection of individuals within households. This procedure might result in the interviewing of the oldest male in one home, the youngest female in the next, the second oldest female in the third, and so on. This selection procedure is used, rather than just interviewing whoever answers the door, to avoid any biases as to which types of people are most likely to be home. For example, young males tend not to be at home as much as other members of a family, but this selection procedure obtains the proper proportion of young males as designated respondents.

If the person to be interviewed is not at home when the interviewer visits, SRC interviewers make an appointment to stop back and interview the designated respondent. If that person is not at home when the interviewer stops back, the interviewer is instructed to call back repeatedly to find the designated respondent. The interviewer cannot just substitute someone else in the household or a neighbor. Call-back and substitution strategies vary across polling firms. Because repeated call-backs are expensive, commercial pollsters generally allow their interviewers to interview anyone who is at home or instruct their interviewers to talk to a neighbor if the designated respondent is not at home. These substitution approaches assume that the not-at-homes will not differ significantly from their neighbors. Respondents can instead be asked whether they were at home at the same time the previous day, and the sample can then be weighted in favor of those who were at home less often, but this procedure does not fully compensate for people who are never at home at that time of day.

Telephone Samples

Telephone interviewing has become an important means of conducting surveys, and sampling for telephone interviewing raises unique problems.

Choosing Telephone Numbers. One way to obtain a sample for telephone interviews is to take a random selection of numbers in local telephone directories and to call those numbers. Unfortunately, this approach has two serious problems. First, some people who have telephones do not list their numbers in directories. Second, telephone directories are a few months out of date by the time they are published and become increasingly out of date as time passes. Because of these factors, in many localities more than 20% of residential telephones are not listed in telephone directories, and this value is above 40% in California.

A slight modification of the use of telephone directories is the **add-a-digit** approach. In this procedure, a set of random telephone numbers is selected from the telephone directory (by using simple random sampling or systematic sampling of every nth number in the directory) and then adding one to that number. For example, if the number 292-6446 is obtained from the directory, the value of 1 is added so that the number to be dialed for the interview is 292-6447. A variant of this approach is to add a random digit from 0 to 9 to the directory number. These add-a-digit procedures make it possible to call unlisted numbers as well as new numbers, although many calls are made to numbers not in service. This is still a reasonable sampling procedure, especially when studying a single community where only one telephone directory is required. It is even feasible when studying a single state where all of the state's directories can be obtained, but it is unmanageable when conducting a national survey. Strictly speaking, this is not a probability sample because the likelihood of each household being selected is not a known nonzero value, so it can produce biased estimates of population values (Kalton, 1983, p. 87).

TABLE 3.2 Part of a Cover Sheet (Items 1-13, 29)

1. **STUDENT**
   Interviewer's Label

3. Your Interview No. _____

4. Date _____

5. Time Started _____

6. Length of Interview _____ (minutes)

7. Location Name _____
   USE THIS NAME WHEREVER
   (CITY/TOWNSHIP) APPEARS

2. **SRC**
   Interviewer's Label

8. Segment No. _____

9. Line No. _____

10. Address (or description) _____

11. Determine if there is more than one HU at the Listing Sheet address referred to in Item 10 above and check one:

    ☐ 1 HU   ☐ There are _____ (SUPPLY NUMBER) HU's at the listed address.

    Make out another cover sheet for each unlisted HU. Add to Item 10 a specific designation of the HU for which this cover sheet is used. On each cover sheet for an unlisted HU, be sure to identify the unit specifically.

12. Call Record:

Call Number	1	2	3	4	5	6	More (specify)
Date							
Day of Week							
Time of Day (+ AM, PM)							
Result of Call							
Int. Initials							

13. Final Outcome:

    Check one after final disposition of cover sheet. For intermediate calls, enter appropriate abbreviation in 12.

    ☐1. INT   Interview completed
    ☐2. HV   House vacant
    ☐3. NER   No eligible respondent
    ☐4. NOC(AT)   No one contacted (any time)
    ☐5. RA   Respondent absent

    ☐6. SLIP   Sample listing isn't proper (no such address, address not a HU, etc.)
    ☐7. REF   Refusal
    ☐8. OTHER   Noninterview for other reasons (specify)

TABLE 3.2 *Continued*

29. List all members of the household.

(a) Household Members by Relationship to Head	(b) Sex	(c) Age	(d) Person Number	(e) Enter "R" to Identify Respondent
HEAD OF HOUSEHOLD				

Persons 18 Years or Older

Persons 18 Years or Younger

For (d) Assign a sequential number to each person in the HU 18 years or older. NUMBER MALES FROM OLDEST TO YOUNGEST, THEN CONTINUE NUMBERING FEMALES FROM OLDEST TO YOUNGEST.

For (e) Use the selection table on the right to determine the <u>number</u> of the person to be interviewed. In the first column of the selection table, circle the number of eligible persons—the highest number assigned in column (d). The corresponding number in the second column of the selection table denotes the person to be interviewed. In column (e) enter letter "R" to identify the respondent.

SELECTION TABLE C

If the number of eligible person is:	Interview the person numbered:
1 _____	_____ 1
2 _____	_____ 1
3 _____	_____ 2
4 _____	_____ 2
5 _____	_____ 3
6 or more _____	_____ 3

30. RECORD RESPONSE TO Q. D10a. HERE:

_____ / _____
STREET ADDRESS   CITY

A commonly used alternative procedure is **random-digit-dialing (RDD)**. This approach uses computers to make up telephone numbers randomly. It is used in many telephone polls, such as the *New York Times*/CBS News poll. In most areas of the country, many telephone exchanges are not used, so completely random dialing would result in many wasted telephone calls to nonexistent exchanges. As a result, RDD is generally limited to exchanges that are in use.

Telephone numbers in the United States are composed of three parts. In the number (614) 292-6446, for example, 614 is the area code, 292 is the central office code (also called the *prefix*), and 6446 is the suffix. It is possible to find out which central office codes are used in a particular area code, either from the local telephone company or from national directories. The researcher can then choose a set of area code-central office codes randomly and add random suffixes to them. In samples from a single community, the local telephone company may be able to provide information on the number of residential telephones per central office code, and then the researcher can stratify by central office code by using that information. Each central office code usually has many unused suffixes, so it is necessary to sample many telephone numbers to obtain the desired interviews. A 5:1 ratio is necessary because only about one fifth of the numbers turn out to be working residential telephones. Telephone calls are then placed until the desired number of interviews is obtained. This is a probability sampling procedure, but it is inefficient because so many numbers are not working residential numbers.

A commonly used variant of this technique that involves fewer wasted calls is known as the **Waksberg method.** The four-digit telephone number suffix (6446 in the above example) can be thought of as having two parts: the first two numbers (64) and the last two numbers (46). Within an area code-central office code combination, randomly choose several banks of the first two numbers (64 could be one). Within each of those banks, select one telephone number randomly (say, 46 is chosen to get 6446). Dial that number. If that number is not a residential number, then reject that bank and dial no more numbers from it. If that number is a residential number, get a specified number of interviews from that bank. The interviewer might keep calling numbers in that bank until, say, eight interviews are taken with working residential numbers. With this system, two thirds of the telephone calls are placed to working residential telephones. This is considered to be a two-stage probability sampling procedure with clustering. The University of Michigan's Survey Research Center is one of the many polling operations to use this method for telephone sampling.

The procedures used for selecting telephone numbers vary tremendously. The Waksberg method is highly regarded, but it is complicated to explain. As a result, many polling companies prefer to use straight random-digit-dialing because they find it easier to justify to their clients. The availability of telephone directories from around the nation on CD-ROMs provides a new means for sampling telephone numbers, although it is difficult to ascertain how current the listings are on those CD-ROMs. The telephone directory CD-ROMs are likely to improve in quality, although they always will be limited to listed numbers.

Survey organizations and market research firms that rely on telephone interviewing often buy their samples from professional sampling firms. Such firms as Survey Sampling, Inc. (SSI) and Genesys Sampling Systems promise to provide lists of telephone numbers that are scientifically sound and that include primarily working residential telephone numbers.[2] They can achieve unusually high "hit rates" by removing business telephone numbers and by checking their lists against computerized yellow page directories. Additionally, they can meet some special sampling needs, such as giving the congressional district of each telephone number or providing a sample of telephone numbers that will have a high likelihood of belonging to African Americans.

Call Dispositions. Survey telephone calls have several possible outcomes (Table 3.3): no answer, a busy signal, or an immediate hang-up, in which cases the number can be tried again later. The number is just set aside if it is a disconnected number, nonworking, or a computer modem. An answered telephone number is also put aside if it turns out to be a pay telephone, a business rather than a residence, outside the intended geographic area, or does not have an eligible respondent. If the call is answered by a nonresident, the interviewer can try phoning back later to see whether someone else answers, which also can be done if the person answering the telephone refuses to cooperate. In addition, study directors have to decide how to handle problem situations, such as answering machines and when the telephone is answered by someone who does not speak English. Finally, designated respondents must be dropped if they are out of town throughout the interviewing period or too disabled to be interviewed. Careful record keeping is required during the telephone calling to keep track of what numbers to try again and to keep statistics on response rates.

When a telephone number does not answer, the survey organization is confronted with a difficult decision: whether to keep calling back or substitute another number. Academic polling operations tend to have interviewers

TABLE 3.3 Sample Interviewer Telephone Codes

INTERVIEW CONDUCTED:

01 - Completed interview

03 - Partial interview, respondent indicated he or she was willing to finish, but we were unable to recontact respondent

06 - Partial interview, respondent refused to complete interview

RESPONDENT CANNOT BE INTERVIEWED:

11 - Too ill; mental disability

12 - Respondent does not speak English

13 - Eligible respondent not available during study

STILL BEING CALLED (RECHECK PERIODICALLY):

21 - No answer

22 - Normal busy signal

23 - Fast busy signal (or strange noise instead of a ring)

24 - Answering service

25 - Answering machine

26 - Temporarily disconnected

27 - Person who answers telephone is unable to help (e.g., child, does not speak English)

28 - Eligible respondent temporarily unavailable (make appointment if possible)

CALL BACK SECOND TIME TO VERIFY PROBLEM WITH NUMBER:

31 - Number changed (do not call new number when random sampling)

32 - Disconnected, cannot be completed as dialed

33 - Wrong number

34 - No ring

35 - Computer number/fax (high-pitched whistle)

NONSAMPLE (DROP, DEPENDING ON PURPOSES OF STUDY):

41 - Business telephone number

42 - Other nonhousehold telephone (car phone or phone booth)

43 - Not a resident of area being sampled

44 - Not a member of the group being surveyed (not eligible)

45 - No one in household 18 years old

46 - No one a citizen of the United States

47 - Works for organization conducting/sponsoring survey

SPECIAL PROBLEMS:

51 - Respondent cannot be reached during regular interviewing hours

TABLE 3.3 *Continued*

REFUSALS BY PERSON WHO ANSWERED THE TELEPHONE (BEFORE RESPONDENT IS SELECTED):

61 - Hang-up during introduction
62 - Verbal refusal during introduction
63 - Hang-up during respondent selection
64 - Verbal refusal during respondent selection

REFUSALS BY THE RESPONDENT (AFTER RESPONDENT IS SELECTED):

91 - Hang-up during introduction
92 - Verbal refusal during introduction
93 - Hang-up after introduction
94 - Verbal refusal after introduction

call the number back repeatedly in case the people return home. Some studies show that repeated call-backs over a period of days are effective, although there is little gain after six call-backs. Commercial polling operations are more likely to make only two or three call-backs and then substitute other numbers for numbers that do not answer, because repeated call-backs diminish their profit margins and take more time.

Call-backs are important if the people who are home less often differ in relevant ways from those who are home most of the time. For example, pollsters sometimes try to gauge public reactions to a presidential speech within 2 hours of the speech, but call-backs are impossible for such polls because of the short interviewing period involved. This limit can bias findings. Thus, when President Clinton went on television to justify the landing of United States troops in Haiti in 1994, a poll reported by the end of that evening indicated that his speech turned public opinion to favor invasion, whereas polls taken over the next few days, which allowed call-backs, consistently found that the majority of the public still opposed invasion.

Procedures differ in how problem situations are handled. Survey organizations often have a few interviewers who are good at getting people to cooperate who initially refuse to give an interview, but polls designed to generate instant results (within a few hours after a news event) do not try to convert refusals. Survey organizations in such states as California, Florida, and Texas usually employ Spanish-language interviewers, whereas those in other states rarely try to get interviews with Hispanic respondents.

Some organizations instruct interviewers to hang up when they reach an answering machine, whereas others have their interviewers read a short statement saying who called, the name of the organization, the purpose of the interview, and their intention to call back later for an interview. The message seems to legitimate the subsequent call-back in about the same way that letters are sometimes sent to respondents so that they expect an interview. A typical message to leave on the answering machine is "Hi, my name is . . . calling from Ohio State University. You have been selected to be included in a study to determine how Ohio residents feel about some important current issues. We will call back at another time. Thank you." It is often possible to get completed interviews from telephone numbers that reach an answering machine during the initial call.

Screening Questions. Some problems with telephone samples can be handled by asking some special screening questions of the person who answers the call. First, if the researcher wants to sample a particular city, the sampling procedures described above are likely to yield some calls to homes that are not in the city. Therefore, the person answering the telephone must be asked whether he or she lives in the desired area, rather than in an adjoining suburb.

Another problem concerns multiple telephone lines. A family with two telephone lines would have twice as great a chance to be included in a sample as a family with just one line. This problem can be handled by asking the respondents how many telephone lines they have. Respondents with two telephone lines would then be given a **weight** of one half, meaning that their data would only be counted half as much as those of respondents with just one telephone line so as to compensate for their greater chance of selection in the sampling.

Screening questions are also used to select the respondent in a household. Studies of households sometimes accept any adult who answers the telephone, even though that means more interviews with women and older people; some other polls try to interview the youngest male in the household to counter that bias. Most surveys instead use random selection of respondents.

Early telephone interviews tried asking people for the full listing of who lives in the household that is obtained for face-to-face interviews (see Table 3.2), but the interviewers soon found that many people would not disclose that information on the telephone. Several alternatives have been developed. One, known as the **Troldahl-Carter-Bryant method,** asks the person answering the telephone how many adults are in the household and how many adult females are in the household. The interviewer then consults a chart (chosen randomly from a set of charts) to decide which person to interview. This method also encounters problems because many people are unwilling to cooperate with interviewers asking about the composition of the household. A less obtrusive method, the **Hagen-Collier method,** is randomly to ask to speak to one of four types of people: the youngest woman over age 18, the oldest woman over that age, the youngest man over that age, or the oldest man over that age. If no person of the designated gender is in the household, the interviewer would then randomly ask to speak to either the youngest or oldest person of the opposite gender. A final system now used frequently is the **next birthday method.** The interviewer simply asks for the person in the household who will have the next birthday, and that person is the designated respondent. A related system is the **last birthday method,** in which the interviewer asks to speak to the person with the last birthday. These last three methods get lower refusal rates than the other methods.

A Sample of Students at a University

How could you draw a sample from the population of all students at a university? You could just use all the students who are taking a particular course for your sample, but they would not necessarily be representative of the total population. A single course would be a haphazard sample, rather than a probability sample, because all students do not have known chances of being included. A probability sample would be preferable.

For conducting a probability sample, you must first obtain a list of all the university students. An up-to-date student directory is perfect for this purpose. If you can gain access to a computerized version of that directory, you can use a computer program to draw a simple random sample. Alternatively, a systematic sample based on the student directory would give a good sample of the student body. There would be less error if you stratify the sample to guarantee proper coverage in the freshman, sophomore, junior, and senior classes, which is possible if the list includes each student's class.

In this example, the list of students (your sampling frame) must match the population of university students as closely as possible. If the list contains a bias, certain types of students will be missing from the sample. For example, a list of students who live in the dormitories would miss students who live off campus. In this case, it would be important to locate many different student lists, investigate the biases of each, and then choose the list that provides the most complete coverage (or use multiple lists together, removing duplicate listings).

Finally, it is important to keep in mind that the population for this study is from a single university, so the results can only be generalized to that university. You should not generalize from results on one campus to the population of college students. The university studied would constitute a haphazard sample of all universities, so generalizations should be limited to that campus.

A Sample of Residents of a City

The sampling problem is somewhat more complicated for a city. You could use a city directory for the listing of the population, but directories are always somewhat out-of-date by the time they are published. Similarly, if you wanted to interview voters a few months before an election, you could sample from the voter registration lists, but the voter registration lists miss people who register just before the election.

The best procedure for selecting a sample for face-to-face interviews is the multistage area sampling approach described above. Obtain lists of neighborhoods of the city and sample those. For each neighborhood in the sample, obtain lists of blocks and sample those. Finally, list the houses and apartments in the blocks that have been chosen and randomly sample those. This procedure guarantees a high-quality sample, although it is so difficult to perform that using directories and/or registration lists is often more convenient regardless of their drawbacks.

Another possibility is to conduct telephone interviews. A sample of numbers from the telephone book can be drawn, adding one to each number to be able to locate unlisted numbers. In many cities, **reverse directories** list houses geographically in order of their addresses and then give the corresponding telephone numbers, and samples can be drawn from these reverse directories. Alternatively, the local telephone company can provide a listing of residential central office codes, and a computer can be used to randomly choose central office codes and four-digit suffixes.

A Sample From a Rare Population

Sometimes, a researcher is interested in a specialized population, such as Jews, people with disabilities, or Vietnam veterans. These are fairly small groups, and it would be very expensive to telephone the general population until one accumulated enough people in these groups. Membership lists of organizations are sometimes useful in locating such people, but this approach still misses people who are not members of organized groups. Polling operations that regularly conduct surveys handle this problem by looking through their past surveys to locate respondents who fall into these groups and then recontacting those respondents.

Another approach to sampling from a rare population is **multiplicity sampling** (also known as **network sampling** or **snowball sampling**). A sample of people might be asked whether their extended family includes any veterans, and those veterans would then be interviewed. This approach is also sometimes used to trace patterns of influence. A random sample of voters might be interviewed and asked with whom they discussed the election most often, and those people might then be interviewed.

Election Exit Polls

One type of poll that involves unusual sampling procedures is the survey taken by the television networks on election day to predict the winners of elections as early as possible. These are generally statewide polls because most American elections are state elections. The networks decide which states to poll. The networks generally want to give early predictions of the results in the large states, but they often are willing to ignore the small states.

In states in which they are polling, the networks draw a sample of the voting precincts. At one extreme, this could be a simple random sample drawn from the list of all the voting precincts in the state, but that approach would allow a sample that would be too urban or too rural. At the opposite extreme, the networks could construct a purposive sample of precincts with known properties (e.g., precincts that usually go with the election winner, a quota sample with the right proportion of black and white precincts), but such nonprobability samples can contain unsuspected biases. The actual sampling procedures generally are stratified random samples, with stratification on urban versus rural precincts and parts of the state (e.g., upstate versus downstate in such states as New York and Illinois). Voting patterns in the sample precincts are examined to make sure the sample has been representative of statewide trends in the past.

In these sample precincts, the networks conduct **exit polls** with voters leaving the polling places. Interviewers might be instructed to take interviews with the fifth person leaving the polls after each quarter of an hour (e.g., 6:00, 6:15, 6:30). The results of these exit polls are telephoned in throughout election day so that network analysts can spot trends long before the polls close. The networks use these exit polls to project election winners, as well as to provide insights into the attitudes of voters.

After the polling places close, interviewers telephone in the official returns for the precinct as soon as they are available. The network analysts sum up those returns for the state and thus provide another means of projecting the vote in the state before the official returns for the whole state are available.

Election projections based on exit polls must be made cautiously because trends at the selected precincts might not be representative of the full range of votes. Absentee ballots are not taken into account in exit polls, and it is common for absentee ballots to favor a different candidate from the one favored by the votes cast on election day. This problem is further exacerbated by the liberalizing of rules for absentee ballots in California, along with the adoption of early voting in Texas. Substantial numbers of ballots are now cast before election day in these states, and particular groups (e.g., Hispanics) may be mobilized for such voting. In close elections, these extra ballots can cause exit polls to call an election wrong. Thus, as appealing as exit polls appear to be, they may not be clearly superior to conventional surveys.

These examples of polling procedures should demonstrate that sampling is a very practical operation. Mathematical theory guides sampling, but taking a sample requires knowledge of what problems are likely to occur. The sampling procedure chosen must handle those likely problems.

Problems in Sampling

The procedures for taking probability samples are complicated, but it is possible to design probability sampling procedures that do not bias the results and that keep costs reasonable. Generally, so long as (a) the interviewer cannot select the respondent, (b) the sample is large, and (c) there are enough clusters, samples will be highly representative of the population. An occasional sample may by chance be far from representative, but such a bad sample can often be detected if the researcher checks whether the sample approximately matches the percentages for each gender, race, and educational level given by the latest data from the Census Bureau. Still, some potential problems require attention.

Noncoverage Error

One complicating problem in sampling is **noncoverage error**—the omission of part of the intended population. Soldiers, students living on campuses, people living in hospitals, prisoners, and residents of Alaska and Hawaii are typically excluded from national samples, as are the homeless. These omissions are unlikely to affect national results by more than 1%, and in some cases they are viewed as completely irrelevant, as in election surveys, because many of these groups have very low turnout rates. Noncoverage error arises in telephone surveys because households without telephone service are not included in the sampling. Noncoverage error also occurs in list samples (e.g., sampling from telephone books or voter registration lists) when the lists are incomplete or out of date.

The Wrong Population Is Sampled

Researchers must always be sure the group being sampled is drawn from the population they want to generalize about. For example, you should not draw a sample of college students if you want to generalize about all college-age persons. A similar problem might arise if city officials were to survey swimmers at the city pool to determine whether the admission price is so high as to discourage use of the pool. The problem with sampling the swimmers is that the officials intend to make a generalization about all potential users, but those potential users who have already found the price too high will not be among the swimmers.

The Response Rate

We have already mentioned the problem of some people never being at home when the interviewer calls or visits. A related problem is some people in a sample refusing to be interviewed because they are ill, are too busy, or simply don't trust the interviewer. The interviewer may employ many kinds of persuasive arguments to get their cooperation, but in the end many people still refuse. In the 1950s, response rates of about 90% were typical. Today, however, people seem less trusting of interviewers, so response rates for door-to-door interviews are in the 70% range.

Response rates for telephone interviews are in the range of 50% to 70% of the answered telephones. This rate requires three to six call-backs at different times of the day and week to numbers that do not answer. Some academic polling operations telephone a number 18 times before dropping it from a sample. About 5% of interviews are not completed because the respondent hangs up in the middle, a higher noncompletion rate than for face-to-face interviews. These response rate figures vary by area, with lower rates in large cities for both face-to-face and telephone interviews.

When telephone interviewing was first being attempted, researchers were concerned because many Americans did not have telephones and would therefore be omitted from survey samples. This became a less serious problem when telephone ownership in the United States reached the 90% level in the 1970s. Response rates in face-to-face interviews fell at that same time and thus made the lack of complete coverage of telephones less serious.

A national experiment by Groves and Kahn (1979) compared demographic characteristics of respondents in face-to-face interviews with those of respondents in comparable telephone interviews. They found telephone respondents to be younger, more urban, and to have somewhat higher incomes and education, but the differences were not large and do not necessarily signify an unacceptable bias in telephone samples. Instead, they reflect reasonable differences in getting people to be interviewed by the two approaches. For example, young people are generally at home less and at more erratic hours than older people, so phoning back several times may be more effective at contacting them than call-back procedures for face-to-face interviews. Similarly, urban residents and people with higher socioeconomic status might feel more threatened by letting interviewers into their houses. They might therefore be more likely to refuse face-to-face interviews but be more approachable by telephone interviews. Thus, the few demographic differences that emerge between face-to-face and telephone interviews may indicate problems with face-to-face interviews as much as problems with telephone coverage.

This finding does not mean that researchers can be entirely sanguine about the demographics of telephone interviewing. As society changes, telephone interviewing may not remain successful. For example, higher telephone costs could cause poor people to drop their telephone service. In fact, the 1985-86 National Health Interview Survey found that 29% of households with incomes under $5,000 were without telephones, versus 1% of those with incomes over $30,000 (Groves, 1989, pp. 117-119). Still, the Census Bureau reports that only 5% of households did not have telephones in the early 1990s; this finding makes noncoverage a minimal problem.

Another problem is that people are becoming more wary of cooperating with surveys because companies often pretend to conduct surveys as a ruse to sell a product (known as **sugging**—*selling under the guise of a survey*). Also, more people are using answering machines to screen their telephone calls; this tactic makes it harder for polling operations to get through to their intended respondents. If these developments continue, nonresponse with telephone interviews may become so serious as to make telephone interviewing less attractive.

Refusals are most likely to occur in "cold contact" situations, when the respondent is not expecting a call. "Warm" telephone interviewing tends to obtain fewer refusals, but it is not always possible to give respondents prior information that they are going to be called. When addresses as well as telephone numbers are available, some survey organizations do send respondents letters in advance, telling them someone will soon be in touch. Some government surveys use face-to-face interviewing for a first interview and then use telephone interviewing for later reinterviews.

Nonresponse can be a problem, although researchers hope that people who refuse to respond do not differ much from those who do respond (other than being less cooperative). The higher the refusal rate, the more important it is to ascertain whether the refusals are concentrated among a certain group. The demographics of the sample can often be compared with census data to determine how representative the sample is, and the data can be reweighted if need be. Brehm (1993) shows that the nonresponse is most likely to be a problem when studying the causes or effects or variables related to survey compliance, such as interest in politics, information level, fear of crime, and general participation. Usually, though, nonresponse is ignored even if it deserves more attention.

_____

Sampling Error

A more basic type of error is **sampling error**—the error that arises from trying to represent a population with a sample. Inevitably, samples differ from populations. Consequently, researchers should not take sample results as absolutes, but rather as approximations. For example, if we find that 67% of a sample favors some program, we have learned that the odds are very high that the proportion favoring the program is near 67%.

The chances of error cannot be calculated for nonprobability samples, but they can be estimated for probability samples. Suppose, for example, a population has 200 people (100 women and 100 men) and we draw a sample of 50. Many different 50-person samples could be drawn, and not all would have the same sex ratio. Most of the samples would have sex ratios close to the sex ratio of the total population. We might draw an all-male sample, but that would be very unlikely.

Simple random sampling permits precision about the representativeness of our sample. If the true proportion of men is 50%, then a sample of 50 people would be expected to have a sex ratio (would have a sex ratio most of the time) within 14% of that value. More precisely, given a 14% margin of error, 95% of the samples would have between 36% (18) and 64% (32) men. This margin of error due to sampling can be determined for probability samples.

To state this technically, if repeated samples of size 50 were taken with replacement from a population with a 50:50 gender ratio, the percentage of males for 95% of the samples would be between 36% and 64%. This is known as the **95% confidence interval.**[3] Of course, we take only one sample, but we hope that our sample is one of the 95%, rather than one of the 5%. A statistician would say that we are taking a 5% chance of drawing a faulty conclusion—and 95:5 isn't bad betting odds.

As an example of a simple random sample with sampling error, it is worth conducting an experiment. Starting with 200 cards, write red numbers (1 to 100) on half and blue numbers (1 to 100) on the other half. Shuffle them well. Draw a card. Record its color. Put it back in the deck. Shuffle again. Draw another card. Record its color. Replace it, shuffle, record, and draw again. Keep doing this until you have drawn 50 cards. You may begin with a run of same-color cards, but you will probably end up with approximately 25 cards of each color. Figure 3.3 shows the probability of having a given number of blue cards in your sample. Because half the cards are blue, the most frequent result will be to have 25 blue cards, the next most frequent results will be to have 24 or 26 blue cards, and the least frequent results will be to have 0 or 50 blue cards. If you add up the probabilities of getting 18 blue cards, 19 blue cards, 20, and so on through 32 blue cards, the total should be about 95%.

Notice that Figure 3.3 shows a normal curve. If you drew a large number of samples from the same population and calculated the mean

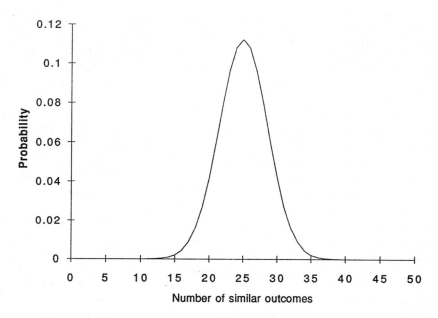

Figure 3.3. Sampling Distribution for Binomial With 50-Case Sample
SOURCE: Generated by the authors, using the binomdist function in Microsoft Excel.

of each sample (e.g., the sex ratio or the number of blue cards in the examples above), the distribution of the sample means has a normal distribution around the population mean. The most likely sample will have a mean precisely the same as the population mean. Values near the population mean are quite likely, whereas values far from the population mean are unlikely. Of course, a researcher only takes one sample, but the odds are that its mean is close to the population mean. According to published tables (e.g., Table 10.1), 95% of the area under the normal curve is within a known distance from its mean, and that is used to generate the margin of error.

Of course, with unusual luck, your sample might be 50 blue cards, but that should not stop you from believing in sampling theory. Just take 100 samples of size 50, and you will find that such eccentric samples will occur in only about 5 of them. Sampling is not magic; mathematical theory ensures that, notwithstanding the chance of getting a bad sample now and then, almost all results will be reasonably on target. Fortunately, researchers are not entirely at the mercy of bad samples. If a researcher knows from past surveys what results to expect, he or she does not trust a poll that departs radically from them. Thus, if one poll predicts a Republican landslide, whereas every other poll taken that year predicts a Democratic victory, you should be suspicious of the inconsistent poll.

Sample Size. The 14% margin of error in this example is high, but we could cut it by taking a larger sample. The key ingredient in determining the error for a simple random sample is the sample size. The more people who are interviewed, the smaller the error. Actually, quadrupling the sample cuts the error rate in half.[4] Surveys generally take more than 100 interviews because the error rate for samples of that size would be too high. But as the number of interviews increases, so does the cost of the study. At some point, added precision is not worth the extra cost. Most national samples use about 1,500 interviews. The margin of error with that size of multistage area sample is generally about 3%. To cut a 3% error to 1.5% would require, not an increase to 3,000 interviews, but an increase to 6,000, and that extra expense would not be justified. Elections can be safely predicted with a 3% to 4% error rate because most are decided by at least that large a margin. Accuracy of 1% is rarely needed.

The Sampling Fraction. The sampling error is also affected by the **sampling fraction**—the percentage of the population that is being interviewed. When the sampling fraction is above 30%, enough of the population has been sampled so that public attitudes are likely to be similar to those of the sample. The error then is less than it would have been for samples of the same size from a larger population. Usually, though, the sampling fraction is very small; few samples include more than 1,500 or 2,000 interviews even when there are millions of people in the population for national samples or hundreds of thousands in the population for surveys of major cities. Thus, the sampling fraction is typically less than 1%, which is too small to matter.[5]

If 1,500 interviews are needed for a representative sample of the 185 million adults in the United States, most people would expect that a sample of 500 or 1,000 respondents would suffice for a sample of the 13 million residents of Florida or of the 725,000 residents of San Francisco County. Because the sampling fraction generally has little effect on the margin of error, however, a big change in population size does not produce a big change in needed sample size. A researcher would need as large a sample to study the attitudes of San Francisco County residents or Florida citizens as for the entire United States. If the researcher uses a smaller sample for studying a smaller area, the error will be higher.

Determining Sampling Error When Stratifying and Clustering Are Used. Notice that when stratifying and clustering are used, the probability of error can still be determined. Clustering increases the sampling error, but stratifying usually reduces it. The error for a cluster design is greater than is the case for a simple random sample, but the multistage area sample is often considered to be preferable because it is much less expensive than a national simple random sample. In the SRC's samples, the margin of error for typical variables is about 3% for a multistage stratified and clustered 1,500-person sample; that is, if they find that 67% of the sample favors a proposal for government medical assistance, then the true population proportion is likely to be within 3 percentage points of 67%. More precisely, in 95 out of every 100 samples, the sample value should be within 3 percentage points of the true population value. The odds that the true population value here is between 64% (67 − 3) and 70% (67 + 3) are 95:5.

Table 3.4 shows the margins of error for various sizes of samples and different sampling procedures.[6] In the table, the error is always lowest with simple random sampling, but the Gallup and SRC procedures are designed to provide more economical samples with sampling error still within reasonable limits. The total survey error is inevitably greater than these sampling errors, as is described in Chapter 16, but it is usually very difficult to estimate the magnitude of the other sources of error in a survey.

Choosing a Sample Size. How does a researcher choose a sample size for a survey? A primary consideration is the margin of error that is tolerable. If you consider a 5% margin of error reasonable, that suggests a particular sample size. The sampling procedure is also relevant in that the margin of error is smaller with simple random sampling than with some other procedures. Additionally, you should consider the error for subgroups that are of particular importance. If you are primarily interested in political participation by women and how it differs from participation by men, you would look at the margin of error for women and men as subgroups. A sample of 400 gives an overall margin of error of 5%, but if about half the sample is female, then any conclusions about women

TABLE 3.4 Maximum Sampling Error for Samples of Various Sizes

| | Sampling Procedure | | |
Sample Size	Simple Random Sample	Gallup Poll	Survey Research Center Survey
960,000	0.1	—	—
200,000	0.2	—	—
100,000	0.3	—	—
10,000	1.0	—	—
4,000	1.6	—	—
3,000	1.8	—	—
2,000	2.2	2.8	3
1,500	2.6	3.0	—
1,000	3.2	4.0	4
750	3.6	4.7	—
700	3.8	4.8	5
600	4.1	5.0	—
500	4.5	5.7	6
400	5.0	6.0	—
300	5.8	7.4	8
200	7.2	9.0	—
100	10.3	12.8	14

SOURCE: The figures in the second column for more than 2,000 cases are based on the *t* distribution; those for under 2,000 cases are exact binomial values.
The figures in the third column were supplied by the Gallup Organization.
The figures in the fourth column are taken from Table 14.1.1, p. 576 in Kish (*Survey Sampling*, by Leslie Kish, Copyright 1965 by John Wiley & Sons, Inc. Reprinted by permission of John Wiley & Sons, Inc.); the latter figures are based on the 1963 Survey of Consumer Finances and may differ from survey to survey; reprinted with permission of the publisher.
NOTE: These are maximum sampling errors because sampling errors depend on the proportion being estimated. Sampling errors are maximal in estimating proportions around 50%. There is less error in estimating proportions less than 30% or above 70%, particularly in estimating proportions less than 10% or above 90%. Yet, in any event, the sample errors are not greater than those shown in the table.

would have a likely error of up to 7%. If you want only a 5% error range for your statements about women, you will require a total sample of 800.

The other major consideration in deciding the size of the sample is the budget. More interviews cost more money, and researchers conduct only as many interviews as they can afford. From this perspective, what size sampling error is tolerable depends on the purposes of the study. If you are trying to predict a landslide election, the 7% margin of error of a simple random sample with 200 interviews could suffice. If you are trying to predict a hard-fought election, even the 3% margin of error with 1,500 interviews may be too large to declare a winner, which is why polls often declare an election to be "too close to call." If you want to measure public attitudes on a matter of public policy, the 5% error with 400 interviews might be adequate.

SUMMARY

The quality of a survey is determined largely by its sampling procedures. Nonprobability samples can give biased results. Probability samples are required for good polls. With such samples, it is possible to estimate statistically the error that results from the sampling. There are other sources of errors in surveys (summarized in Chapter 16), but sampling error is particularly important because the margin of error due to sampling can be estimated mathematically.

Sampling methods will continue to evolve because applied sampling involves compromises between probability theory and practical problems. Researchers want to minimize sampling errors but are constrained by cost considerations. Increased use of unlisted numbers and the advent of answering machines, caller ID, call-forwarding, fax machines, and mobile cellular telephones are examples of the many practical problems that researchers must contend with in telephone sampling. Consensus may be reached on how to handle these matters, but changing technology and social conditions will inevitably create further problems for applied sampling.

Further Readings

Sampling

Hess, I. (1985). *Sampling for social research surveys, 1947-1980.* Ann Arbor: University of Michigan, Institute for Social Research.

Kalton, G. (1983). *Introduction to survey sampling.* Beverly Hills, CA: Sage.

Kish, L. (1965). *Survey sampling.* New York: John Wiley.

Lee, E-S., Forthofer, R. N., & Lorimor, R. J. (1989). *Analyzing complex survey data.* Newbury Park, CA: Sage.

Notes

1. A careful study using a 1937 Gallup survey that asked about participation in the 1936 *Literary Digest* poll (Squire, 1988) found that both the sample and the response (with only a quarter of 10 million mailed postcard ballots being returned) were biased.

2. A description of the SSI and Genesys sampling procedures, along with those used by the *New York Times*/CBS News, Gallup, and Harris in the early 1990s, is provided by Voss, Gelman, and King (1995).

3. To simplify this example, we are assuming the sample is "with replacement." After we draw a name, that name is thrown back into the pool so that each drawing has identical probabilities. Sampling with replacement is unusual. When the population of interest is large relative to the sample, however, the chance of drawing the same person twice is negligible, so the effect is the same as sampling with replacement.

4. The margin of error is

$$\pm t \sqrt{\frac{p(1-p)}{(N-1)}} \sqrt{1-f}$$

where t approaches 1.96 for the 95% confidence interval with large samples; f is the sampling fraction (sample size divided by population size); p is the sample proportion; and N is the sample size. The $\sqrt{1-f}$ term is ignored when sampling with replacement. The t term is larger than 1.96 for small samples: for example, 2.01 for a sample size of 50, 2.09 for a sample of size 20, 2.26 for a sample of size 10, and 2.77 for a sample of size 5. The full t distribution is shown in Table 10.2.

To illustrate the formula, let's return to the example above of selecting 50 cards from a deck of cards; however, it requires that we phrase the problem slightly differently. If we took a sample (with replacement) of 50 cards and found 25 to be blue (the proportion of blue cards, $p = .5$), how much confidence could we have in that number? The formula is

$$\pm 2.01 \sqrt{\frac{p(1-p)}{(N-1)}} = \pm 2.01 \sqrt{\frac{.5(1-.5)}{(50-1)}} = \pm 2.01 \sqrt{\frac{.25}{49}} = \pm .14$$

Hence, there is a 95% chance that the population proportion is between $.5 \pm .14$, or .36 and .64, so the number of blue cards is between $(.36 \times 50) = 18$ and $(.64 \times 50) = 32$. Notice that the sampling fraction is omitted because the sampling is with replacement.

5. The sampling error depends on the sample size, the sampling fraction if it is large, and the amount of variation in the variable being measured. Throughout this discussion, we have assumed some variation of the variable. If there were no variation (e.g., if everyone's party affiliation was the same), a sample of one would be sufficient, and there would be no error. Most of the variables that social scientists deal with, however, have considerable variation. The confidence interval and sampling error figures in the text assume a population proportion of .5, which yields the maximum error.

6. The values in the simple random sample column for $N > 100$ in Table 3.4 are maximal margins of errors using the formula

$$1.96 * \sqrt{\frac{(.5 * .5)}{(N-1)}} = \frac{.98}{\sqrt{(N-1)}}$$

The error in cluster samples can be much larger (three or four times these values) for geographic variables related to the clustering—such as the rural-urban variable.

☑ EXERCISES

1. If the margin of error is 1% and you found that the proportion of respondents favoring government restrictions on abortion is 45%, that finding means that

    a. the true proportion is probably between 43% and 47%.

    b. the true proportion is probably between 44% and 46%.

    c. there is only a 1% chance that the population proportion is not 45%.

    d. you have made a 1% error in your sampling, so the true proportion is 44%.

2. According to your analysis of a survey, there is only 25% support for government health insurance among the eight Southern college-educated white respondents with income over $15,000. What do you conclude from this?

3. Sampling error is most affected by the

    a. proportion of the population sampled.

    b. response rate.

    c. number of people sampled.

    d. size of the population.

4. Cluster sampling is used in face-to-face interviewing rather than simple random sampling to

    a. increase precision of surveys.

    b. cut transportation costs.

    c. get better estimates of attitudes in neighborhoods.

    d. get the proper representation of different regions of the country.

5. Sampling error is caused by which of the following? (Circle all correct answers.)

    a. refusal of some people to be interviewed

    b. differences between the sampling frame and the intended population

    c. interview with the wrong respondent

    d. attempts to describe a population with only a sample

6. The margin of error with 1,500 interviews using the SRC or Gallup sampling procedure is about _____ %.

4  Questionnaire Construction

☑ The preceding chapter addressed the issue of *whom* to ask; now we take up the issue of *what* to ask. What forms should the questions take? How should questions be worded? What response choices should be offered? In what sequence should the questions be asked? To conduct a survey, these practical matters must be settled.

Survey questions should be directly related to the theory and concepts you are investigating. Great care must be exercised in writing questions to get the information you are seeking. Naturally, the first step in writing questions is to spell out precisely what it is you want to learn from each question or set of questions. Once this is done, you can construct the questionnaire.

Question Form

When constructing a questionnaire, the first decision to make is what form of question will be used to measure each variable. There are two basic forms: closed-ended and open-ended. **Closed-ended questions** offer a series of alternative answers among which the respondent must choose, like a multiple-choice examination question. **Open-ended questions** allow people to answer in their own words, like an essay examination question.

Open-Ended Questions

Examples of open-ended questions are listed below:

What do you like about the Republican Party? What do you dislike about it?
What do you like about the Democratic Party? What do you dislike about it?
What do you think is the cause of the crime and lawlessness in this country?
What do you consider to be the most important problem facing the nation today?

In these questions, respondents can reply by using any framework they choose.

Open-ended questions have the advantage of allowing respondents to express their thoughts and feelings in their own words instead of in words chosen by the researcher. Thus, these questions permit the analyst to study how the public thinks, rather than just what their opinions are. For example, the question series asking what the person likes and dislikes about the political parties can be used to assess how positively or negatively a person feels about each political party. But that series can also be used to reveal the terms in which people think about politics: Do they mention ideological concepts? Specific issues? Do they justify their opinions with lots of information?

Thus, one advantage of open-ended questions is that researchers can see how respondents actually think about the topic. Another advantage is that different analysts with different research interests can find information of value to them from the answers to these same questions. The accompanying disadvantage, however, is that different respondents may approach the same question from different perspectives, so their answers are not fully comparable.

Open-ended questions are more difficult to analyze than closed-ended questions. This is so because researchers must code respondents' answers to open-ended questions into categories before analysis can begin. This coding involves grouping together respondents who provided similar answers. Because no two respondents ever give identical answers, researchers must often fill in missing details of an answer by making guesses about what a respondent meant to say. Closed-ended questions are easier to analyze because the respondents code themselves into categories.

Closed-Ended Questions

Examples of closed-ended questions are listed below:

Do you think the penalties for selling marijuana should be made stricter, should be made less strict, or should remain as they are now?

Which do you think is more responsible for crime and lawlessness in this country—individuals or social conditions?

Which of the following is the most important problem facing the country today: inflation, unemployment, the federal budget deficit, or the threat of nuclear war?

In each of these questions, respondents are asked to choose one from among a set of response alternatives.

A common format for closed-ended questions is to read a statement and ask the respondent to agree or disagree. Simple agreement or disagreement with a statement, however, gives no clue as to the intensity of the person's views. Intensity can be measured by asking whether the respondent

Agrees strongly
Agrees
Neither agrees nor disagrees
Disagrees
Disagrees strongly

This is a **rating scale.**

Rating Scales. Rating scales are ubiquitous in daily life. Restaurant reviewers, for example, give an establishment a certain number of stars to indicate its quality; more stars indicate higher quality. In surveys, many variables can be measured by using rating scales. For instance, people can be asked to indicate how much they like a person (e.g., a political candidate) or a group of people (e.g., blacks, Catholics, police) on a 6-point scale with end points labeled *like a great deal* and *dislike a great deal* (Table 4.1). Alternatively, respondents could be asked to indicate their

TABLE 4.1 Rating Scale					
How much do you like the Republican Party?					
1	2	3	4	5	6
Dislike a great deal					Like a great deal

feelings toward a person or group by using a **feeling thermometer** (Figure 4.1), on which a rating of 0° means they feel very cold, 50° represents the neutral point, and 100° is a very warm rating.

Tables 4.2, 4.3, and 4.4 show three other popular rating scales. For the **card sort** (Table 4.2), the person is handed a set of cards with statements such as "I like the Republican Party" on them and is asked to sort these cards into seven boxes. The **semantic differential** approach (Table 4.3) has the person rate entities such as the Republican Party along several 7-point bipolar scales such as good-bad, strong-weak, and fast-slow by checking the appropriate boxes. A common **7-point scale** (Table 4.4) calls for stating two opposite extremes—"Some people think that women

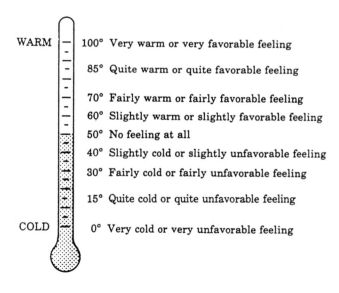

WARM
    100° Very warm or very favorable feeling

    85° Quite warm or quite favorable feeling

    70° Fairly warm or fairly favorable feeling

    60° Slightly warm or slightly favorable feeling

    50° No feeling at all

    40° Slightly cold or slightly unfavorable feeling

    30° Fairly cold or fairly unfavorable feeling

    15° Quite cold or quite unfavorable feeling

COLD
    0° Very cold or very unfavorable feeling

Figure 4.1. Feeling Thermometer

TABLE 4.2 Card Sort

How strongly do you agree or disagree with the following statement:
Marijuana should be legalized.

Strongly Agree					Strongly Disagree
+ + +	+ +	+	−	− −	− − −

TABLE 4.3 Semantic Differential

Here is a list of words you might use to describe political groups, and between each pair is a measuring stick of seven lines. Taking the first pair of words—"Good/Bad"—as an example, the line on the extreme left would mean the group concerned is very good, the next line would mean it was fairly good, and so on. The words at the top of your card will help you in choosing the line you think is appropriate.

Now, will you tell me which line you would use to describe the Republican Party?

	Very	Fairly	Slightly	Neither	Slightly	Fairly	Very	
Good:	:	:	:	:	:	:		:Bad
Weak:	:	:	:	:	:	:		:Strong
Fast:	:	:	:	:	:	:		:Slow

TABLE 4.4 7-Point Scale

(HAND R CARD G10) Recently, there has been a lot of talk about women's rights. Some people think that women should have an equal role with men in running business, industry, and government. Others think that women's place is in the home.

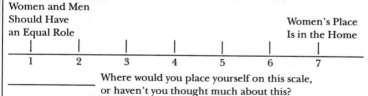

Women and Men
Should Have   Women's Place
an Equal Role   Is in the Home

1   2   3   4   5   6   7

_____   Where would you place yourself on this scale,
or haven't you thought much about this?

should have an equal role with men in running business, industry, and government. Others think that women's place is in the home"—and then asking the respondent to indicate his or her position along a numbered 7-position scale with the two end points labeled to represent those two extremes.

If a rating scale is to be used, three decisions must be made. The first decision to make is how many points to include in the scale. Because psychological research has shown that people have difficulty reliably making more than seven distinctions (G. Miller, 1956), it is usually not a good idea to construct scales with more than seven points. Indeed, if respondents are expected to remember the answer categories in a telephone survey, it is safer to use only five response categories. When people are given a 101-point scale like the thermometer (Figure 4.1), they typically simplify their task by using only the few points that are labeled and ignoring the rest.

The second decision to make is whether to provide a middle alternative. The feeling thermometer in Figure 4.1 includes one (50 = no feeling at all), whereas the 6-point scale in Table 4.1 does not. It is generally good to include a middle alternative because it represents the best description of some respondents' feelings. In some situations, however, researchers prefer to force respondents to take a stand one way or the other.

The third decision to make is how many points to label with words. You could label only the end points with words and label the other points with numbers (Table 4.1). You could put verbal labels on the end points and on some of the points in between (Figure 4.1). Or you could label all the scale points with words (Table 4.2). In general, verbal labels clarify the meanings of scale points for respondents, but they may be distracting for respondents in some cases. It is best to include them only when necessary.

If verbal labels are used, they must be chosen carefully, a process that is sometimes difficult. For example, should people be given the chance to evaluate the president's performance in office as *very good, good, bad,* or *very bad,* or does a different set of descriptors work better? Research on this topic has found that people see little difference between *very good* and *good.* A better set of labels is *excellent, good, so-so, bad,* and *terrible.* These terms capture the gradations from one end to the other better than the *very good* through *very bad* scale. If a researcher wanted even more extreme terms for the two ends of the scale, *perfect* and *disgusting* could be used as anchors (Lodge, Cross, Tursky, & Tanenhaus, 1975).

At the same time, caution is required in preparing closed-ended questions. Respondents tend to use the offered alternatives even when these do not represent their true views. For example, a study (Schuman,

Ludwig, & Krosnick, 1986) compared answers to the usual open-ended most important problem question ("What do you think is the most important problem facing this country today?") with a closed-ended version in which the respondents were given more specific choices ("Which of the following do you think is the most important problem facing this country today—the energy shortage, the quality of public schools, legalized abortion, or pollution—or if you prefer, you may name a different problem as most important"). Fully 60% of the sample accepted one of the four offered alternatives in the closed-ended version, whereas only 2.4% of an equivalent sample mentioned these problems in the open-ended version. Thus, answers to closed-ended questions can be misleading if the closed-ended alternatives are not selected carefully.

Remembering Response Alternatives. During a face-to-face interview, the respondent can be handed a show card on which are printed the response alternatives for a particular question. This is a useful technique when the choices are difficult to remember after just hearing them read aloud. Before telephone interviews are conducted, respondents are sometimes mailed sets of show cards so that they are on hand when the interviewer calls. Most often, though, telephone interviews are conducted without show cards. Therefore, response categories used in telephone interviews must be easy to remember.

One way to help telephone interview respondents answer closed-ended questions is to use a **branching format.** For example, asking whether a person "strongly agrees, moderately agrees, slightly agrees, neither agrees nor disagrees, slightly disagrees, moderately disagrees, or strongly disagrees" with a statement can lead to unnecessary confusion. It is better to ask first whether the respondent agrees or disagrees. Then, respondents who say they agree can be asked whether they agree strongly, moderately, or only slightly, and similarly for respondents who disagree. This is called a branching format because which questions are asked depends on the respondent's answers to earlier questions (see Aldrich, Niemi, Rabinowitz, & Rohde, 1982). If several questions using the same branching format are asked, many respondents will become familiar enough with the categories to give the complete response at once. Krosnick and Berent (1993) found that the branching format gives more reliable answers than does verbal labeling.

Response Choice Order. Unfortunately, the order in which answer choices are presented to respondents can affect their answers to closed-ended questions. The effect of order seems to depend on whether answer choices are read aloud to respondents (as occurs in face-to-face and telephone interviews) or are presented in written form (as occurs in self-administered questionnaires and in face-to-face interviews using show cards). When answer choices are read aloud to respondents, they are more likely to choose alternatives at the end of a list. When answer choices are printed on a questionnaire or on a show card, respondents are more likely to choose the alternatives at the beginning of the list. These order effects seem most likely to occur when many answer categories are offered to the respondent, so it seems better to offer only a few alternatives that are easy to remember (Krosnick & Alwin, 1987; Schuman & Presser, 1981).[1]

Choosing a Question Format

The main advantage of the closed-ended question format is that it provides the same frame of reference for all respondents to use in determining their answers. It is also easy and inexpensive to work with the resulting data. If the closed-ended format is chosen, however, care must be taken in writing the answer choices so that all possible opinions are included and none of the categories overlap.

Open-ended questions take more time to analyze, so if instant analysis is required, closed-ended questions are better. Commercial pollsters who have to meet client deadlines use closed-ended questions almost exclusively. Academic researchers, who can take years to analyze interview data, use open-ended questions more often.

Wording Questions

Once the investigator has decided which question forms to use in measuring each variable, the specific wording of each question must be worked out. When wording a survey question, a number of general rules should be kept in mind.

Ambiguous Wording

The meanings of words in survey questions must be clear to all respondents. For example, if a researcher asked respondents about their use of butter, the question wording should be clear whether use of margarine is or is not to be included. Or take a question asking whether respondents favor or oppose racial integration. This question is likely to be confusing to some respondents because it is not completely clear what is meant by "racial integration." Does it mean African Americans and whites eating in the same restaurant? Or does it mean blacks and whites living in the same house? If different respondents interpret the meaning of a question differently, their answers will be difficult to interpret.

To avoid ambiguity, survey questions should be short and direct. Also, the researcher must keep respondents' cognitive abilities in mind. When interviewing a sample of physicists about their work, it may be perfectly appropriate to use jargon to save time. But when interviewing a representative sample of Americans, the interviewer should use ordinary, everyday language and should avoid social science jargon or technical terms. Misunderstandings and confusion produce useless data.

A notable ambiguous question is one that was used by the University of Michigan's Center for Political Studies: "How many public officials do you think are a little bit dishonest—most, some, a few, or none?" Researchers included this question in surveys for years to measure how cynical Americans were about politicians. Needless to say, they were surprised to learn from a test of the questionnaire that some very cynical people were answering "none" because they believed that most public officials are very dishonest and that none are only a little bit dishonest! As a result, this question was changed to, "Do you think that quite a few of the people running the government are crooked, not very many are, or do you think hardly any of them are crooked?" As this case clearly illustrates, questions should be examined carefully for unintended double meanings.

In addition to agreeing with question writers about the meanings of words, respondents must share assumptions of those who write the questions. Unfortunately, this is not always the case. For example, political scientists generally agree on the meanings of the words *liberal* and *conservative* and often speak about how liberal or conservative political candidates are. Members of the public may not see candidates in this way, however, so asking them to report their perceptions of how liberal or conservative a candidate is might not yield useful results.

Another ambiguity in question wording pertains to descriptions of periods of time. Questions often ask people about their activities in the past few months or their plans for the next few years, but these are ambiguous time frames that different respondents will interpret differently. The phrase "over the past few years" might mean as few as 2 years to some people but more than 10 to others. It would be better to be precise about time frames than to use terms that are ambiguous.

Survey designers must be careful to avoid writing biased questions. Biased questions are those that make one response more likely than another regardless of the respondent's opinion. Examples of biased questions (taken from actual questionnaires) are "Do you favor murdering babies in the womb?" and "Should we continue disarmament so as to give this country to the Communists?" The bias in these questions is obvious, but unfortunately, subtle forms of bias can creep into survey questions despite researchers' best efforts to be objective.

One subtle form of bias results from citing authority figures such as the president. If the president is popular, the question, "Do you support the president's position on aid to India?" is likely to attract more support than stating the president's position without mentioning him and then asking respondents whether they support it. Generally, questions that identify the president with a program will bias support for that program, in comparison with questions asking about the program without mentioning him.

How a question is worded sets a frame of reference for the respondent. Thus, asking about forced busing frames the problem differently than does asking about school integration. People may think about those two topics differently, so which frame is used in a question may determine the answer. Close inspection of poll results reported in newspapers often reveals that wording of the question may evoke one answer more than another.

An important rule in question wording is that it should be as easy for a person to say no to a question as to say yes to it. Rather than just ask whether the person agrees with the proposed policy, the question can indicate that there is a legitimate disagreement on the proposal so the person will not think that automatic approval is required. So, instead of asking, "Should penalties for selling marijuana be made stricter?" it is preferable to say, "Some people think the penalties for selling marijuana should be made stricter, and other people think they should be made less strict. Do you favor stricter penalties, less strict penalties, or do you think the penalties for selling marijuana should remain as they are today?"

Some survey questions produce useless data because of **social desirability bias.** This occurs when respondents are unwilling to admit certain behaviors or attitudes because they are not considered to be socially acceptable. As a result, when polling about sensitive topics, it is important to make it easy for the respondent to give a truthful answer. For example, simply asking people whether they voted in the last election makes it difficult for some people to admit they did not vote. Instead, it is common to assure people that such behavior is reasonable, as in the question, "In talking with people about elections, we often find that a lot of people were not able to vote because they weren't registered, they were sick, or they just didn't have time. What about you—did you vote in the last election?"

Over the years, survey researchers have found that some question wordings yield more biased results than others. For example, people may round or understate their ages but generally will report their birthdates accurately. Similarly, people often refuse to tell strangers their income, but they are more willing to state the range in which their income falls (a. less than $10,000, b. $10,000 to $20,000, . . ., i. over $80,000, with people being asked to give the letter corresponding to their income bracket).

The problem of biased wording is seen in a survey sponsored by Ross Perot during the 1992 presidential campaign. Respondents mailed in replies to a questionnaire printed in *TV Guide*. A typical question asked, "Should laws be passed to eliminate all possibilities of special interests giving huge sums of money to candidates?" When phrased in this way, 99% of those responding answered yes. This result partly reflected the use of volunteer respondents, but the proportion answering yes was still 80% when a poll for *Time* and CNN by Yankelovich and Partners asked the same question to a half-sample of a regular cross-section survey. The *Time*/CNN poll asked the other half-sample a more neutrally phrased question, "Should laws be passed to prohibit interest groups from contributing to campaigns, or do groups have a right to contribute to the candidate they support?" and only 40% wanted contributions prohibited (Wilber, 1993). The difference in responses in the two half-samples shows how easy it can be to word survey questions in a biased manner to make it appear there is overwhelming support for a position that is, in fact, more controversial.

Double-Barreled Questions

It is important to avoid **double-barreled questions**—those that ask two questions at once: for example, "Do you favor reducing American use of gasoline by increasing our taxes on foreign oil?" There are two issues here: One is whether to reduce gasoline consumption, and the other is whether to use taxes on foreign oil as a means of accomplishing that end. Some respondents might say no to the question because they do not believe consumption should be reduced; others might say no because they believe some other means of reducing consumption should be used. Asking two questions would be better: (a) "Do you think that American use of gasoline should be reduced?" If the person answers yes, ask, (b) "Do you favor or oppose a tax on foreign oil as a way to cut gasoline use?"

Another version of this problem sometimes occurs with 7-point scales. When respondents are given two opposite sides to an issue and are asked to locate their own position along a scale (Table 4.4), it is important that the two extremes really be opposites in the minds of the respondents. If respondents do not see them as mutually exclusive, then answers will be meaningless. For example, during the Vietnam War days, the National Election Studies included a 7-point scale asking people whether they favored immediate American withdrawal from the war on the one hand, or the pursuit of military victory on the other hand. It has become apparent that many respondents actually favored both of these supposedly polar extremes over what they considered to be the unacceptable status quo: fighting on in an indecisive war.

_____

Double Negatives

Another question-wording problem is the use of double negatives. Such question wording can be confusing to respondents who do not know which answer represents their view. An extreme example comes from a 1992 survey on anti-Semitism done by the Roper Organization for the American Jewish Committee. Among the many questions asked in this survey was, "Does it seem possible or does it seem impossible to you that the Nazi extermination of the Jews never happened?" Remarkably, 22% of the public said it is "possible that it never happened," and another 12% answered don't know. The original poll result received much press play as a sign of rising anti-Semitism, but polling professionals were worried about the double negative in the question.

To test the question-wording effect in this instance, the Gallup Organization later asked two versions of the question to half-samples. A third of the public said it was possible that the Holocaust never happened when asked the double negative version, compared with only one tenth of the public when asked directly, "Do you doubt that the Holocaust actually happened, or not?" The double-negative phrasing of the original

Roper question resulted in a confusing stimulus that many respondents misinterpreted (Ladd, 1994).

No-Opinion Options

Another decision one must make in designing questions is whether to include a "no opinion" response option. Sometimes, respondents are asked whether they have an opinion on an issue before they are asked what that opinion is. For example, an interview might begin with a filter question, "Have you been interested in the issue of capital punishment enough to favor one side or the other?" Alternatively, a question could read, "Do you favor capital punishment, oppose capital punishment, or haven't you thought much about this issue?" Either of these approaches tells respondents it is legitimate and acceptable for them to indicate that they have no opinion on an issue. And doing so typically raises by 15% to 20% the proportion of people saying they have no opinion on an issue.

Some researchers advise the use of no-opinion options to prevent people from giving meaningless answers; that is, respondents may feel pressure to answer opinion questions even when they are not familiar with the issues just to avoid looking foolishly uninformed. Or, respondents may believe that providing an answer is more polite and does the interviewer a favor. Also, interviewers sometimes press respondents to offer opinions whenever possible, rather than accept don't-know answers right away. But if the questions explicitly indicate that not everyone will have opinions on the issues, then respondents may be more comfortable saying they have none, and interviewers may be less likely to press for opinions.

No-opinion options also have a down side, however: They sometimes discourage respondents from reporting meaningful opinions they do have. This can happen when a strongly worded filter implies that a great deal of thought is necessary to form an opinion on an issue; this wording may intimidate some people who have thought a bit about it and have formed meaningful opinions. And no-opinion options are attractive choices to respondents who may not be highly motivated to think carefully about a survey question in order to report their opinions precisely.

Consequently, it seems best to omit no-opinion options if asking about well-known issues with which most respondents are likely to be familiar. But such options may be useful when asking about issues that are relatively obscure and on which many respondents will be completely uninformed.

Hypothetical Situations

Another problem involves asking about how the respondent would behave in a hypothetical situation. Respondents may answer the question, but the answers may tell little about how they actually behave. For example, asking legislators whether they vote their own minds or follow constituents' wishes produces meaningless results. At best, the legislators give answers that will put them in a good light. A better tactic is to ask them what they considered in deciding how to vote in a recent specific vote in the legislature. Dealing with a specific case is more likely to get meaningful answers than asking hypothetical questions.

Importance of Question Wording

Even after taking account of all the question-wording problems described so far, there is no way to word a question perfectly. The same question can be asked in different ways, all of which seem good, and the different wordings may yield different results.

For example, pollsters Gallup and Harris ask questions monthly that measure the president's popularity, but they ask different versions. The Gallup Poll asks, "Do you approve or disapprove of the way the president is handling his job as president?" The Harris Poll asks, "How would you rate the job the president is doing—excellent, pretty good, only fair, or poor?" Harris then combines *excellent* with *pretty good* to yield *positive,* and *fair* with *poor* to yield *negative.* These questions generate different results. For example, 1 year after Gerald Ford became president, Gallup reported a 45% presidential approval rating, whereas Harris found only a 38% positive rating.

Consider another example. On the face of it, answering yes to "Do you think the United States should forbid public speeches against democracy" seems equivalent to answering no to "Do you think the United States should allow public speeches against democracy?" However, only 20% of respondents in a 1976 survey said yes to "forbidding" such speeches, compared with 45% who said no to "allowing" such speeches (Schuman & Presser, 1981, pp. 276-280). It is difficult to know why people answered these two questions differently, but this example illustrates how even trivial changes in question wording can substantially alter answers.

As a final example, polls routinely find much greater support for a constitutional amendment "protecting the life of an unborn child" than for a constitutional amendment "prohibiting abortion." People on both sides of the abortion issue can find poll evidence showing public support for their point of view because question wording can be manipulated to yield results that favor either.

In these examples, question wordings are logically equivalent but different versions produce different results. It is certainly natural to wonder which wording of each question is the "correct" one, but it is impossible to decide which result is right. It therefore seems best to recognize that there is no such thing as a correctly worded question. Instead of looking for perfect questions, researchers have learned to measure attitudes by using a variety of question wordings and to interpret the results of polls cautiously because they can be sensitive to rewording of questions.

Therefore, researchers tend not to try to determine how many people favor or oppose legalized abortion, for example. Instead, they study which types of people are more favorable and which types are less favorable, how opinions change over time, and what causes these opinions. Researchers generally believe that the same results regarding group differences, change, and cause will be obtained regardless of the exact question wording used. For example, if Protestants and Catholics differ in terms of favorability toward abortion, any wording of an abortion question probably will reveal that difference. Similarly, changes in attitudes over time and the cause of attitudes should be apparent regardless of the attitude measure used.

Using Standard Questions

A useful shortcut to wording your own questions is to use standard questions that have been developed and employed by major survey organizations. Through extensive experience, these organizations have refined measures of political and psychological concepts (D. Miller, 1991), as well as standard background questions about income, age, occupation, education, and so on. A survey researcher can benefit from the experiences of others by using their questions and by modifying these only when necessary to suit particular objectives. Using questions that have been used in previous surveys allows comparison of new results with older ones to study changes in attitudes over time. This use also permits replication of findings of previous research, a task that is important in science but that is rarely done.

When designing a survey, a constant tension exists between the desire to use standard questions for comparing results with those of previous surveys and the desire to improve the wording of questions. After some experience using a standard question, researchers sometimes realize that it could be improved through rewording. Changing wording, however, makes it more difficult to examine attitude change because the stimuli given to respondents are different. This difference means that minor tinkering with the wording of standard questions is not worthwhile; standard questions should be reworded only if serious problems are found with them.

Sometimes, rewording questions is necessary because of changes in the meanings of words or in the acceptability of certain terms. For example, it was common to refer to blacks as Negroes in the 1950s. Asking a question about Negroes today would seem odd to many respondents. Therefore, if a researcher were tracking changes in racial attitudes over time, it would have been necessary to replace the word *Negroes* with the word *blacks* at some point since the 1950s.

Another reason for rewording questions pertains to changing meanings. Consider a question that asks respondents whether they favor or oppose racial integration. In the 1950s, most Americans probably interpreted the term *racial integration* as referring to whites and African Americans eating in the same restaurants, sleeping in the same hotels, and so on. Today, most respondents would be unlikely to think of *racial integration* as referring to these circumstances because most people take them for granted. Instead, it is more likely that people will think of controversial aspects of racial integration, such as busing children to integrate schools. To track changes in attitudes toward the same concept, it is necessary in cases like this to reword the survey question.

It is useful to think of a survey question as a **stimulus** to which respondents respond. To track variations in attitudes across groups or changes in attitudes over time, the same stimulus must be presented to respondents in all groups and at all times. It is tempting to think of the stimulus as the *wording* of a question, but it seems more appropriate to think of the stimulus as the *meaning* of the question. Wording should therefore be changed when necessary to keep meaning constant.

Batteries of Questions

It is often impossible to measure a complex concept with only a single question, so several questions may be needed to measure the various aspects of the concept. For example, if researchers wanted to measure how cynical people are about government, they might ask, "How much of the time do you feel you can trust the government in Washington to do what is right? Do you think that people in the government waste a lot of the money we pay in taxes, waste some of it, or do not waste very much of it? Do you think that quite a few of the people running the government are a little crooked, not very many are, or do you think hardly any of them are crooked?" No one of these questions provides a perfect measure of political cynicism, but the set of questions can be combined into an overall index of cynicism. The results produced by this index are not as influenced by the wording of particular questions as would be the case if only one question were used.

Tailoring Questions to Respondents

Questions should be written specifically for the group being interviewed. For a sophisticated political elite, the questions could be phrased differently than for the general public. Legislators, for example, could be asked their opinions on specific policies that would be meaningless to most people. Of course, questions asked of the mass public cannot be compared directly with questions asked of elites if the two sets of questions are worded differently.

When dealing with the mass public, it is important to keep questions at a level the respondents understand. Minimally, this means avoiding social science jargon and terms the public would not recognize. It also argues for phrasing questions and alternative responses in the way the public thinks about the topic, rather than in the way researchers think about it.

Evaluating Questions

Once a survey question has been written, the investigator must evaluate how well it does what it is intended to do. That requires assessing the reliability and the validity of each question.

For a survey question to be useful, it must be reliable, meaning that people should answer it the same way each time they are asked. Imagine measuring the length of a pencil with an elastic ruler. One person may measure its length to be 4 inches, whereas another person may find its length to be 3 inches because he or she stretched the ruler. This is an example of an unreliable measure. Using a reliable measure, repeated measurements of the same object produce similar results, as is the case when measuring the length of a pencil with a wooden ruler.

The best way to assess the reliability of a question is by comparing answers people give to it on one occasion with the answers those same people give to it a short time later. Of course, if the time interval is too short, the apparent reliability of a question may be exaggerated because people simply repeat what they remember saying the first time they were asked. If the time interval is too long, people's answers may change because their attitudes have changed and thus caused the question's apparent reliability to be artificially low. If answers to a question are quite consistent over a period of a few weeks, the question is probably adequately reliable, but if people's answers are very different on the two occasions, the question must be rewritten.

A battery of questions measuring the same concept is considered to be reliable if a person's answers to them are consistent with each other. For example, on the cynicism battery described above, if the people who give cynical answers to one question are trusting on a second question, whereas those who give trusting answers to the first question are cynical on a second question, then the two questions are not consistent. The researcher should try to determine which question is least consistent with the remaining questions and drop that question to improve the overall reliability of the battery.

Good survey questions must also be valid, meaning that they should measure the concepts they are intended to measure. Sometimes, a question may actually measure a related concept, rather than the one the researcher wants to measure. The validity of a survey question may be evaluated in a number of ways, the simplest of which is to assess its **face validity**—the degree to which it seems to measure the appropriate concept on its face. For example, to measure how cynical people are about politics, asking whether all politicians should be trusted has more face validity than asking whether all politicians should be jailed. Yet, face validity is a subjective matter, so it should not be the only test of a question's validity.

Two other sorts of question validity are **convergent validity** and **divergent validity.** The principle underlying these forms of validity is that measures of the same concept should receive similar answers, whereas measures of different concepts should receive different answers. Convergent validity is achieved when measures of the same concept have similar patterns of correlation with other variables. Divergent validity is assessed by comparing people's answers to a question measuring one concept with their answers to a question intended to measure a different concept. For example, questions on political cynicism should not yield identical answers when compared with questions on political efficacy (whether people think they can influence government actions); if answers are not highly similar, they are said to have high divergent validity. Questions with low convergent or divergent validity must be rewritten.

Another form of validation is **criterion validity,** which can be assessed by comparing people's answers to a survey question with a direct measure of the concept of interest. For example, a question asking people whether they voted in an election can be validated by checking official records in voting registration offices. Unfortunately, it is impossible to obtain official criteria for most survey questions, particularly those measuring attitudes. When it is possible to assess criterion validity, though, it often turns out to be surprisingly low. It is therefore important to assess criterion validity whenever possible in order to identify inadequate questions.

Sometimes, a survey includes a battery of questions intended to measure different aspects of the same concept. Investigators speak of the **content validity** of such sets of questions, the degree to which they measure all the important aspects of the concept. For example, if a researcher wants to measure how knowledgeable respondents are about politics, a single question asking how many justices are on the U.S. Supreme Court would be insufficient. Obviously, other questions should be added, perhaps asking how many years a senator's term in office is, how many times a person can be reelected president, and so on. If a battery of questions lacks content validity, the survey designer can solve the problem by adding new questions to measure additional aspects of the concept.

A final form of validity is **construct validity.** A theory may indicate how the concept being measured should be related to other concepts. If the measure of the concept is not related to other concepts as the theory suggests, then either the theory is disproved or the measurement is invalid. If the theory is widely accepted, the construct validity of the measure is considered to be low. As an example, suppose that much previous research shows that people who are more cynical about politics are less likely to vote but that you find the opposite in your survey. This could be a disproof of the theory, but it is more likely that the construct validity of your cynicism and/or voting turnout measures is low.

Always be cautious in interpreting survey results because those results may be the product of poor question wording. Before taking the results literally, make some appropriate checks. Does the question wording really seem reasonable (have good face validity)? Does it give results similar to the results of other measures of the same concept (have good convergent validity)? Does it give results different from questions that are supposed to be measuring different concepts (have good divergent validity)? Can it be compared against a direct measure of the concept (have good criterion validity)? Does it measure the full breadth of the concept (have good content validity)? Does it relate to other variables as theory and previous research suggest it should (have good construct validity)?

Constructing the Questionnaire

After deciding on the wording of each question, the questionnaire must be assembled. This involves deciding on the order of topics to be discussed and the order of questions on each topic.

Topic Order

The organization of questions in the questionnaire is extremely important, partly because the interview may be terminated at the beginning if it starts with questions that anger or embarrass the respondent. Also, a respondent may not give candid answers to personal questions unless he or she has developed some rapport with the interviewer. Therefore, interviews should begin with general warm-up questions that put respondents at ease and show that the interviewer or researcher is interested in learning their views, rather than in testing their knowledge. Open-ended questions encourage people to speak freely and help them become comfortable, so they make good early questions.

It is especially important that the early questions in an interview correspond closely to the purpose of the survey as it was originally described to the respondent. So many salespeople call or visit homes, claiming to be conducting a survey and later switching to a sales pitch, that people may distrust surveys until the interviewer has proved that the study is legitimate by asking many questions on the stated topic. Trust between interviewer and respondent is more difficult to establish on the telephone than in person, so early questions in telephone interviews must be especially good at building rapport.

Routine demographic background questions (e.g., about the person's education, occupation, and religion) are usually placed toward the end of a questionnaire. Questions that might anger or embarrass some respondents or that they might be reluctant to answer (e.g., questions about their income) are customarily put at the end of the interview as well.

Question Order

Each question in a questionnaire should flow naturally from the previous one. It is confusing to people if the questionnaire skips around from topic to topic, so questions on the same topic should be grouped together. Each section should begin with an introductory sentence telling the respondent the topic of the next series of questions ("Now we will turn to some questions about politics"), particularly when there is a sharp change in subject matter.

The order in which questions on the same topic are asked sometimes makes important differences. Asking one question before a second can yield different results from asking the second question first. This possibility is especially important in the presence of **consistency bias**—the desire of respondents to appear consistent to the interviewer by answering related questions in a consistent manner. For example, studies find that people are more likely to agree that Japan should have the right to limit its imports if they are first asked whether the United States should have the right to limits its imports. Consistency bias is reduced if people do not notice that separate questions are interrelated. Still, it is worth avoiding this problem by not asking a series of questions that might make respondents think they are being tested for the consistency of their answers.

Early questions can affect what comes to mind for the respondent when asked a later question. Suppose you wanted to measure what people consider to be the most important problem facing the country (measured via an open-ended question) and how they feel about specific policy questions such as foreign aid, our relations with Russia, and the state of the economy (measured with closed-ended questions). If the most important problem question is asked late, people will naturally think back to their answers to the specific policy questions and will often choose from among the issues mentioned in those earlier questions. To avoid inadvertently structuring responses in this way, open-ended questions should be asked before closed-ended questions on similar topics.

Response Choices

Some further question-wording problems arise from the response choices in a survey. It is useful to have some consistency in scales used in a study. Respondents are likely to become confused if they are asked to use a 5-point scale on one set of questions, then a 101-point thermometer scale, followed by a 7-point scale for another set of questions, some branching questions, more 5-point scales, and so on. Some variety in scales might help keep a respondent's attention, but switching back and forth can be very confusing.

A final question-wording problem is related to a sequence of questions that all use response options such as yes/no or agree/disagree. Sometimes, people do not seriously consider each question but are just in an acquiescent mood and simply say yes or agree to all the questions. This problem, called **response set,** can seriously distort results. Suppose you have a series of yes/no questions designed to measure how conservative a person is, with a yes on each question being the conservative response. An acquiescent person would be scored as extremely conservative. The impact of response sets can be reduced by introducing some variety into the questions so that, for example, yes is the conservative response to some questions and no is the conservative response to others. An acquiescent person would then be scored as conservative on some questions, liberal on others, and therefore be viewed as neither conservative nor liberal. Overall, the result would be a more accurate measure of conservatism.

Number of Questions

Researchers invariably want to ask more questions than possible in a single survey. If too many questions are asked in face-to-face or telephone interviews, many respondents will terminate their interviews early. Similarly, the proportion of returned forms decreases as the length of mailed questionnaires increases. There are no firm guidelines for how many questions can be asked, but survey organizations develop experience in how long they can keep interviews going.

The problem of having too many questions has several possible solutions. One is to ask some questions of only half-samples; that is, half of the sample is asked some questions and the other half is asked other questions. Door-to-door interviews often have two forms of questionnaires to accommodate such half-samples. Computer-assisted telephone interviewing permits even more complicated questionnaire design, with many questions asked of different half-samples.

NORC's General Social Survey (GSS) has been particularly inventive in finding ways to stretch the number of questions it asks. GSS conducts yearly interviews to monitor social trends, but it would take too much time to ask every question every year. Furthermore, if each question had to be asked each year, there would not be enough space in the interview to try out new questions. GSS handles this problem by asking each question 2 years out of each 3 on a rotational basis. This strategy allows GSS enough space to have a special topical module for each survey, such as religion one year, occupational prestige another year, and intergroup relations another. Additionally, GSS includes experiments most years, including multiple forms trying different wording of some questions and varying question order. In 1994, GSS switched to a biennial, split-sample design, with two samples of 1,500 each being interviewed every other year with the same core questions but different topical modules.

Questionnaire Layout

After the questions and their order are determined, it is necessary to lay out the questionnaire so that it can be read easily. If the physical layout of the questionnaire is too confusing, even a good interviewer will skip questions by accident. This is especially a problem with self-administered questionnaires because there is no way of calling to the respondent's attention a question that was missed.

A good questionnaire is laid out so that the pages are not overly cluttered. Arrows may help the interviewer follow the intended question sequence. Important questions should not be hidden at the bottom of the page.

Pretesting the Questionnaire

Questionnaire construction is really an art, much of which is learned through practice. In fact, it is so difficult that researchers rarely use a questionnaire in a survey without first pretesting it. They interview some people who will not be in the final sample to try out the questions. Taking 25 to 75 pretest interviews for a major survey has been recommended (J. Converse & Presser, 1986), but minimally it is important to try out the questionnaire on at least a few people just to make sure it works.

Pretest interviewers generally report to the researchers at a debriefing, when they indicate any difficulties they encountered with the questions. Often, unexpected problems are found with some questions. After the debriefing, the questionnaire is revised and may be pretested again if substantial changes are made.

Pretesting can be used as a tool in question formulation. Suppose a researcher wants to use closed-ended questions so that answers can be tabulated quickly but is unsure about which issues people have opinions on. A pretest could include an open-ended question asking people what issues they consider to be important, and the issues mentioned most frequently could be examined by using closed-ended questions in the final study.

Pretests are also useful for determining how long it will take to administer a questionnaire. Inevitably, researchers want to ask more questions than can be fit into the short amount of time most respondents will give them. Pretests often force questionnaire designers to be realistic about the length of a questionnaire and to drop questions for reasons of time.

More complex and formal pretesting methods have been developed that some researchers think can help improve questionnaires. One is **cognitive think-aloud** pretesting. To do this, a set of pretest respondents are asked to think aloud as they proceed through an interview, verbalizing their thoughts about the questions as well as their answers. Although most people find this difficult to do at first, some can learn to do it well, and it allows researchers to identify some potential problems in questions that might not otherwise be apparent.

Another pretesting method involves studying the respondent's behavior while answering questions. If a respondent asks for questions to be read again, or if he or she pauses for a long time or says "uhh" or "umm," this may indicate problems with a question that should be fixed. Pretest interviews are sometimes audio- or videotaped for later analysis because it is difficult for interviewers to take extensive notes on respondent behavior while asking questions and recording answers.

SUMMARY

The general rules of questionnaire design are as follows: (a) Use open-ended questions to let respondents define their own frame of reference for the answer, but use closed-ended questions when a quick tabulation of results is required; (b) word the questions simply and avoid bias; (c) avoid questions that are too sophisticated or complex for respondents; (d) organize the questions so that they flow smoothly, so that early questions are not threatening, and so that early questions do not direct later answers.

Remember, what you ask is what you get. Ask a good question, and you get useful information. Ask a bad question, and you get useless information. Questions must be structured with the purposes of the survey clearly in mind, so be tenacious in asking yourself, What is it that I really want to know? How will I use this information when I get it? What is the purpose of this question? and Does it accomplish that purpose?

Finally, you cannot take survey results as absolute because they are dependent on the wording of questions. Slightly different wordings can yield results that differ by 5% to 10% and sometimes more. But if the wording is reported, readers can form their own ideas about how valid the questions are. All surveys have flaws, but high-quality surveys make an honest attempt to accomplish their purposes with accurate, unbiased questions.

Further Readings

Questionnaire Design

Bradburn, N. M., Sudman, S., & Associates. (1981). *Improving interview method and questionnaire design*. San Francisco: Jossey-Bass.

Converse, J. M., & Presser, S. (1986). *Survey questions: Handcrafting the standardized questionnaire*. Beverly Hills, CA: Sage.

Fox, J. A., & Tracy, P. E. (1986). *Randomized response*. Beverly Hills, CA: Sage.

Krosnick, J. A., & Fabrigar, L. R. (in press). *Designing good questionnaires: Insights from psychology*. New York: Oxford University Press.

Labaw, P. (1985). *Advanced questionnaire design*. Cambridge, MA: Abt.

Schuman, H., & Presser, S. (1981). *Questions and answers in attitude surveys.* San Diego: Academic Press.

Reliability and Validity

Carmines, E. G., & Zaller, R. A. (1979). *Reliability and validity assessment.* Beverly Hills, CA: Sage.

Note

1. A meta-analysis (Bishop, 1990) found that the effects of offering a middle alternative and of giving counterarguments are greater for those with lower involvement on an issue, whereas question order and response order effects are no greater for those with low involvement.

☑ EXERCISES

1. Suppose you are designing a survey on attitudes toward various lifestyles and expect educational differences to be a major factor in determining people's attitudes. To test this hypothesis, you want to measure each person's education. First, list the different things that might be meant by "the person's education." The term has at least three major meanings. Write a question (or series of questions) to use in asking about a person's educational background that would permit analysis of the effects of all of these aspects of education.

2. It is very difficult to phrase unbiased questions on emotionally charged issues. Suppose you want to study people's opinions on abortion; more precisely, you are interested in the circumstances in which people would permit abortion. What are the most basic types of circumstances that should be included in a question? (There are many distinct alternatives, so concentrate on a few major types.) How would you phrase a closed-ended question on this topic?

5 ☐☑ The Data
☑☐ Collection Stage

☑ Once the questionnaire has been prepared, the next stage in a survey is to collect the data. The three primary methods for survey data collection are face-to-face interviewing, telephone interviewing, and self-administered questionnaires. In this chapter, we describe the mechanics involved in each method and compare their strengths and weaknesses. Telephone interviewing now predominates over the face-to-face approach, but understanding face-to-face interviewing helps clarify the advantages and disadvantages of the telephone approach.

Face-to-Face Interviewing

Historically, face-to-face interviewing has been the most common method of survey data collection, and some commercial survey organizations still make frequent use of this approach. To use this method, an organization begins by hiring a staff of interviewers and teaching them how to conduct interviews. Letters describing the purpose of the survey and telling residents to expect a visit from an interviewer are then mailed to all the residences (e.g., houses, apartments, mobile homes) where interviews are to take place. Each interviewer is given a set of blank questionnaires and is assigned a set of residences to visit; after the interviews are completed, the questionnaires are returned to the survey organization office for data processing.

Selection of Interviewers

Regardless of how much care is taken in drawing the sample and in writing the questions, the success of a survey is in the hands of the interviewers. They ask the questions and record the responses by writing them on the questionnaires. If they do a good job, the study is in good shape; if they do a poor job, the results are meaningless.

Because getting in the door for an interview can be difficult, one of an interviewer's most important tasks is to get respondents to agree to participate in the survey. Even when the interviewer identifies herself, shows credentials, and reminds the resident about the letter he or she presumably received a few days earlier, it is natural for the person to wonder whether the interviewer is being truthful. Magazine salespeople often claim to be taking a survey until they are well into their sales pitch, so it is not surprising that many people are suspicious of interviewers.

People who seem credible and who do not make respondents feel threatened are most likely to obtain entry into homes. Because initial perceptions of an interviewer's credibility and threat are based largely on appearance, survey organizations prefer to hire middle-class, middle-aged women. (Thus, we refer to interviewers as female.) Young people and men have a harder time gaining access to people's homes, and men with long hair or a beard are especially likely to have trouble obtaining interviews. Interviewers of an ethnic minority are typically employed in predominately ethnic minority neighborhoods because these individuals are more likely to gain entry there.

A second primary task of the interviewer is to measure respondents' attitudes as accurately as possible. To do so, the interviewer must gain the trust of the respondent and must induce him or her to speak freely. Understandably, most people are reluctant to express their opinions to a person they do not know at all, but candid responses are essential for survey data to be useful. Respondents speak most freely with interviewers whom they believe have opinions similar to their own, a judgment that is also made partly on the basis of the interviewer's appearance. This is another reason why white interviewers are usually assigned to interview white respondents, black interviewers are usually assigned to interview black respondents, Hispanic interviewers are usually assigned to interview Hispanics, and so on.[1]

Once interviewers are chosen, they must be taught general procedures for obtaining good interviews, as well as specifics about the current
questionnaire. They are shown how to initiate interaction with a potential respondent and how to administer the questionnaire. The training
usually begins with showing the interviewers some play-acted interviews
so that they can see which interview practices are successful. Survey
organizations often use their own training videotapes that illustrate good
and bad interviewing procedures and that show how to handle particular
problem situations. During the training, interviewers are taught a number of basic rules for obtaining the interviews.

Interviewers must also become familiar with the questionnaire being
used in the study. They are briefed on the purposes of the study and on
the objectives of each question. This knowledge helps them handle
problems they may encounter during interviews. Finally, they conduct
practice interviews to familiarize themselves with the questions before
they take the real interviews.

One distinction between the best survey organizations and the rest is
the amount of effort they give to this training phase. It is easy to hire
people to do interviewing, but training is required to yield quality
interviews.

Organizations that regularly conduct surveys hire a permanent staff of
interviewers in their primary sampling units. The same interviewers are
used for several different surveys. This use leads to better trained interviewers than would be obtained by hiring new interviewers for each study.

Obtaining the Interview

It might sound as if face-to-face interviewing is easy, that the interviewer just goes to the person's home and conducts the interview.
Survey research is never that simple, however. Instead, the interviewer
must handle a number of preliminary problems before starting the
interview.

Initiating Contact. When an interviewer rings a doorbell and someone
comes to the door, the interviewer must make sure the person does not
slam the door in her face. Usually, she begins by introducing herself and
showing some credentials from the survey organization. She explains the
nature of the study in general terms ("We are getting information on

how people feel about important problems facing the country today") and assures the person that the opinions collected will be kept confidential. Finally, the interviewer tells the person how his or her home was chosen ("We talk with people of different ages and walks of life in all parts of the country and put their answers together to get a cross section of the people").

Sometimes, an interview gets no further than this stage. The person may not trust the interviewer's explanation or may be fearful of being interviewed. Further explanations or assurances may help, but sometimes the refusal is adamant and the interview terminates. If the interviewer came at an inconvenient time, perhaps a later appointment can be made for the interview. Occasionally, interviewers encounter situations that do not permit interviews: The respondent may be mentally or physically ill, drunk, or so busy that the interview is constantly interrupted. Every survey loses a few interviews for these reasons.

The problems inherent in interrupting someone's life should not be minimized. People are always doing something when an interviewer knocks on their door. Most people stop what they are doing to answer the door, and most agree to be interviewed, but sometimes a respondent is caught in an embarrassing moment. Every survey organization has a story about the interviewer who rings a doorbell and is greeted by a naked person. The story often continues that the interviewer explains that she is not permitted by her organization to take interviews unless the person is clothed. Usually, the individual agrees to get dressed. If an interview is truly impossible at a given time, the interviewer is instructed to excuse herself politely and return later to try again.

Selecting a Respondent. Once the person who answers the door agrees to speak with the interviewer, she asks who is living in the home and what their genders and ages are. Using the household listing, she follows instructions and selects the person to be interviewed—perhaps the oldest male (if there is one) in the first household, the youngest female over age 18 (if there is one) in the next, and so on. It is important to the sampling that the interviewer carry out this respondent selection procedure carefully.

After the respondent has been selected, a time for the interview must be agreed on. If the person who answers the door is the person to be interviewed, the interview is usually conducted at that time. If the person to be interviewed is not at home, an appointment can be made for the interviewer to return to the home.

Setting Interview Conditions. Whenever possible, interviews should be conducted without an audience. If friends or family members are present, the respondent might give the answers that these people would approve of instead of report his or her own attitudes. Furthermore, children playing in the same room can be distracting and can therefore decrease the quality of answers. Unfortunately, it can be difficult to get the respondent alone, so in some national studies as many as half of the interviews are taken with family or friends present.

Getting Informed Consent. The participation of respondents in surveys should be voluntary and based on an understanding of the nature of the research project and of any risks involved. The more the interviewer reminds people that they need not participate, however, the less likely they are to do so. The lower response rates that result from stressing voluntary participation make the research findings less generalizable to the population of interest. As a result, interviewers typically mention the voluntary character of participation only briefly while attempting to secure the person's cooperation.

At the beginning of interviews, respondents are usually told what topics will be covered and are given a rough idea of the length of the interview. They should also be apprised of what rights they have in the interview situation. This is done by saying something like, "Feel free to ask any questions at any time. If you do not wish to answer a particular question for any reason, just let me know and we'll go on to the next question."

Guidelines for Interviewing

A variety of guidelines for interviewing are designed to help get candid answers from respondents.

Asking the Questions. Generally, the interviewer is expected to read the questions by using the same wording and in the same order as they appear in the questionnaire. Because even small changes in question wording or order of questions can sometimes change respondents' answers dramatically, it is essential that all interviewers administer the questionnaire in an *identical* manner. Chaos would result if every interviewer asked a different variant of the same question or changed the order of questions to suit her tastes.

Recording the Answers. Interviewers usually record respondents' answers exactly, including a verbatim record of open-ended answers. This practice allows researchers to analyze the respondent's answers in whatever manner they desire, without being dependent on the interviewer's interpretations of those answers. Imagine a respondent giving a lengthy answer explaining why government regulation hurts the economy only to have the interviewer simply write down "big government." The richness of an answer can be preserved only by recording it in full, which permits a researcher to study how people think by evaluating their choice of words. Although it may seem sensible, tape-recording interviews is rare in surveys of the general public because many people are uncomfortable being recorded, some are unwilling to be recorded, and transcription of the recordings is costly and time-consuming.

A new development in the field of face-to-face interviewing is computer-assisted personal interviewing (CAPI). Notebook computers can be brought to the interview. The questionnaire can be computerized, which helps the interviewer follow complicated question branching. The interviewer can read the questions off the computer screen and type the answer directly into the computer. The direct entry of answers into the computer permits faster tallies of responses. This procedure is used in many large interviews, such as the National Longitudinal Study of Youth that the National Opinion Research Center (NORC) conducts using the CAPI program developed by the Center for Human Resource Research at Ohio State University.

Not Giving Opinions. The primary purpose of an interview is to measure the respondent's attitudes. This means the interviewer should simply ask the questions and not express her own opinions to the respondent. If the interviewer expresses her own attitudes, the respondent might feel pressure to give answers the interviewer will like. If this pressure actually influences some respondents' answers, validity is compromised. On occasion, a respondent will pressure an interviewer for her opinions. In such a case, the interviewer is trained to say that she is not permitted to state her own opinions during the interview but that she would be happy to discuss the issue at the end of the interview. Interviews sometimes conclude with an informal conversation, during which the interviewers express some of their own attitudes.

Building Rapport With the Respondent. Obviously, the interview situation is unusual for respondents. Rarely do strangers come to a person's door and inquire about his or her opinions. Indeed, the respondent may not be used to stating his or her opinions on political or other controversial matters, so he or she must be made to feel comfortable in this unusual situation. Furthermore, respondents sometimes feel inadequate; they may be afraid that they do not know enough to give an answer or that they might give the "wrong" answer.

Ideally, the respondent should find the experience pleasurable and should feel happy that someone is interested in his or her opinions. For this to occur, the interviewer must build rapport with the respondent; that is, both people should develop feelings of confidence, understanding, and trust. Two ways that an interviewer can build rapport are by expressing appreciation for each answer (e.g., saying thank you, nodding affirmatively) and by permitting the respondent to talk as much as he or she wants. It is also important to assure respondents that there are no right or wrong answers to most survey questions and that the researcher is interested in their opinions. One common way that interviewers reassure respondents is borrowed from psychotherapy: a nondirective "uh-huh." Using this and other techniques, interviewers should be good listeners; they should inspire trust and encourage expression of frank opinions.

Probing. Researchers need clear, complete, and relevant answers to their questions. Often, a respondent's initial reply to an open-ended question is unclear, is just a fraction of his or her views, or is off the track. When any of these occur, the interviewer must probe, getting the person to clarify his or her answer. Questionnaires sometimes list additional questions the interviewer may ask to clarify unclear answers. Also, interviewers are taught a set of general techniques to be used whenever necessary: saying yes, pausing, repeating the question, repeating the respondent's answer, asking "How do you mean that?" or "Anything else?" or "Could you tell me more about what you mean?" Some fairly standard probes are shown at the top of Table 5.1. (The bottom part of the table shows some phrases that interviewers can use when respondents have difficulty answering a question or to reinforce useful answers.)

The most common answer that requires probing is "I don't know" because it has so many possible meanings. It may mean the person has never thought about the question and has absolutely no opinion. At the opposite extreme, it may be just a phrase the respondent uses while thinking for a moment before giving an answer. In response to a closed-ended question, "I don't know" may mean a respondent knows exactly

TABLE 5.1 Standard Probes and Interviewer Remarks

OPEN-ENDED PROBES:

Anything else?

Any others?

Any other reasons?

PROBES FOR VAGUE OR ONE-WORD ANSWERS:

How do you mean?

Would you tell me more about you're thinking on that?

Does a particular aspect of that problem stand out in your mind?

Could you give me more information about your thoughts on . . . ?

Thinking about _____ a bit more, what else about it concerns you?

Could you tell me a little more about that?

Would you tell me what you have in mind?

Could you elaborate on . . . ?

GENERAL REMARKS:

Let me repeat the question.

Let me repeat the choices.

Of course, no one knows for sure.

There are no right or wrong answers.

We're just interested in what you think.

STANDARD CLARIFICATIONS:

Whatever _____ means to you.

Whatever you think of as _____.

It is important that the question be answered as best you can in terms of the way it's stated. Maybe I could read it to you again.

Could I reread the question and the answer I've written down just to be sure I have everything you wanted to say?

FEEDBACK PHRASES:

It's important to find out what people think about this.

I see, that's helpful to know.

That's useful/helpful information.

Thanks, it's important to get your opinion for our research.

TASK-RELATED COMMENTS:

Let me get that down.

I want to make sure I have that right. (REPEAT ANSWER)

We have touched on this before, but I need to ask every question in the order that it appears on the questionnaire.

You've told me something about this, and the next question asks . . .

how he or she thinks about on the issue but isn't sure which answer choice fits that opinion best. Respondents should not be badgered to determine the meaning of "I don't know," but the interviewer should not accept don't-know responses too easily. An important part of interviewer training sessions is to help interviewers learn the fine line involved in probing without becoming overly demanding.

Dealing With a Refusal. Another problem that sometimes occurs is the respondent's refusal to answer a particular question. This rarely occurs, but when it does, the interviewer should try to get the answer. However, she should not try so hard as to jeopardize the rapport for the rest of the interview.

Interviewing Elites. When surveying members of elite groups, such as politicians or civic leaders, some exceptions are made to the usual interviewing rules. For example, in these situations, it is common for interviewers to memorize the questions and ask them in whatever order the conversation follows. The argument behind this practice is that members of an elite group are not likely to accept interviews that are not tailored directly to them.

Another exception is that writing down the respondent's answers during such an interview is uncommon because it is thought that doing so would be viewed as a discourtesy and a distraction and take away from the flow of the interview. Instead, the interviewers usually record a few key phrases during the interview to aid their memories and then transcribe the interview immediately afterward, while the experience is still fresh in their memories. Political elites are used to being interviewed by reporters using tape recorders, so they are often willing to have the interviews taped once they are sure of the purposes and confidentiality of the interview.

Providing Benefits to the Respondent. Perhaps most important, interviewers must bear in mind that respondents should benefit from the experience. People usually think an interview is valuable and useful mainly to the researcher who is gathering the information. But surveys would not be possible if the benefits were only one-sided. Surveys offer respondents opportunities to speak to a good listener, to reflect on things, to reminisce about past experiences, to be stimulated intellectually by thinking about issues they don't often consider, and to express attitudes candidly without fear of the consequences. When an interviewer does her job well, the experience is a pleasant break in the respondent's daily routine.

Supervision of Interviewers

Most survey organizations sooner or later discover that a few of their interviewers fake interviews. Often, this is apparent from the completed questionnaires: Real people tend to have somewhat inconsistent attitudes; fake interviews tend to be too consistent. Also, interviews often include a question designed to check some known information about the respondent; a wrong answer recorded here can be a clue that the interview is a fake. Survey organizations increasingly employ some technique to validate each interview, usually either sending a letter or making a telephone call to the respondent to verify that the interview took place. In general, though, interviewers who are paid good wages almost never fake interviews.

Confidentiality

When survey interviews address sensitive topics, respondents run the risk of being injured if their responses were to become public. Imagine, for example, that a newspaper publishes a survey detailing the extent of drug use on a college campus and that the local police subpoena the questionnaires to identify respondents who admitted illegal drug use. Or imagine a survey in which respondents reported their family incomes, the results of which the Internal Revenue Service subpoenas in order to identify tax evaders. Or imagine a survey of political attitudes, the results of which are subpoenaed by the Federal Bureau of Investigation to identify people who have committed crimes. Respondents are well aware of this danger and are usually reluctant to discuss such topics with interviewers.

The best way to handle this problem is to explain to respondents that their responses will be kept confidential and that only statistical analysis of the results will be published. Names and other identifying materials (addresses, phone numbers) are generally removed from interview schedules after the interview has been conducted and validated. From that point on, each questionnaire can be identified with a unique number, with the respondent's identity being kept confidential.

Telephone Interviewing

At a superficial level, telephone interviews are very similar to face-to-face interviews. In both cases, interviewers read questions to respondents and record their answers. However, many aspects of these two data collection methods are quite different. Below, we describe the most notable procedural differences between face-to-face and telephone interviewing.

Interview Administration

Telephone interviews are generally conducted from a single site. Most major survey organizations have many telephones located in the same room from which all interviewers make their calls. Even a national sample can be interviewed from a single location by using relatively inexpensive WATS (wide area telephone service) lines. For example, the *New York Times*/CBS News poll does its interviews from a New York City location that is convenient for the unemployed Broadway actors and actresses it sometimes hires as interviewers.

Conducting all the interviews from a single site also increases the amount of supervision that is possible. Supervisors often listen in on another phone to check how the interview is being conducted. Thus, they can notice problems when they occur, and unanticipated problems can be dealt with immediately. In some cases, this response might mean further training for a particular interviewer; in other cases, it might mean adding new instructions for all of the interviewers.

Data collection through telephone interviews is often done by using computer-assisted telephone interviewing (CATI). Instead of reading questions out of a booklet and writing down answers with a pencil, interviewers read questions displayed on a computer video screen and type responses on a computer keyboard. CATI programs became available in the late 1970s and became prevalent with the move to personal computers in the 1980s. CATI is the state of the art for telephone interviews. Major CATI programs include CASES (developed by the Survey Research Center of the University of California at Berkeley) and Ci3 (from Sawtooth Software).

CATI has numerous advantages. First, the data are recorded directly into a computer, which eliminates the time usually spent transferring written responses to computers for analysis and eliminates errors made in this transferring process. Second, the computer can immediately inform the interviewer whether an invalid response has been recorded. Third, the computer can be programmed to implement skip patterns or branching, changing the questions to be asked on the basis of answers a respondent has already given. Computers can make these decisions more quickly and accurately than a person can and thus save time and eliminate error. CATI systems are often used for survey experiments, as when different respondents are asked different versions of questions to check the effect of question-wording choices. Also, CATI programs help manage the sample, keep track of interview scheduling, and maintain records of the outcomes of calls. The best CATI programs can handle such problems as the need to go back when a respondent changes an answer to an earlier question, the disposition of interviews that are broken off prior to completion, and the occasional need to call back a respondent to complete a partial interview.

The disadvantage of CATI is that it is costly and time-consuming to set up the system. Programming a complicated survey in CATI requires going through it several times to check whether possible skip patterns are processed correctly. As a result, CATI would not be reasonable for doing a small survey; its use makes most sense for survey organizations that can capitalize on their investment over a long time period. Even these problems may be solved by new CATI systems that use object-oriented technology with a graphic user interface to simplify the programming of questions and with reusable code to permit assembling a questionnaire from questions that worked properly in past surveys.

Telephone interviewing is now often conducted by small research organizations from a room with perhaps a dozen stations. Each station is equipped with a telephone (usually with a comfortable headset for the interviewer) and with soundproofing between the stations. A CATI station also has a computer with a monitor that shows the questions and a keyboard for the interviewer to type the responses. Large research firms have similar operations, but they may have as many as 100 stations in the same room.

Telephone interviewing of the mass public is usually done in the evenings (5:00 p.m. to 9:00 p.m., local time) on weekdays plus weekend afternoons. Friday and Saturday evenings are usually not productive times for interviewing because many people go to social events or entertain. Weekend afternoons and Monday evenings are problematic during seasons when many people—especially young males—watch televised sports. It is possible to conduct telephone interviews with the mass public during weekday afternoons, but less success in getting respondents at home should be expected. Many national survey operations are based in the Midwest or in Western states, so interviews can be taken throughout the country before it gets too late in the evening. Telephone surveys of businesses can proceed during normal working hours.

The guidelines described above about good face-to-face interviewing technique are generally applicable to telephone interviewing, although there are some necessary differences. Of course, because the respondent cannot see the telephone interviewer, nonverbal gestures are not possible. Furthermore, the telephone requires a somewhat different start to the conversation between interviewer and resident.

A telephone interview begins with an introduction and explanation to convince the answerer that the call is legitimate. Generally, interviewers begin by asking whether they have reached the number they intended to call; needless to say, the call is terminated if a wrong number has been reached. Next, the interviewer must determine whether the number reached is a business or a residence. Most surveys involve residences only. Screening questions might also be asked at this point to make sure the residence reached is located in the area targeted for the survey. For example, for a study of Tucson, Arizona, interviewers might need to confirm that the number they have reached is located in Tucson or one of its suburbs. The interviewer would politely terminate the call if the person lives in a suburb not to be included in the survey.

If the correct number has been reached and the residence is within the region to be sampled, the interviewer then identifies herself, identifies the organization for which she is calling, and explains that it is conducting a survey on a specified topic. At this point, the interviewer checks whether the person who answered the telephone is the proper respondent (see Chapter 3). If the proper respondent is someone else, the interviewer asks to speak with that person; if the person is not home, the interviewer makes an appointment to call back at another time. From this point on, telephone interviews closely resemble face-to-face interviews.

Respondents often are suspicious of telephone interviews, so interviewers are given standard instructions on how to handle particular problems. Respondents often want to know how their number was obtained, particularly if the number is unlisted. A standard response to this question is, "All of the telephone numbers we use were created by a computer to cover listed and unlisted numbers alike. Your telephone number will not be given to any other organization, and we will not keep records of it." If people ask about their names being used, they are assured that the interview is anonymous and that results will be released only in percentages, without identifying who gave which answer. Inter-

---

TABLE 5.2 Refusal Conversion Guide

Respondent: I'm too busy.

Interviewer: I think you will find this interview to be worth your time. We ask questions and talk about issues that are really timely and interesting, and it's important that we include busy people like you so that our results don't just include very young people or retired people. So we don't want to miss your opinion, and if you could help us out, we'd really appreciate it. Other people we've interviewed have said the interviews go much faster than they expected because the questions are interesting and move right along. For instance, the first one asks . . .

Respondent: I don't want any.

Interviewer: Let me reassure you I'm not selling anything. I'm calling from ____ . This is a research project. We're just looking for your personal opinions on some topics of current interest, and if you would help us out, we'd really appreciate it.

Respondent: You're invading my privacy.

Interviewer: I can certainly understand; that's why all our interviews are completely confidential. Protecting people's privacy is one of our major concerns. Everything is also completely anonymous. All results are released in a way that no single person can ever be identified, so you don't need to be concerned. And if I happen to ask you something that you don't want to talk about, just let me know and we'll move on to something else. So if I have your permission, our first question asks . . .

Respondent: I'm too old.

Interviewer: Your opinions are very important to us. We need to hear from people of all ages in order for our sample to be representative. We really need your opinion so that we could benefit from your experiences. If you could help us out, we'd really appreciate it.

Respondent: I don't know enough.

Interviewer: Let me reassure you there are no right or wrong answers to our questions and they are not difficult. They concern how you feel, rather than how much you know about certain things. Some of the people we have already interviewed had the same concern as you have, but once we got started, they didn't have any difficulty answering the questions. Maybe I could just read a few of the questions so that you can see what they are like . . .

---

viewers are also told how to answer questions about the sponsorship of the survey and whom to contact with questions about it.

TABLE 5.2 *Continued*

Respondent: I object to telephone surveys.

Interviewer: One of the reasons we do telephone surveys is because everything is kept confidential. For instance, with mailed-out surveys, we have to know people' names and addresses. Telephone calls also cost much less than going door to door. Your opinions are very important to our study, and this way we can keep our costs down too. So if you could help us out, we would really appreciate it, and if I happen to ask you something that you don't want to talk about, just let me know and we'll move on to something else.

Respondent: We don't do surveys.

Interviewer: This particular study that we are doing here at _____ is very important, and let me reassure you that we are not selling anything. We are just looking for people's opinions and feelings about current issues. Also, everything is kept completely confidential and anonymous. All results are released as group data, such as the percentage of people who agreed or disagreed with a particular question. There isn't any way any individual can be identified. And if I happen to ask you something that you don't want to talk about, just let me know and we'll move to something else.

Respondent: I'm not feeling well.

Interviewer: I'm sorry to hear that. I would be happy to call you back in a day or two. Would that be okay? When would be a better time to call back?

SOURCE: Based on a handout prepared by Dr. Kathleen Carr and Kristi Pope of the Polimetrics Laboratory for Political and Social Research at Ohio State University.

Interviewers are also given standard ways to deal with potential refusals. Table 5.2 lists some potential excuses and replies used by interviewers for the Center for Survey Research (Polimetrics) at Ohio State University. The response is read up to the point that the respondent agrees to conduct the interview, with consent often being given after only the first two or three sentences are read.

Interviewer Effects

The controlled atmosphere of telephone interviews permits more tests of the effects of interviewers than are usually possible with face-to-face interviews. In particular, some studies have taped telephone interviews and then analyzed those tapes. For example, one study found that interviewers performed unwanted behaviors in more than half of the questions asked, including asking more than a third of the questions not exactly as written. The specific problems included reading errors, speech variations, improper probes, and unprogrammed feedback to the respondent. Surprisingly, interviewers with more experience seemed to be more likely to engage in such behavior, reflecting a less formal approach to interviewing. These verbal behaviors did not, however, necessarily affect the responses that were obtained. Also, interviewers who expected accurate reports or overreports of sensitive behavior (e.g., use of alcohol, drugs, and sex) tended to obtain reports of a greater frequency of such behavior than interviewers who expected underreports. Thus, interviewers do have some effect on the responses obtained in surveys (Bradburn, Sudman, & Associates, 1981, Chaps. 3-4; see also Fowler & Mangione, 1990).

Interviewer-related errors can be decreased by care in selecting, training, and supervising interviewers. More specifically, interviewers should be given guidelines about how to handle the questions and answers (to read questions exactly, to record answers exactly, and to probe nondirectively) and how to deal with the respondents (to be neutral, to reinforce desired behavior, and to give the respondents the impression that high-quality answers are desired). Additionally, care in question wording helps diminish interviewer-related errors, particularly when questions are worded well so that they can be read easily and interpreted clearly by the respondent.

At the extreme, a survey operation can try to standardize the interviewing completely. The interviewer would just read the questions verbatim and record the answers without in any way personalizing the interviewing experience. Some specialists (e.g., Fowler & Mangione, 1990) argue in favor of such a completely standardized approach, but others believe that a skilled interviewer who is free to customize can obtain better quality answers. The research literature on survey methods has not yet provided a definitive answer to the circumstances under which each approach is better.

Self-Administered Questionnaires

The third method through which survey data can be collected involves giving questionnaires to respondents to fill out. Typically, questionnaires are distributed to respondents by one of three methods. First, question-naires can be mailed to individuals or delivered to their homes. People are asked to fill out the questionnaires and either to mail them back to the researcher or to give them to a messenger who returns a few days later. Second, people may be stopped on the street or in public places such as shopping malls and be asked to complete the questionnaires on the spot. Third, people can be assembled in groups in large rooms and can be asked to complete questionnaires at that time. This meeting can be ar-ranged most easily in institutional settings, so this approach is commonly used to survey schoolchildren, members of the armed forces, employees of a company, and so on. With this method, only a few staff people are required to distribute questionnaires to respondents, answer any ques-tions they might have, and collect the completed questionnaires.

When questionnaires are distributed in institutional settings or in such places as shopping malls, the person distributing them usually explains the purpose of the study to respondents and asks them to participate. If necessary, the distributor can give the questionnaire to only certain types of people. In contrast, when questionnaires are mailed to respondents, the purpose of the study is typically explained in a cover letter, and respondent selection is much more difficult. Usually, re-searchers using mail questionnaires do not ask a particular person to complete the questionnaire, but instead simply ask anyone who lives at the address to fill it out.

In institutional settings and when respondents are recruited on the street, response rates tend to be reasonably high. Unfortunately, though, many people throw into their wastebaskets any questionnaires they receive in the mail; response rates for mail questionnaires tend to be between 10% and 50%. Mail questionnaire return rates have never been high, but they have been further threatened by the frustration that many people have with fund-raising attempts masquerading as surveys (also known as "frugging"—*fund-raising under the guise of research*).

Survey researchers compensate for low mail return rates in several ways. First, they send questionnaires a second, third, or even fourth time to households that do not return them. Included in the follow-up mailings are letters asking respondents to reconsider participating in the survey. Second, some survey organizations include small amounts of money (e.g., $1) or material incentives with the questionnaire as a way of thanking respondents in advance for their time. Over the years, material incentives have included golf balls, letter openers, tobacco pouches, photograph holders, pens, lottery tickets, pencils, instant cof-fee packages, stamps, tie clasps, books, and key rings. Such incentives have been shown to increase response rates when few follow-up mailings are conducted, but the effect of incentives is eliminated if multiple follow-ups are implemented (Dillman, 1978; Nederhof, 1983). Through the use of follow-up mailings and incentives, response rates as high as 70% can be achieved for mail questionnaires.

Don Dillman's (1978) **total design method** (TDM) is intended to boost response rates for mail questionnaires. The idea is (a) to make it look easy to fill out the questionnaire, (b) to give social rewards for filling it out (e.g., giving thanks, according the person individual attention), and (c) to establish trust by official sponsorship. TDM involves paying attention to every detail of questionnaire construction and survey implementation that would improve response rates. For example, questionnaires are prepared as $6\frac{1}{2} \times 8\frac{1}{4}$-inch booklets. The front cover is designed to attract interest, with a title, illustration, and instructions; the back cover invites further comments and thanks the respondent. The questionnaire is accompanied by a 1-page cover letter that explains the importance of the survey, emphasizes that the respondent is important, and states who should answer the questions. A postcard follow-up is sent 1 week after the questionnaire. A second questionnaire and cover letter are mailed 2 weeks later to those who did not respond, and a third questionnaire is sent through certified mail 4 weeks later to those who still have not responded. As an example of the level of detail of the TDM implementation procedures, cover letters are addressed to the respondents personally and are signed with ballpoint pen. These procedures are expensive, but they are claimed to yield response rates as high as the 70% range. Unfortunately, some direct mail advertisers emulate these techniques by using computers to personalize letters. As people may get used to this approach, the effectiveness of TDM may decrease.

A meta-analysis of mail questionnaire response rates (Fox, Crask, & Kim, 1988; see also Yammarino, Skinner, & Childers, 1991) found some factors that are consistently influential across different research efforts. University sponsorship increased response rate by 9% (as compared with commercial sponsorship), prenotification by letter of the survey had an 8% enhancing effect, a stamped return envelope had a 6% enhancing effect, and a postcard follow-up had a 4% effect. Smaller but significant effects were also found for using first-class postage in the mailing to the respondent and for using colored questionnaires. Cash incentives were found to increase response rates, with a $1 incentive increasing responses by about a third.

TABLE 5.3 Comparison of Interviewing Situations

Feature	Administration Method		
	Mail	Telephone	Face-to-Face
Cost of interviewing	Inexpensive— no interviewers	Inexpensive— no transportation	Expensive
Response rate	Very low without reminders and/ or incentives	Good: 60%	Highest: 70%
Length of interview	Short	Medium: 20 to 30 minutes	Long: up to an hour
Candor of interview	Limited	Good on sensitive items	Good
Data collection time	Several weeks	Less than a week	Intermediate
Interviewer supervision	—	Good	Minimal
Respondent selection	Low-SES* bias; hard to control who fills out questionnaire	High-SES* bias	Good
Quality of interview	Good candor; cannot probe	Terse answers	Good rapport

NOTE: *Socioeconomic status.

Choosing an Administration Method

Having reviewed procedures for face-to-face interviews, telephone interviews, and self-administered questionnaires, a natural question is, Which is the best procedure to use? The answer is that it depends. In designing any study, a researcher must balance considerations of cost, speed, length of interview, and quality of data. The best choice in one setting will not necessarily be the best choice in another setting. Table 5.3 presents a summary of some considerations that have been discussed in this chapter and introduces some further points mentioned below.

Practical Differences

Expense. Procedures differ in cost; mail questionnaires are the least expensive, even after taking into account the expense of postage and wasted questionnaires. Face to-face interviews are the most expensive because interviewers and supervisors must be paid and because of transportation costs.

Telephone interviews are about half as expensive as face-to-face interviews. The smaller required number of interviewers sharply cuts the costs of hiring, training, and supervising interviewers. Transportation costs, often one of the most expensive aspects of face-to-face interviewing, are eliminated when telephone interviews are conducted. Indeed, most other components of the data collection process are less expensive with telephone interviews, including the pretest, debriefing of interviewers, verifying that interviews were not forged, printing, field office expenses, record keeping, salaries, and sample selection. Communication costs are, of course, higher for telephone interviews, but that greater expense is more than balanced by the decreased travel costs. Telephone interviewing costs vary with how many interviews are to be taken, how long the interview takes, how many call-backs are desired, and how much screening is necessary to find a respondent who qualifies for the survey. A short survey of a few hundred people without call-backs in which any adult can be a respondent is fairly inexpensive, whereas a long survey of several thousand people with a dozen call-backs before discarding a telephone number as not working and with extensive screening (e.g., to find Vietnam veterans) would be much more costly.

Response Rates. Response rates are best for face-to-face interviews. Telephone interviews do reasonably well, but it is so easy for people to terminate a call by hanging up that response rates are lowered by break-offs. If something important comes up, it is apparently easier to hang up on an interviewer than to ask one sitting in your living room to leave. As a result, completion rates are about 60% for national telephone interviews, still respectable but less than the 70% obtained for face-to-face interviews. Mail questionnaires typically have the lowest response rates, although the response rates can be increased by persistent mailings to uncooperative respondents and by including incentives with the questionnaires.

Interview Length. Face-to-face interviews allow for longer interviews. The main expense in face-to-face interviews is getting the interviewer to the person's home. It is not worth the trouble of sending out interviewers and persuading people to be interviewed for only a 5-minute interview. Consequently, face-to-face interviews tend to average an hour in length. Researchers initially assumed that telephone interviews had to be kept short, just 5 to 10 minutes. As researchers gained more experience writing questionnaires that are effective on the telephone and as interviewers gained more experience in building rapport in telephone interviews, interview length has increased. Now, 20- to 30-minute telephone interviews are common. Self-administered questionnaires pose the greatest length difficulty. The researcher always wants to add more and more pages of questions, but the longer the questionnaire, the less likely it is that the respondent will bother to fill it out. Consequently, they tend to be short.

To give an idea of how some of these considerations combine, in 1987 the University of Michigan's Survey Research Center estimated its interviewing costs at $150 to $170 for a 1-hour face-to-face interview, compared with $65 for a half-hour telephone interview. Even though these figures increase with inflation over the years, their relative sizes are informative. The longer face-to-face interview provides more information, but many more people can be interviewed within a fixed budget with telephone interviews.

Data Collection Time. Using self-administered questionnaires distributed in institutional settings can save a great deal of time because hundreds of people can fill them out simultaneously. Self-administered questionnaires distributed by mail take much longer to implement, especially if researchers try to improve response rates through follow-up mailings to those who have not sent back the questionnaire.

When face-to-face interviewing is used, the geographic dispersion of the sampled residences limits the number of interviews that any one interviewer can take. The interviewer must spend time driving from one area to another, and interviewers sometimes visit a residence many times before they finally find someone home. As a result, these studies are generally in the field for between 1 week and 2 months. With a telephone, an interviewer can conduct many more interviews in a short period of time. Calling a residence at which no one is home wastes less than a minute. Consequently, telephone interviewing requires much less time for data collection and requires fewer interviewers. In a national study, for example, four times as many interviewers are needed for face-to-face interviews as are needed for telephone interviews.

Because telephone surveys require less time than face-to-face surveys, the former are especially attractive to news organizations that want to publish up-to-the-minute polling results and to researchers who want to study the impact of an event immediately after it happens. For example, telephone surveys are frequently used by politicians to measure public reactions immediately. A president may give a speech and have a pollster measure the public's reaction that same night, expecting to get a report on public attitudes the next morning. Television and newspaper polls are often conducted to assess immediate reactions to dramatic political events, something that was not possible before the advent of telephone polling.

Telephone surveys are also used for tracking purposes. The ability to take a random sample of a few hundred people every day permits daily tracking of trends. Political candidates sometimes contract for daily tracking of their popularity. This tactic permits their strategists to follow the effects of their speeches and campaign appearances, as well as those of their opponents and of events during the campaign. In some cases, these tracking polls have been large enough that the strategists can check the effectiveness of targeting particular groups. Similar tracking polls are common in the business world, with companies doing continuous tracking of customer satisfaction.

Interviewer Supervision. One advantage of telephone interviewing over face-to-face interviewing is that supervisors can easily monitor each interviewer's telephone conversations. This supervision permits quality control that is not feasible when face-to-face interviews are conducted. If the supervisor notices some problem in the way an interviewer conducts herself, it can be corrected at once, either by telling the interviewer what she is doing wrong or by changing the instructions that all the interviewers receive. Intensive interviewer supervision is impossible when face-to-face interviews are conducted in respondents' homes.

Interviewer Effects. Interviewer bias is another important form of bias in a survey. The interviewer-respondent interaction is an unusual interaction in the life of the respondent, and the respondent often does not know just how to act. Some respondents will try to please the interviewer in their answers and avoid giving answers the interviewer might not approve. The interviewer may also inadvertently ask a question differently from how it is written or ask the question in such a tone that one answer seems preferred. These are all sources of interviewer bias. Such bias can never be eliminated, but it is minimized by care in the selection and training of interviewers.

One advantage of self-administered questionnaires is that responses are not influenced by interviewer effects because there are no interviewers. Questions in self-administered questionnaires appear identical to all respondents, whereas interviewers read questions slightly differently from each other. When filling out questionnaires, however, respondents can make mistakes that could be avoided if a face-to-face or telephone interview were conducted.

Interviewers hired for face-to-face interviews require the most training because personal interviews are so sensitive to how the interviewer handles the interpersonal relations involved. Telephone interviews tend to require less interviewer training. Unfortunately, the fact that telephone surveys typically use fewer interviewers than do face-to-face interviews increases the risk that a single interviewer's style of asking questions will distort the final results of a telephone survey. If a particular interviewer happens to ask questions in a way that biases answers, the effect on results will be relatively small when 50 other interviewers are collecting data for the study. When this interviewer is one of only 15, however, a greater proportion of interviews will be biased. The closer supervision possible in telephone interviewing probably allows researchers to identify and eliminate many of these biases, but some are so subtle that they cannot be detected by supervisors.

Respondent Selection. Some sampling issues involved in a choice among face-to-face interviews, telephone interviews, and self-administered questionnaires were discussed in Chapter 3. To summarize briefly, studies (e.g., Groves & Kahn, 1979, pp. 94-97) show that telephone interview respondents tend to have somewhat higher income and education levels than face-to-face interview respondents and that mail questionnaire respondents have even lower income and education levels. Still, with 95% of the households in the United States having telephones, the choice of procedure today has less effect on the demographic composition of the sample than it once did.

A disadvantage of mailed self-administered questionnaires is that it is impossible to coordinate respondent selection the way an interviewer can. In most telephone and face-to-face interviews, the interviewer obtains a household listing and uses a selection table to select one adult to be interviewed, or the interviewer can use the "next birthday method" to ask to speak with the adult in the household with the next birthday. Obviously, this procedure cannot be done with mail questionnaires. In homes where more than one adult lives, the decision who will fill out the questionnaire is made by the residents. Therefore, respondent sampling is less controllable with this data collection method, and sampling is likely to be biased as a result.

Differences in Respondent Satisfaction

Respondents say they prefer face-to-face interviews over telephone interviews. The rapport with the interviewer is greater in the former case, and people are more comfortable giving open-ended comments in the face-to-face interview. Differences between the two types of interviews are not substantial, however, so telephone interviewing is done widely. When asked to compare self-administered questionnaires to interviews, respondents generate some reasons in favor of each. On the one hand, they say, a self-administered questionnaire gives a person more time to think about each question and allows the respondent to complete the questionnaire at his or her convenience. On the other hand, self-administered questionnaires are said to require more effort than interviews and to feel less personal (Martin, 1983, p. 724).

Differences in Results

When telephone interviewing was first being tried, researchers were concerned about the validity of data gathered over the telephone. Some studies have compared the results of surveys done with face-to-face and telephone interviewing and found that the two methods produce similar results for the most part. However, there are a few important differences.

People typically provide more information in face-to-face interviews than in telephone interviews. For example, more people refuse to reveal their incomes during telephone interviews, although this reluctance to reveal sensitive information does not seem to extend to other items. Some research suggests that people are more likely to answer sensitive questions and less likely to give socially acceptable answers on mail questionnaires. Apparently, respondents give more candid answers when they can fill out the questionnaire in complete privacy, both from other people in the household and from the interviewer as well. Research is even beginning to show that mail questionnaires can predict election outcomes better than can telephone interviews.

Similarly, telephone interviews obtain fewer comments in response to open-ended questions. This is especially true among people who have more difficulty expressing their thoughts verbally. Because respondents are more terse in answering questions on the telephone, face-to-face interviews are preferable if open-ended material is critical. Self-administered questionnaires obviously are not useful when the researcher thinks that probes of respondent answers are important.

Another interesting difference between results obtained by face-to-face and telephone interviews concerns the use of rating scales. When respondents are presented with scales on which some but not all of the points are accompanied by verbal labels, face-to-face interview respondents tend to use the points with verbal labels more often than do telephone interview respondents. As a result, responses from the latter group are spread more evenly across the points of the rating scale.

Otherwise, telephone interviews seem to obtain responses that are just as valid and sometimes more valid than responses from face-to-face interviews. For example, a study of crime victimization found that people reported more incidents of crime directed against them when interviewed on the telephone than in person. People seem unwilling to mention to an interviewer in their homes some crimes that they were willing to mention on the telephone. This difference, in part, may be because of the greater secrecy associated with telephone interviews: It is sometimes impossible to conduct a face-to-face interview without other members of the family present, whereas in telephone interviews, the respondent can answer yes or no without other members of the family knowing what the question was. This increased privacy during telephone interviews may yield more candid data in response to some questions.

Survey Organizations

Survey units vary considerably along several dimensions. Nearly all survey organizations have telephone banks for telephone interviewing, and most are equipped to do large-scale mailed questionnaires. A few of the larger operations also maintain field staffs for face-to-face interviewing. The University of Michigan's Survey Research Center and the University of Chicago's NORC keep interviewers around the country on their payrolls, as do the Census Bureau, Gallup, Roper, and a few other commercial pollsters. A few survey units have field staffs for statewide or local face-to-face interviews. Survey organizations also are often able to run focus groups.

Survey units also differ in terms of how they obtain business. University-based survey units generally conduct many of their surveys for grants, as when a faculty member's research proposal involving polling is funded by a grant agency. Contract research is also very prevalent; government units frequently request proposals from survey operations to conduct surveys on specific topics and then select the organization to be given the contract on the basis of the bids they receive. In the market research field, it is common for a company to have a long-standing relationship with a survey firm that conducts its polling on a regular basis. Ideally, survey groups have some large regular polls to sustain their operation and then seek other surveys that they find especially interesting.

Survey units vary from the multimillion-dollar firms to small store-front operations. Many smaller survey companies have been set up by a single entrepreneur, often someone who has learned about surveys in a graduate training program or as an employee in another survey firm. All that these firms require are funds for a medium-sized room equipped with a dozen soundproof cubicles for telephone connections plus a modern personal computer operation for processing the data.

Several personnel positions are common across survey units. Some people are assigned to solicit business and to give budget estimates to potential clients. Project managers watch over each individual survey. An office manager is responsible for the paperwork involved in hiring and paying interviewers and billing clients. A statistician does the sampling and computes any needed sample weights. A trainer teaches interviewers how to conduct interviews. Interviewing supervisors monitor the actual interviewing. Coders code answers to open-ended questions. Data entry people type the completed interviews into a computer if a CATI system is not being used. Computer professionals maintain the needed computer systems. Data analysts perform statistical analyses and write reports for clients. One person might perform several of these roles in a small survey unit, whereas the largest survey operations would have multiple people performing each of these functions. Small survey units tend to hire added workers, such as interviewers, coders, and data entry personnel, on an as-needed basis. Larger survey organizations treat these positions as more permanent, frequently using performance-based incentives to retain the most productive workers.

Organizationally, survey operations typically have a fairly lean bureaucracy, often following the team approach associated with total quality management (TQM). For example, the Gallup Organization does not use a hierarchical organizational model, but instead organizes itself into teams for specific clients and projects.

Finally, every survey operation faces the trade-off between quality and cost. Commercial survey units are more likely to take the shortcuts necessary to keep their expenses down.

SUMMARY

Over the years, researchers have learned many valuable lessons about how to conduct surveys. The procedures used by survey organizations across the country for obtaining interviews and for administering questionnaires are remarkably similar and successful. Good interviewing requires careful selection, training, and supervision of interviewers. Interviewers must ask the questions as written, record the answers exactly, not give their own opinions, build rapport with the respondents, probe answers where they are unclear, and not accept refusals too easily.

Choosing a method for collecting survey data is a complex decision involving considerations of expense, response rates, the sorts of questions being asked, and the amount of information needed. Face-to-face interviews were once seen as the only way to obtain high-quality data, but telephone surveys are now used extensively because they are less expensive, faster, and can be carefully supervised. Self-administered questionnaires are also useful, although extra effort is necessary to get an acceptable response rate from mail questionnaires. Different types of people may respond in face-to-face, telephone, and mail studies, so researchers should compare the demographics of their samples with census statistics to detect any biases that result.

Further Readings

Interviewing

Converse, J. M., & Schuman, H. (1974). *Conversations at random*. New York: John Wiley.

Dexter, L. A. (1970). *Elite and specialized interviewing*. Evanston, IL: Northwestern University Press.

Fowler, F. J., Jr., & Mangione, T. W. (1989). *Standardized survey interviewing*. Newbury Park, CA: Sage.

Guenzel, P. J., Berkmans, T. R., & Cannell, C. F. (1983). *General interviewing techniques: A self-instructional workbook for telephone and personal interviewer training*. Ann Arbor: University of Michigan, Institute for Social Research.

Kahn, R. L., & Cannell, C. F. (1967). *The dynamics of interviewing*. New York: John Wiley.

Saris, W. E. (1991). *Computer-assisted interviewing*. Newbury Park, CA: Sage.

Telephone Polls

Frey, J. H. (1983). *Survey research by telephone.* Beverly Hills, CA: Sage.

Groves, R. M., Biemer, P. N., Lyberg, L. E., Massey, J. T., Nichols, W. L., II, & Waksberg, J. (Eds.). (1988). *Telephone survey methodology.* New York: John Wiley.

Groves, R. M., & Kahn, R. L. (1979). *Surveys by telephone: A national comparison with personal interviews.* San Diego: Academic Press.

Lavrakas, P. J. (1993). *Telephone survey methods: Sampling, selection, and supervision* (2nd ed.). Newbury Park, CA: Sage.

Note

1. As an example of this effect, one study found that blacks are more likely to report that they feel particularly close to blacks if the interviewer is black rather than white. An apparent decrease in 1984 in the number of blacks feeling close to blacks turned out to be due to a decline in the number of blacks interviewing blacks (Anderson, Silver, & Abramson, 1988). Another study (Finkel, Guterbock, & Borg, 1991) found that Southern whites were more likely to say they were planning to vote for a black Democrat gubernatorial candidate when the interviewer was black, a social desirability effect that may partly explain why preelection polls often predict a higher vote for a black candidate than that candidate actually receives.

☑ EXERCISES

What should the Interviewer (I) do next in each of the following three exchanges with the Respondent (R)?

1. I: What do you think are the most important problems facing this country?

   R: Our relations with Russia.

2. I: Now looking ahead, do you think that a year from now you (and your family) will be better off financially, or worse off, or just about the same as now?

   R: Hmmm. Let me see about that. I don't know.

3. I: What is your main occupation?

   R: Engineer.

6 ☑☐ ☑☐ Coding Practices

☑ Unfortunately, it is impossible to analyze a set of interviews simply by leafing through them. Computers are required for analyzing the large amount of data in large-scale surveys. To use a computer to analyze survey data, the verbal answers to survey questions must be translated (coded) into numbers in the computer's memory.

In this chapter, we describe the coding process, which usually has three parts. First, the researcher must develop the coding scheme for each question and decide which numbers correspond to which answers. Second, a codebook must specify where each question's answers will be recorded on coding sheets. Third, numbers representing each questionnaire's answers must be written on the coding sheets and entered into the computer.

Coding Schemes

Procedures for developing codes differ for closed-ended and open-ended questions. Let's take a look at them.

SURVEY DESIGN

Closed-Ended Questions

It is much easier to develop coding schemes for closed-ended questions than for open-ended ones because all the possible answers to a closed-ended question are known before the interviews take place. Each possible answer is printed in a box on the questionnaire, with a number corresponding to that particular answer. When a respondent answers a question, the interviewer checks the box corresponding to the respondent's answer. As an example, Table 6.1 displays the coding format of an election study question asking how respondents voted in the congressional election. If a respondent says he or she voted for the Democrat, the interviewer should check Box 1; Box 2 should be checked for respondents who voted for Republicans; and so on.

The numbers in the questionnaire boxes are used to code answers to closed-ended questions. These response categories for each question must be **mutually exclusive** so that no answer can fit more than one category, and the categories must be **exhaustive** so that every answer fits some category. Sometimes, additional coding categories must be assigned after the interviews have been conducted to handle unanticipated responses to closed-ended questions. Also, if an interviewer does not record a respondent's answer to a particular question for some reason, the respondent must be assigned a code for that question, describing why no answer was recorded.

Table 6.2 shows the coding scheme that could be used for the vote question. It corresponds closely to the original questionnaire but also includes additional coding categories. For the coding categories to be exhaustive, allowance was made for respondents who refused to say for whom they voted, who voted for other candidates, who did not remember how they voted, who did not vote for a congressional candidate, and who—accidentally or not—were not asked the question. Categories 6, 7, 8, 9, and 0 handle these special situations. When a question has five or fewer alternative answers, it is conventional to use 6 for "refused to say," 7 for "other," 8 for "don't know," 9 for "not ascertained," and 0 for "inappropriate." When a closed-ended question has more than five possible answers, these situations are often assigned codes of 96, 97, 98, 99, and 00, respectively.

Categories 9 (for questions with 5 or fewer valid answers) and 99 (for questions with 6 to 99 valid answers) are used to code lack of response for a question. This lack could occur if a respondent terminated the interview prior to being asked the question or if a coffee stain made it

TABLE 6.1 Congressional Vote Question

Whom did you vote for in the election for the House of Representatives?		
1. Democratic candidate	2. Republican candidate	7. Other, Specify: _____

impossible to read what the person's response was. In any case, the number of responses coded "not ascertained" is usually quite small.

The 0 category is required when a question is asked of some but not all respondents. This code is most often used when an answer to a preceding question causes the interviewer to skip a later question because it is inappropriate for a particular respondent. For example, people who say they did not vote in the election are not asked for whom they voted. We use the 0 code for those not-appropriate or not-applicable cases. (Non-academic surveys often leave "blanks" for these situations.) The 0 code can also be used in panel studies if a respondent has not been reinterviewed. For example, the American National Election Study interviews the same people both before and after presidential elections. Some people interviewed before the election cannot be contacted for a reinterview, however, so they are also given the 0 code for all the reinterview questions.

Open-Ended Questions

Open-ended questions are usually the most interesting (and possibly the most valuable) questions in a survey. Respondents say whatever they

TABLE 6.2 Closed-Ended Question Code

(If reports voting in 1992)
Which party did you vote for in the election for the U.S. House of Representatives?
1. Democrat
2. Republican
6. Refused to say whom voted for
7. Other
8. Don't know
9. Not ascertained
0. Inappropriate—did not vote for House (or no postelection interview)

wish in response to these questions, and interviewers record the answers verbatim. These questions allow respondents to express themselves; if respondents give inconsistent, bigoted, witty, dumb, sophisticated, or knowledgeable answers, all of that is preserved on the questionnaire. Because people give a variety of answers to these questions, most of which could not be anticipated, researchers develop coding categories for them only after the interviews are completed.

Code categories should satisfy the objectives of the question. If a question has more than one objective, the same answers might be coded in more than one way. For example, answers can be coded in terms of either manifest or latent content. **Manifest** coding focuses on the content of the respondent's answer to a question; **latent** coding focuses on the style of the person's answer. Consider a survey that asked respondents how they decided which presidential candidate to vote for. Obviously, the manifest reasons that respondents give would be coded, and it might also be useful to code evidence about *how* each respondent thinks about politics. If a respondent used the word *liberal* or *conservative,* his or her answer might be coded as having ideological content. Often, the same open-ended question is coded at the manifest level and at one or more latent levels.

Manifest codes for open-ended questions can be developed in two ways. The first way is the **theoretical or a priori method:** The researchers develop the codes, based on the answers they expect, in advance, just as they do with closed-ended questions. For example, suppose respondents in a survey were asked, "What do you think this country will be like in 10 years?" If the researchers wanted to know simply whether people are optimistic or pessimistic, they could develop code categories (optimistic and pessimistic) before seeing the respondents' answers. A second way to develop manifest codes for open-ended questions is the **contextual method:** Researchers read a large number of answers and develop codes by grouping similar answers together. If they were working on the above question, they might find overcrowding and increasing land values mentioned by a number of respondents, so a category would be created for each.

Researchers usually combine these methods to develop code categories for open-ended questions. Researchers almost never let data speak for themselves (by using only the contextual method) and almost always impose their own theoretical or a priori view to some extent. In other words, researchers usually look in the data for things they are interested in. An economist might code the question about the future in economic terms; a sociologist might look for references to changes in the racial and ethnic character of the country; and a psychologist might mine the data for information about whether the respondent feels threatened by the changes. In the end, coding schemes always depend on the researchers' objectives.

Consider the question, "What is the most important problem facing the country today?" The manifest coding scheme for answers to this question is complicated because so many different problems are mentioned by respondents. Furthermore, various coding schemes for the latent content of answers are conceivable. For example, answers could be categorized according to whether the researchers believe the problem can be solved by government, business, or not at all. Or answers could be categorized as social, political, economic, or structural problems.

Table 6.3 shows the outline of the code categories used by the National Election Studies (NES) in coding this question. The responses are sorted into basic types. One range of code numbers represents social welfare problems (e.g., aid to education, helping the poor), another range of numbers represents various agricultural and natural resource problems, and so on. To illustrate the detailed codes more directly, Table 6.3 also lists some of the NES codes relating to problems involving the functioning of government. There are several specific codes for particular problems plus a general code (800) for a respondent who makes a nonspecific reference about government power and a catchall code (890) for references to government problems other than those being coded specifically. Notice the variety of missing-data codes that are available if a person (a) gives an answer beyond the basic types being coded, (b) says "I don't know," (c) is not asked the question by accident, or (d) is not asked the question for some other reason.

Developing coding schemes for open-ended questions is often difficult. People sometimes give answers that cannot easily be put into simple categories, and their answers sometimes span several categories. The coding scheme in Table 6.3 seems relatively simple to use, yet what if someone answers that the major problem facing the country today is "all the crooked politicians in control of those big fancy corporations." Is that an 810 answer (honesty) or an 871 (lack of devotion to general welfare)? The best coding schemes make it easy to categorize answers.

Researchers usually try to preserve as much detail as possible in their codes to open-ended questions. For example, the question about major problems could be coded into hundreds of detailed categories or a few general headings. On the one hand, if only general codes were created in the first place, a later decision to capture more detailed information would require repeating the coding process, a very expensive move. On

TABLE 6.3 Part of an Open-Ended Code

What is the most important problem facing the country today?

General Category Codes

001-099	Social welfare problems
100-199	Agricultural and national resource problems
200-299	Labor problems, union-management problems
300-399	Racial and public order problems
400-499	Economic and business problems; consumer protection
500-699	Foreign affairs problems
700-799	National defense problems
800-899	Problems relating to the functioning of government
900-999	Miscellaneous and missing data

Some Detailed 800-999 Codes

800	Power of government; general reference
805	Government control of information; secrecy
810	Honesty in government; ethics in government
811	Lack of personal ethics of people in government
815	Media bias
819	Other specific references to honesty in government
820	Campaign donations
830	Confidence/trust in political leaders
831	Increased trust in political leaders
832	Decreased trust in political leaders
833	Quality, efficiency, cost of government

the other hand, if detailed coding is done initially, a later decision to move to a higher level of abstraction requires simply combining detailed codes into general categories, a fairly inexpensive process.

An extreme solution to this problem is to record the entire open-ended answer verbatim into a computer file so that researchers can develop their own coding schemes each time they analyze the data. The researchers make up specific instructions indicating that answers using some words (e.g., *liberal* or *conservative*) go into one category, those using other words go into another category, and so on. Computer content analysis obviously lacks the discernment of human coding, but it has the advantage of permitting different researchers to use different coding schemes on the same answers without requiring a costly rereading of all the original questionnaires.

TABLE 6.3 *Continued*

What is the most important problem facing the country today?

834	Increased quality/cost of government
835	Decreased quality/cost of government
836	Compensation of government employees
837	Waste in government
840	Size of federal government
841	For a more powerful federal government
842	Against power of federal government
850-859	Power of president, Congress, Supreme Court
860-869	Apportionment and election procedures
870	Other qualities of political leaders
871	Lack of devotion to general welfare
872-882	Comments on current president
885	Public apathy
886	Getting people together; unity of people
890	Other specific references to functioning of government
995	"There were no issues"
996	"There was no campaign in my district"
997	Other
998	Don't know
999	Not ascertained
000	Inappropriate; no problems mentioned; no further mention

SOURCE: Adapted from the codebook for American National Election Study.

The Codebook

Once the coding schemes for a survey's questions are specified, the researcher constructs a **codebook.** The codebook lists the questions, shows what codes are used for each one, and shows the locations of each question on the coding sheets onto which the numbers representing answers are written. In a small study, this codebook might fit on a single sheet of paper; in large studies, the information is put into books. The coders use an early version of the codebook when they do the coding.

TABLE 6.4 Codebook Entry for Closed-Ended Question

Variable 5623   Name: Respondent's vote for House of Representatives

Question: (If reports voting for House of Representatives) Who did you vote for in the election for the House of Representatives?

812	1. Democratic candidate
558	2. Republican candidate
	6. Refused to say who voted for
22	7. Other
57	8. Don't know
7	9. Not ascertained
1029	0. Inappropriate—did not vote for House (or no postelection interview)

SOURCE: 1992 American National Election Study codebook.

As an example, Table 6.4 reproduces part of a page from the codebook for a National Election Study, which is several hundred pages long. The valid responses to the congressional-vote question are shown in this table. Congressional vote is listed as variable number 5623, a unique number representing this variable. In analysis of the data, a researcher would direct the computer to analyze variable 5623.

Notice that the codebook has been annotated to show the number of people who gave each response. Needless to say, this is done after the data are all coded. The "refused" category was not employed. Incidentally, the reason for the large number of inappropriate responses is that many respondents did not vote, did not remember whether they had voted, or accidentally were not asked the question. Also, there was no postelection interview with some people who were interviewed prior to the election.

Coding Mechanics

Two coding procedures are described here: (a) a mechanical procedure using coding sheets and (b) a computerized version. The computer approach is being used more and more, but coding sheets are still used frequently and give the novice a better idea of what is involved in coding.

When completed questionnaires are given to the coding department after interviews, coders read through them and write the numbers for each person's responses onto coding sheets (Figure 6.1). Each row of a coding sheet has many columns; exactly one single-digit number is written in each cell. In large surveys, more than one row is used for each respondent's data.[1]

Each respondent is given an identification number to preserve confidentiality and to allow comparison of the computer's record of what someone said during an interview with his or her questionnaire (on which the same interview number is written) if necessary. To keep track of which rows on the coding sheet correspond to which person's data, the respondent identification number is written near the beginning of each row of data. To keep each person's rows in order, a row number is also written near the beginning of each row. The row number ranges from 1 to the number of rows used for each person's data.

As an example, Figure 6.1 shows a coding sheet. The respondent's identification number (0638) appears in columns 7 through 10 of every row of that person's data. The row number, which ranges from 1 to 25, appears in columns 5 and 6. Also, a number identifying this particular survey (say, 7010) appears in columns 1 through 4 of every row for every respondent. The numbers corresponding to people's answers to the survey questions appear in columns 11 through 80 of every row.

How exactly do the coders work? First, they write the identification numbers, row numbers, and study numbers in the first few columns of each row. Then, they page through the questionnaire and write the numbers representing the answers in the appropriate columns. For example, here's what coders for an election study might do to code the 638th respondent's report of her vote for Congress. Let's say the coding instructions indicate that the vote question is to be coded in column 70 of row 12. So, for respondent 638, a 2 is put into that column of that row because she reported voting for the Republican candidate. The coders go through the questionnaire sequentially, so 11 full rows and 69 columns of the 12th row would be filled up when they reached the vote question. Therefore, they do not have to check the coding instructions to find where the answer to each question goes; it goes in the next empty column.

It might seem that it would simplify the coding process if a blank on the coding sheet were used to indicate that a respondent did not answer a particular question. However, there are three reasons not to do so. First,

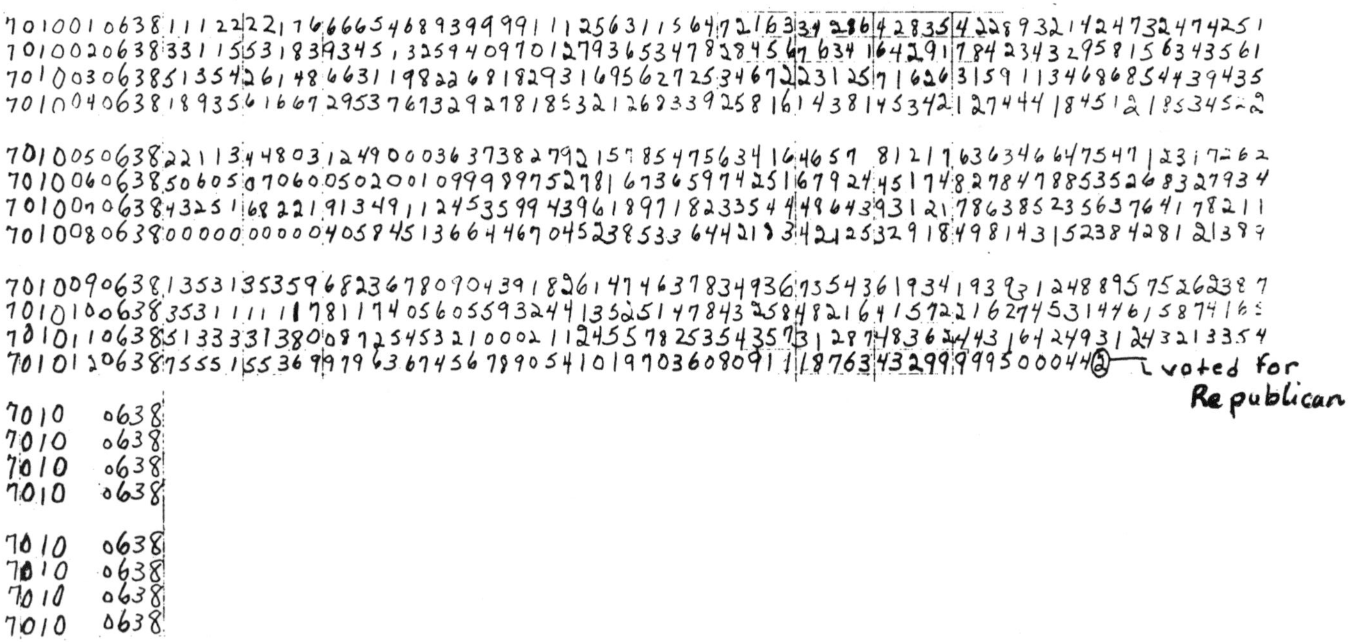

140

Figure 6.1. A Coding Sheet

leaving a column blank is a good way to indicate the coder was not sure which code was appropriate, so a supervisor can scan the completed sheets and find the blanks to be filled in. Second, it makes it easy for the coder to keep his or her place and hence reduces coder error. Third, some computers do not read blanks accurately, so the data may not be easily analyzed. Therefore, it is better to code all responses and nonresponses with numbers.

The coding of some variables is complicated by the possibility of the respondent giving more than one valid answer. For example, the question might ask people what the major problems facing the country are, and the interviewers might be instructed to prompt to obtain three answers per respondent, as by asking, "And what else do you consider to be an important problem facing the country today?" The coder would code up to three responses per respondent. Physically, that would mean setting aside three separate coding fields (e.g., columns 15 through 17, columns 18 through 20, and columns 21 through 23) for the three responses. For the sake of completeness, a special code would be created for no second or third response.

An alternative to using coding sheets is to write the code numbers in the margin of each page of the questionnaire. **Edge coding,** as this practice is called, can be faster than using coding sheets, although it is easy to miss questions. The data are then entered into the computer right off the actual questionnaires.

Data Entry

Once all respondents' answers have been translated into numbers on coding sheets, those numerical codes are entered into a computer's memory banks to be analyzed. The methods used for entering data into computers have changed in recent years. In the 1950s, the numbers on coding sheets were punched onto computer cards by using special "keypunch" machines; the holes in these cards were read by a "card reader" machine into a computer's memory bank. Computer card technology went out of fashion by the 1970s.

It is now common for a typist to sit at a computer terminal and type the numbers from the coding sheets into the computer. Indeed, improvements in computer technology now allow survey organizations to enter survey results into computers even more quickly through a process called **direct data entry** (DDE). Coding sheets are no longer required. The coder sits at a computer and types each person's answers directly into the computer from the completed interview schedules. The questions are displayed on the screen in order, along with the appropriate answer categories. The coder reads each person's answers directly from the questionnaire and types the appropriate numbers. An extreme form of direct data entry is CATI, computer-assisted telephone interviewing. Telephone interviewers read the questions on the computer screen and type respondents' answers into the computer during the interview, instead of writing the answers down on paper.

DDE speeds up data processing a great deal. Also, as detailed in the next section, accuracy is increased because the computer checks each number typed in to make sure no obvious errors are made in coding the data. The major extra expense for DDE is programming a computer to display the questionnaire.

A new approach for data entry is to enter the data into a **spreadsheet** on a computer. A spreadsheet is essentially a grid with a column for each variable and a row for each respondent. The spreadsheet columns are usually designated by letters, and the rows by numbers, so cells can be uniquely identified by a letter-number combination, such as D6 to designate the cell corresponding to column D and row 6 of the spreadsheet. Figure 6.2 shows part of a spreadsheet. The rows are labeled with the respondent numbers (in column A). If variable D is congressional vote, then the 6th row shows that respondent number 1006 voted Republican (a code of 2). Spreadsheet programs, such as Microsoft Excel, LOTUS 1-2-3, and Quattro Pro, are used extensively in business. Statistics programs on personal computers generally permit data to be imported from such spreadsheet programs, and most (including SPSS for Windows) also provide for entry of data into a spreadsheet in the statistics programs.

The spreadsheet entry of data is more intuitive than earlier ways of entering data, in that the focus is on entering variable values rather than digits. This way is probably most useful for a researcher entering a small amount of data by hand. Spreadsheet entry is less efficient for entry of large amounts of data from major surveys, however, and it does not lend itself to procedures for verifying the accuracy of the data entered.

Coding Accuracy

After carefully collecting a set of data, it is important to avoid errors during the coding and data entry stages. Let's see how this can be accomplished.

	A	B	C	D	E	F	G
1	1001	3	14	2	90	9	5
2	1002	2	25	1	75	8	3
3	1003	1	36	3	55	5	4
4	1004	3	28	2	45	3	2
5	1005	4	15	1	35	2	1
6	1006	5	05	2	20	1	3
7	1007						
8	1008						
9	1009						

Figure 6.2. A Data Spreadsheet

Coding Reliability

Coding closed-ended questions is a simple process. Nonetheless, a bit of human error always creeps into the computer data file. The interviewer may check the wrong box—a nonrecoverable error. The interviewer's check mark may be so unclear that the coder may misread which box is checked. The coder may write down the wrong number even if the interviewer's mark was clear. This last error may be found by having a second coder check over the coding, but such clerical error is so slight (less than 1% on closed-ended questions) that code checking is rarely done. Unlike other types of error, this type of error is unlikely to introduce any substantial bias into survey results because the errors are likely to be infrequent and random.

Coding open-ended questions requires the coder to make judgments, so this process is more subject to error. The coder reads the responses to each open-ended question and must decide which category is best for each response. The better the coding scheme, the easier it is for the coder to choose a category for each response. Coders are often told about the objectives of the questions and of the coding schemes so that the coding process will be easier and less prone to errors.

Coding schemes for open-ended questions are constantly evaluated while the coding goes on, and they are sometimes revised midstream. Usually, a preliminary coding of a few interviews is done to test the open-ended codes, just as a pretest is used to test the questionnaire before the actual interviewing. Then, researchers observe the coding process to spot coding schemes that do not work well. If coders frequently ask about how to code answers to a particular question, the coding scheme for that question will probably be revised. Additionally, coders keep track of responses that do not fit the established categories, so the researchers can add new categories when an unanticipated response appears frequently.

An open-ended coding scheme not only must be easy to use but also must produce reliable results; that is, different coders ought to reach the same decisions about how to code particular answers. If this is not the case, the coding scheme is too ambiguous. One means of assessing the reliability of a coding scheme is to have several people code the same set of interviews. If they all code the questions the same way, then the researcher can be confident the codes are good. If each coder puts an answer into a different category, however, then either the coders are not doing a good job or, as is more likely, the codes have not been adequately constructed. The researcher may compute a measure of the intercoder reliability of each open-ended question on the basis of the extent of agreement between two coders on that question. In some studies based on small numbers of interviews with elites, researchers actually have two or three coders code each question so that the intercoder reliability of the open-ended questions can be fully measured.

Data Entry Errors

Once the numbers representing responses have been entered into a computer, the resulting data file must be cleaned. Many errors can be made during data entry because typing thousands of numbers per hour can be very boring work. Therefore, it is essential to check the data file for errors. When numbers on coding sheets were punched onto cards, cleaning could be done partly by repunching each card on a verifying machine that would signal the operator whenever a typed number differed from the number already on the card. When DDE is employed, the data can be entered into the computer a second time, and the computer signals the operator whenever the new numbers differ from the ones typed in first. Although this method is extremely effective at catching errors, it is expensive because each data point must be typed twice.

Verifying at the data entry stage is a way to catch some errors, but errors made during coding and during data collection cannot be spotted this way. Therefore, once a set of survey responses is in a computer's memory, **wild code checking** must be performed. This is done by having the computer list all the numbers entered into the data set for each question in the survey. These are then compared to the codebook, which lists all the valid codes for each question. If some invalid codes occur, the researcher must locate the original questionnaires and correct the values in the computer file. DDE programs can prevent wild codes by storing in the computer a list of acceptable code values for each variable and then having the computer alert the typist to invalid entries.

Another form of error elimination is **consistency checking.** Some combinations of responses are logically impossible, so if they are observed, an error was made. For example, something would certainly be wrong if a data file indicated that a respondent said no to the question, "Did you vote in the most recent presidential election?" and then said he voted Democratic in that election in answer to the question, "For whom did you vote?" Computers can locate such logical inconsistencies in responses. The analyst must then fix each one by consulting the questionnaires. Again, DDE systems can be programmed to check for inconsistencies while the data are being entered, so the coder must correct such errors.

SUMMARY

Coding is the conversion of verbal responses into a set of numbers representing mutually exclusive and exhaustive categories. The codes may represent manifest or latent information, and they must be reliable. Testing and revision of the code categories may be required, along with careful training of coders, but the added expense is justified.

Open-ended questions are much more difficult and expensive to code than are closed-ended questions. Also, coding a large study with many open-ended questions takes months. Although these questions permit great flexibility, including latent coding at various levels of abstraction, the most interesting abstract codes may well have the least reliability. Therefore, many researchers prefer to use closed-ended questions, which allow respondents to code their own answers into a preestablished set of categories. Clearly, each question form has its advantages, and the decision whether to use open-ended or closed-ended questions must be made on the basis of considerations unique to each survey.

After the codes are constructed, they are assembled into a codebook. The coding can be done manually on coding sheets, in the margins of the questionnaires, or directly into a computer. It is important to check coding consistency, especially for open-ended questions. When intercoder reliability is low, it is necessary to train the coders better or to improve the coding scheme. Computers can be programmed to check for some trivial data entry errors.

Further Readings

Writing Style

Krippendorff, K. (1980). *Content analysis: An introduction to its methodology.* Beverly Hills, CA: Sage.

Weber, R. P. (1990). *Basic content analysis* (2nd ed.). Newbury Park, CA: Sage.

Note

1. The columns originally corresponded to the 80 columns of information that used to be punched onto computer cards (see the discussion below).

☑ EXERCISE

Construct a code for the following question: "If you could vote for anyone, who would be your first choice for president?" You might try out this question on a few people to get an idea of the variety of possible responses before writing out the code. Make sure to provide an easy way to differentiate Republican and Democratic candidates. Also, you might choose to construct more than one code for this question.

7 ☑☐☐☑ Designing a Survey

☑ We have traced the major steps in conducting a survey: sampling, questionnaire construction, interviewing, and coding. We can use that information to describe how best to design a survey.

Unfortunately, there are no simple rules about good and bad survey designs. Instead, the best design for a survey is determined by its goals; different goals require different designs. In Chapter 1, we listed four main goals of surveys: (a) to measure the prevalence of attitudes, beliefs, and behavior; (b) to determine the amount of change over time in those attitudes, beliefs, and behavior; (c) to examine differences between groups, as between men and women; and (d) to analyze the causes of attitudes, beliefs, and behavior. The best design depends on which goal is predominant. For example, to predict the winner of an election, researchers would design the study differently than if their goal were to examine the relationship between union membership and election turnout.

Measuring the Prevalence of
Attitudes, Beliefs, and Behavior
_____

_____
Measuring Behavior

Surveys are frequently used to measure the frequency with which people have performed certain acts. For example, people can be asked how many times they visited a physician during the last year, and it would seem likely that they can provide accurate information. This is true especially when the behavior in question was performed recently. Good examples of this are the exit polls taken by the news media on election days, in which interviewers approach people as they leave the polling area and ask them how they voted. Exit polls are typically highly accurate because people remember how they voted a minute earlier and are generally willing to disclose that information.

When people are asked to recall behavior performed long ago, though, their reporting typically becomes much less accurate. This is especially true when a particular time frame is involved. For example, if you asked people the number of times they went to a physician in the past year, they would probably forget some visits that were several months earlier and would be unsure about exactly when other visits occurred. Because long-term recall is difficult, it is best to ask people only about recent behavior.

People sometimes misremember past events as having occurred more recently than they actually did (**forward telescoping**) or longer ago than they actually did (**backward telescoping**). A good strategy is to set the time frame for people, possibly by beginning with a throw-away question (e.g., how often they visited a physician in the previous month) and then asking them the real question (say, how often they visited a physician during the current month).

Sensitive Topics. Although people are usually able to report their behavior accurately, they are sometimes unwilling to do so. This is true especially when people believe they will look more respectable to an interviewer if they say they behaved or will behave in a certain way. When asked whether they voted in the last presidential election, more respondents claim to have voted than official records show actually did (Clausen, 1968-69). Also, more people report having voted for the winner of an election than actually did, particularly when the winner's performance in office since the election has been good. Similarly, high school students seem to overreport their use of alcohol and drugs rather than not sound "with it." Questions about sensitive behavior can be asked, but the resulting data may not be valid because of respondents' desires to present themselves favorably to the interviewer.

Fortunately, survey researchers have developed several techniques to improve the validity of reports of behavior on sensitive topics. One such technique is called the **bogus pipeline technique.** Interviewers ask respondents for permission to check an official record of their behavior (e.g., a voting record, medical records) to validate their report of it. When this is done, the accuracy of peoples' reports increases.

Another way to improve the validity of reports of sensitive behavior involves giving respondents lists of acts and asking how many they have performed. The lists include several nonsensitive behaviors (e.g., having visited Europe). A random half of the sample is given a list that includes the sensitive behavior of interest (e.g., having used cocaine), whereas the other half of the sample is given the same list except for that sensitive behavior. This latter group is the control group. Because the two samples differ only by chance, it is expected that they are similar in terms of having visited Europe and other nonsensitive acts. Therefore, any difference in numbers of acts performed between the two samples should be because of the sensitive behavior. As an example, if the "average" person in the group asked about the sensitive behavior performed 2.72 of the acts versus 2.31 acts for the "average" person in the control group, then 41% (2.72 – 2.31) of the sample would be estimated to have performed the sensitive behavior. Using this system, researchers cannot know *which* people performed the sensitive behavior, but they would be able to estimate *how many* did.

A particularly ingenious means of measuring sensitive attitudes or behavior is the **randomized response technique.** Suppose a researcher wanted to know how many people cheated on their federal income tax returns. The respondent could be handed a coin and a card on which is printed:

(A) Did you cheat on your last year's federal income tax return?
(B) Did you fill out your last year's federal income tax return honestly?

Then the respondent is told to flip the coin and to conceal the result from the interviewer. The respondent is then told to answer Question A if the coin turns up heads and to answer Question B if the coin turns up tails. Using this procedure, the interviewer and the researcher never know which question the respondent answered. After all the answers are tallied, however, the researcher can use a mathematical formula developed by Warner (1965; Fox & Tracy, 1986) to calculate how many people cheated on their taxes.[1]

The randomized response technique may be implemented in other ways, but all of them involve a randomizing device, such as a flipped coin and a set of questions on a show card. This technique has been found to yield more honest answers regarding sensitive behavior and attitudes than does direct questioning. It does not, however, allow the researcher to determine whether any particular respondent performed the behavior of interest. It can only reveal the proportion of all respondents who performed it.

Beliefs About Others' Attitudes. Surveys often ask questions about facts, which on closer inspection turn out to be questions about what the respondent believes to be true. Researchers should not believe answers to such questions when the respondents are not likely to possess the information needed to answer the questions. Asking people about the attitudes of others, for example, is not likely to be fruitful because they are unlikely to know those attitudes. Studies of parents and their high-school-aged children, for example, have found that neither group has very accurate knowledge of the political views of the other. Parents are likely to think their children agree with them on politics even when that is not the case. At best, these questions show how parents believe their children think or perhaps what parents want their children to think, not how they actually think. If the researcher wants to know someone's opinions on a matter, it is best to ask that person directly.

Predicting Behavior

Another task for which surveys are frequently used is to predict people's behavior. These predictions often are based on people's beliefs about what their actions are likely to be.

Election Predictions. Perhaps the most widely known examples of this use are surveys conducted to forecast the outcomes of elections. Every 4 years, the Gallup, Harris, and other polls track candidate popularity as the U.S. presidential campaign progresses, in an attempt to predict the winner before election day. Pollsters must contend with a 3% to 4% margin of error, so no poll can reliably predict very close races, but predictions of presidential election outcomes are usually remarkably

TABLE 7.1 Gallup Poll Accuracy in Presidential Elections

Year	Election Winner	Gallup's Predicted Percentage for Election Winner	Actual Vote Percentage for Election Winner	Over-/ Underprediction of Winner's Vote in Percentages	Winner Prediction
1936	Roosevelt	55.7	62.5	−6.8	accurate
1940	Roosevelt	52.0	55.0	−3.0	accurate
1944	Roosevelt	51.5	53.3	−1.8	accurate
1948	Truman	44.5	49.9	−5.4	WRONG
1952	Eisenhower	51.0	55.4	−4.4	accurate
1956	Eisenhower	59.5	57.8	1.7	accurate
1960	Kennedy	51.0	50.1	.9	accurate
1964	Johnson	64.0	61.3	2.7	accurate
1968	Nixon	43.0	43.5	−.5	accurate
1972	Nixon	62.0	61.8	.2	accurate
1976	Carter	48.0	50.0	−2.0	accurate
1980	Reagan	47.0	50.8	−3.8	accurate
1984	Reagan	59.0	59.1	−.1	accurate
1988	Bush	56.0	53.9	2.1	accurate
1992	Clinton	49.0	43.2	5.8	accurate

SOURCE: Adapted from *Gallup Poll Monthly,* November 1992, p. 33.
NOTE: "Accurate" is recorded when the poll did not proclaim the wrong winner. Percentages are based on two-party vote, except in 1948, 1968, 1976, 1980, and 1992. Gallup did not correctly estimate the 1992 Perot vote among those who claimed to be undecided.

accurate. As Table 7.1 shows, the Gallup Poll has been nearly perfect in forecasting the winner of recent American contests.

These predictions are based largely on what people say they will do in the voting booth, and fortunately people are good at predicting which candidate they will prefer on election day. People are not so good, however, at predicting whether they will vote. Most people want to appear as good citizens to survey interviewers, so almost everyone says he or she expects to vote in the upcoming election even though only about half the nation's eligible voters actually participate in elections these days. To predict an election's outcome, a pollster must use only the predictions made by respondents who are most likely to make it to the voting booth. The challenge for the pollster is to figure out which respondents are likely to vote in the election and which are not.

As might be expected, people are better at predicting their behavior a short time into the future than a long time into the future. Polls are therefore more accurate if the election is the next day than if the election is 1 month later. Election standings always change as the campaign progresses, in part, because many people flirt with voting against their own party early in the campaign but vote for it in the end. Because the popularity of candidates inevitably changes throughout the campaign, trying to predict the outcome of an election long in advance is unlikely to work.

American pollsters learned this lesson in an embarrassing way in 1948. It took a long time to interview large samples of respondents and to analyze the data in those days, so the last poll conducted was done several weeks before the presidential election. The results of the final poll suggested that Thomas Dewey would win the election easily, a prediction that pollsters made publicly. Unbeknownst to them, though, Harry Truman's campaign caught on in the final weeks before the election, after interviewing had ended. As a result, Truman won the election and the pollsters' prediction was wrong. Now, polling routinely continues until election eve. Even so, the polls were unable to predict the Perot vote accurately in 1992, possibly because many people who would not otherwise have been expected to vote decided in the last few days of the campaign to turn out and vote for Perot as a means of registering their dissatisfaction with politics as usual.

Another factor that makes it difficult to predict the outcomes of elections is that many respondents say they are undecided. Usually, these people split their votes fairly evenly between the two candidates, but this isn't always the case. Consider, for example, the 1980 presidential contest between Jimmy Carter and Ronald Reagan. Polls conducted close to election day showed a fairly tight race, but many voters were undecided. In this case, most of the undecided voters ended up voting for Reagan, so he won the contest in a landslide. Fortunately for the polling industry, that was an unusual event; the vote of the undecided is rarely so one-sided.

Different survey organizations rarely make identical predictions of election outcomes. This is true partly because of sampling error, differences in wording of questions, and different interview dates. It is also true partly because of how different organizations decide which people are likely to vote and what undecided voters will do on election day. When different pollsters make similar predictions, they are likely to be correct. But when the polls disagree with one another, it is safest to assume that none is exactly correct and that the truth lies somewhere near the average of their forecasts.

Sensitive Topics. Predictions of behavior can also be inaccurate if one answer is seen as sensitive. For example, surveys in California predicted in 1982 that black Los Angeles Mayor Tom Bradley would win the governorship, but instead he lost by several percentage points. By all accounts, many white California Democrats were reluctant to tell interviewers they were unwilling to vote for a black for governor.

Another factor that makes it difficult to measure people's predictions of their own behavior in emotionally charged situations is the bias of rationality (J. Converse & Schuman, 1974, pp. 72-74). The formality of the questions reduces the spontaneity of the interview; the one-to-one discussion eliminates the group influences that can incite action and violence; and the reasonable tone of the interviewer makes it harder to express unreasonable views. Thus, if a researcher wants to know whether a person is likely to participate in an urban riot, survey interviewing may be too cool a methodology (Riesman, 1958, p. 291). The artificial interview situation inhibits a range of emotional responses that occur in other settings. As a result, surveys may be least useful for the study of beliefs and future behaviors that are emotionally charged.

Measuring Attitudes

Certainly, the most common goal of surveys is to measure attitudes. There is always the possibility, however, that questions intended to measure attitudes instead measure **nonattitudes.** When respondents are asked questions on topics they have thought little about, the best answer is probably "I don't know." But instead of saying this, some respondents generate opinions on the spot even though the responses they give are not indicative of preexisting, well-thought-out opinions. These answers, possibly developed to avoid appearing uninformed to the interviewer or to be polite to an interviewer who is expecting an answer, represent what pollsters call *nonattitudes* (Converse, 1964). Surveys that query the public about such obscure topics as U.S. policy toward Nepal may mainly measure nonattitudes. Although this example is stark, focusing on nonattitudes diverts attention from the fact that attitude strength and intensity are actually continuua. As a result, recent work in social psychology has paid less attention to the nonattitude topic and more to the importance of considering attitude strength.

Attitude Strength. Although a person may have opinions on a wide range of issues, he or she may not necessarily feel strongly about all of them.

This is variation in what social scientists call **attitude strength.** Strong attitudes are stable over time, resistant to change, and shape a person's thinking and actions, whereas weak attitudes can be changed easily and have few if any effects.

An attitude can be strong for any number of reasons. For example, people might become very knowledgeable about an issue through numerous stories in newspapers and on television, and they might be very confident in the validity of their opinions as a result. Or, an issue might be deeply important to a person personally because it is related to his or her personal values. So, racial discrimination might be an important issue to a person who values "social equality" a great deal and who sees equality as being violated by discrimination. Even if this person has very little factual knowledge about the history of discrimination, he or she may nonetheless have strong opinions on affirmative action and other policies addressing racial discrimination.

Attitude strength can be measured in a number of ways in surveys. People can be asked how important an issue is to them personally, or how knowledgeable they feel on the issue, or how certain they are of their opinion, or how much they have thought about the issue. People who indicate involvement in an issue for any of these reasons tend to have stronger attitudes than do people who are low in importance, knowledge, certainty, and thought. It is also possible to measure attitude strength more surreptitiously by measuring the length of time it takes a person to answer an attitude question: The longer it takes, the weaker the person's opinion typically is.

An interesting approach to testing the strength of attitudes is to give counterarguments and see what effect that has on the expressed opinion (Sniderman, Brody, & Tetlock, 1991, Chap. 12). For example, people may first be asked whether they think the government should increase spending for programs to help blacks or whether they think blacks should rely only on themselves. Those who favor increased spending are next asked, "Would you still feel the same way even if government help means people get special treatment just because they are black, or would that change your mind?" Those who originally favored self-reliance are instead next asked, "Would you still think that way even if it means that blacks will continue to be poorer and more often out of work than whites, or would that change your mind?" In other contexts, these question wordings would be viewed as leading and biased, but here they are used to see how firm the original attitude was.

It is important to measure the strength of peoples' attitudes. Some people may give an answer to a question but not really care much about it, whereas other people may care passionately about their view on the same question. Take the issue of gun control. Surveys routinely show that a majority of Americans favor stricter gun control laws. Yet, gun control legislation has had a very hard time getting passed in Congress. One reason is that the anticontrol people have much greater strength in their attitudes than the procontrol people. Those opposed to gun control are more willing to finance and support large lobbying efforts to influence Congress, and they have, on occasion, cast single-issue votes against members of Congress who have supported gun control. As a result, members of Congress have learned that votes for gun control can threaten their reelection to Congress regardless of the majority support for gun control in public opinion polls. This is a case in which public opinion polls should show the strength of public attitudes, as well as their direction.

A special problem that occurs is to distinguish between initial views that are just first impressions based on little information and more formed opinions. For example, early polls reported widespread public support for President Clinton's health care reform plan in 1994. But at that time, people didn't know much about the specifics of the plan and its possible consequences. As such information was publicized, more people became opposed to the plan. Similarly, unknown candidates running for public office sometimes do poorly in early polls because people don't know them, but once people become better informed, the candidates' popularity may skyrocket. Such opinion change can occur even if no new information is distributed; people may simply be induced to think about an issue to which they had previously devoted little thought. Thus, to interpret the results of a poll, it is important to keep in mind how strong people's opinions are likely to be: The stronger the opinions, the more stable and consequential they are likely to be. Asking people how much they have heard about the issue or candidate can help in assessing this aspect of attitude strength.

Weakly held attitudes are not very useful for predicting people's behavior, a common goal for survey researchers. For example, survey-based predictions may overestimate support for civic improvements because questions usually do not force the respondents to take account of the costs of such projects. Respondents who say they support building a bridge may vote against it when they realize that taxes would have to be raised to cover the costs. Thus, a survey question may tap one attitude although actual behavior may be based on another, more complex attitude. For this reason, social scientists should exercise caution when inferring behavior from survey reports of attitudes unless they have evidence indicating that the reports are not of nonattitudes.

Disagreement About the Meanings of Words. Another warning about interpreting poll results on attitudes: The attitudes that analysts think they are measuring may not be those they are, in fact, measuring. It is natural to read the report of a survey and then to assume that respondents interpret the questions just the way you do, but that is not always true.

Consider the case of ideology. Politicians, academicians, and journalists often use such ideological terms as *liberal* and *conservative* in their discussions of politics. These professionals view liberals as people who favor big government and who favor the welfare state, whereas they view conservatives as people who oppose big government and who favor free enterprise unconstrained by government regulations.

For many years, the Gallup Poll has asked Americans whether they consider themselves to be liberal or conservative. Almost one third of respondents say they think of themselves as neither; this finding suggests that these people do not think of themselves in these terms. Because reports of liberalism/conservatism from the other two thirds of respondents are quite stable over time, they seem not to reflect nonattitudes (Levitin & Miller, 1979), but it turns out that many of the respondents who call themselves either liberals or conservatives do not mean what journalists and scholars assume. Most people think of liberals as people who spend money freely and think of conservatives as tightwads. This example illustrates how careful a researcher must be when interpreting the results of attitude measures. Results that seem to mean one thing can, in fact, mean something quite different.

Changing Frames. Another reason to be careful in interpreting poll results about a news story is that the story can be reinterpreted over time. Attitudes measured during the initial flurry of media attention might not be representative of the views that form later. In particular, the "frame" through which the event is described in the media can change.

A pair of examples may help illustrate this reframing effect. The first involves President Bush's 1991 nomination of Clarence Thomas to be a justice on the Supreme Court. In the midst of the Senate's confirmation process, Anita Hill accused Thomas of sexual harassment. The Senate Judiciary Committee held televised hearings on these allegations, and Thomas was a salient feature of them. He made an effective appearance, arguing that they amounted to a "high-tech lynching." Public opinion polls showed that most Americans believed Thomas over Hill, and that result held for blacks as well as whites. The Senate confirmed Thomas's appointment, with many senators justifying their vote in terms of the public opinion polls.

Yet, by the 1992 election, when Thomas and his testimony were no longer salient, the public's view had shifted. Perhaps partly because news coverage had highlighted sexual harassment in many segments of society, public opinion polls showed that more people believed Hill than Thomas. Dissatisfaction with how Hill had been treated by the Senate Judiciary Committee fueled Senate campaigns by several women and helped turn the 1992 election into "the year of the woman." Thus, public attitudes changed over this period as the event was reframed.

Senators might have followed public opinion at the time, but those attitudes had been formed in just a few days during the hearings. Once the charges moved off the front pages and more conventional political processes took over, the incident was reinterpreted, and public views correspondingly changed. It is interesting to see what the public thinks about a political event as it occurs, but that preliminary view is not necessarily the public's final judgment.

A similar point can be made about the reactions of the American public to the war with Iraq. Iraqi leader Saddam Hussein's army invaded Kuwait in the fall of 1990. The United States put together a coalition of nations to force Iraq out of Kuwait, and the Desert Storm War began in January 1991, with the coalition forces bombing Baghdad. A ground invasion followed, and the Alliance forces won in just 100 hours. Public opinion polls showed substantial American support for the war effort, with President Bush riding American support for U.S. troops to record heights for the personal popularity of a president.

Yet, less than 2 years later, Bush was defeated for reelection, receiving only 38% of the vote. Not only had public attention shifted from foreign policy to the domestic economy, but the coalition's success in the war had also been reinterpreted. Most people thought that Bush had ended the war too early, that the Alliance forces should have taken Baghdad, and that Saddam Hussein should have been removed from power. Public opinion had changed. Supporting U.S. troops during war conditions was no longer a salient consideration; instead, the question was whether Bush had squandered an opportunity to achieve a larger victory.

In summary, instant poll readings during (or immediately after) a news event can elicit transient feelings. Public opinion can change as events are reframed in the popular press and in political discourse. Attitudes do not gel overnight, so instant readings of public opinion should be considered to be just that.

Measuring Change

Imagine picking up the morning newspaper and seeing the headline "President's Popularity Increases." You begin to read the article and find that it reports the results of a recent survey in which respondents were asked whether they approve or disapprove of the president's handling of his job. The article says that 60% of Americans approve of the president's performance today, whereas only 56% approved of his performance last month when a similar survey was conducted. Is the conclusion that presidential popularity has increased a valid one on the basis of this evidence? That is a very complex question.

Attitude Recall Data

You might think that the simplest way to assess whether attitudes have changed over time is to ask people. Respondents can be asked about their past attitudes, as well as their current attitudes, and the difference could be attributed to attitude change. For example, people can be asked how they felt about legalized abortion last year and how they feel today so that changes in attitudes can be assessed.

Unfortunately, though, attitude recall data are frequently inaccurate. When asked how they felt a year ago, people tend to assume they believed then just what they do today. As a result, attitudes seem more stable than they really are. For this reason, attitude recall data should be interpreted cautiously and should be avoided whenever alternative methods for measuring attitude change are available. Minimally, a researcher should check whether people's recollections correspond with other evidence from the earlier period, such as surveys conducted at that time with different individuals, before accepting the recall data as valid.

Comparisons of Repeated Cross-Sectional Surveys

A much more useful way to determine whether public attitudes on a particular issue have changed over time is to survey the topic at different times and compare the results. The researcher should be careful, however, when studying attitude change with this approach. What may seem to be attitude change may reflect a change in methodology or the effect of sampling error. To evaluate whether an apparent change in attitudes is real, four questions should be asked:

1. Did the same organization conduct both polls by using the same interviewing methods?
2. Was the same population sampled in the same manner on both occasions?
3. Were the questions worded in the same way on both occasions?
4. Is the size of the observed attitude change larger than could result from sampling variation alone?

We discuss each of these issues below.

Surveys Conducted by Different Organizations. Survey organization all have their own idiosyncratic procedures for drawing samples and for conducting interviews. Some use primarily middle-aged women interviewers, whereas others use many more young men when conducting telephone interviews. Even such seemingly simple decisions as how many times to call a telephone number before giving up are made differently by different organizations. As a result, even if the sampling procedure used for two surveys were the same, the implementation of that sampling procedure or the interviewing procedure or both could be different. Changes in sampling or in the interviewing procedure could easily ruin the comparison.

Consider two telephone surveys on attitudes toward capital punishment conducted 2 weeks apart by different organizations. In the first survey, interviewers called homes three times before giving up, whereas in the second, the same telephone number was called back six times. Suppose further that the first survey found more people to be favorable toward capital punishment than did the second. This result could simply reflect the different call-back procedures. Wealthy people tend to be home less often than poor people, so the former are harder to get in touch with by telephone. As a result, fewer wealthy people probably were interviewed in the first survey than in the second. Because wealthy people tend to be less favorable toward capital punishment, their greater presence in the second survey could account for the apparent difference in results. Thus, the comparisons of the two surveys' results might reflect the fact that call-back procedures changed while attitudes remained constant.

Another example of this problem pertains to don't-know rates. Some survey organizations instruct their interviewers to discourage don't-know responses as much as possible and to encourage respondents to choose one of the alternatives offered by closed-ended questions. Other organizations tell their interviewers to accept don't-knows immediately and not to press respondents for substantive responses. Therefore, if one survey finds 15% of its sample saying they have no opinion about capital punishment, whereas a later survey done by a different organization finds 25% of people without opinions, it would be inappropriate to claim that people have become less opinionated on the issue; the apparent change could actually be due to different interviewing practices.

Therefore, if two survey organizations conducted the surveys, their results should not be directly compared. If an analyst were able to obtain lots of information about the two organizations' interviewing procedures and found that they were identical, it would be legitimate to compare their results. It is rarely possible to obtain such detailed information, however, and even rarer to find two organizations that use identical procedures. Thus, it is safest to compare only surveys done by the same firm.

Comparing Different Populations. Another problem in comparing trends over time occurs when the polling organization changes the population being studied. This occurred during a key part of the 1992 presidential campaign. Bill Clinton held the lead over George Bush in virtually all the polls taken after the Democratic convention in July. The tracking poll taken by the Gallup Organization for CNN/*USA Today,* however, showed that the Clinton lead narrowed considerably in the last week before the election. Part of that change turned out to be a change in the results being reported. The earlier polls showed the preferences of all respondents, but in the last week they showed only the intentions of likely voters. Democrats generally vote at a lower rate than Republicans, so the Democratic lead decreased when only likely voters were considered. Gallup argued that likely voters were the appropriate population for reports close to the election, but changing the base created an impression of changing electoral dynamics. Unfortunately, changes in the population studied are usually technical details that are not noticed in poll reports.

Comparing Different Questions. Even if two surveys are conducted by the same organization, it is inappropriate to compare their results if different questions were asked in the two surveys. Unfortunately, the survey literature is filled with examples of people trying to assess attitude change by using different questions at different times. For example, a researcher trying to determine whether whites' attitudes toward blacks are different in the 1990s from what they were in the 1950s may compare current results to those of a poll conducted 40 years before. Most often, the exact questions were not asked in both polls, so the researcher compares questions on the same topic even though they are phrased slightly differently.

Such comparisons are risky. As you know from Chapter 4, even slight changes in a question's wording can produce dramatic changes in the distribution of answers. When substantial changes are made, it is impossible to anticipate what effects they will have on answers. Therefore, researchers can easily be misled about attitude change if they compare answers to different questions.

For example, the University of Michigan's Survey Research Center found that fewer people said they supported federal aid to education in the early 1960s than had done so previously. Some observers viewed this finding as evidence of changing attitudes. It is important to note, however, that the wording of the question was revised in 1964. Before that time, people were asked to indicate whether they agreed strongly, agreed but not very strongly, were not sure, disagreed but not very strongly, or disagreed strongly with the following statement: "If cities and towns around the country need help to build more schools, the government in Washington ought to give them the money they need."

In 1964, the question was changed to the following: "Some people think the government in Washington should help towns and cities provide education for grade and high school children; others think that this should be handled by the states and local communities. Have you been interested enough in this to favor one side or the other? (IF YES) Which are you in favor of?"

Even though the question wording was not changed a great deal, it is different in a number of ways. Perhaps most obviously, acquiescence bias might have led some people to agree to the old form of the question, whereas they were forced to make a choice in responding to the second. Therefore, at least some, if not all, of the differences between responses to these questions are probably attributable to changes in the question, and not to changes in attitudes.

To make things more difficult, even if a question is worded exactly the same in both surveys, the social and political environments may have changed so much over time that the question means something different during the first interview than during the second. For example, in the 1960s, if people were asked whether they favored or opposed civil rights, they probably thought of integration of restaurants, public transportation, and so on. If they were asked the same question in the 1990s, however, they were more likely to think of school busing, Afrocentric schools, and affirmative action. Answers to the same question may be different because it is interpreted differently. The longer the time period between two surveys, the greater the chance for this type of change of interpretation to occur.

Successive Cross Sections. A relatively safe procedure for studying attitude change is to compare surveys of the public conducted by the same organization using the same questions. Fortunately, some organizations have asked the same questions in many surveys over the years. Different samples were interviewed in each case, but the same population was sampled each time, and the sampling procedure was the same. The results for one survey of a cross section of the public can therefore be compared with those for earlier cross sections.[2]

Figure 7.1 shows an analysis of Americans' trust in government, using this strategy. These results are based on identically worded questions used in surveys by the University of Michigan's Survey Research Center. Therefore, we can be confident that the trends shown here are not due to methodological artifacts. According to these results, Americans' trust in their government declined considerably during the 1960s and 1970s. Interestingly, this trend reversed in the 1980s but resumed in 1992.

Be careful not to overinterpret minor fluctuations in successive cross sections of this sort. As you saw in Chapter 3, no survey produces perfectly accurate results because of sampling error. A drop of 3% or more from one reading to the next might be totally attributable to sampling. Unfortunately, newspaper stories on presidential popularity polls frequently emphasize minor fluctuations, which could be caused by random differences in sample selection, rather than by real attitude change. When studying trends in attitudes, focus on major trends. Thus, the results in Figure 7.1 are useful because the major trend is clear and is therefore unlikely to be the result of sampling error.

Figure 7.1 provides a nice illustration of time-series analysis. However, it also shows the limits to such analysis. Studies of change over time can be relatively atheoretic. A researcher can locate the timing of changes, but that does not tell the reasons for those changes. Theory is required for interpreting the changes.

One drawback inherent in comparing successive cross-sectional surveys is that the analyst can only assess net change and cannot estimate the degree of gross change. Imagine that you conduct a survey and find that 40% of a national sample say they favor capital punishment and 60% say they oppose it. Imagine further that you asked the same question of

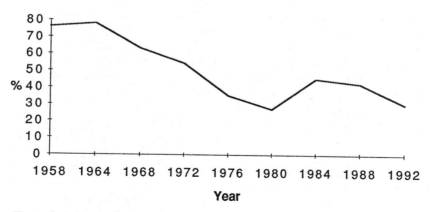

Figure 7.1. Trust in Government*

SOURCE: American National Election Studies, as shown in Asher (1992, Table 1.1), updated on the basis of subsequent election studies.
NOTE: *Proportion of the public who think they can trust the government in Washington to do what is right "always" or "most of the time."

a different national sample 1 year later. If, between the times of the two surveys, 10% of the public became more favorable toward capital punishment and 10% became more unfavorable and 80% did not change their attitudes, you would find the same distribution of attitudes at the time of the second survey: 40% in favor and 60% opposing. On the basis of this evidence, it would be fair to conclude that the distribution of attitudes in the nation did not change, but it would be wrong to conclude that no one's attitude changed. If a researcher wants to assess the extent of gross change in people's attitudes, a series of cross-sectional surveys will not do the trick. Instead, the same people must be interviewed on several occasions.

Panel Studies

The best way to measure gross attitude change by using surveys is to interview the same people a number of times. Repeated interviewing of the same respondents, referred to as a **panel,** reveals the amount of individual-level attitude change that occurred between the waves of the survey. For example, the University of Michigan's Center for Political Studies conducted a panel study in which researchers interviewed a group of people in 1992 and 1994. From those data, it is possible to assess how many people who voted Democratic for Congress in 1992 also voted Democratic in 1994, how many switched to a Republican vote in 1994, and how many did not vote. Similarly, it is possible to examine the voting behavior in 1994 of people who voted Republican for Congress in 1992.

Long-term panel studies have rarely been conducted because they are very expensive and labor intensive. Because people often move from one address to another, it can be difficult to locate a respondent years after a first interview. Also, people are sometimes unwilling to be interviewed repeatedly, particularly if they were not interested in the subject of the interview in the first place. As a result, considerable **mortality** is common in panel studies, with smaller and smaller proportions of the original sample interviewed at each successive wave.

Another common problem in panel studies is that the wrong person is sometimes interviewed; instead of reinterviewing a man, an interviewer might mistakenly interview his wife at the second wave of a panel study. For example, in a 1960 panel survey conducted by the University of Michigan's Survey Research Center, 1% of respondents are recorded as being a different gender at the postelection interview than at the preelection interview. In all likelihood, either a recording error was made at one of the waves or the wrong person was interviewed at the second wave. There is usually no way to correct for this because it is impossible to reconstruct what error occurred, but it reminds us that small amounts of error are present in all questions in surveys—even the seemingly obvious, such as the gender of the respondent.

Panel sample mortality decreases the representativeness of the sample at later waves. The people who are found for reinterviews tend to differ in some respects from a random cross section of the public. They tend to move their residence less often, which means they include fewer young people, and they tend to have more interest in and knowledge about the topic of the survey. Fortunately, it is possible to assess whether the part of a sample that was successfully followed up at later waves is unrepresentative of the original full sample. This assessment can be done by comparing the first-wave answers given by respondents who were successfully reinterviewed to the first-wave answers given by those who were not. Unfortunately, most reports of studies analyzing panel data report results based only on respondents who were successfully reinterviewed and do not report how representative they were of the original sample.

Another possible problem with panel designs is that the first interview may affect respondents' attitudes and behavior. For example, interviewing people for an hour about an upcoming election increases their interest in politics and therefore causes more of them to vote in the election than would have had they not been interviewed. Thus, because of the earlier interview of the panel sample, the behavior patterns apparent at the second wave of a panel survey may be slightly different from the behavior patterns of a representative sample interviewed at the same time. In the case of voting, the effect is not large, but it illustrates a possibly larger problem in some panel surveys.

Instant Polls

Often, there is interest in tying observed change to a particular event, such as the effects of a televised speech, without other factors intervening. The news media have been experimenting with techniques to conduct instant polls. As an example, CBS News conducted an interactive poll to gauge public reaction to President Clinton's 1994 State of the Union speech (Frankovic & Arendt, n.d.). A random sample was interviewed during the weeks leading up to the speech, and sample participants were asked to call a toll-free telephone number after the speech. Respondents with touch-tone phones were given a computer-administered survey with answers given by punching the appropriate key, whereas live operators administered the survey to callers from rotary-dial telephones. This procedure allowed responses to be tabulated in time for presentation on the network's postspeech analysis program. Furthermore, touch-tone callers were asked to stay on the line and to respond to questions that news anchor Dan Rather read on the air; results were broadcast 2 minutes later.

This example provides a good illustration of advantages and disadvantages of interactive polls. The technological ability to obtain an instant reading of public opinion is amazing. The technology permits weighting respondents according to known population parameters (so that young and elderly respondents are given extra weight to make up for the fact that people in those age groups are least likely to participate in the phone-in poll), but there is no guarantee that the respondents who called in have attitudes that are representative of people who did not call in. The immediate judgment of people who have just listened to a speech may differ from the view that develops in the public in the next few days after the speech. Thus, President Clinton's 1995 State of the Union address received very positive reactions in a similar instant poll taken that year, but surveys taken the following weekend showed that his popularity level remained low regardless of the speech.

A final point to make about measuring change is the importance of using longitudinal data when the focus is on change. Sometimes, researchers try to make statements about change from a single cross-sectional study, but such conclusions are often incorrect. As a classic example, American surveys routinely show that the voting turnout rate of people with high levels of education is greater than that of people with less education. It is tempting to conclude from that cross-sectional relationship that education leads to voting. That appears true, however, only when one looks a single cross-sectional survey. If compared across time, educational levels have increased dramatically in this country during the past century and even during the past 40 years, whereas voting turnout has declined. A relationship found in a cross-sectional study may not hold longitudinally. Longitudinal data are necessary if change is the focus of the study.

As another example of this problem, look back at the article on guns reprinted in Figure 1.1. The headline writer titled this article "Guns Don't Help People Feel Safer." That is ostensibly a claim about changes in attitudes, but the survey being reported is only a single cross-sectional survey. The article does show that people who owned guns did not feel safer than people who did not own guns at the time of the survey, but it is different from showing that there is no change in feelings of safety because of purchasing guns.

In summary, conducting surveys to measure attitudinal and behavioral change is tricky business. People's recall of their earlier views and actions is often faulty. Results of two surveys of different samples can be compared, but care must be taken that the differences found are not because of changes in the questions or different sampling or interviewing procedures. Panel studies provide the best evidence of change, but they are used infrequently because they are costly and difficult to implement. Cross sections provide untrustworthy evidence of changes over time.

Making Subgroup Comparisons

Surveys are frequently used in comparing the attitudes, beliefs, and behavior of subgroups. This use may seem routine, but sometimes it has special implications for sampling. Suppose you are interested in a subgroup that is relatively small in size, such as blacks, Hispanics, or Jews. In a representative national sample of 2,000 people, you would not obtain enough interviews in these categories to be able to compare them accurately with the rest of the population.

One approach sometimes taken to remedy this problem is to oversample a group of interest. To assess blacks' attitudes, for example, it might be worthwhile to **double-sample** blacks. All of the interviews with blacks would then be used to make generalizations about blacks' attitudes. To describe the entire sample, the surveyor would use only half of the blacks' interviews, weighting the interviews with blacks to their proper proportion.

Another approach is to combine samples in a **pyramiding** strategy. Lacking enough Hispanics in one national sample to draw valid conclusions about their attitudes, it might be reasonable to combine a series of surveys, perhaps even taken over a period of years, so long as those surveys contained identical questions and used similar sampling and interviewing procedures. Thus, combining the 1972 through 1992 American National Election Studies might produce a large enough sample of Hispanics to draw conclusions about their attitudes. Of course, this strategy would not be useful if attitudes changed drastically over that period.

Incidentally, many of the potential difficulties discussed earlier in this chapter are less severe when the goal is to compare subgroups. For example, the problem of people forgetting some of their actions of a year earlier than the survey would be a serious problem if we were trying to estimate what proportion of people did something (e.g., voting in an election a year earlier), but it is much less of a problem if we were trying to determine whether one group was more likely to take that action than another group. The relationship between union membership and voting, for example, can be assessed fairly safely a year after the election as long as we do not have any reason to expect that union members are more or less likely to forget their previous behavior than are non-union members. Thus, subgroup differences can often be assessed more accurately than the marginal proportions of respondents giving each answer on the survey.

Subgroup comparisons are an important part of surveys and survey reports. Procedures for comparing subgroups are explained more fully in Chapters 11 and 13.

Assessing the Causes of Behavior

A final common goal for surveys is to understand why people say or do certain things. It may seem reasonable simply to ask them. Unfortunately, though, people often do not know the reasons for their own actions, so their reports can be inaccurate (Nisbett & Wilson, 1977). Typically, the answers that people offer are rationalizations post hoc for behavior—their best guesses about what the causes of their behavior might have been. Apparently, people make up convincing explanations that appear rational to the interviewer. The explanations that people offer may make sense and sound reasonable, but they often have nothing to do with the actual causes of behavior. It is therefore best not to ask people directly about the reasons for their behavior when the reasons are likely to be complex.

The better strategy for assessing the causes of behavior with surveys is to think through the different possible causes of the behavior, to ask about those different possible causes, and then to analyze the results. Thus, surveys usually do not ask people why they voted as they did, but instead ask people about their feelings on the issues, the candidates, and the parties. Statistical analysis of these answers can reveal the relative importance of issues, candidates, and party in the vote decision. The general problems of explanation and causation are treated more fully in the next chapter.

SUMMARY

Surveys can be used to measure the prevalence of attitudes, beliefs, and behavior. Survey researchers have learned that measuring these variables can sometimes be difficult and that some ways to do so are better than others. Similarly, some ways of using surveys to assess change over time in attitudes, beliefs, and behavior are better than others. In this chapter, we have described some of the advantages and disadvantages of particular survey designs for accomplishing these goals.

Further Readings

Poll Results

Converse, P. E., Dotson, J. D., Hoag, W. J., & McGee, W. H., III. (1980). *American Social Attitudes data sourcebook, 1947-1978.* Cambridge, MA: Harvard University Press.

Gallup, G. H. (Ed.). (various years). *The Gallup Poll: Public opinion.* Wilmington, DE: Scholarly Resources.

Miller, W. E., & Traugott, S. A. (1989). *American National Election Studies data sourcebook: 1952-1986.* Cambridge, MA: Harvard University Press.

Niemi, R. G., Mueller, J., & Smith, T. W. (1989). *Trend in public opinion: A compendium of survey data.* Westport, CT: Greenwood.

Robinson, J. P., Rusk, J. G., & Head, K. B. (1968). *Measures of political attitudes.* Ann Arbor: University of Michigan.

Public Opinion Quarterly. (A scholarly journal published by the American Association for Public Opinion Research [AAPOR].)

Public Perspective magazine, Roper Center, Storrs, CT.

Advanced Topics in Survey Research

Brehm, J. (1993). *The phantom respondents.* Ann Arbor: University of Michigan Press.

Groves, R. M. (1989). *Survey errors and survey costs.* New York: John Wiley.

Rossi, P. H., Wright, J. D., & Anderson, A. B. (Eds.). (1983). *Handbook of survey research.* San Diego: Academic Press.

Singer, E., & Presser, S. (Eds.). (1989). *Survey research methods: A reader.* Chicago: University of Chicago Press.

Turner, C. F., & Martin, E. (Eds.). (1984). *Surveying subjective phenomena* (2 vols.). New York: Russell Sage.

Notes

1. Several variants of this procedure have been developed to try to counteract the distrust of respondents who worry that they are being tricked; one common variant is to use for statement (B) on the show card a nonsensitive item whose probability is known, such as "I was born in November."

2. Several useful compendia of survey results over time are available: The University of Michigan's National Election Studies and Survey Research Center surveys are summarized in P. Converse, Dotson, Hoag, and McGee (1980) and W. Miller and National Election Studies (1993). Similarly, the General Social Surveys are summarized in Davis (1993). Also see Niemi, Mueller, and Smith (1989).

☑ EXERCISES

Suppose that you are an expert in survey research and that you have been asked to evaluate the following survey results. What would you question about the studies?

1. A survey of high school seniors found that a majority of young people have experimented with drugs.

2. A survey of members of Congress shows that a majority believe they should follow the wishes of their constituents rather than their own attitudes when the two are in conflict.

3. A survey finds that when legislators in Germany and the United States are asked what their goals are, 20% more in Germany gave ideological goals than did in the United States.

PART

2

DATA ANALYSIS

8 The Process of Data Analysis

☑ The analysis of data gathered for a large research project can take years; it requires careful planning. In this chapter, we describe a general approach to analyzing survey data. This involves three steps: (a) stating hypotheses in theoretical terms, (b) operationalizing the concepts in the hypotheses, and (c) testing the hypotheses.

Stating Hypotheses

Analysis of survey data can be either descriptive or explanatory. The news media often use poll results only for description. For example, a reported poll may describe what proportion of the public supports the president, whether that support is increasing or decreasing, and whether some types of people are more likely to support the president than are others. Before examining the results of a poll, an investigator might formulate some hypotheses about the expected results. If support for the president is being studied, the investigator might speculate on the basis of recent political events that support for the president will be falling and is especially low among blue-collar workers as compared with white-collar workers. These are descriptive hypotheses.

In addition to describing, polls are often used for explanation: to understand the causes of people's beliefs, attitudes, and behavior. Usually, researchers seek to test generalizations that account for the attitudes

173

and behavior of aggregates of individuals—generalizations derived from theories of human behavior. Thus, poll results are used to answer such questions as, What factors determined which candidate each citizen voted for in the last presidential election? Why do some people oppose capital punishment for convicted murderers, whereas other people favor it? Why do some people vote in presidential elections, whereas others do not? These are examples of questions requiring **explanations.**

Causal Explanations

When seeking explanations, social scientists attempt to find the **causes** of social phenomena. What is a cause? Causation has a number of meanings; in scientific usage, its meaning is similar to that of "producing" (Blalock, 1964, p. 9; Bunge, 1959, pp. 46-48; cf. King, Keohane, & Verba, 1994, Chap. 3). One thing is a cause of another thing if a change in the first produces a change in the second. Therefore, it is appropriate to say that the weather causes human behavior. When it starts to rain, people put up umbrellas when they walk outside. Thus, a change in the weather produces a change in behavior.

Social scientists' causal hypotheses usually posit relationships between **variables.** A variable is something that varies from person to person or across situations. Social scientists study such types of variables as behavior, beliefs, attitudes, and background characteristics such as race, gender, educational attainment, family income, and religion. The variable the researcher wants to *explain* is called the **dependent** variable. For example, many studies of voting behavior seek to explain why some people vote Republican and others Democratic. In those studies, whom a person voted for is the dependent variable. The other variables used in hypotheses, called **independent** variables, are examined to discover whether they are causes of the dependent variable. In our example, independent variables such as religion and race might be used to explain a person's vote. In short, a dependent variable is an effect, and an independent variable is a suspected cause. A hypothesis states that one variable may cause another.

A few variables that social scientists frequently study are almost always independent. These are demographic variables, such as race, gender, and age. Social scientists are seldom interested in the causes of these variables (although gender was treated as a dependent variable by geneticists who studied what causes some babies to be male and others to be female), so social scientists' hypotheses generally treat these variables as independent. In contrast, some variables are nearly always dependent variables in social scientists' hypotheses. Political scientists, for example, often study the causes of such behavior as voter turnout, vote choice, and political participation. Many other variables may be independent or dependent, according to the context in which they are studied. For example, party identification (whether the person thinks of him- or herself as a Republican or a Democrat or an Independent) would be a dependent variable if we were studying the effect of income on party identification, but it would be an independent variable if we were analyzing the effect of party identification on a person's vote.

Explanation is not just a concern for academic social scientists. Politicians hire pollsters to provide campaign advice by explaining people's voting. Marketing firms want explanations of people's buying behavior. Public policy analysts want explanations of people's responses to various welfare programs. These examples illustrate how explanation is always crucial to providing advice and evaluating solutions.

Necessary and Sufficient Conditions. In thinking about causation, many people find it useful to distinguish between necessary conditions and sufficient conditions. A **necessary condition** is required for an effect to occur, but by itself it does not guarantee that the effect will occur. For example, it is necessary in most American states to register in order to vote; one cannot vote in those states without first registering. Some people who are registered do not vote, however, so registration is not a complete cause of voting.

By contrast, a **sufficient condition** guarantees that the effect occurs, although the effect may also occur without it. Suppose we are studying the weather—in particular, we are examining precipitation. The occurrence of snow is a sufficient condition of precipitation because when it snows, there is precipitation. Precipitation can occur without snowing, however, as by raining, so it is not a necessary condition.

In some cases, a researcher will find a condition that is both necessary and sufficient. In that case, the effect occurs **if and only if** the condition occurs. If the presumed cause is always followed by the presumed effect, and if that effect occurs only when that presumed cause precedes it, then the researcher has identified a **necessary and sufficient condition.** Obviously, it would be ideal if researchers could always identify necessary and sufficient conditions for the dependent variables they are studying, but causation is not that simple. When causation is complicated, they may be able to identify necessary conditions or sufficient conditions, but not both.

Multiple and Indirect Causes. A single independent variable almost never accounts fully for a dependent variable. Any given attitude or behavior is likely to have many causes that work simultaneously. Because of the typically complex effects of social science variables on one another, researchers usually try to identify causal processes, rather than single causes.

Causal processes may work indirectly. For example, consider a social scientist studying cigarette smoking among adolescents. Most people believe that this behavior is caused by peer pressure. Put more formally, this hypothesis states that the smoking behavior of an adolescent's peers causes his or her smoking behavior. This causal influence may operate indirectly via the adolescent's beliefs about popularity; that is, an adolescent whose friends smoke may believe that he or she will be more popular if he or she smokes. In contrast, an adolescent whose friends do not smoke might believe that he or she will be more popular if he or she does not smoke. Therefore, it might be that peer smoking behavior causes an adolescent's beliefs about popularity, which cause his or her smoking behavior.

Arrow Diagrams. Causal processes can be represented by arrow diagrams (Figure 8.1). An arrow means that one variable is thought to affect the other; the direction of the arrow shows the presumed direction of influence. Such arrow diagrams are generally read from left to right and from top to bottom.

Figure 8.1 shows an example of a causal process by which some theories explain voting behavior. Evaluation of the candidates is portrayed as a cause of voting choice, and reactions to candidates are shown to have their own causes. Some causes are shown to have indirect effects, such as issues affecting the vote through their effect on the evaluation of candidates. Party identification is shown to affect the vote directly and also indirectly, through its effect on evaluations of the candidates.

This model posits **reciprocal causation,** whereby two variables cause each other. In this case, evaluations of the candidates affect party identification, and party identification affects evaluations of candidates. Another possible reciprocal causal relation would be the claim that vote choice may be affected by party identification and may affect party identification. This occurs when people who have always considered themselves to be Democrats happen to vote Republican in a series of elections and then begin to think of themselves as Republicans.

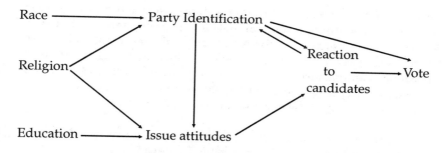

Figure 8.1. A Causal Model of Voting

When planning an analysis, it is often useful to draw such arrow diagrams. This exercise forces the planner to think in causal terms, to consider the full range of variables that should be included in an explanation, and to map out the presumed causal process.

Testing Causal Hypotheses

The relationship between two variables must pass four tests for causation to be possible. If any is not satisfied, then the variables do not have a causal relationship.

Association. First, a causal relationship between two variables is unlikely to exist unless there is some tendency for a change in one variable to be **associated** with a change in the other. Imagine, for example, that we were interested in the hypothesis that income causes educational attainment; that is, perhaps the amount of money a family earns determines whether children in that family go to college. For this hypothesis to be true, children in families with large incomes must go to college more often than children in families with smaller incomes. If this is the case, we cannot be certain that income causes educational attainment. But if this is not the case, we can be relatively certain that income does *not* cause educational attainment.

Two variables can be related in a simple linear fashion or in a more complex way. In the simplest form of association, a one-unit change in one variable would always be associated with a certain number of units of change in the other variable. For example, such an association would exist if 1 additional year of education is always associated with an average increase of $2,400 in a person's annual income. Such simplicity, however, is rare in human society. A more complex possibility is that an increase from 1 year to 2 years of education may produce an average increase of only $600 in annual income and that an increase from 12 to 13 years may produce an average increase of $4,200 in annual income. This is an example of a nonlinear association between two variables.

Temporal Order. Second, we can speak of causation only when the cause precedes the effect. Temporal succession of cause and effect is implicit in the notion of causation; that is, a change in the suspected cause must precede observed changes in the suspected effect. When surveys are used to test causal hypotheses, both variables are usually measured at essentially the same time—during the interview. Thus, it is impossible to assess whether changes in one variable occur before changes in another. Therefore, to test for temporal ordering in surveys, a researcher must interview a sample many times and observe when changes in variables occur.

In many cases, it is reasonable to assume that changes in one variable preceded changes in the other. A researcher can ask people how many years they went to school and what their annual income is today because it is probably safe to assume that their formal education preceded the attainment of their current income level. When it is difficult to justify assumptions about temporal ordering, however, it is essential to use repeated surveys.

A change in one variable may at some times precede a change in the other and at other times follow it. This occurrence may signify that these two variables are unrelated, but it may also indicate that each of the two variables affects the other. In such cases of reciprocal causation, the back-and-forth interplay is usually clear: A change in the first variable produces a change in the second, which in turn produces later change in the first, and so on.

Alternative Causes. Third, even if two variables are found to be associated and if change in one always precedes change in the other, it is possible that the one to change first does not cause the one that changes second. Instead, it could be that they are both caused by some third variable. For example, imagine that a researcher was interested in the relationship between the size of families' houses and how often they take vacations in Florida. The investigator finds that families who live in bigger houses tend to take vacations in Florida more frequently and that when families move from one house into a larger one, they tend to take a vacation in Florida soon thereafter. Would this finding prove that size of house causes vacation behavior? Of course not, because both house size and vacation behavior may be caused by family income; that is, every time a family experiences a large salary increase, they may move into a larger house and then take a vacation in Florida. If this were the case, the investigator would conclude that the relation between house size and vacation behavior is not causal, but **spurious.**

It is therefore important to test alternative explanations for an observed relation between two variables. This is done by positing reasonable alternative hypotheses and attempting to disprove them. Unfortunately, because it is practically impossible to test every possible third-variable cause, researchers can never completely rule out the possibility that an observed relationship between two variables is spurious. Thus, they can never be absolutely sure that a relationship is causal. Ruling out many other variables, however, allows them to become more confident about a causal hypothesis.

Causal Mechanism. Another way to acquire confidence in causal hypothesis is to develop an understanding of the **causal mechanism** involved. If A seems to cause B, how might that happen? Ideally, it should be possible to deduce the causal mechanism from a theory. If the investigator cannot think of a plausible causal mechanism relating the variables, then the apparent relationship might just be coincidence.

A classic example of a relation between two variables without an apparent causal mechanism is the fact that the Republican Party has usually won the presidential election in the years that the National League has won the baseball World Series. This finding satisfies the first three necessary conditions of causation: there is association, the National League victory precedes the Republican victory, and there are no plausible third-variable causes. Yet, it is difficult to believe that a National League victory causes the Republicans to win the presidency. Because there is no plausible causal mechanism connecting the outcomes of the World Series and the presidential election, any apparent relationship is probably just coincidence. In cases in which the investigator can posit a causal mechanism, it is easier to have confidence that a causal relation has been identified.

Summary. Testing of a causal explanation requires four steps: (a) checking to see whether the variables are associated with one another, (b) verifying that change in the presumed cause precedes change in the presumed effect, (c) eliminating alternative explanations, and (d) generating a plausible causal mechanism.

Operationalizing Concepts

In order to use survey data to test a causal hypothesis, the researcher must operationalize the concepts in the hypothesis. That requires choosing survey questions to measure each variable addressed by the hypothesis. When doing so, it is important that the questions accurately measure variables that correspond to the theoretical concepts of interest. Investigators who design their own surveys accomplish that when writing the questions.

Secondary Analysis

Operationalization is more difficult for the secondary analyst who analyzes a survey that was designed by someone else. Different researchers approach the same problem from different perspectives and with different philosophies and ideologies, so the secondary analyst may sometimes be dissatisfied with the original investigator's questions. Secondary analysts are often interested in hypotheses different from those of the original investigators. Consequently, some needed questions may be either missing or not asked in the most desirable way. Secondary analysis therefore often requires compromises, using the available questions that come as close as possible to those desired. In addition, the secondary analyst may sometimes have to use several surveys, testing with one study the hypotheses that cannot be adequately tested with another study.

The secondary analyst must be particularly concerned with the validity of the measures. He or she may be interested in one concept, whereas the questions in the survey actually measure a different concept. Too often, the secondary analyst employs the questions that come closest to his or her concepts without recognizing that the wrong concept is being measured. As a result, secondary analysis sometimes does not provide such sharp tests of hypotheses as does primary analysis, wherein the researcher devises survey questions to correspond identically to the concepts.

An important aspect of operationalizing concepts is ascertaining the level of measurement of the variables. Many different statistical tests can be computed, and which statistic to compute depends partly on the types of variables being examined. Statisticians distinguish among four basic levels of measurement of variables: (a) nominal, (b) ordinal, (c) interval, and (d) ratio. Each level requires a different type of statistical analysis.

Nominal Variables. **Nominal variables** are made up of distinct categories that are not related in any numerical or orderly fashion. One example of a nominal variable is religion. A person may be Catholic, Protestant, Jewish, a member of another religion, or a member of no organized religion. Nothing about these categories is numeric, although coders may number the categories to enter data into a computer. Region is another nominal variable. A person may live in the North, East, South, or West, but nothing about these categories is numeric. Even if such categories have been numbered, arithmetic operations such as averaging are not appropriate.

Ordinal Variables. The second type of measurement occurs when ordered categories do not have any intrinsic numeric qualities. People may be asked whether they "strongly agree, agree but not strongly, are neutral, disagree but not strongly, or strongly disagree" with a statement. These responses are intrinsically ordered from most favorable to least favorable.[1] The options in **ordinal variables** do not have numeric properties because it would be unreasonable to assume that the psychological differences between successive categories are the same. For example, the difference between strong and weak agreement to a statement may be more or less than the difference between weak agreement and neutrality. Ordinal measurement is sometimes used in surveys when categoric responses are thought to be easier to obtain than are numeric responses, such as when people are asked what range their income falls in, rather than their exact income.

Interval Variables. Variables that are intrinsically numeric but that lack a meaningful zero point are called **interval variables.** Interval measurement requires numeric responses with the distances between the successive numbers being equal. The standard example of an interval-level variable is temperature as measured by the usual Fahrenheit scale. A temperature of 64°F is 1° warmer than a temperature of 63°F. However, 0°F does not signify the absence of temperature, so 64° is not twice as hot as 32°. (The zero point is meaningful for the Kelvin scale of absolute temperatures, so that is, instead, a ratio scale.)

Ratio Variables. Variables that are intrinsically numeric with a meaningful zero point are known as **ratio variables.** Age and height are examples of ratio variables. Because they have meaningful zero points, it is possible to compare values through ratios, such as saying that one person is twice as old as another or twice as tall as someone else.

Interval-level and ratio-level variables are both "metric data" that can be manipulated arithmetically by addition and subtraction; averages can be calculated, and more complex statistical techniques can be used. Survey researchers who want to use these statistical techniques often try to measure attitudes numerically, such as by using numbered response scales as described in Chapter 4. The difference between interval and ratio data rarely matters in the choice of statistical techniques, so these two levels will not be distinguished throughout the rest of this book and are referred to as "interval data" or "interval/ratio data."

The distinctions among nominal, ordinal, and interval/ratio measurement reappear continually in statistics, so it is important to understand the differences. Consider some possible questions concerning religion:

1. What is your religion? Are you Protestant, Catholic, Jewish, a member of another religion, or a member of no religion?
2. How religious do you consider yourself to be? Do you consider yourself to be very religious, somewhat religious, or not at all religious?
3. How many times a month do you usually go to religious services?

The first question is aimed at classifying people in terms of nominal categories. The second seeks to determine religiosity on an ordinal continuum. The third measures attendance at religious services in ratio terms.

Choice of Measurement Level. These levels of measurement represent a hierarchical set. The highest levels—ratio and interval data—can be divided into ordered categories and treated as ordinal data, a lower level, although the usual rule is to keep the analysis level as high as possible. Similarly, ordinal data can be treated as nominal data, the lowest level. Shifts in the opposite direction are generally not possible without special justification,[2] however, although exceptions to this rule are discussed in Chapter 14.

Different types of statistics are appropriate for different levels of measurement. Throughout the remainder of this book, we refer to levels of measurement when we describe how to decide which statistical procedures are appropriate in particular research situations.

It is useful to note that level of measurement does not matter for dichotomous variables—those with only two categories. Gender, major party vote (Democratic or Republican), and whether or not a person voted are three examples of such variables. They can be treated as interval, ordinal, or nominal without any loss of meaning, although performing significance tests (as described in the next section) on them requires making assumptions about their distribution.

Testing Hypotheses

Once the variables for the analysis are selected, the analyst can test the hypothesis. When using a sample to test hypotheses about a population, the survey researcher must employ a special logic.

The Logic of Null Hypotheses

Hypotheses are propositions that are deduced logically from theory; in the social sciences, hypotheses are based on theories of human behavior. A hypothesis posits something about a variable, such as its mean value or its relationship to another variable. For example, theories of voting behavior suggest the hypothesis that political party identification causes voting behavior: Identifying with the Democratic Party leads people to vote for Democratic candidates, whereas identifying with the Republican Party leads people to vote for Republican candidates.

When testing hypotheses like this one, avoid committing what logicians term **the fallacy of affirming the consequent.** Consider the claim that Condition A causes Condition B. Observing that Condition B has occurred may seem to suggest that Condition A should also exist. This argument is fallacious, however, because it might be that Condition C also causes Condition B. Observing that Condition B has occurred does not indicate whether Condition A or C caused it. For example, consider the claim "cities with heavy rain have high annual precipitation counts."

Discovering that a city has a high precipitation count does not prove that it has heavy rain, because heavy snow also leads to high precipitation counts. Observing a high precipitation count does not indicate whether heavy rain or heavy snow is the cause.

Returning to the voting example, finding that Democrats voted for the Democratic candidate in a particular election more than did the Republicans does not prove the generalization that Democrats are more likely than Republicans to vote for Democratic candidates. It should be clear that verifying that Democrats did vote in a greater proportion for the Democratic candidates in a particular election than did Republicans does not prove that the research hypothesis (Democrats are *always* more likely than Republicans to vote for Democratic candidates) is correct. The research hypothesis states a generalization, and there are data on only one particular instance.

The rules of logic permit a different type of proof. **Denying the consequent** is a valid form of argument. Consider again the claim "Condition A causes Condition B." If this claim is true and if Condition B has not occurred, it is certain that Condition A has not occurred. If cities with heavy rain have high precipitation counts, then a low precipitation count for a city proves that it does not have heavy rain. Similarly, finding that Republicans voted in a greater proportion for the Democratic candidates in an election than did Democrats would show that the claim that Democrats are more likely than Republicans to vote for Democratic candidates is false. The rules of logic are different for proof and disproof, and as a result, science proceeds by a series of disproofs rather than by direct proofs.

Because a research hypothesis cannot be proved but only disproved, scientists have developed the notion of the **null hypothesis.** The null hypothesis is usually the opposite of the research hypothesis. In our example, the null hypothesis is "Republicans are as likely as Democrats to vote for Democratic candidates." Most often, the null hypothesis states that no relationship exists between two variables or that one variable does not affect another variable. After stating a null hypothesis, researchers try to disprove or **reject** it. Disproving a null hypothesis offers some support for the research hypothesis.

Remember, however, that disproving the null hypothesis does not prove the research hypothesis. At best, by offering evidence that the null hypothesis is not true, the researcher shows that the research hypothesis may be true. Despite this warning, many researchers speak of "accepting" the research hypothesis. We use this terminology as well, but readers

TABLE 8.1	Error Conditions When Accepting or Rejecting a Null Hypothesis, Depending on Whether the Null Hypothesis Is True or False	
	H_0 true	H_0 false
accept H_0	Correct	Type II Error
reject H_0	Type I Error	Correct

should bear in mind that accepting the research hypothesis does not mean that it has been proved to be true.

Types of Error

When a researcher decides whether to reject a null hypothesis, two types of errors can be made (Table 8.1). First, a true null hypothesis may be rejected by mistake. Falsely rejecting a true null hypothesis is known as a **Type I error.** Second, a null hypothesis may be accepted when it is false. Accepting a false null hypothesis is known as a **Type II error.** Social scientists strive to avoid both types of errors.

The two types of errors are related. The more stringent the criterion for rejection of the null hypothesis, the fewer true null hypotheses the researchers will mistakenly reject (fewer Type I errors), and the more false null hypotheses they will keep by accident (more Type II errors). The same criterion that protects researchers from wrongly rejecting a true null hypothesis (wrongly accepting a research hypothesis) also causes them to err more often by accepting a false null hypothesis. Thus, there is a trade-off between these two types of errors.

Scientists generally view Type I errors as the more serious. In medicine, for example, one would not want to change treatment if the new treatment were not a real improvement over a safe, widely used treatment. Therefore, one would not want to take a large chance of falsely rejecting a true null hypothesis of no difference between the treatments. If one has to make a mistake, continuing with the old treatment when the new one is better is preferable to switching from a widely used treatment to one that may prove worse. Therefore, a slight chance of a

Type I error together with a larger chance of a Type II error is preferred over the reverse.

In science, new studies sometimes contradict previous results, but researchers should not toss out the established wisdom in a field on the basis of weak evidence. The null hypothesis in this situation is that the previous results are correct. If the findings of the new research challenge those results, investigators have to decide whether the evidence is strong enough to publish the new findings. The new findings could be wrong, in which case publishing them would constitute rejecting a true null hypothesis (Type I error). Or the new conclusion might be right, in which case not reporting it would constitute accepting a false null hypothesis (Type II error). The usual conservative statistical procedure is to take only a small chance of making a Type I error even if doing so entails a large chance of a Type II error. Thus, researchers are stringent in publishing new results even if that occasionally means not publishing some correct findings. Presumably, if the null hypothesis is incorrect, some later study will reject the null hypothesis more conclusively, so there is no lasting harm in avoiding Type II errors.

Statistical Inference

When testing a null hypothesis, a researcher must decide how big a chance of making a Type I error he or she is willing to take. Usually, in the social sciences, investigators are willing to take a 5% chance; that is, tests are set up so that there is only a .05 probability of rejecting a true null hypothesis. The likelihood of a Type II error is usually ignored in this procedure. Sometimes, researchers employ more stringent levels, such as the .01 level or even the .001 level, but usually .05 is sufficient.

To illustrate this approach to testing a hypothesis, imagine that 54% of a survey sample favor a proposed government program. A researcher might want to test the hypothesis that this program has majority support—that is, to know whether the true proportion in favor is more than 50%. The null hypothesis corresponding to this hypothesis is that the true population proportion in favor is 50% or less. Thus, disproving the null hypothesis would mean that there is majority support for the program. A researcher computes a **test statistic** to determine whether the null hypothesis should be rejected. The test statistic can be used to determine the probability that the observed proportion would be 54%

if the true proportion in the population is 50% or smaller. If the probability is less than 5%, the researcher would reject the null hypothesis. Otherwise, he or she would accept it.

The test of a hypothesis described above is only one way to draw a statistical inference. Another is the **confidence interval.** When using this method, the researcher determines an interval in which the population value is likely to fall, given an observed proportion. For example, if an investigator obtained a sample proportion of 54% with a margin of error of 7%, there is a 95% chance that the true population value is between 54% − 7% and 54% + 7%. More precisely, in 95 out of 100 samples of the same size, the sample mean would be within 7% of true population mean. From this perspective, the researcher would decide that the sample result is not significantly different from 50% because the 95% confidence interval extends from 47% to 61%, which includes 50%.

Whichever method is used, the question usually being asked is whether a result is likely to hold for the population of interest. If a survey finds 54% of the sample favoring the proposed program, does that mean a majority of the population favors it? Phrased more technically, is 54% significantly greater than 50%? As you saw in Chapter 3, whether 54% is significantly greater than 50% largely depends on how large the sample is. A large sample is more likely to be representative of the population, so large samples have small sampling errors; this allows the researcher to detect small differences between observed proportions and hypothesized ones.

Even if a result is statistically significant, researchers often argue about whether it is substantively significant. Even if our sample is so large that 54% is statistically significantly greater than 50%, we still may believe that the 4% difference is not significant in a substantive sense. After all, 54% is so close to 50% that it would be more appropriate to describe the public as evenly split on the program than to say a majority favors it. Deciding what is important is not just a technical statistical issue; it depends on the researcher's substantive understanding of what is being studied. Statistical inference is useful for determining how to interpret a set of results, but the researcher must always assess substantive significance as well.

In designing an analysis, the researcher must decide whether to employ significance tests and what types to employ. When dealing with large samples, researchers often decide not to employ formal significance tests and instead simply describe the sample results.

SUMMARY

Analysis design consists of the three steps described in this chapter: (a) the specification of the hypotheses to be tested, (b) the operationalization of the specific concepts, and (c) the selection of appropriate statistical tests. These steps must be carefully meshed. Variables must properly operationalize the concepts in the hypotheses, and statistical techniques must be appropriate for the variables and their measurement level. These three steps for analysis design should be followed whether analyzing primary survey data or doing secondary analysis of surveys others have taken.

The chapters that follow explain common statistical analysis procedures. An analysis usually begins by counting and rendering into percentages the responses to single questions (Chapter 9) and then examines relationships between pairs of variables (Chapters 11, 12, and 14). Often, alternative hypotheses are tested by seeing whether two-variable relationships are different for people who differ on other variables (Chapters 13 and 14).

Further Reading

Measurement

Zeller, R. A., & Carmines, E. G. (1980). *Measurement in the social sciences: The link between theory and data.* Cambridge, UK: Cambridge University Press.

Notes

1. Assigning numbers to categories in a systematic way does not suffice to make the variable ordinal. A variable is still nominal if the categories are not ordered along some dimension. For example, ZIP codes were assigned to areas in the United States according to systematic rules, but ZIP codes are only a nominal measure because low-high ZIP codes do not measure any dimension. (What does it mean, saying that your ZIP code is higher than someone else's?)

2. Categorical variables can be treated as ordinal if a theory orders the categories along some dimension. For example, religion might be treated as ordinal if a theory orders the amount of ritual each religious denomination involves. Some analysts are willing to treat ordinal data as interval, especially if the underlying variable being measured is continuous.

☑ EXERCISES

1. Construct a model of the causal process that determines a person's income. Use age, education, and parent's social class as predictors. What other explanatory variables might be useful? (To avoid some definitional problems, assume a restriction to people over 25 years of age.)

2. Construct a model of the causal process that determines a person's political party preference. Use parent's social class, parent's party preference, and the person's social class as predictors. What other predictors might be included in the model?

3. Construct a model of the causal process that determines a person's attitude toward legalized abortion. Include as predictors the person's religion, age, and extent to which the person has traditional values. What additional predictors might be included?

4. What level of measurement is each of the following variables?

   a. The number of states the Republicans won in the last presidential election

   b. A person's marital status, coded as married, never married, separated, divorced, or widowed

   c. Whether a person reads the daily newspaper every day, frequently, occasionally, seldom, or never

5. A trial jury must decide whether the defendant is guilty or not guilty. What two types of errors can be made in this situation? Which type of error do liberals tend to view as more serious, and which do conservatives tend to view as more serious? Which type of error is minimized by requiring unanimity by juries for conviction?

9 ☑☐ Single-Variable
☐☑ Statistics

☑ The first step in analysis of survey data is to examine one variable at a time. This task can consist of tallying up the responses to a particular question on a survey or calculating the average age of respondents. In this chapter, we present the procedures for analyzing single-variable statistics, along with procedures for changing and combining variables.

Frequency Distributions

The simplest display of results for a single variable is a list showing the number of people giving each answer to the variable—the distribution of the frequency of each response. This information is sometimes called the **marginals** because the frequency distribution is often printed in the margin of the codebook. Table 9.1 displays some hypothetical data in the form of a frequency distribution.

Table 9.1 shows a majority of respondents supporting the idea of government health insurance. Of 1,303 people, 863 supported government health insurance; 863 is clearly bigger than 440, the number that opposed government health insurance. This approach summarizes the

190

TABLE 9.1 Attitudes on Government Health Insurance
"Would you support or oppose having the federal government take over health insurance in this country?"
Support   863
Oppose   440
1,303

results nicely, except that it does not indicate whether 863 is a very large majority of 1,303 or not.

Percentage Distributions

It is usually more effective to present the frequency distributions in percentage form. For example, the proportion supporting the program in Table 9.1 is $(863/1,303) \times 100 = 66.2\%$. The proportion opposing it is $(440/1,303) \times 100 = 33.8\%$. Table 9.2 reports exactly the same data as does Table 9.1; however, this time the display is in percentages. The percentage table shows at a glance that government health insurance commands support from approximately a two-thirds majority.

The number of cases (often called N) is listed under the percentages in Table 9.2 so that the reader knows how much confidence to place in the results. Two thirds is a large majority, but we have much greater confidence that the results reflect the nation's attitudes accurately when we know there were 1,303 respondents, rather than just 30 or 40. Listing the number of cases also allows the reader to compare the numbers of people who gave each response.

TABLE 9.2 Attitudes on Government Health Insurance
"Would you support or oppose having the federal government take over health insurance in this country?"
Support   66.2%
Oppose   33.8%
Total   100.0%
(Number   (1,303)
of cases)

TABLE 9.3 Attitudes on Government Health Insurance

"Would you support or oppose having the federal government take over health insurance in this country?"

Support	863
Depends	223
Oppose	440
No opinion	350
Not ascertained	18
Total	1,894

Missing Data

Unfortunately, survey results are never as cut-and-dried as those in Tables 9.1 and 9.2; extra categories may be needed. For example, some respondents may say they would support the program only as long as private insurance were still permitted; in other words, it **depends.** Many people have not thought about the problem, and many of them will admit they have **no opinion.** Sometimes, the interviewer forgets to read a question or the respondent terminates the interview before the interviewer has managed to ask this particular question. If so, the respondent's attitude on this issue is **not ascertained.**

If we included these categories in the frequency distribution, we might obtain the results shown in Table 9.3. How do we summarize opinion in this table? The largest problem is the lack of answers from the no-opinion and not-ascertained categories.

Not Ascertained. The phrase "not ascertained" shows that the question was not asked of everyone. Therefore, the people in that group could certainly be treated as having missing data and be dropped from the table. Replacing the remaining numbers with percentages would give us Table 9.4. Notice that the number of cases on which Table 9.4 is based is less than the number on which Table 9.3 is based because the not-ascertained category has been subtracted.

Incidentally, why do the percentages in Table 9.4 add to 100.1%, rather than to 100.0%? We have rounded each percentage to one digit after the decimal point, and the rounded percentages sum to 100.1. It is common in such tables for percentages to add to 99.9% or 100.1%

TABLE 9.4 Attitudes on Government Health Insurance

"Would you support or oppose having the federal government take over health insurance in this country?"

Support	46.0%
Depends	11.9%
Oppose	23.5%
No opinion	18.7%
Total	100.1%
(Number of cases)	(1,876)

instead of 100.0 because of the effects of rounding to the nearest ¹⁄₁₀th of a percent. Similarly, if the percentages are rounded to the nearest whole percent, the total might be 99% or 101%. This error because of rounding should not be of any concern.

Table 9.4 gives an honest rendition of the results. More people support government health insurance than oppose it. But many have intermediate views, and many have not made up their minds yet. Those supporting the program are not a majority, but they could form a majority by attracting some of those with no opinion or by accommodating those who say it depends.

No Opinion. The "no opinion" category shows to what extent opinion has crystallized on the question. A large number of people saying they don't know suggests that most of the people have not made up their minds on an issue. However, it is still interesting to know the distribution of opinion among those who have made up their minds. We might ask, Of those who had an opinion and answered the question, how many support government health insurance? This means treating the no-opinion category as a missing-data category and excluding it from the table. Thus, we get Table 9.5.

Of those with an opinion, a majority support the government health insurance plan and fewer than 30% oppose it. Table 9.5 does not indicate how many people are undecided on the issue, but it does show a summary of the views that were stated. A researcher should present a table without the no-opinion category when the assumption is that undecided respondents will eventually be distributed in about the same way as the opinion of those who now have opinions. In other words, a table like 9.5 is based

TABLE 9.5 Attitudes on Government Health Insurance

"Would you support or oppose having the federal government take over health insurance in this country?"

Support	56.6%
Depends	14.6%
Oppose	28.8%
Total	100.0%
(Number of cases)	(1,526)

on the assumption that about 56.6% of the people with no opinion will eventually support government health insurance. Although that is the most likely assumption, several other assumptions also prompt researchers not to report the no-opinion category. Imagine a policymaker who takes a survey to help with a decision that must be made soon so that it is safe to ignore respondents who have no opinion. Another example is provided by a survey taken the day before an election; it is doubtful that those who have no opinion about the candidates will take part in the election.

Under certain circumstances, the no-opinion category should not be omitted. Dropping the no-opinions would be misleading if there were reason to suspect that these respondents did or will have a particular opinion. For example, a researcher might not want to drop the no-opinions on a question concerning racial issues if he or she had reason to believe that it was a covert racist answer—the respondent claimed to have no opinion rather than give the interviewer a racist answer. This is rarely a serious problem, although it often makes sense to consider whether "no opinion" has a concealed meaning. Also, "don't know" may be a meaningful answer, as on questions of political information such as how many justices are on the United States Supreme Court. The don't-knows are not missing data, but rather an indication of the fact that the respondents did not know the correct answer. It would thus be a mistake to drop that category from a summary table. Another circumstance in which a researcher should not drop the missing-data category is when the proportion of respondents falling into the category is quite large in comparison with the proportion endorsing the substantive categories. That usually indicates some problem with the questions, and the reader should be made aware of it.

TABLE 9.6 Attitudes on Government Health Insurance

"Would you support or oppose having the federal government take over health insurance in this country?"

Support	56.6%
Depends	14.6%
Oppose	28.8%
Total	100.0%
(Number of cases)	(1,526)
(No opinion)	(18.7%)
(Total number of cases)	(1,876)

Notice that Tables 9.1 through 9.5 are all based on the same set of responses, those listed in full in Table 9.3. The tables differ in only two respects: (a) whether the results have been expressed as percentages or numbers of cases and (b) which categories have been omitted. Table 9.2, 9.4, or 9.5 could be published as "The Distribution of Public Opinion on Government Health Insurance," yet the three tables give somewhat different views. When you read a poll result, it is worth checking whether intermediate categories (e.g., *depends*) and the missing-data categories were included.

As another means of displaying the same data, Table 9.6 gives the distribution of opinions plus an indication of how many respondents offered no opinion. This may be the most helpful way to display the results.

Graphic Displays

A final way of presenting frequency distributions is graphically. Graphic presentations usually are the most effective mode of presentation. Readers who find frequency tables hard to understand usually can understand graphs easily. To paraphrase the old saying, A graph is worth a thousand numbers.

Several graphic forms have been developed for displaying frequency distributions. Figures 9.1 through 9.3 present three common forms. The pie chart in Figure 9.1 displays how many people gave an answer by the area in the circle for each category. Nearly twice as many people support government health insurance as oppose it, according to these hypotheti-

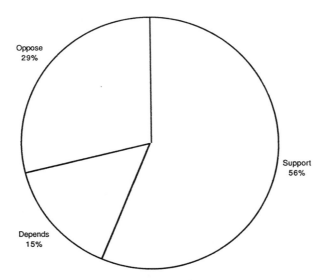

Figure 9.1. Pie Chart of Attitudes on Government Health Insurance

cal data, and that is represented by the relative areas for the supporting and opposing groups.

The bar chart in Figure 9.2 represents how many people gave an answer by the height of the bar for each category. The height bar for "support" is nearly twice as tall as that for "oppose" to show how many more people support government health insurance than oppose it.

The frequency polygon in Figure 9.3 also uses height to represent the frequency of responses. The response categories are ordered along the horizontal axis, and the height of the line above each category shows how popular it is. The frequency polygon is usually used for ratio, interval, and ordinal data, whereas the bar chart and pie chart are used for nominal data. Modern personal computer programs for statistics, spreadsheets, and presentations make drawing presentations like those of Figures 9.1 to 9.3 quick and easy.

Interpreting Frequency Distributions

Do not take the percentages in such tables and graphs to be perfect descriptions of opinions. They are affected by many factors other than the attitudes being measured. One factor discussed in Chapter 3 is

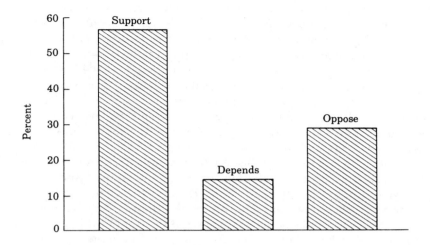

Figure 9.2. Bar Chart of Attitudes on Government Health Insurance

sampling error, the error that occurs when a sample of people is not perfectly representative of the population. It depends mainly on the sampling procedures and the sample size. With 1,526 interviews, the

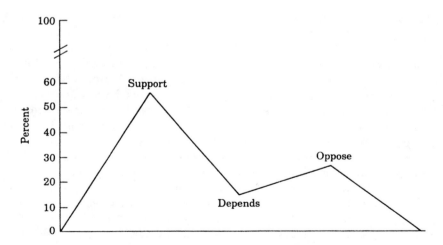

Figure 9.3. Frequency Polygon of Attitudes on Government Health Insurance

margin of error is approximately 3% or 4%, which means that the actual percentage in the population supporting government health insurance is probably between about 53% and 60%. Even with this potential error, it is clear that the program had majority support of those with opinions.

The second important factor (discussed in Chapter 4) is the **wording of the question.** Do not take the observed distribution of responses too literally, because they depend on the wording of the questions (or code categories). What if the question on health insurance had been, "Would you prefer government health insurance or private health insurance in this country?" It is not unreasonable to expect a 10% to 20% difference due solely to the question wording. Sometimes, there is no difference at all between the results of different wordings, but never assume that question wording does not matter. Thus, Table 9.6 should be interpreted as showing public support for government health insurance, but do not give too much emphasis to the 56.6% level of that support.

In general, when constructing frequency distributions, it is most important to include sufficient information to illustrate the important substantive point. Often, what you want to show with the data will determine how much detail (and, in fact, which details) should be included in a table. Readability is usually improved by showing percentages rather than raw frequencies, although the number of cases underlying the percentages should be given so that the reader can reconstruct the raw frequencies if necessary.

Measures of Central Tendency

It is easy to examine Table 9.6 (or any of the preceding tables in this chapter) to get a quick impression of the distribution of public attitudes. Consider, however, Table 9.7. This table has a rather large number of substantive categories. The reader can examine the full set of percentages, but it would be useful to summarize the results more compactly. When the responses are tallied and a frequency distribution produced, responses may be summarized statistically—for example, to report the average response or to give some idea of how unified the public is in its attitudes. This point gets us into the realm of statistics.

The simplest type of summary measure is the **central tendency,** which indicates how the typical person behaves or what the typical value of a variable is. Summary measures that are appropriate to the analysis of some variables, however, are inappropriate for analysis of others. For

TABLE 9.7 Ideal Family Size	
"How many children would you consider to be the right number for a family?"	
None	10.5%
One	22.1%
Two	35.2%
Three	21.6%
Four	5.8%
Five	3.1%
Six	1.6%
Eight	0.1%
Total	100.0%
(Number of cases)	(1,404)

example, we could calculate from Table 9.7 the average number of children mentioned as the ideal, but we could never calculate the "average religion" of respondents. Although the average may be a useful concept in analyzing some variables, it cannot and should not be calculated for others. What measures are appropriate depends mainly on the level of measurement of the variables as discussed in Chapter 8.

The Mean

The most familiar measure of central tendency is the arithmetic average, known technically as the **mean.** A mean can be calculated only for interval- and ratio-level variables. To compute it, add up the values of the variable for each case and divide that by the number of cases. Thus, if a survey found that 6 people attended religious services 0, 1, 3, 3, 5, and 8 times per month, respectively, add these numbers together to get a sum of 20 and divide by 6 (the number of people) to get a mean of 3.33. The average number of times these people went to church is 3.33. Table 9.8A illustrates the above calculation.

We need a more concise way of describing the information in Table 9.7. The mean should help. Although the mean for Table 9.7 takes longer to calculate than that for Table 9.8A, the process is the same. After adding up the number of children mentioned by each of the 1,404 respondents and dividing that number by 1,404, a mean of 2.06 results.

TABLE 9.8 Central Tendency Measures

(A) Interval Variable: Frequency of Attendance of Religious Services

	Times per Month	Frequency	(Times × Frequency)
x_1	0	1	$(0 \times 1) = 0$
x_2	1	1	$(1 \times 1) = 1$
x_3, x_4	3	2	$(3 \times 2) = 6$
x_5	5	1	$(5 \times 1) = 5$
x_6	8	1	$(8 \times 1) = 8$
		6	$\overline{20}$

$$\text{Mean} = \overline{X} = \frac{\sum\limits_{i=1}^{N} x_i}{N} = \frac{20}{6} = 3.33$$

(B) Ordinal Variable: Religiosity

	Proportion	Cumulative Proportion
Very religious	40%	40%
Somewhat religious	35%	75% (50% point)
Not at all religious	25%	100%

Median: Somewhat religious

(C) Nominal Variable: Religion

	Proportion
Protestant	45%
Catholic	30%
Jewish	5%
Other	10%
None	10%

Mode: Protestant

It is useful to understand some of the mathematical notation that is often used to describe the mean. Researchers often speak of the observations of the variable X as x_1 (the first person's value), x_2 (the second person's value), $x_3, \ldots, x_N$. We would say that there are N observations of x, where N is the number of people. The sum of those N observations of x can be written:

$$x_1 + x_2 + x_3 + \ldots + \sum_{i=1}^{N} x_i$$

This is read as follows: "The sum of the x-sub-i's, where i ranges from 1 to N." The mean of X, often written $\overline{X}$, can be expressed:

$$\overline{X} = \frac{\sum_{i=1}^{N} x_i}{N}$$

Alternative Measures

The average is only appropriately calculated for interval and ratio data; other measures are available for ordinal and nominal data. If a variable is ordinal, one can examine the **median**—the middle position. If 40% of the sample indicate they consider themselves to be very religious, 35% somewhat religious, and 25% not at all religious, then the middle person in the sample considers him- or herself to be somewhat religious. That is the median response (Table 9.8B). Technically, the median response should have half the responses below it and half above it. Frequently, though, the median falls in a large group of other responses, so the numbers of responses above and below are not exactly equal. In these instances, the median is the category that comes closest to being in the middle of the distribution.

If a variable is nominal, the **mode**—the category that occurs most frequently—can be located. If more people in the United States consider themselves to be Protestants than Catholics, Jews, members of other religions, or members of no religion, then the modal religion is Protestant (Table 9.8C).

Choice of Central Tendency Measure

Sometimes, the mode and the median are also used for numeric variables. For example, Table 9.7 on ideal family size might best be summarized by saying that both the modal number and the median number of children desired is 2. The mean number of children desired in this case is also quite close to 2; it is 2.06. In some instances, the mean can be distorted by a few extreme values of the variable that are outside the normal range of the values. Suppose, for example, a few people said that 20 children would be ideal; that response might raise the mean a great deal. In such a situation, the median or the mode would be a much more reasonable measure of the "average" person's preference.

Whereas the mode and the median can be used for nominal data, the mean should not be used for nonnumeric data, and the median should not be used for nominal data. Thus, for a nominal variable such as region, a researcher might find which region of the country most people live in (the mode), but it would not make sense to speak of the mean region or the median region even if numbers had been assigned to the regions in the coding process.

The mean can be used for dichotomous variables. Suppose, for example, that gender has been coded 0 for male and 1 for female, and suppose that 55% of the sample is female. Then, the mean of gender would be 0.55. Thus, calculating the mean on a dichotomous 0/1 variable correctly shows what proportion of people fall into the 1 category.

Incidentally, if you are using a computer for data analysis, do not automatically think you can use a statistic just because the computer printed it. People who write computer programs often have the computer automatically print a wide range of statistics and expect the researcher to decide which are appropriate. Thus, do not assume that you have a true interval- or ratio-level measurement on a variable just because the computer calculated a mean for it.

Finally, in computing any of these measures of central tendency, always be sure that the missing data have been excluded. For example, a set of data might have the symbol 99 coded for a person who was accidentally not asked a question (not ascertained). That 99 should not be allowed to affect the calculation of, say, the average number of children a person wants!

Measures of Dispersion

Social scientists often seek to account for differences among people. The **variance** is a measure of how different the scores are for interval and ratio variables. Not everyone has the same score, so there is variance. If everyone had the same score, it would be the mean and there would be no variation. **Variation** is a measure of how dispersed the cases are from

TABLE 9.9 Variance of Age			
Age	Frequency	(Age – Mean)	(Age – Mean)²
20	1	(20 – 24.33) = –4.33	$-4.33^2 = 18.75$
23	1	(23 – 24.33) = –1.33	$-1.33^2 = 1.77$
30	1	(30 – 24.33) = 5.67	$5.67^2 = 32.15$
Total	3	0.01	52.67

$$\overline{X} = 24.33 \qquad s^2 = \frac{\displaystyle\sum_{i=1}^{N} (x_i + \overline{X})}{N} = \frac{52.67}{3} = 17.56$$

the mean. The smaller the variance, the closer the cases are to the mean; the larger the variance, the more widely they are scattered.

You might imagine measuring the dispersion around the mean by subtracting it from each value and summing those differences. You would find, however, that the sum would always be zero (within rounding error) because the sum of the differences for the cases above the mean is the same as the sum of the differences for the cases below the mean (with the opposite sign). This can be seen in the third column of Table 9.9.

This problem can be handled in at least two ways. One is to take the absolute value of the differences; the other is to square them. Although it would make little difference for present purposes, statisticians prefer working with the squared values when they generalize the variance concept to more than one variable. Therefore, the variance is customarily defined as the average squared deviation from the mean:[1]

$$s^2 = \frac{(x_1 - \overline{X})^2 + (x_2 - \overline{X})^2 + \ldots + (x_N - \overline{X})^2}{N} = \frac{\displaystyle\sum_{i=1}^{N} (x_i - \overline{X})^2}{N}$$

Table 9.9 illustrates this calculation. The mean is subtracted from each person's score; the resulting differences are squared, summed, and then divided by the number of people. For the first person, the mean of 24.33 is subtracted from the score of 20. That yields a deviation of –4.33, which when squared, is 18.75. Similar calculations for the second and third

TABLE 9.10 Income of Two Groups	
Group A	*Group B*
$9,800	$5,000
$9,900	$7,500
$10,000	$10,000
$10,100	$12,500
$10,200	$15,000
$\overline{X}$ = $10,000	$\overline{X}$ = $10,000
x^2 = 20,000	x^2 = 12,500,000
s = 141	s = 3,535

persons give squared deviations of 1.77 and 32.15, respectively. These squared deviations sum to 52.67. The variance is 52.67 divided by 3 (the number of people), which is 17.56.

Because we squared the differences between each value and the mean before we added them, the measurement scale of the variance is the square of that of the original variable. It is hard to interpret a squared variance of 17.56^2 years in our example, so it makes more sense to move back to the original unit of measure. As a result, statisticians suggest that it is more meaningful to look at the square root of the variance. The resulting statistic is the **standard deviation.** In our example, the square root of 17.56 is 4.19. We would speak of these people as having a mean age of 24.33 with a standard deviation of 4.19 years.

It is useful to see how the variance and standard deviation contrast instances of small and large variation. The example in Table 9.10 illustrates two sets of data on income with the same number of people (5) in each set and the same mean income ($10,000) but with quite different dispersions. Group A has a variance of 20,000, whereas Group B has a variance of 12.5 million. The standard deviations for the two groups are 141 and 3,535, respectively. Both the variances and the standard deviations report that the incomes for Group A are substantially less dispersed than those for Group B.

At this stage, you might wonder how these dispersion measures are used and why they are important. It would be premature to explain at this point, but we repeatedly make use of them in dealing with statistical inference and correlation/regression (see Chapters 10 and 14, respectively).

Two final cautions. First, the variance and the standard deviation can be computed only for interval and ratio variables because the data must be actual numbers. For ordinal and nominal data, there are no common measures of dispersion, but you can still look at graphic displays of each variable to see how much dispersion exists. Second, you will occasionally encounter variables with little or no variance; that is, the responses are all nearly the same. These variables are not useful in data analysis. Because social scientists usually want to explain variation, there is little to explain in these instances. Also, variables with no variance have no explanatory potential. As an example, there is no reason to try to explain the vote for president of Republicans in 1984 because more than 95% of the Republicans voted for Ronald Reagan that year.

Computer Analysis

Social science data analysis is now routinely performed on computers. We give little attention to this aspect of data analysis in this book because of the tremendous variability in computer systems. It is useful to introduce the topic here, however, with some attention to single-variable statistics as an example of computer analysis.

Computers range from large mainframe computers with enormous capacity generally available only in large organizations such as corporations or university computer centers to small desktop personal computers. Social science data analysis was originally done exclusively on mainframe computers, but it is shifting increasingly to personal computers.

To analyze a set of survey data, it is necessary to obtain access to it. When the analysis is on a mainframe computer, this usually amounts to being told how to access the desired data. For example, it is common to store surveys on magnetic tape, which is similar to tapes used in tape recorders. If the data are on tape, the analyst must find out how to access the tape and how to locate the survey on the tape (because usually several different data files are on the same tape). When the analysis is on a personal computer, the data can generally be handed to the analyst as a file on a small diskette or a CD-ROM.

The analyst also must obtain the codebook for the study. The codebook will indicate what variables are in the data set and what each is called. For example, it might be necessary to refer to V5623 to access congressional vote, or the data might be set up so that one can simply refer to CONGVOTE or a similar shortened name. It is also important to inspect the codebook for relevant sampling information about the study. If the sampling procedure in the study is unusual, the analyst may have to take special steps. For example, some studies purposely oversample some groups, such as double-sampling blacks so that enough blacks are in the sample to provide valid estimates of their attitudes. Such studies include a special **weight** variable (which counteracts the oversampling) that has to be specified in the analysis when valid estimates are desired for the complete sample.[2]

The next step is to use a statistical analysis program. Most installations maintain several such programs on their mainframe computers. Common statistical analysis programs for mainframes are SPSS (Statistical Package for the Social Sciences), SAS (Statistical Analysis System), and BMD (Bio-Medical). Statistical analysis programs are also available for personal computers; three of the more common programs are MINITAB, SPSS, and SYSTAT. Using these programs requires instructions on how to operate the computer, how to access the program, how to read the data into the program, and how to use the specific analysis procedure.

As a brief example, consider the SPSS procedure for finding the frequency of people who have given each response for a question. The example shown below would produce the frequencies for congressional vote and race (V4202) using the previously saved file ELEC92.

```
TITLE VOTE AND OTHER FREQUENCIES
GET FILE=ELEC92
FREQUENCIES VARIABLES=V5623,V4202/
 BARCHART/
 STATISTICS=MEAN
FINISH
```

In the first line, TITLE is used to label the output of the program so that the analyst can tell different analyses apart. In the second line, GET FILE tells the program the name of the data file. In the third, FREQUENCIES indicates the type of analysis that is to be done *and* the variables to be analyzed. BARCHART asks for a graph of the distribution of each variable. STATISTICS requests that statistics (here, the mean) be calculated for each variable. FINISH completes the SPSS run.

The specific instructions for data analysis differ from computer to computer and from program to program, but this example shows several common aspects: labeling for program output, telling the program how to access the data file, indicating the type of analysis that is desired and what variables to analyze, choosing particular options to tailor the analysis to one's needs, and choosing which statistics to employ from long lists of available statistics.

Statistical programs on computers that use the Macintosh or Windows operating systems usually permit the analysis to be directed through use of pull-down menus instead of special syntax like that shown above. The user might pull down a Graph menu, select Barchart from that menu, and click on the name of the variable to be graphed.

The important thing to remember about computer analysis is that computers are only tools. They are useful tools because they can process huge amounts of data quickly and accurately. They cannot decide what analysis is appropriate for a set of data, however, nor can they interpret the results. The analyst must still decide which procedures to use; which statistical tests are appropriate, given the level of measurement of the data; and whether weighting is required by the sampling design. In some cases, the program may print out many different statistics (e.g., the mean, median, and mode), and the analyst has to decide which are really appropriate for the data. Computers are very useful, but the analyst must still make sure the analysis makes sense.

Modifying Variables

So far, we have assumed that the variables in the data can be used as is. However, it is frequently necessary to modify variables prior to analysis. The variables in the data file may not be identical to those the analyst wants to study. The concepts in the theory suggest certain types of operational indicators, which can be derived from (but are not identical to) the variables in the data file. In these cases, it is necessary to change the variables prior to generating the desired set of tables, correlations, or controls. In this section, we review procedures for changing variables through recoding, index construction, and scaling.

Recoding

Modifying a Variable. The first case of this type is when variable recoding is required. For example, the data may include a variable named party

identification that shows to which political party the respondent feels
closer. The variable may be coded as follows:

0. strong Democrat
1. weak Democrat
2. Independent, leaning to Democrats
3. Independent, leaning to neither
4. Independent, leaning to Republicans
5. weak Republican
6. strong Republican
7-9. missing data

But the theory being investigated may pertain to strength of partisanship, rather than to its direction. For example, the theory may be that
the longer a person has identified with a party, the stronger that identification. The dependent variable for that relationship is strength of
partisanship without a direction component. Ideally, strength of partisanship would be coded as follows:

0. strong identifier
1. weak identifier
2. independent leaner
3. pure independent
7-9. missing data

By a process of combining categories, a strength of partisanship
variable can be determined from the original party identification variable available in the data set:

new 0 = old 0 or old 6
new 1 = old 1 or old 5
new 2 = old 2 or old 4
new 3 = old 3
new 7 = old 7
new 8 = old 8
new 9 = old 9

The new category 0 (strong identifier) includes those coded 0 (strong
Democrat) or coded 6 (strong Republican) on the original list. Similarly,
the new category 1 (weak identifier) consists of those coded 1 (weak

Democrat) or 5 (weak Republican) on the party variable. The other categories have been transformed in the same way. Conceptually, nothing about this single-variable recoding is complicated, although it is important that the computer program used have an easy way of doing it.

Most statistical computer programs can transform variables in this manner, although they differ in the way they accomplish the recoding. Once a variable is recoded, the new variable may be used in any table or analysis (or other recoding) in which any of the original variables might have been used.

Combining Two Variables. A more difficult but nevertheless useful type of recoding is **bivariate recoding,** in which two variables are recoded together to yield the variable of interest. For example, you might have a theory that older citizens vote against their party less often than younger ones. The study would have a variable showing the party the person identifies with (coded as in the previous example) and a variable showing how the person voted, but no variable showing whether the person voted with his or her party. If this last variable is needed, you would have to construct it from party identification and vote.

To do so, list the desired categories for the new variable, being sure to include all necessary missing data codes:

1. vote with party
2. vote against party
9. no party, no vote, or missing data on either question

Suppose the vote is coded as follows:

1. Democrat
2. Republican
5. did not vote
8. don't know
9. missing data

The appropriate recoding would be as follows:

new 1 (vote with party) = party identification 0, 1, or 2
                          and vote 1 (Democrats voting Democratic) or
                        = party identification 6, 5, or 4
                          and vote 2 (Republicans voting Republican)

new 2 (vote against party)   = party identification 6, 5, or 4
                                         and vote 1 (Republicans voting Democratic) or
                                   = party identification 0, 1, or 2
                                         and vote 2 (Democrats voting Republican)
new 9 (missing data)   = party identification 4, 7, 8,
                                         or 9 (independent or missing data on party) or
                                   = vote 5, 8, or 9 (did not vote or missing data
                                             on vote)

The result of the recoding is a new variable we might call defection, showing whether the person defected from the party with which he or she identifies.

Index Construction

The recoding process can be built up beyond two variables. New variables can be some combination of several variables. This knowledge is especially useful when a survey includes a battery of questions measuring a complex concept. As Chapter 4 indicated, this strategy makes the results less dependent on the wording of particular questions than when only a single question is used. A special way of combining such questions is to build **additive indices.**

For example, our survey might ask people four questions concerning whether or not they obtained news about the election campaign from television, radio, newspapers, and magazines. For some purposes, we would want to keep the differentiation among the four media, for example, to see whether those who rely on television differ in their behavior from those who rely on newspapers. For other purposes, it would be useful to know from how many media the person obtains news. People who pay attention to several media could differ in their behavior from those who employ only a single news medium. Therefore, we would want a count of how many news media the person employs.

Suppose that each variable is coded as follows:

1. employs this medium
0. does not employ this medium
9. missing data

We might make an index from the four separate media variables by adding up each person's scores on the four separate variables. A person who employs all four media would get a score of 4, 3 would mean the person employs any three media, and so on.

Missing Data. Missing data can be handled in several ways. We might give a missing-data code to anyone with missing data on any one of the four questions. Or, more likely, we might decide not to count the 9s when adding the variables, but to give a respondent a score of 9 on the index if he or she has missing data on all four questions.

The final result if we used the second approach to handling the missing data would be a variable coded as follows:

4. employs four media
3. employs three media (possibly missing data on the fourth)
2. employs two media (possibly missing data on others)
1. employs one medium (possibly missing data on others)
0. employs no media (possibly missing data on some)
9. missing data on all four media

This would be an additive index of the four media questions, with a minimum assignment of cases to missing data. Remember that when analyzing this variable, the 9 signifies missing data, rather than 9 media used.

More Than One Dimension. One problem with additive indices is that different variables may be tapping wholly different concepts. Consider, for example, category 2 on our media index. Respondents who employ only the print media—newspapers and magazines—would receive a score of 2 on the index, as would respondents who employ only broadcast media—television and radio. These two types of people would have the same score for two very different forms of behavior. It is not difficult to imagine that different types of people employ only print media or only broadcast media. We would expect, for example, the broadcast media people to have received less total information about a political campaign than if they had read detailed articles in the print media. In other words, in this example, the index may be measuring two different underlying concepts or **dimensions**—a broadcast media dimension and a print media dimension. Because of the possibility of more than one dimension, we cannot expect all the respondents coded 2 on the index to be similar. A researcher must therefore be careful to create indices only using variables that all tap the same concept.

Guttman Scaling

Clearly, it is of value to know whether an index is **unidimensional** (composed of only one dimension). Guttman scaling was developed to determine whether a set of variables measures a single concept or dimension and thus whether they can be combined. It should be emphasized from the outset that Guttman scaling is only one way to assess the unidimensionality of a set of variables. Guttman scaling does not measure some other meanings of unidimensionality. Guttman scaling is still useful, however, in beginning to suggest what dimensionality is and why it is important to check the dimensionality of a set of variables.

Let's use our example above to illustrate scaling. Suppose television is the easiest medium to use, so most people use it first; radios are the next easiest; newspapers the next; and magazines the hardest. If media use were unidimensional, no one would employ a more difficult medium without also employing all of the easier ones. No one would use newspapers for campaign news unless he or she also used radio and television. People who used magazines would use all of the other media. Thus, if media use were perfectly unidimensional in the Guttman sense, these are the only patterns that would appear:

4. uses all media
3. uses television, radio, newspapers
2. uses television, radio
1. uses television
0. uses no media
9. missing data

Table 9.11 illustrates the same notion in a slightly different form. Each column gives data from a set of respondents. The columns headed by the letters A through E correspond to the perfectly cumulative categories. Below these columns are shown the ordinal scores (4, 3, 2, 1, 0) of the persons in each category on a Guttman scale. If only the cumulative patterns A through E appeared in the data, then a perfect Guttman scale would be formed. The appearance of the other possible response patterns (e.g., W through Z) is counted as an "error"—that is, as a divergence from the perfect Guttman scale.

TABLE 9.11 Media Use Scale

Medium Used	Valid Patterns					Error Patterns				Marginals	Largest Marginal	Total
	A	B	C	D	E	W	X	Y	Z			
Television	yes	yes	yes	yes	no	no	no	no	yes	78-22	78	100
Radio	yes	yes	yes	no	no	yes	no	yes	?	60-39	60	99
Newspapers	yes	yes	no	no	no	yes	yes	no	yes	42-58	58	100
Magazines	yes	no	no	no	no	yes	no	yes	yes	23-77	77	100
Frequency	20	19	19	19	19	1	1	1	1			100
Score	4	3	2	1	0	4	0	?	4			4
Number of errors	0	0	0	0	0	1	1	2	0			4
Number of yeses	4	3	2	1	0	3	1	2	?			
Second error count	0	0	0	0	0	2	2	2	?			6

Guttman's
method: Number of errors = 4

Number of responses = (Number of people)
$\times$ (Number of items) – Amount of missing data
$= (100) \times (4) - 1 = 399$

CR = Coefficient of reproducibility $= 1 - \dfrac{\text{(Number of errors)}}{\text{(Number of responses)}}$

$= 1 - \dfrac{4}{399} = .99$

MMR = Minimum marginal reproducibility =

$\dfrac{(78 + 60 + 58 + 77)}{399} = .68$

Coefficient of scalability $= \dfrac{\text{CR} - \text{MMR}}{1 - \text{MMR}} = \dfrac{.99 - .68}{1.00 - .68} = .97$

Alternative
method: 6 errors, 396 responses; Reproducibility = .98

NOTE: "?" is used to represent missing data.

Measuring the Extent of Cumulation. To determine the extent to which a set of questions forms a Guttman scale, it is necessary to count the number of errors that occur in the responses. The number of errors for a pattern is the least number of responses that must be changed to obtain a valid pattern. Consider, for example, pattern W. Because that pattern most closely matches valid pattern A (except that the person does not watch television), it scores 4 with one error. X most closely resembles valid pattern E, so it is scored 0 with one error. Sometimes, an error pattern is equally close to more than one valid pattern. Thus, pattern Y could be scored 4 with two errors, 2 with two errors, or 0 with two errors. Scoring where data are missing is often possible, as with pattern Z, which fits pattern A without errors. Altogether, four errors are present, given the frequencies of each response pattern in Table 9.11. The proportion of the total number of responses that fit the valid patterns is known as the **coefficient of reproducibility.** Its calculation is illustrated beneath Table 9.11. When the coefficient of reproducibility is 1.00, each person's responses are perfectly reproducible from the person's score on the scale.

Louis Guttman originally suggested that a reproducibility of at least .90 should be required for a good scale. Experience with that criterion, however, suggests that it is too low and that a .95 criterion might be more realistic. The coefficient of scalability shows how much better a scale's reproducibility is than the minimum reproducibility that would be expected given the marginal frequencies of the responses to each question in the scale. The point behind this measure is that if, say, 90% of respondents give the same answer on a question, then at most 10% of the responses on that question can produce scale errors (because there would be no error if all the responses were identical). Consequently, we can find the lower limit of the coefficient of reproducibility, given the numbers of respondents that answered the questions in each way. We could then compute the improvement of the actual reproducibility over that minimum value. The coefficient of scalability is the ratio of the actual improvement to the maximum potential improvement.

For example, although the coefficient of reproducibility for Table 9.11 is .99, it could not possibly be lower than .68, given the marginal distributions of the answers. The actual improvement in reproducibility is $.99 - .68 = .31$, whereas the maximum potential improvement is $1.00 - .68 = .32$. Thus, the actual improvement is 97% (.31/.32) of the potential improvement, and the coefficient of scalability has a value of .97. Generally, the coefficient of scalability should be at least .60 for a good scale.

Because the scoring and error-counting procedures outlined so far are difficult and time-consuming, a simpler and quicker procedure is often substituted. This second procedure is used in most computer programs for Guttman scaling. Although both procedures are usually referred to as Guttman scaling, they do give slightly different results. For example, with the fast procedure, pattern W would receive a score of 3 because the respondent uses three media. The fast procedure, however, would treat this as having two errors because pattern W differs from the valid pattern with three media used (pattern B) by using magazines (one error) but not television (a second error). Similarly, pattern X would be given a score of 1 (because one medium is used) but with two errors, and pattern Y would be given a score of 2 with two errors. Also, to speed calculation, patterns containing missing data are dropped from the analysis in the second procedure. This rapid Guttman scaling procedure does produce some scores that differ from those produced by classical Guttman scaling, but the two sets of scores would be highly correlated with each other. They also have similar correlations with other variables. The quick procedure yields an error count that is about twice as high as the classical Guttman count; this difference obviously lowers the reproducibility. Under this error-counting procedure, a .90 reproducibility is considered to be good.

Number of Dimensions. The essential difference between an index and a scale is that index construction simply adds together the scores on the individual questions, whereas scaling is concerned with the pattern of responses. According to the Guttman scaling logic, if the responses do not fit a cumulative pattern, then they do not measure the same underlying concept or dimension and should not be combined into a Guttman scale. Sometimes, it makes sense to drop a variable that is not cumulative with the remaining variables. At other times, it might be possible to construct two separate dimensions, such as one for print media and one for broadcast media.

Whether or not a set of questions can be formed into a Guttman scale is an empirical question. A scale with a sufficiently high coefficient of reproducibility may or may not be useful and valid. In fact, researchers are sometimes interested only in whether a set of questions constitutes a Guttman scale. In such a circumstance, the researcher might argue that the questions in a set on government policy all represent the same dimension. For example, a researcher might argue that attitudes toward a set of policies represent a liberal-conservative dimension because they form a Guttman scale. In other situations, however, the researcher forms the scale as the first step in a more complex scheme of analysis. For example, individuals could be scored on a liberal-to-conservative scale so that these scores can be related to income and education.

Often, it is impossible to account for a set of attitudes with a single Guttman scale. For example, if we had a set of questions on international and domestic policy, we might find that people who are liberal on domestic issues are not necessarily liberal on international issues. Separate Guttman scales would then be needed for domestic and international issues. We would say that two dimensions underlie the data. In other circumstances, more than two dimensions may be required.

Incidentally, there are several ways besides Guttman scaling to examine the dimensionality of data. These procedures can handle interval and ratio variables, as well as ordinal measures and dichotomous data. The other scaling procedures, however, are more complicated than we can consider in this book.

SUMMARY

Statistical analysis of a single variable begins with generating its frequency distribution and possibly displaying it graphically. The next step is computing an appropriate measure of central tendency, usually the mean for numeric variables, the median for ordinal variables, and the mode for nominal variables. The variance and standard deviation are measures of dispersion for numeric variables.

Researchers often require forms of variables different from those available in the data set. Simple recoding often suffices to construct the needed variables. Additive indices are also useful. When several variables are combined into an index, however, it makes sense to check first whether they all pertain to the same dimension. Guttman scaling is one test of such dimensionality.

Data analysis should involve more than single-variable statistics. However, inspection of these statistics for each variable should be a routine part of any data analysis. They give the researcher an extra chance to check for data errors that might escape detection in a multiple-variable analysis. Additionally, they help the researcher in understanding the variables to be used in further analysis.

Further Readings

Basic Statistics

Blalock, H., M., Jr. (1979). *Social statistics* (rev. 2nd ed.). New York: McGraw-Hill.

Hays, W. L. (1973). *Statistics for the social sciences* (2nd ed.). New York: Holt, Rinehart & Winston.

Lewis-Beck, M. S. (1995). *Data analysis: An introduction.* Thousand Oaks, CA: Sage.

Moore, D. S. (1991). *Statistics: Concepts and controversies* (3rd ed.). New York: Freeman.

Moore, D. S., & McCabe, G. P. (1989). *Introduction to the practice of statistics.* New York: Freeman.

Weisberg, H. F. (1992). *Central tendency and variation.* Newbury Park, CA: Sage.

Indices and Scales

Jacoby, W. G. (1991). *Data theory and dimensional analysis.* Newbury Park, CA: Sage.

McIver, J. P., & Carmines, E. G. (1981). *Unidimensional scaling.* Beverly Hills, CA: Sage.

Spector, P. E. (1992). *Summated rating scale construction.* Newbury Park, CA: Sage.

Secondary Analysis

Hyman, H. H. (1972). *Secondary analysis of sample surveys: Principles, procedures, and potentialities.* New York: John Wiley.

Kiecolt, K. J., & Nathan, L. E. (1985). *Secondary analysis of survey data.* Beverly Hills, CA: Sage.

Survey Analysis

Bourque, L. B., & Clark, V. A. (1992). *Processing data: The survey example.* Newbury Park, CA: Sage.

Lee, E-S., Forthofer, R. N., & Lorimer, R. J. (1989). *Analyzing complex survey data.* Newbury Park, CA: Sage.

Notes

1. Notice that the denominator of the variance in this equation is N because this is the variance for a population. Some versions of the formula have $N - 1$ in the denominator; technically, those refer to samples. Usually, the number of respondents in a survey is so large that the numerical difference between the two formulas can be ignored. When we are specifically discussing a sample, we use the $N-1$ version; otherwise, we use N.

2. The common statistical computer programs do not properly adjust statistical significance tests for weighted data.

☑ EXERCISES

Partisanship

Republican	250
Independent	350
Democrat	400

1. What is the total number of cases in this table?

2. What proportion of the people are Republicans?

3. What proportion are Democrats?

4. What proportion are Independents?

5. What categories have probably been omitted from this table?

6. What is the partisanship of the "average" American, according to these data?

7. Suppose five people gave the incumbent president the following thermometer ratings: 95, 85, 80, 75, and 65. Find the group's mean thermometer score, the variance, and the standard deviation.

8. Suppose you want to determine whether young people are more likely than older people to consider themselves to be political independents. However, the only available measure of partisan-

ship is coded (0) strong Democrat, (1) weak Democrat, (2) Independent leaning to Democrat, (3) pure Independent, (4) Independent leaning to Republican, (5) weak Republican, (6) strong Republican. Construct a new variable coded (1) Independent (including Independent leaners), (2) partisan.

9. Suppose you want to determine if strength of partisanship is related to whether a person votes a split ticket (votes Republican for some offices and Democratic for others). However, the only measures of voting are presidential vote, coded (1) Democrat, (2) Republican, (3) not vote; and congressional vote, coded (1) Democrat, (2) Republican, (3) not vote. Construct a new variable coded (1) straight ticket, (2) split ticket, (3) skipped voting for at least one race.

10. Suppose you hypothesize that a person's education affects his or her amount of campaign participation. However, the available participation questions are separate questions on attendance at political meetings, coded (1) yes, (0) no, (9) missing data; working for a party or candidate, coded (1) yes, (0) no, (9) missing data; and giving campaign contributions, coded (1) yes, (0) no, (9) missing data. How would you construct an additive index from these questions to yield an overall measure of campaign participation?

11. If the above questions about campaign participation formed a Guttman scale, with party meetings being the most frequent activity and campaign contributions being the least frequent activity, then what response patterns would fit the scale perfectly?

10 ☑☐ Statistical Inference
☑☐ for Means

☑ When studying a sample, it is important that the results observed are not due to chance. If the sample is small, the odds that it is atypical are great. Another sample of the same size might give different results. Consequently, a researcher does not want to overgeneralize on the basis of small samples. In this chapter, we describe procedures for statistical inference that are used for small, simple random samples to determine what inferences to the target population safely can be made.

Probability Theory

To understand statistical inference, it is necessary to be familiar with probability theory. Let's review it.

The Meaning of Probability

People often speak of the probability of an event, such as the probability of drawing a red card if one randomly selects a card from an ordinary deck of playing cards. What is a **probability?** It is a number between 0 and 1 that is associated with an event. These numbers are assigned so that they indicate how likely it is that the event will occur under certain conditions. A common interpretation of probabilities (though not the only interpretation) relates to the **relative frequency** of events. For example, the relative frequency of red cards in a deck is the ratio of the number of red cards (26) to the total number of cards in the deck (52): 26/52 = .50; the probability of drawing a red card from a full deck is .50. By similar logic, the probability of drawing a black card from the deck is also .50, the probability of drawing a heart is .25, the probability of drawing a diamond is .25, the probability of drawing an ace is 4/52 = .08, and so on.[1]

If you draw one card from the deck, replace it, shuffle, draw again, and keep doing this sampling with replacement many times, the proportion of times that you draw a red card will be very close to .50. Thus, probabilities can refer not only to the relative frequency of events but also to long-term rates of occurrence of events.

Events are considered to be the **complements** of each other if it is certain that one or the other occurs. For example, drawing a red card and drawing a black card are complements because the card drawn must be either red or black. Probabilities of events that are complements add up to 1.00, or certainty. That means the probability of the complement of an event is 1 minus the probability of that event. Thus, the probability of drawing a black card is 1 minus the probability of drawing a red card: 1.00 − .50 = .50.

Two events are described as **mutually exclusive** if both cannot occur at once. For example, drawing a heart and drawing a diamond are mutually exclusive because when one card is drawn, it cannot be both a heart and a diamond. Probabilities of mutually exclusive events can be added up, so the probability of drawing either a heart or a diamond is .25 + .25 = .50, the probability of drawing a red card.

Probabilities of events that are not mutually exclusive cannot be added together. For example, drawing a heart and drawing an ace are not mutually exclusive because drawing an ace of hearts would satisfy both events at once, so the probability of drawing either a heart or an ace (16/52) is the proportion of cards that are either hearts or aces or both. This does not equal the sum of their separate probabilities (13/52 + 4/52 = 17/52).

A set of events is called **exhaustive** if all possible outcomes are accounted for by the events. Drawing a red card and drawing a black card are exhaustive events because any card drawn from the deck satisfies one event or the other.

A **probability distribution** states the probabilities of a set of mutually exclusive and exhaustive events. For example, the probability distribution associated with the color of a card in an ordinary deck of playing

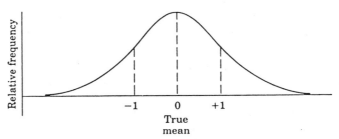

Figure 10.1. The Normal Distribution

cards is .50 for a red card and .50 for a black card. Similarly, the probability distribution for the suit of a card in an ordinary deck of playing cards is .25 for a heart, .25 for a diamond, .25 for a club, and .25 for a spade. Notice that the probabilities sum to 1.00 in each case because the events are mutually exclusive and exhaustive.

Normal Probability Distribution

Some theoretical probability distributions are particularly important in statistics. The most important one is the **normal distribution.** The shape of the distribution follows a precise mathematical equation that is graphed in Figure 10.1. The horizontal axis shows the value of the variable; the vertical axis is the relative frequency of each value.

The horizontal axis of Figure 10.1 is calibrated in standard deviation units from the mean, called z scores. Recall from Chapter 9 that the **standard deviation** is a measure of the dispersion of the values of the variable. A z score is computed according to the following formula:

$$z = \frac{(x - \overline{X})}{s}$$

where $\overline{X}$ is the mean value of the variable X and s is its standard deviation. For example, if the mean of a variable is 10 and its standard deviation is 5, then a score of 15 would be 1 standard deviation unit above the mean ($z = +1$), a score of 20 would be 2 standard deviation units above the mean ($z = +2$), a score of 5 would be 1 standard deviation unit below the mean ($z = -1$), and so on. A z score of 0 always represents the mean of the variable.

If a variable has a normal distribution, then its mean is at the center of the normal curve. Values of the variable closest to the mean occur most frequently; values farthest away occur least frequently. For example, if the variable is a set of test scores with a normal distribution, scores near the mean occur more frequently than scores far above or below the mean.

Areas Under the Normal Curve. The normal curve is constructed so that the area between it and the horizontal axis is one unit. The area under the curve is interpreted as a probability. For example, the probability of a value of a variable falling between the lowest possible value on the horizontal axis and the highest possible value on the horizontal axis is the area under the entire curve, or 1.0—certainty.

Because the mean is at the center of the distribution, the probability of a value being higher than the mean equals the area under the curve to the right of the mean, or half the total area under the curve—.50. The curve is symmetric, so the probability of a value being lower than the mean is exactly the same as the probability of its being above—.50.[2]

The probabilities of other values of the variable can also be obtained by examining the normal curve. For example, the probability of obtaining a value more than 1 standard deviation below the mean is .16; that is, the area under the curve to the left of 1 standard deviation unit is .16. Because the curve is symmetric, the probability of obtaining a value more than 1 standard deviation above the mean is also .16. Thus, the probability of obtaining a value no greater than 1 standard deviation unit on either side of the mean is (1.0 − .16) − .16 = .68.

Let's consider an example. Suppose that scores on the Graduate Record Examination (GRE) are normally distributed with a mean of 500 and a standard deviation of 100.[3] The probability of a score under 400 (the mean of 500 minus 1 standard deviation) would be .16, the probability of a score above 600 (500 + 100) would be .16, and the probability of a score between 400 and 600 (plus or minus 1 standard deviation unit around the mean) would be .68. These values are shown in Figure 10.2. This does not mean that a person has a .16 chance of scoring below 400 on the GRE. Instead, it means that 16% of the students taking the exam score below 400, so the probability that a randomly chosen individual has a score below 400 is .16.

Notice that the values in the tails of the distribution (the parts farthest from the center) are particularly unlikely. Extreme values are much less likely than moderate values. In fact, the probability of obtaining any range of values declines as the range moves away from the mean either below (to the left) or above (to the right). The probability of obtaining a value more than 1.96 standard deviation units below the mean is only .025, as is the probability of obtaining a value more than 1.96 standard deviations above the mean. Therefore, the probability of obtaining a value not more than 1.96 standard deviation units from the mean in either direction is $(1.0 - .025) - .025 = .95$ (see Figure 10.3). In the GRE example, this corresponds to a .95 probability of obtaining a score between 304 [which is $500 - (1.96 \times 100)$] and 696 [which is $500 + (1.96 \times 100)$]. The chance of obtaining extreme scores below 304 and above 696 is only .05.

Because it is difficult to read the area from a curve such as shown in Figure 10.1, statisticians have constructed tables from which the area can be read more easily. Table 10.1 gives the probabilities of particular ranges of values under the normal curve. To read the table, choose a number of standard deviation units (z) above the mean. The table shows what proportion of the area under the normal curve is above that z value. For example, to find the area above the mean, look under 0.00 standard deviations above the mean, and you will find in row 0.0 and column 0.00 the number .5000, indicating that half the area is above the mean. To find the area above 1 standard deviation unit, look under z of 1.00—row 1.0 and column 0.00—and you will find the number .1587, which we rounded to .16 for Figure 10.2 and in the above example. To find the area above .45 standard deviation units above the mean, use row 0.4 and column 0.05 to find the value .3264.

The normal-curve table can also be used to obtain the z values (number of standard deviation units above the mean) associated with certain areas. To find the z value for which there is only a .025 probability of higher values, find 0.025 in the body of the table; it is in row 1.9 and column 0.06, so the z value is 1.96. Similarly, to find the z value for which there is only a 0.005 probability of higher values, find 0.005 in the body of the table; it is in row 2.5 and between column 0.07 and 0.08, so the z value is about 2.575. (More precise tables indicate it is actually 2.576.)

The table gives probabilities only for positive z's. The symmetry of the normal curve, however, permits the same table to be used for negative z's. If you want to know the proportion of the area under the curve less than $z = -1.28$, you would look under row 1.2 and column 0.08 to get the value 0.1003.

Importance of the Normal Distribution. The normal curve is important for a number of reasons. First, some variables, such as standardized test scores, have normal distributions, although most social science variables

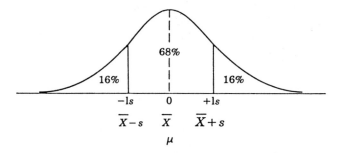

Figure 10.2. One Standard Deviation Range for the Normal Distribution

do not have normal distributions. Second, researchers often assume that the errors in measurements for a variable have a normal distribution. That assumption considerably simplifies the mathematics in some statistical proofs. Third, the normal distribution often serves as a good approximation to other distributions, such as the number of heads in 50 tosses of a coin. Finally, and most important, even when a variable does not have a normal distribution, the mean of that variable for a large sample can be regarded as having come from a normal distribution of sample means. This result is known as the **central limit theorem.**

Central Limit Theorem

Sampling Distribution. To explain the central limit theorem, we need some additional terminology. In a population, there is a distribution of cases on a variable, such as the one shown in Figure 10.4. In a random

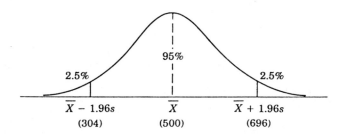

Figure 10.3. 95% Range for the Normal Distribution

TABLE 10.1 Areas Under the Normal Curve. (Entries show the probability of obtaining a z value above z^0. Areas for negative values of z^0 are found by symmetry.)

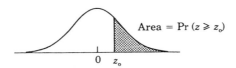

Area $= \Pr (z \geqslant z_o)$

					Second Decimal Place of z					
z	0.00	0.01	0.02	0.03	0.04	0.05	0.06	0.07	0.08	0.09
0.0	.5000	.4960	.4920	.4880	.4840	.4801	.4761	.4721	.4681	.4641
0.1	.4602	.4562	.4522	.4483	.4443	.4404	.4364	.4325	.4286	.4247
0.2	.4207	.4168	.4129	.4090	.4052	.4013	.3974	.3936	.3897	.3859
0.3	.3821	.3783	.3745	.3707	.3669	.3632	.3594	.3557	.3520	.3483
0.4	.3446	.3409	.3372	.3336	.3300	.3264	.3228	.3192	.3156	.3121
0.5	.3085	.3050	.3015	.2981	.2946	.2912	.2877	.2843	.2810	.2776
0.6	.2743	.2709	.2676	.2643	.2611	.2578	.2546	.2514	.2483	.2451
0.7	.2420	.2389	.2358	.2327	.2296	.2266	.2236	.2206	.2177	.2148
0.8	.2119	.2090	.2061	.2033	.2005	.1977	.1949	.1922	.1894	.1867
0.9	.1841	.1814	.1788	.1762	.1736	.1711	.1685	.1660	.1635	.1611
1.0	.1587	.1562	.1539	.1515	.1492	.1469	.1446	.1423	.1401	.1379
1.1	.1357	.1335	.1314	.1292	.1271	.1251	.1230	.1210	.1190	.1170
1.2	.1151	.1131	.1112	.1093	.1075	.1056	.1038	.1020	.1003	.0985
1.3	.0968	.0951	.0934	.0918	.0901	.0885	.0869	.0853	.0838	.0823
1.4	.0808	.0793	.0778	.0764	.0749	.0735	.0721	.0708	.0694	.0681
1.5	.0668	.0655	.0643	.0630	.0618	.0606	.0594	.0582	.0571	.0559
1.6	.0548	.0537	.0526	.0516	.0505	.0495	.0485	.0475	.0465	.0455
1.7	.0446	.0436	.0427	.0418	.0409	.0401	.0392	.0384	.0375	.0367
1.8	.0359	.0351	.0344	.0336	.0329	.0322	.0314	.0307	.0301	.0294
1.9	.0287	.0281	.0274	.0268	.0262	.0256	.0250	.0244	.0239	.0233
2.0	.0228	.0222	.0217	.0212	.0207	.0202	.0197	.0192	.0188	.0183
2.1	.0179	.0174	.0170	.0166	.0162	.0158	.0154	.0150	.0146	.0143
2.2	.0139	.0136	.0132	.0129	.0125	.0122	.0119	.0116	.0113	.0110
2.3	.0107	.0104	.0102	.0099	.0096	.0094	.0091	.0089	.0087	.0084
2.4	.0082	.0080	.0078	.0075	.0073	.0071	.0069	.0068	.0066	.0064
2.5	.0062	.0060	.0059	.0057	.0055	.0054	.0052	.0051	.0049	.0048
2.6	.0047	.0045	.0044	.0043	.0041	.0040	.0039	.0038	.0037	.0036
2.7	.0035	.0034	.0033	.0032	.0031	.0030	.0029	.0028	.0027	.0026
2.8	.0026	.0025	.0024	.0023	.0023	.0022	.0021	.0021	.0020	.0019
2.9	.0019	.0018	.0018	.0017	.0016	.0016	.0015	.0015	.0014	.0014

NOTE: Generated by the authors, using the normdist function in Microsoft Excel.

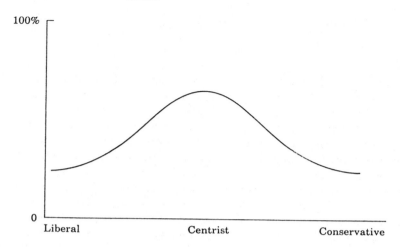

Figure 10.4. Population Distribution on a Variable

sample of cases from that population, there is a distribution of sample values on the variable—the sample distribution. That distribution can be graphed in a fashion similar to that used in Figure 10.4, and the mean for that sample can be calculated.

Suppose we calculate the mean for a second independent random sample, a third, and so on for a large number of samples. If we look at the means of all these samples together, we have a distribution of sample means, known as the **sampling distribution of means,** or often simply as the **sampling distribution.**

According to the central limit theorem, for very large numbers of large samples, the sampling distribution of means is approximately normal; that is, it is approximately the same shape as the normal distribution. As an example, assume GRE scores have a true mean of 500 and a standard deviation of 100 in the population. We give this test to one sample of people and get a mean of 510 for that sample. Another sample might have a mean of 485, and so on. If our samples are large and if we take a lot of them, these means would have a normal distribution. That distribution of sample means is what we call the sampling distribution.

Standard Error. The mean of the sampling distribution is the same as the population mean of the variable. The standard deviation of the sampling distribution is called the **standard error of the mean:**[4]

$$s_m = \sqrt{\frac{s^2}{(N-1)}} = \frac{s}{\sqrt{(N-1)}}$$

For a sample of 26 students for the GRE example above, the standard error would be 20 (the standard deviation of 100 divided by the square root of $26 - 1$).

We now know that GRE sample means have a normal distribution with a mean of 500 and a standard error of 20. Recall our earlier results on the probability of values with a normal distribution. The probability of a value being within 1 standard deviation of the mean is .68; hence, the probability of the sample mean being between 480 and 520 for samples of size 26 is .68. The probability of a value being farther than 1.96 standard deviations away from the mean is only .05, so the probability of the sample mean being below 460.8 [which is $500 - (1.96 \times 20)$] is .025 and the probability of it being above 539.2 [which is $500 + (1.96 \times 20)$] is .025.

You may be wondering why we are using 20 for our calculation of the range of sample values for the mean in this last example but used 100 in the earlier example. In the earlier example, we were examining the distribution of cases, so we used the standard deviation (100). When we examined the distribution of possible means in the more recent example, we used the standard error of the mean (20), an estimate of the standard deviation of the sampling distribution.

Notice that the larger the sample, the smaller the standard error. As a result, the bounds on the sample means will be narrower for larger samples. If the sample in the GRE example were 101 students, the standard error would be 10. The probability of the sample mean being between 490 and 510 would be only .68, and the probability of the sample mean being either below 480.4 or above 519.6 would be only .05. A sample has to be nearly four times as large to cut the standard error in half. This is what we should expect: There should be less chance of a large sample giving an atypical mean (a mean far away from the population mean) than of a small sample giving an atypical mean.

The **law of large numbers** makes this point more generally. For random samples, the larger the sample size, the more likely it is that the sample mean is very close to the population mean. A small sample can have an atypical mean, but it is less likely that a large sample will. Of course, if the sample is large enough to include the entire population, then there will be no difference between the sample mean and the population mean.

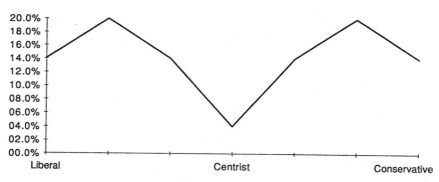

Figure 10.5. A Bimodal Distribution of Opinion

The law of large numbers states that when repeating a random experiment many times independently the mean observed value approaches the expected value. This law is not only of interest in theoretical statistics—it is the basis of gambling and insurance businesses. It allows casinos to compute the expected value of their games and insurance actuaries to compute the expected pay-out on their policies, so they can price them so as to be guaranteed a profit in the long run. Note that this law holds only in the long run, so that a casino or an insurance company can experience bad losses in a short time frame even though it has a guaranteed long-term profit.

We have noted the standard error's dependence on the sample size. The standard error of the mean also depends on the standard deviation of the variable. The more dispersed the observations, the less confidence one can have that the observed mean is the correct one. Conversely, if there is little dispersion in the observations, one can have more confidence in a sample of the same size.

Assumptions. The central limit theorem makes no assumptions about the shape of the variable's distribution. Even if a variable has a distribution that is very different from the normal curve shape (as in Figure 10.5, where the variable is bimodal so it takes on mainly very small or very large values but rarely moderate values), the means of large samples will be very close to the population mean, and the distribution of means of the samples will approximate a normal distribution. Thus, the central limit theorem makes the normal distribution important for data analysis even if the variables themselves do not have normal distributions.

The central limit theorem requires that the population variance of the variable be known. Rarely are researchers in a position to know the true population variance for a variable. For large samples, this is no problem; the normal distribution still holds even when the researcher must estimate the population variance with the sample variance. For small samples, the sampling distribution of means has a shape nearly that of the normal distribution but not exactly the same. The distribution of means for small samples has the shape of the t distribution. We present this distribution in greater detail later in this chapter. Statistical inference with the t distribution is very similar to statistical inference with the normal distribution, except that there is a slightly greater chance for extreme means.

So far, we have assumed that the population mean is known. We have looked for the probability of an atypical sample mean, given a known population mean. In practice, the population mean is not known, and it is too costly to take repeated samples to get a sampling distribution of means. Usually, researchers have only a single sample mean and its standard deviation. In statistical inference, analysts reverse the central limit theorem. They act as if their one sample mean is a sample from a normal distribution of means. The central limit theorem indicates that if the population mean were known, a sample mean far away from it would be unlikely. Even if the population mean were not known, it should be rare for the population mean to be far away from the sample mean. Therefore, analysts make inferences about the population mean on the basis of the sample mean.

Statistical Inference

There are actually several approaches to statistical inference. We begin by describing the most classical: hypothesis testing.

Hypothesis Testing

As an example of hypothesis testing, assume that we know that scores on the GRE have a normal distribution and a standard deviation of 100. We take a sample of size 26 from your university and obtain a sample mean of 541. We know that the national average on the test is 500. Does the sample show that your school differs from the national value?

   The null hypothesis is that the population mean for your school is 500. The hypothesis-testing procedure is therefore useful. As shown in the previous section, the standard error of the mean for this example is 20. Thus, our sample mean is more than 2 standard error units away from the null hypothesis mean. If the null hypothesis were correct, the probability of a sample mean more than 2 standard error units away would be less than .05, so we can reject the null hypothesis at the .05 level. Your school's mean is significantly different from the national mean of 500.

   Incidentally, the use of the .05 significance level here is arbitrary. With the .05 level, there is only a 5% chance of obtaining the observed results by chance, and this is usually considered to be decent betting odds in statistical inference. Such fields as medicine, however, often demand more stringent testing and therefore use the .01 level or even the .001 level. By contrast, some exploratory studies are less stringent, using the .1 level. The example here would not be found significant if the .01 or .001 levels were being used, but is significant at the .1 and .05 levels. If the analyst chose the significance level after conducting the test, it would be possible to manipulate which results are found significant, so it is important to choose the significance level before inspecting the results. The .05 level is the most conventional in surveys, so we use it throughout the remainder of the text.

Critical Ratio. To perform hypothesis testing more formally, the analyst would compute a **test statistic** known as the **critical ratio,** or **z.** The critical ratio is the difference between the sample mean ($\overline{X}$) and the null hypothesis mean (which we denote by the Greek letter mu, μ) divided by the standard error of the mean: $z = (\overline{X} - \mu) / s_m$. The normal-curve table gives the z values required for different levels of significance. **Statistical significance** at a particular level means that the probability of rejecting a true null hypothesis is less than or equal to that level. The z value required for significance at the .05 level is 1.96. In our example, the z value is $(541 - 500)/20 = 2.05$. Because it is greater than 1.96, we would reject the null hypothesis. If z were less than 1.96, we would not reject the null hypothesis.

Critical Region. An equivalent procedure for hypothesis testing involves setting up a **critical region** (or **rejection region**); a sample mean in this region would justify rejection of the null hypothesis. For a normal distribution, the chance of obtaining a value more than 1.96 standard

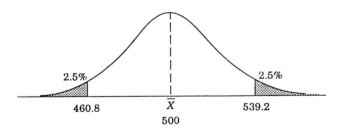

Figure 10.6. Critical Region at the .05 Level

errors from the population mean is 5% (or .05). When the population mean for the GRE is 500 (the null hypothesis) and the standard error is 20, the chance of obtaining a sample-mean GRE below 460.8 [which is $500 - (1.96 \times 20)$] or above 539.2 [which is $500 + (1.96 \times 20)$] is .05. Therefore, the critical region in which we would reject the null hypothesis is below 460.8 and above 539.2. The critical region corresponds to the darkened area in Figure 10.6. In our example above, the sample-mean GRE was 541; hence, we would reject the null hypothesis and again conclude that your school's mean is significantly different from the national mean of 500.

The critical region immediately indicates what action to take for any sample mean. For example, we would not reject the null hypothesis if the sample's mean GRE were 535; we would reject the null hypothesis if the sample's mean GRE were 455; and so on. Thus, the critical-region calculation provides all the information of the critical-ratio test and is simple to use.

Probability Value

The critical ratio and the critical region share a disadvantage: They are tied to a particular level of significance (the .05 level, in our example). A researcher who wants to use a different level of significance from one used in a published research report would be unable to quickly employ the new level. An alternative is to calculate the probability value for the sample mean.

The probability-value approach is an equivalent method of hypothesis testing. The normal-curve table shows the probability of different z values. In our example, we had a z value of 2.05. Table 10.1 indicates only a .02 chance of obtaining a z value above 2.05 by chance and only a .02 chance of obtaining a z value below -2.05 by chance. So, the overall probability of a sample mean at least 2.05 standard error units from the population mean is $.02 + .02 = .04$, the probability value or p **value**. The p value is the probability that the null hypothesis is true. If the p value is less than .05, we would say the result is significant at the .05 level.

If we decided to use the .05 significance level, we would reject the null hypothesis because the p value is less than .05. This is entirely consistent with the results of the critical-ratio and critical-region procedures. However, the p value permits other researchers who believe that the .01 level is more appropriate to decide not to reject the null hypothesis. The probability-value procedure relieves some of the arbitrary character of significance levels, so many researchers prefer to report probability values instead of hypothesis tests. Computer programs frequently report the p values for results, which makes this approach easy to apply.

Notice that if our data did not contradict the null hypothesis, we would accept the null hypothesis. We could never prove the null hypothesis because we can never prove the population's mean GRE is 500 (or any other value) on the basis of a sample. At most, we can say the sample is not inconsistent with such a possibility. As we argued in Chapter 8, science proceeds by a series of disproofs rather than proofs. This is part of the reason that Type II error is deemphasized. After all, if the null hypothesis is really wrong, a later study is likely to disprove it conclusively.

Many researchers are dissatisfied with the asymmetry between the two types of errors. Other researchers want more information about the population mean than just whether an arbitrary null hypothesis is rejected. As a result, hypothesis testing is not very popular in some social science fields. An alternative way of reporting statistical inferences is to establish confidence intervals for the unknown population mean. This approach is based on the same statistical theory as hypothesis testing but yields a range of possible values for the mean, rather than a test of whether the mean has a specific value.

Confidence Intervals

If we are willing to accept a 5% chance of making an error, we can construct a **95% confidence interval.** This is a range of values in which

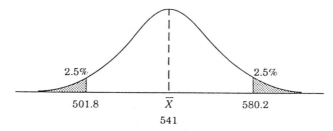

Figure 10.7. 95% Confidence Interval for the Mean

we can be 95% sure that the true population mean falls. If we took a large number of random samples and constructed confidence intervals for all of them, 95% of them would contain the population mean. The 95% confidence interval extends 1.96 standard error units on either side of the sample mean.

In our example, the sample mean for your university was 541 and the standard error was 20. Therefore, the confidence interval would range from 501.8 [which is $541 - (1.96 \times 20)$], to 580.2 [which is $541 + (1.96 \times 20)$]. On the basis of our sample of only 26 cases, we should be able to conclude at a high level of confidence (95%) that the population-mean GRE for your university is between 501.8 and 580.2 (see Figure 10.7).[5]

The calculation of the confidence interval is similar to the calculation of the critical region. Both involve a radius of 1.96 times the standard error. The critical region was centered around the null hypothesis value (500 in our example) and indicated which sample means would lead to rejection of the null hypothesis (those below 460.8 and those above 539.2). By contrast, we do not require a null hypothesis in order to compute a confidence interval. It is centered around the sample mean (541 in our example). It indicates the region (501.8 to 580.2) in which the population mean is 95% likely to fall. Notice that our earlier null hypothesis value of 500 does not fall within the confidence interval. The two procedures always lead to identical conclusions with the type of test described so far. That is not the case in making directional tests, as described in the next section.[6]

Directional Tests

In the hypothesis-testing procedure considered above, the sample mean could be either above or below the hypothesized mean. In some situations, however, the researcher is interested in only one of those possibilities. Suppose, for example, the GRE is known to have a mean of 500 for the population of college seniors. If we had a sample of students from elite universities, we might be interested only in whether their abilities are significantly greater than those of the population. We would strongly believe that the mean for the population of students from which our sample was selected could not be less than 500. We want to test the null hypothesis that the mean for the population of elite universities is 500 or less against the research hypothesis that the mean is greater than 500.

Our previous significance testing involved **nondirectional tests,** or **two-tailed tests,** in which we were interested in whether our sample deviated significantly in either direction from the population mean. We looked at the probability of a sample mean at least 1.96 standard error units less than the population mean, as well as the probability of a sample mean 1.96 or more standard error units above the population mean. The probability of these two extreme conditions together was .05. In **directional,** or **one-tailed,** tests, only one of these possibilities is of interest. The chance of obtaining a sample mean 1.96 standard error units above the population mean is .025. So, to operate at the .05 level of significance, we would have to modify the value 1.96. The normal-curve table indicates a .05 chance of obtaining a z value greater than 1.645. Therefore, for the same level of significance, in directional tests we substitute +1.645 for +1.96 and −1.96.

We can use any of our earlier hypothesis-testing procedures for a directional test. First, we can calculate a critical ratio and see whether it is greater than 1.645. Second, we can establish a critical region greater than 1.645 standard errors above the null hypothesis mean. Third, we can use the normal-curve table to find the probability of a z value more extreme than our obtained z value and then see whether it is less than .05. If we chose to construct a 95% confidence interval, however, we would still construct it 1.96 standard error units around the sample mean, so the confidence interval would not be identical to directional hypothesis testing.

Because the sample mean of 541 in our example was significant at the .05 level with a nondirectional test, it would also be significant with a directional test. After all, if the z value or critical ratio is greater than 1.96, then it certainly is greater than 1.645. Assume instead that the sample's mean GRE is 535. We would not reject the null hypothesis with a sample-mean GRE of 535 for a nondirectional test. What about a directional test? For 535, the z value would be 1.75. That is greater than 1.645; therefore, we would reject the null hypothesis that the population mean

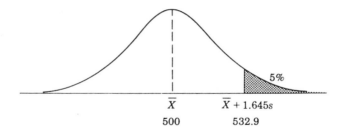

Figure 10.8. Critical Region for Nondirectional Test

is 500 or less. With a sample of 26, a sample-mean GRE of 535 would be enough to show a 95% chance that the population mean is greater than 500. The critical region (Figure 10.8) for this test would involve rejecting the null hypothesis for sample means above 532.9 [which is 500 + (1.645 × 20)]. If the null hypothesis were true, the probability of a sample-mean GRE of 535 would be .04 (the value in Table 10.1 for a z of 1.75); hence, we would reject the null hypothesis at the .05 level.

Thus, a mean that is not significant in a nondirectional test can be significant in a directional test. Because nondirectional tests are more conservative, it would be wrong to use directional tests if the researcher has no idea of which direction to test until after seeing whether the sample mean is above or below the hypothesized mean. In some substantive situations, however, one direction may make no sense or the researcher may be certain of the direction. In these cases, directional tests should be used.

The t Distribution

The above discussion has assumed that the population standard deviation is known. Researchers rarely know the population standard deviation; they can only estimate it on the basis of a sample. The sampling distribution of means is not exactly normal, however, when dealing with an estimated standard deviation. Instead, it has what is known as the t distribution. That distribution has a shape (see Figure 10.9) very much like the normal distribution, except that extreme values are slightly more likely. To complicate matters further, there is not one t distribution but several, depending on the sample size. We define the **degrees of freedom** for a t distribution as the sample size minus 1. In significance testing and for establishing confidence intervals, researchers use the t distribution

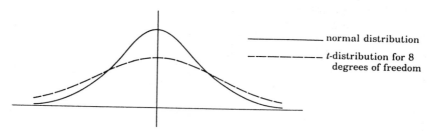

Figure 10.9. A Comparison of *t* Distribution and Normal Distribution

for the appropriate degrees of freedom instead of the normal distribution. It happens, though, that with a large number of cases, the *t* distribution is virtually identical to the normal distribution. Therefore, the normal distribution can still be used for large samples of size 120 or more. Researchers switch to the *t* distribution only for smaller samples.

We now return to the nondirectional null hypothesis of a mean GRE of 500. Suppose a sample of size 26 leads to a mean of 541 with an estimated standard error of 20. In that case, the appropriate test would involve the *t* distribution based on ($N-1$ =) 25 degrees of freedom. Table 10.2 shows that a value of 2.06 would be required for significance in this instance, rather than the 1.96 used for the normal distribution. Our *t* value would be 2.05 [which is $(541-500)/20$], less than the 2.06 required for significance at the .05 level. Therefore, we would not reject the possibility that the mean GRE is 500. Table 10.2 also shows that a value of 1.71 is required for a directional test for 25 degrees of freedom. Because our *t* value in this instance (2.05) is greater than the value required at the .05 level (1.71), we reject the null hypothesis for the directional test; hence, we conclude that the mean GRE is greater than 500.

Conclusions

If all this seems complicated, the procedure is actually fairly straightforward in practice. First, consider whether the sample size is large (120 or greater). If it is, use the normal distribution. If it is small and if the population standard deviation is known, use the normal distribution. If the sample size is small and the population standard deviation is not known, use the *t* distribution.

TABLE 10.2 Critical Ratios for the *t* Distribution. (Entries show the *t* ratio required for significance.)

d.f.	Pr	0.05 Directional	0.05 Nondirectional	0.01 Directional	0.01 Nondirectional
	1	6.314	12.706	31.821	63.656
	2	2.920	4.303	6.965	9.925
	3	2.353	3.182	4.541	5.841
	4	2.132	2.776	3.747	4.604
	5	2.015	2.571	3.365	4.032
	6	1.943	2.447	3.143	3.707
	7	1.895	2.365	2.998	3.499
	8	1.860	2.306	2.896	3.355
	9	1.833	2.262	2.821	3.250
	10	1.812	2.228	2.764	3.169
	11	1.796	2.201	2.718	3.106
	12	1.782	2.179	2.681	3.055
	13	1.771	2.160	2.650	3.012
	14	1.761	2.145	2.624	2.977
	15	1.753	2.131	2.602	2.947
	16	1.746	2.120	2.583	2.921
	17	1.740	2.110	2.567	2.898
	18	1.734	2.101	2.552	2.878
	19	1.729	2.093	2.539	2.861
	20	1.725	2.086	2.528	2.845
	21	1.721	2.080	2.518	2.831
	22	1.717	2.074	2.508	2.819
	23	1.714	2.069	2.500	2.807
	24	1.711	2.064	2.492	2.797
	25	1.708	2.060	2.485	2.787
	26	1.706	2.056	2.479	2.779
	27	1.703	2.052	2.473	2.771
	28	1.701	2.048	2.467	2.763
	29	1.699	2.045	2.462	2.756
	30	1.697	2.042	2.457	2.750
	40	1.684	2.021	2.423	2.704
	60	1.671	2.000	2.390	2.660
	80	1.664	1.990	2.374	2.639
	100	1.660	1.984	2.364	2.626
	120	1.658	1.980	2.358	2.617
	100000	1.645	1.960	2.326	2.576

SOURCE: Generated by the authors, using the tinv function in Microsoft Excel.

Next, decide whether to use a directional or nondirectional test. Nondirectional tests are preferred because they are more conservative. In situations in which one direction makes no sense, however, the test should be directional. Then, determine the value required for significance with the distribution that you have chosen.

A final caution is appropriate. If several significance tests are run, the probability is high that at least one will be significant by chance alone. The data analyst who runs 100 significance tests and reports the 5 that turn out to be statistically significant at the .05 level is forgetting that 5 out of 100 tests will be significant by chance. Looking at all the possible tests to see which are significant can thus lead to incorrect conclusions.

Comparing Two Means

So far, we have described how to test whether an observed sample mean is different from a specified value. In this section, we describe how to test whether two observed sample means are different.

To illustrate the problem, suppose a simple random sample of 18 colleges, divided into private and public colleges, have mean GREs as shown in Table 10.3. The average GRE score for the public colleges is 520, and that for the private colleges is 525, so the difference in the average GRE for the two types of colleges is 5. The important statistical question is whether that difference is real or whether it could be due to chance. Might the difference of 5 be due to the fact that we have examined only a sample of colleges, rather than have data for the entire population of colleges? Or is the difference of 5 statistically significant? A difference-of-means test is required to answer these questions.

Hypothesis Testing

To determine how to test the statistical significance of the difference between two means, recall how the significance of a single mean was tested above. A critical ratio was computed; the ratio was the difference between the observed and hypothesized means divided by the estimated standard error of the mean: $(\overline{X} - \mu) / est\ s_m$. The test for the significance of a difference of means is similar in form. A critical ratio is computed. The numerator is the observed difference of means instead of the difference between an observed mean and its hypothesized value. The denominator is an estimated standard error of the difference: $(est\ s_{\text{diff}})$. Thus, the critical ratio is $(\overline{X}_1 - \overline{X}_2) / (est\ s_{\text{diff}})$.

240

DATA ANALYSIS

TABLE 10.3 GRE Scores by Type of College	
Public	*Private*
510	515
509	514
511	516
520	525
519	524
521	526
530	535
529	534
531	536
$\overline{X}_1 = 520.00$	$\overline{X}_2 = 525.00$
$s_1^2 = 67.33$	$s_2^2 = 67.33$
$s_1 = 8.21$	$s_2 = 8.21$

$$\overline{X} = 522.50$$
$$s^2 = 73.58$$
$$s = 8.58$$

What is an **estimated standard error of the difference,** and how is it computed? The significance of the observed difference of means depends on the dependent variable's variance. In Table 10.3, the observed difference of means is 525 − 520 = 5. Whether a difference of 5 is large depends on how much variance is in the GRE scores. If the GREs have little variance, then 5 may be a large difference. If the GREs have great variance, then 5 may be a small difference. More precisely, the significance of the observed difference of means depends on the dependent variable's variance within each category. If there is little variance in mean GREs among private colleges and little variance in mean GREs among public colleges, then 5 may be a large difference. If the mean GREs in either (or both) type of college have great variance, then 5 may be a small difference. The difference between types of colleges is considered to be large only if it is large with respect to the differences within each type.

As was shown above, statistical testing requires knowing something about the sampling distribution of the statistic to be tested. In this case, we need to know about the sampling distribution of the difference between two means. The sample represented in Table 10.3 gives the difference of means for one possible sample. A different sample would probably yield a different difference of means. If we took a very large number of samples of the same size of the same population and examined the difference of means for each sample, we would have a sampling distribution for the difference between two means. If the sample size were large, the distribution would be normal. If not, it would be approximated by the t distribution. In any case, the standard deviation of that distribution is useful for inferential statistics, and it is called the **standard error of the difference of means.**

For separate independent samples from two groups whose populations variances are unknown, the standard error of the difference is as follows:

$$est\, s_{diff} = \sqrt{s_{m_1}^2 + s_{m_2}^2}$$

or, using the formula for the standard error of the mean:

$$est\, s_{diff} = \sqrt{\frac{s_1^2}{N_1 - 1} + \frac{s_2^2}{N_2 - 1}}$$

If we make the assumption that the variances of the two populations are equal but unknown, we can use both samples' standard deviations to estimate the one underlying population standard deviation:

$$est\, s_{diff} = \sqrt{\frac{N_1 s_1^2 + N_2 s_2^2}{N_1 + N_2 - 2}} \sqrt{\frac{1}{N_1} + \frac{1}{N_2}}$$

$$= \sqrt{\frac{\sum (X_{1i} - \overline{X}_1)^2 + \sum (X_{2i} - \overline{X}_2)^2}{N_1 + N_2 - 2}} \sqrt{\frac{1}{N_1} + \frac{1}{N_2}}$$

where X_{1i} is the GRE for the i-th private college, $\overline{X}_1$ is the private college mean, and X_{2i} and $\overline{X}_2$ are similarly defined for public colleges. The first term is the combined or "pooled" estimate of the standard deviation of the dependent variable.

Returning to the example, the pooled estimate of the standard deviation is as follows:

$$\sqrt{\frac{9\,(8.21)^2 + 9\,(8.21)^2}{(9 + 9 - 2)}} = \sqrt{\frac{606 + 606}{16}} = \sqrt{\frac{1212}{16}} = 8.70$$

Therefore, the estimated standard error of the difference is

$$est\ s_{diff} = 8.70\ \sqrt{\frac{1}{9} + \frac{1}{9}} = 8.70\ (.47) = 4.10$$

The critical ratio for a 5-unit difference is then $5/4.10 = 1.22$. To determine whether this is statistically significant, we employ a t test using 16 degrees of freedom $(N_1 + N_2 - 2)$. According to Table 10.2, a critical ratio of at least 2.12 would be required for statistical significance at the .05 level with 16 degrees of freedom, so the difference is not significant at the .05 level; that is, there is more than a 5% chance of obtaining the observed difference by chance in our sample if the two types of colleges had the same average GRE. Therefore, we conclude that the data do not demonstrate that public and private colleges have significantly different GREs.

Confidence Intervals

It is also possible to construct a confidence interval for the difference between two means. The confidence interval is the observed difference $\pm\ t(est\ s_{diff})$, where the estimated standard error of the difference is computed as above.

The example in Table 10.3 has 18 cases, so the number of degrees of freedom for the t value would be $18 - 2 = 16$. According to Table 10.2, a t value of 2.12 corresponds to a 95% confidence interval with 16 degrees of freedom. Because the estimated standard error of the difference was found to be 4.10, the confidence interval is the observed difference, $5 \pm 2.12\ (4.10)$, or 5 ± 8.69, or -3.69 to 13.69.

In other words, we would expect that, 95% of the time, the means for the two types of colleges would differ by as much as 8.69 because of random fluctuations in the sample. We conclude, therefore, that the means in Table 10.3 may differ by as much as they do by chance alone. Another way to say this is to note that the confidence interval includes zero, so we cannot be sure the two population means differ from one another.

The confidence interval indicates the maximum amount of difference that may be expected because of chance. Generally speaking, differences larger than that are statistically significant, and smaller ones are not. An observed difference less than t times $(est\ s_{diff})$ may represent no actual difference between the two population means. Thus, in the present example, the observed difference in means would have to be larger than 8.69 (or smaller than -8.69) to be statistically significant.

The t distribution has been used so far in this section because of the small sample sizes. For large samples, the normal distribution is used.

Also, if the population variance is known, then the population standard deviation is substituted for the pooled standard deviation in the formula for the standard error of the difference.[7] Where population variances are both known and different:

$$s_{diff} = \sqrt{\frac{s_1^2}{N_1} + \frac{s_2^2}{N_2}}$$

Where population variances are equal and known:

$$s_{diff} = s \sqrt{\frac{1}{N_1} + \frac{1}{N_2}}$$

Even using the t distribution, it is necessary that the populations be normally distributed and that the population variances be nearly equal. Fortunately, these assumptions can be violated without harm if the sample sizes are large (for the assumption of normality) and of equal size (for the assumption of equal variance).

Finally, it would be wrong to do a large number of t tests (or confidence intervals) at the .05 level and report only those that are statistically significant. After all, 5% of the tests will be significant by chance alone. Even more than 5% will be significant by chance if the tests are not independent of one another, as if we separately tested the significance of the difference in mean tax rates between religious and nonreligious private colleges, religious and public colleges, nonreligious and public colleges. When comparing several means, "analysis of variance" procedures (which are beyond the scope of this book) must be used.

SUMMARY

When dealing with samples, it is necessary to check whether results are statistically significant, particularly when the samples are small. According to the central limit theorem, the sampling distribution of means has a normal distribution regardless of the distribution of the variable, with a standard error that depends on the standard deviation of the original variable and the sample size. This result is used to test the significance of sample results.

In testing the null hypothesis, the deviation of the sample mean from the null hypothesis mean in standard deviation units is compared with the value required for statistical significance at the chosen significance level to decide whether to reject the null hypothesis. Alternatively, the probability value of a particular standardized deviation from the null hypothesis mean can be obtained from the normal-curve table. Confidence intervals can be used to find regions of values in which the population mean is likely to fall. In dealing with small samples with unknown variances, the t distribution is used, rather than the normal distribution. Finally, related tests can be used to test the significance of the difference between a pair of means.

Further Readings

Significance Testing

Mohr, L. B. (1990). *Understanding significance testing.* Newbury Park, CA: Sage.
Morrison, D. E., & Henkel, R. E. (Eds.). (1970). *The significance test controversy.* Chicago: Aldine-Atherton.

Notes

1. There are two common interpretations of probability in addition to the relative frequency interpretation in the text. One is **long-term frequency,** such as deciding that a coin is biased when it lands heads up 75% of the time in a series of 1,000 coin flips. The other is a **subjective interpretation,** as when people guess the likelihood that the vice-president will succeed the president.

2. What about the probability of obtaining *exactly* the mean value? The normal curve is used with continuous numerical variables, such as length. The probability of a pencil being exactly 3 inches long is exactly zero. It might be 3.00012358 inches, but the chances of it being any particular value is infinitesimal. Therefore, an analyst can disregard the possibility of the variable having a value exactly equal to the mean. More generally, the normal curve shows the probability of values falling into particular ranges, not the probability of specific values.

3. We use this example because several common standardized tests, including the Scholastic Aptitude Test (SAT), as well as the GRE, are normed to have means of 500 and standard deviations of 100.

4. The s in this formula is the popular standard deviation from Chapter 9 that had N in its denominator. More generally,

$$Sm = \sqrt{\frac{\sum(x_1 - \overline{X})^2}{N(N-1)}}$$

5. Because the national mean of 500 does not fall into this 95% confidence interval, you can see once again that the mean for your school is significantly different from the national mean.

6. The margin of error explained in Chapter 3 is a special case of this procedure. The margin of error given there was actually 1.96 times the standard deviation of a proportion, so the confidence interval could be obtained by just subtracting and adding the margin of error from the observed proportion.

7. Actually, it is not quite that simple; the $N-1$ in the denominator should be replaced by N.

☑ EXERCISES

1. According to the normal-curve table, what proportion of the area under the normal curve is above $z = .50$?

2. Suppose a variable has a normal distribution with a mean of 75 and a standard deviation of 10.

   a. What is the probability of a value being above 95?

   b. What is the range within which 95% of the cases will fall?

3. Suppose a variable has a normal distribution with a mean of 75 and a standard deviation of 10, and also suppose a sample of size 101 is taken.

   a. What is the standard error of the mean?

   b. Would a sample mean of 78.5 be significantly different from a hypothesized mean of 75 at the .01 level?

   c. What is the 99% confidence interval for a sample mean of 78.5?

4. Suppose a variable has a normal distribution with a mean of 75 and a standard deviation of 10, and also suppose a sample of size 26 is taken.

   a. What is the standard error of the mean?

   b. Would a sample mean of 78.5 be significantly different from a hypothesized mean of 75 at the .05 level?

    c. What is the 95% confidence interval for a sample mean of
       78.5?

5. Suppose a variable has a t distribution with a mean of 75 and a
  standard deviation of 10, and also suppose a sample of size 26 is
  taken.

    a. What is the standard error of the mean?

    b. Would a sample mean of 78.5 be significantly different from
       a hypothesized mean of 75 at the .05 level?

    c. What is the 95% confidence interval for a sample mean of
       78.5?

11 ☐☑ Two-Variable
☐☑ Tables

☑ Researchers are interested in more than describing popular attitudes and behavior for the full sample. They are also interested in understanding what causes attitudes and behavior. As we have said, one studies the causes of an attitude or a behavior by examining what other variables are associated with it. Researchers are also interested in comparing attitudes, beliefs, and behavior for different groups, and this too requires examining the pairs of variables together. In this chapter, we begin our description of how to study relations among variables by discussing how to study a pair of nominal or ordinal variables.

Contingency Tables

A common way of studying the relation between two nominal or ordinal variables is to construct a **bivariate frequency distribution,** which is also called a **cross-tabulation, cross-tab,** or **contingency table.** Table 11.1 is an example of a cross-tab constructed from hypothetical data.

Cross-tabs are very informative if read correctly, but they are often misread. The table shows that more people were hurt crossing the street at the corner than were hurt jaywalking. In fact, 60% of those hurt crossing the street crossed at the corner. Is it more dangerous to cross at the corner? A quick glance at the data would seem to suggest that it is.

TABLE 11.1 Pedestrian Accidents by Location of Pedestrian			
	Crossing at Corner	*Jaywalking*	*Total*
Safe	1,997,000	198,000	2,195,000
Hurt	3,000	2,000	5,000
Total	2,000,000	200,000	2,200,000

Intuition tells us, however, that it is more dangerous to jaywalk—and so does the table, if we read it correctly. Notice that 10 times as many people crossed at the corner as jaywalked and that only 1.5 times as many people were hurt at the corner. Clearly, your chances of being hurt are greater if you jaywalk.

This example illustrates how survey data can be used to mislead people. Imagine that a group of people wanted to eliminate all cross-walks. They could argue that people should not cross the street at the corner because 60% of accidents occur there. Without seeing the entire table, it is easy to accept such a false conclusion. A real-life example of this pertains to speed limits. Many people argue that when the speed limit on U.S. highways was lowered to 55 in the 1970s, the number of deaths per year caused by traffic accidents dropped dramatically. These advocates claimed this finding showed that a lower speed limit saves lives. Some critics argued, however, that when the speed limit was lowered, people drove less frequently on highways. In fact, they said the number of traffic deaths per highway mile driven did not change when the speed limit was lowered. This example shows why it is important to look at the entire contingency table and read it carefully.

Percentage Tables

It is generally easier to interpret a table if the data are expressed in percentages, rather than in raw frequencies, like those in Table 11.1. Because we are interested in the danger of crossing the street at the corner relative to that of jaywalking, we compare the proportion of jaywalkers hurt with the proportion of people who crossed at the crosswalk who were hurt. We can begin to do so by calculating the percentage of people who crossed at the corner who were hurt and the percentage who were

TABLE 11.2 Pedestrian Accidents by Location of Pedestrian

	Crossing at Corner	Jaywalking
Safe	99.85%	99.00%
Hurt	0.15	1.00
Total	100.00%	100.00%
(N)	(2,000,000)	(200,000)

safe. Next, we calculate the percentage of people who jaywalked who were hurt and the percentage who were safe. Then, we can compare the jaywalkers' percentages with those for crosswalk users. In this way, we can assess the relation between the location at which one crosses the street and the likelihood of being hurt. As Table 11.2 illustrates, 1% of those who jaywalked were hurt, and only 0.15% of those who crossed at the corner were hurt. Crossing at the corner is almost seven times safer than jaywalking.

This hypothetical example illustrates some of the comparisons that can be made with data in table form. It is usually better to compare percentages than raw numbers as long as the percentages are calculated correctly. For example, the statement that 60% of those hurt were crossing at the corner was correct but misleading. The percentages should be calculated so that they add up to 100% for each category of the independent variable. Recall that independent variables are used to explain the dependent variable. In this example, the dependent variable being explained is whether a person is hurt crossing the street, and the independent variable is where the person crossed the street. In Table 11.2, percentages were calculated within categories of the independent variable. Calculating percentages in this way allows a researcher to assess how much effect the independent variable might have on the dependent variable.

Comparing Percentages

Researchers examine tables to determine how much effect one variable has on another. This determination requires calculating the percentages in the right direction and comparing those percentages. In this

TABLE 11.3 Turnout by Race, 1992

(A) Column Percentages

	Whites	Blacks
Voted	78%	70%
Did Not Vote	22	30
Total	100%	100%
(Number of Cases)	(1,879)	(286)

(B) Row Percentages

	Voted	Did Not Vote	Total	Number of Cases
Whites	78%	22	100%	(1,879)
Blacks	70%	30	100%	(286)

SOURCE: 1992 American National Election Study.

section, we explain how the size of a relation between two variables is gauged from a table. Our examples are based on data from the 1992 American National Election Study.

Percentage Differences

Table 11.3 reports 1992 data on voter turnout separately by race. A researcher would construct such a table to study the causes of turnout rates—the proportion of people who go to the polls and cast a vote. That is the dependent variable. Our independent variable in this instance is race because we suspect that racial differences may cause turnout differences. (It is difficult to imagine turnout causing racial differences.) The table shows that 78% of whites reported voting in the 1992 presidential election, as compared with 70% of blacks.

Percentage Direction. Notice how Table 11.3 percentages were figured according to the rule described above. We could have calculated the proportion of voters who were white and the proportion who were black. Instead, we figured the percentages within the categories of the independent variable. Race is the independent variable, one category of which is whites. We calculated the percentages of whites who voted and who did not. Then, similar calculations were done for blacks.

Two forms of the cross-tabulation are shown in Table 11.3. Notice that Table 11.3A has the independent variable as the column variable and that Table 11.3B has the independent variable as the row variable. Either way, the interpretation of the table is the same. Generally, tables with the independent variable as the column variable are easier to read. An exception to this rule is made when one of the independent variables has many categories; then, it is put on the rows because it is easier to fit the table onto a sheet of paper. Regardless of the choice, adopting a consistent table format within a paper or article is recommended. And always be sure to figure percentages within categories of the independent variable.

Comparison Direction. Because we calculated percentages within the categories of the independent variable, we can compare the percentages across categories to assess the effect of the independent variable (race) on the dependent variable (turnout). In the present example, 78% of whites voted and 70% of blacks voted. Subtracting the second percentage from the first, we find an 8% difference. This is sometimes summarized by saying that the turnout rate for whites is 8 points higher than that for blacks. The 8% difference is presumed to be the effect of race on turnout.[1] The percentages must be calculated in the correct direction for the percentage difference to show the effect of the independent variable on the dependent variable.

Size of the Percentage Difference. Table 11.3 also reports the number of cases in each category of the independent variable. The sample contains 1,879 whites and 286 blacks. These values are large enough to permit a great deal of confidence that there was a difference in the actual percentages of whites and blacks who would claim to have voted in the 1992 election. This is so because the margin of error with 1,879 whites and 286 blacks is smaller than the 8% difference in the turnout rates. Given the large sample size in this table, it is unlikely to obtain an 8% difference by chance. If only 40 people were in each category, we would place little trust in the percentage difference.

How strong is the relationship between race and turnout? The difference could have been 100% if all whites had voted and no blacks had voted; similarly, the difference could have been 0% if whites and blacks had voted in equal proportions. The 8% difference found in the table falls near the low end of this 0-to-100 continuum. It obviously shows a relatively weak relation.

TABLE 11.4 Maximal Sampling Errors for Differences in Proportions

Size of Other Sample or Group	Size of One Sample or Group									
	3,000	2,500	2,000	1,500	1,000	750	500	300	200	100
3,000	2.53	2.65	2.83	3.10	3.58	4.00	4.74	5.94	7.16	9.97
2,500		2.77	2.94	3.20	3.67	4.08	4.80	5.99	7.20	10.00
2,000			3.10	3.35	3.80	4.20	4.90	6.07	7.27	10.05
1,500				3.58	4.00	4.38	5.06	6.20	7.38	10.13
1,000					4.39	4.74	5.37	6.46	7.60	10.29
750						5.06	5.66	6.70	7.81	10.45
500							6.21	7.17	8.21	10.76
300								8.02	8.97	11.35
200									9.83	12.05
100										13.94

SOURCE: Generated by the authors, using a *t* test for independent proportion in Microsoft Excel.
NOTE: The figures in the table are maximal because they represent the sampling errors for proportions in the range of 35% to 65%. The sampling errors decline when the proportions are more extreme, especially when the proportions are below 10% or above 90%. The values in the table are for simple random samples; the sampling errors for complex probability samples are higher than shown here.
  The obtained difference in proportions must be larger than that shown for the numbers of cases for a two-tailed 95% confidence range. For example, with 750 cases in both groups, a difference must be more than 5% for significance.

Survey data on attitudes rarely reveal large percentage differences. A 60% difference would be relatively enormous, and most researchers would consider a 30% difference to be large. A 5% to 10% difference is relatively small; it may even be the result of sampling error if the sample size is around 1,500. A quick way to determine whether a percentage difference is greater than sampling error is to consult a table like Table 11.4. It shows the maximal sampling errors for percentage differences between two groups of specified sizes. If an observed percentage difference is smaller than its associated sampling error, a researcher cannot be confident that it did not occur by chance. If a percentage difference is greater than its sampling error, however, a researcher can be confident that the two groups really differ on the dependent variable. For example, with 1,000 whites and 1,000 blacks, the margin of error is no greater than 6%; that is, there are just 5 chances out of 100 of getting a difference as large as 6% by chance alone.[2] The values in Table 11.4 are a special application of the difference-of-means test presented in the previous chapter, this time applied to differences in proportions and percentages.

Even if a percentage difference is very close to its sampling error, the reader need not discount it as due to chance if it is consistent with data from other surveys. For example, all the surveys during elections prior to 1992 show that a greater percentage of whites than blacks voted. Therefore, we can have some confidence that whites were more likely than blacks to vote in 1992 even though the observed 8% difference is close to its sampling error.

Missing Data

The problems with missing-data categories described in Chapter 9 must be faced with cross-tab tables. Researchers generally omit categories for missing data when computing percentage tables. For example, in Table 11.3, people of other races were omitted, as were people whose race was not determined by the interviewer. As in Chapter 9, though, the decision about whether to omit a category of respondents must be based on whether the category of missing data is substantively important. If it is important, it should be included. On the one hand, when data are missing because of interviewer failure to determine race or to ask a particular question, they are usually omitted. On the other hand, some researchers prefer to include don't-know responses to attitude questions.

Even when missing data are included in a table, though, they are generally omitted from the percentages. The decision about whether to include a category in percentages must again be made on the basis of the substantive significance of the category. In Table 11.3, people who were neither white nor black were omitted because some of the categories had very few cases. If we were interested in thoroughly analyzing the relation of turnout to race, we would want to include the data for the other races as well.

One problem with missing data in cross-tab tables does not arise with one-variable distributions. In the present case, a respondent must have a value on each of the two variables in order to contribute to our understanding of the relation between the two variables. Therefore, if a person is missing a value on either one, he or she is usually excluded from the table.[3]

TABLE 11.5 House Vote in 1992 by Party Identification				
Congressional Vote	Strong Democrat	Weak Democrat	Independent	Weak Republican	Strong Republican
Democrat	89%	82%	64%	35%	19%
Republican	11%	18%	36%	65%	81%
Total	100%	100%	100%	100%	100%
Number of cases	(283)	(230)	(405)	(209)	(191)
SOURCE: 1992 American National Election Study.					

Larger Tables

Table 11.3 is a relatively simple table because both race and turnout have only two categories. Table 11.5 shows a more complex table—the relation between party identification and vote in the 1992 U. S. congressional election. Here, we want to explain the respondents' votes, so voting behavior is the dependent variable. A person's party identification is presumed to be a cause of voting behavior; therefore, it is the independent variable.[4] This table contains five categories of party identification and two categories of vote.

Because Table 11.5 is more complex than the preceding tables, it provides more information than a two-by-two table, such as Table 11.3. Table 11.5 tells us a number of things. First, party identification is associated with voting behavior. Second, Democrats were more loyal to their party than were Republicans. Although 89% of strong Democrats and 82% of weak Democrats voted for a Democratic House candidate, only 81% of strong Republicans and 65% of weak Republicans voted for a Republican House candidate. Third, Independents were much more likely to vote for a Democrat than for a Republican.

Notice that looking at relationships, rather than at simple percentages, reduces the impact of certain types of errors. For example, say that Republicans were oversampled: Assume that, in 1992, the sample had twice as many Republicans as it should—800 instead of the 400 reported in Table 11.5. As Table 11.6 shows, our total percentage vote for a Republican would be distorted in this case, but the relationship between party identification and vote might be the same as in Table 11.5. Thus,

TABLE 11.6 House Vote in 1992 by Party Identification, with Double-Sampling of Republicans

Congressional Vote	Strong Democrat	Weak Democrat	Independent	Weak Republican	Strong Republican
Democrat	89%	82%	64%	35%	19%
Republican	11%	18%	36%	65%	81%
Total	100%	100%	100%	100%	100%
Number of cases	(283)	(230)	(405)	(418)	(382)

SOURCE: Hypothetical.

the relationship between two variables is minimally affected by oversampling or undersampling on the independent variable.

As the number of categories of variables in a cross-tab table increases, summarizing the patterns of relationship in the table becomes more difficult. Graphs are sometimes employed to solve this problem. For example, Figure 11.1 presents the results in Table 11.5 in a graphic fashion. Obviously, the figure does not present all of the information in the table; rather, it makes the important patterns easy to read.

Interpreting Relationships

Group differences are almost always smaller than researchers expect them to be. As an example, consider survey evidence on attitude differences between social groups. People's stereotypes lead them to assume that everyone in a group thinks alike and that opposite groups differ a lot from one another. In fact, attitude differences between men and women, between blacks and whites, and between young and old are usually relatively small. As Table 11.7 shows, in 1992, social-group differences on many political issues were small. Racial differences are larger than gender gaps and generational cleavages on three of the six issues shown. Gender has a large effect on views toward permitting gays to serve in the military, whereas age has a large effect on feelings about traditional family values, but sex and age have only limited effects on other attitudes. None of these social differences has much effect on the abortion-policy issue.

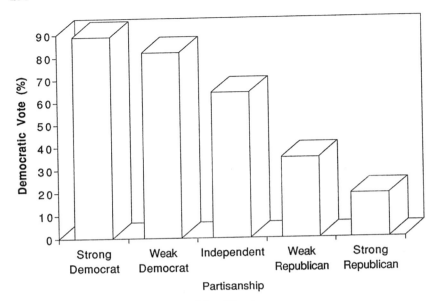

Figure 11.1. House Vote by Party Identification
SOURCE: Based on the 1992 American National Election Study.

Table 11.7 uses a common notation system to show which differences are statistically significant. One asterisk indicates the difference is significant at the .05 level; two asterisks show less than 1 chance out of 100 of getting that large a difference by chance alone; and three asterisks show the probability of such a large difference is less than 1 in 1,000.

Thus, Table 11.7 shows where large differences emerge and that differences do not exist where we might expect them.[5] The table has only a single difference as large as 25%. This analysis illustrates one valuable effect of survey data—correcting stereotypes by demonstrating that differences between social groups in terms of attitudes are relatively small in contemporary America.

SUMMARY

Cross-tab tables are used to determine whether a relation exists between two nominal or ordinal variables. Percentage tables can be read most easily, and the percentages must be calculated within categories of

TABLE 11.7 Group Attitude Differences in 1992 (in percentages)

Question	Age			Sex			Race		
	18-24	>24	Difference	Women	Men	Difference	Blacks	Whites	Difference
Homosexuals should be allowed to serve in the armed forces	58	59	−1	68	47	21***	61	58	3
Favor preferential hiring and promotion for blacks	26	18	8**	21	18	3	56	13	43***
Favor making English the official language	63	65	−2	65	65	0	54	67	−13***
This country would have fewer problems if there were more emphasis on traditional family values	64	84	−20***	82	81	1	74	82	−8**
Favor government health insurance rather than private health plans	48	52	−4	55	48	7**	61	49	12***
Favor state law requiring parental consent for a minor to have an abortion	72	75	−3	73	77	−4*	75	75	0

SOURCE: 1992 American National Election Study.
NOTE: *$p < .05$; **$p < .01$; ***$p < .001$.

the independent variable. It is important to remember that even if a relation between two variables is found in this fashion, that does not prove that the independent variables caused the dependent variable. The role of other variables in affecting the dependent variable must be examined before one can assess causality with any confidence. As you will see in Chapter 13, taking additional variables into account can change the apparent importance of the two-variable relation shown in a cross-tab. Thus, examining such tables is only the beginning of statistical analysis.

Notes

1. The turnout variable is actually based on respondents' reports of their voting behavior. Unfortunately, some respondents report voting when they actually did not. Consequently, turnout figures derived from surveys are usually somewhat higher than actual turnout percentages.

2. The error for percentages below 35 and above 65 is smaller than shown in Table 11.4. The values shown are for simple random sampling; comparable values for complex sample designs can theoretically be less but are often 30% higher. More complete tables are given in Warwick and Lininger (1975, p. 313).

3. Some researchers would instead try to "assign" the person a value on the missing variable, such as the mean of that variable.

4. It is often difficult to be sure that the independent variable is the cause of the dependent variable, particularly when both are measured in the same survey. In this example, some respondents might first decide whether to vote Republican or Democratic and then report that as their party identification. Thus, voting would cause party identification. Because the dominant theory of voting behavior is that partisanship precedes vote decision for most respondents, we take that view and construct our analyses accordingly.

5. One reason why the differences between groups are not large is the groups overlap. For example, you might expect that young people, women, and blacks have different issue positions from older people, men, and whites. But what about white women? Older blacks? Young whites? The expectations for these overlapping groups are contradictory, and that lessens the overall differences between young and old people, between women and men, and between whites and blacks. Social group differences are muted when many people fall into groups with contradictory tendencies.

☑ EXERCISES

1. What is the independent variable in Table 11.8?

2. What is the dependent variable in Table 11.8?

3. Are the percentages in the correct direction in Table 11.8?

TABLE 11.8 U.S. Relations With Russia				
Education	Less Militant (%)	Status Quo (%)	More Militant (%)	Total (%)
College	30	30	40	100
High school	35	30	35	100
Grade school	40	30	30	100

4. The 40% in the College row and More Militant column means that:

   a. 40% of the respondents are people with a college education who want a more militant stand toward Russia.

   b. 40% of those wanting a more militant stand have a college education.

   c. 40% of the college educated want a more militant stand.

   d. 40% of the college educated who want a more militant stand voted in the last election.

5. Does Table 11.8 suggest that those with more formal education want a more militant stand or less militant stand toward Russia, as compared with those with less formal education?

6. Is the relationship between formal education and position on relations with Russia large or small according to Table 11.8?

7. What simple piece of information is missing from Table 11.8 but is necessary in evaluating the importance of these results?

12 ☑☐ Measures
☐☑ of Association

☑ In Chapter 11, we described cross-tab tables—a way to
determine whether two variables are associated with one
another. Associations between variables vary in strength:
Some are strong, others are weak. Therefore, once a researcher has determined that two variables are related to
one another, it is useful to determine how strongly they are
related. Researchers compute **measures of association** to
do so. A measure of association is a single number that
summarizes the information in a cross-tabulation in simpler form.

Logic of Measures of Association

Two Models of Association

What is meant by **association** between variables? The usual way to
think of a relationship is in terms of **covariation**—the extent to which a
change in one variable is accompanied by a change in another variable.

If two variables vary or change together, either in the same direction or in opposite directions, we say they covary and are associated or related. If an increase in the independent variable is always accompanied by an increase in the dependent variable, we call that a **perfect positive relationship.** Similarly, a **perfect negative relationship** is one in which an increase in the independent variable is always accompanied by a decrease in the dependent variable. We say that **no relationship** exists if the dependent variable is equally likely to increase, decrease, or remain the same when the independent variable increases.

Another common way to think of a relationship is in terms of **predictability.** How well can a person's category on the dependent variable be predicted from his or her category on the independent variable? In a perfect positive relationship, knowledge of the independent variable permits perfect prediction of the value of the dependent variable. If there is no relationship, knowledge of the independent variable does not provide any information with which to predict the value of the dependent variable.

In most respects, the covariation model and the prediction model are the same; throughout the introductory material in this chapter, we do not draw distinctions. Later, we discuss the differences between these models.

Extreme Relationships

Table 12.1 illustrates a perfect relationship for both the predictive and covariation models. The predictor variable here is education, and the dependent variable is the respondent's answer to a survey question asking to which social class he or she belongs. According to these hypothetical data, people with a grade school education consider themselves to belong to the working class; those with a high school education consider themselves to belong to the middle class; and those with a college education consider themselves to belong to the upper class. Knowing a person's education level allows a researcher to predict perfectly the person's class identification. As education increases, so does subjective social class. Consequently, there is a perfect positive relationship between education and subjective social class for both models. The relationship is positive because as education increases, so does subjective social class.

We would say that the relation is negative if as education increases, subjective social class decreases. Table 12.2 illustrates a hypothetical

TABLE 12.1 Perfect Relationship Between Education and Class

	Education		
Class	Grade School	High School	College
Working	100%	0%	0%
Middle	0	100	0
Upper	0	0	100
Total	100%	100%	100%
N (total 2,262)	(381)	(778)	(1,103)
	$\tau\text{-}b = 1.00$	$d_{rc} = 1.00$	$\gamma = 1.00$
	$\lambda_{rc} = 1.00$	$\tau\text{-}c = .923$	

SOURCE: Hypothetical.
NOTE: The coefficients of correlation $\tau\text{-}b$ and $\tau\text{-}c$ are explained later in the chapter. The reader will be referred to this table.

perfect negative relationship. This relationship is perfect in the predictive sense, in that class can be predicted perfectly from education. But this relationship is negative because *higher* education is associated with *lower* subjective social class. In reality, education and social class would be expected to have a positive relationship like that in Table 12.1 (the higher the education, the higher the class), only weaker. Table 12.2 is provided merely as an example of what a negative relationship would look like.

By way of contrast, Table 12.3 illustrates no relationship between two variables. Of those with grade school education, 30% consider themselves to be part of the working class, as do 30% of those with a high school education and 30% of those with a college education. Of those with a grade school education, 50% consider themselves to be part of the middle class, and the same holds true for the higher education levels. Finally, 20% of each education group consider themselves to be part of the upper class. A higher education does not lead to a higher subjective social class, according to these hypothetical data. Instead, the two variables are unrelated: People with little or no education are as likely to consider themselves to be members of a particular class as those with more education. Education and class are **statistically independent** here, meaning that the proportions reading down each column are identical.

TABLE 12.2 Negative Relationship Between Education and Class

Class	Education Grade School	High School	College
Working	0%	0%	100%
Middle	0	100	0
Upper	100	0	0
Total	100%	100%	100%
N (total 2,262)	(381)	(778)	(1,103)
	$\tau\text{-}b = -1.00$	$d_{rc} = -1.00$	$\gamma = -1.00$
	$\lambda_{rc} = 1.00$		
		$\tau\text{-}c = -.923$	

SOURCE: Hypothetical.

Because knowledge of a person's education provides no information about his or her class, this is an example of no relationship.

Subjective social class and education are unlikely to be totally unrelated, as in Table 12.3, and they are unlikely to be perfectly related, as in Table 12.1. Instead, the relationship is probably somewhere between those shown in the tables. Because most relationships between variables are neither perfect nor null, it is useful to summarize how strong they are.

TABLE 12.3 No Relationship Between Education and Class

Class	Education Grade School	High School	College
Working	30%	30%	30%
Middle	50	50	50
Upper	20	20	20
Total	100%	100%	100%
N (total 2,262)	(381)	(778)	(1,103)
	$\tau\text{-}b = .000$	$d_{rc} = .000$	$\gamma = .000$
	$\lambda_{rc} = .000$		
		$\tau\text{-}c = .000$	

SOURCE: Hypothetical.

TABLE 12.4 Reversed Relationship Between Education and Class

	Education		
Class	Grade School	High School	College
Working	0%	0%	100%
Middle	0	100	0
Upper	100	0	0
Total	100%	100%	100%
N (total 2,262)	(381)	(778)	(1,103)
	$\tau\text{-}b = -1.00$	$d_{rc} = -1.00$	$\gamma = -1.00$
	$\lambda_{rc} = 1.00$	$\tau\text{-}c = -.923$	

SOURCE: Hypothetical.

Features of Measures of Association

Measures of association indicate how strong a relationship is—how close to perfect or null. To convey the information with a single number, the following conventions are usually followed:

■ The absolute value of a measure of association equals 1.0 if there is a perfect relationship between two variables.
■ The measure equals zero if there is no relationship.
■ The larger the measure's absolute value, the stronger the relationship.
■ A value greater than zero represents a positive relationship.
■ A value less than zero represents a negative relationship.

It is meaningful to talk about the direction of a relationship only when the categories of both variables are ordered in some way. Therefore, the distinction between positive and negative relationships is made only when the variables involved are ordinal, interval, or ratio, and not when they are nominal.

Caution is required in dealing with the sign of the measure of association. It indicates the direction of the relationship between the variables *as they are coded.* For example, a researcher might set up a table involving education so that the first category is college, the second is high school,

TABLE 12.5 Actual Relationship Between Education and Class in 1992

Class	Education		
	Grade School	High School	College
Working	66.6%	64.8%	36.5%
Middle	33.4	35.2	63.5
Total	100%	100%	100%
N (total 2,262)	(381)	(778)	(1,103)
	$\tau\text{-}b = .264$	$d_{rc} = .238$	$\gamma = .453$
	$\lambda_{rc} = .271$	$\tau\text{-}c = .293$	

SOURCE: 1992 American National Election Study.

and the third is grade school (Table 12.4). Is this a positive or a negative relationship? The measure of association for Table 12.4 as presented will have a negative sign. Substantively, the table represents a positive relation between education and class, as does Table 12.1. The measure of association is negative here because the categories of education have been reversed. If you verbalize the structure of the table—"greater educational background is associated with higher social class identification"—you will clearly understand the table regardless of the sign of the measure.

It is easy to get confused about the direction of a relationship between two variables. It is therefore a good idea to verbalize the structure of cross-tab tables before looking at measures of association. Also, always set up tables so that the categories of the row variable increase as they go down the page and the categories of the column variable increase as they go from left to right. If a measure of association is negative even though the substantive relationship is positive (or vice versa), either the columns or the rows can be reversed and the sign changed.

Table 12.5 illustrates the relationship between education and subjective social class as based on data from the 1992 National Election Study. This table has only two class categories because only a handful of people considered themselves to be members of the upper class. The relationship in Table 12.5 is positive: Higher education is associated with higher class identification. The relationship is neither perfect nor null, so a measure of association summarizing it will be some number between 0 and 1.

Many different measures of association might be used to summarize the relationship shown in Table 12.5. Different measures have been developed because researchers have different needs at different times. Specifically, one basis for deciding which measure to use is the level of measurement (interval/ratio, ordinal, or nominal) of the variables involved. Different arithmetic operations are appropriate for the different levels of measurement. In this chapter, we describe measures of association appropriate for ordinal and nominal data.

Ordinal Measures

The three most commonly used measures of association at the ordinal level are "tau" "*d*," and "gamma." They have much in common and usually have similar values, although each has its own purpose. Unfortunately, there is no simple rule for determining the appropriate statistic to use, nor is one or the others always best. In fact, there is no general consensus among researchers on which measure is best.

Kendall's tau (τ, hereafter referred to simply as "tau") is probably the most frequently used ordinal measure of association. It measures the extent to which a change in one variable is accompanied by a change in another variable. It precisely fits the covariation model discussed earlier. Because tau measures covariation, or how two variables vary together, it always has the same value regardless of which variable is the independent variable and which is the dependent. Therefore, tau is called a **symmetric** measure.

Having calculated a value of tau, the researcher must judge the importance of that value. We know that 1.0 is a perfect relationship and that 0.0 indicates no relationship at all, but it is usually useful to specify how strong the relationship is. As a rough guideline, we would call a tau above .7 high, a tau between .3 and .7 moderate, and a tau between 0 and .3 small. In fact, values higher than .3 are rare in survey research, so correlations of even .1 are reported as important. Much depends on the state of knowledge in the field and whether the proper predictors are known. Ideally, only correlations of .3 or stronger should be emphasized, but smaller relationships can sometimes still be of interest; in such cases, it is important to recognize that a relationship is small.

The tau statistic actually has different forms. Tau-b can obtain a value of 1.0 only if there are an equal number of categories of each of the two variables (e.g., when there are two partisanship categories and two vote categories). Tau-c corrects for unequal numbers of variable categories and can attain a value of 1.0 if there are unequal numbers of independent variable and dependent variable categories. Only tau-b need be calculated if the variables have the same number of categories. In fact, if tau-c is used when the variables have the same number of categories, as in Table 12.1, it will not always produce a value of 1.0 when there is a perfect relationship. As a result, tau-b seems to us to be the more generally useful measure.

The tau-b value for Table 12.5 is .26, which shows a small relationship between education and class. The tau-c value for the same table is .29, which is close enough to suggest a similar conclusion. Because the table has an unequal number of rows and columns, some would consider tau-c to be more appropriate.

Notice that we report the tau values with two digits after the decimal point. Computers often provide more digits (e.g., .26382), but reporting those additional digits is unnecessary. Given the amount of error in any set of survey data, more than two- or three-digit accuracy should not be taken seriously.

A Measure of Difference Between Percentages

Somer's d (hereafter referred to as "d") is another ordinal measure of association. It is a generalization of the logic of differences between percentages that we used to compare categories of the independent variable in Chapter 11. There, because the independent and dependent variables each had two categories, a single percentage-difference figure could be derived from a cross-tab table in a simple fashion. Things become more complex when variables have more than two categories. Somer's d summarizes percentage differences under these conditions. The value of d is an indicator of how much the dependent variable changes for each change in the independent variable. For the data in Table 12.5, d is .24, which indicates a weak relationship.

Recall that when the data in a table are presented in percentages, the percentages should be calculated within the categories of the independent variable; otherwise, the comparisons are not informative of causal relationships. Because d is based on the same logic, it is calculated according to whether the column or the row variable is the independent variable. Statistics like d, which have different values depending on which variable is independent, are called **asymmetric measures.** Because there are two d values for any table, a system is needed to distinguish them: "d_{rc}" is used to indicate the value of d when the row variable is dependent; "d_{cr}" denotes the opposite—the column variable is dependent.

Computer data analysis programs generally calculate both d_{rc} and d_{cr}. The researcher must decide which is correct for the table being analyzed. For Table 12.5, d_{rc} =.24 and d_{cr} =.29. It would be fallacious to report both values because only one of the variables is dependent. Here, subjective social class—the rows—is the dependent variable; hence, d_{rc} is the appropriate measure. It can be shown that a relationship exists between Somer's d and tau-b discussed above: tau-$b^2 = d_{rc}d_{cr}$. As a result, the value of tau-b for a table always falls between the values of d_{rc} and d_{cr}. Tau-b for Table 12.5 is .26, which is between d_{rc} =.24 and d_{cr} =.29.

A Measure for Scale Relationships

Goodman and Kruskal's gamma (γ) statistic is another measure of association for ordinal variables. Instead of measuring the effects of independent variables on dependent variables, a researcher might want to know whether two variables measure the same underlying dimension, as discussed in Chapter 9. Suppose we suspect that interest in a political campaign and concern about its outcome are two measures of the same underlying dimension, which we call *political involvement.* We might hypothesize that people who are not involved in politics will also show little interest and little concern, that people with great involvement might be expected to show substantial interest and concern, and that people with medium involvement might show high concern but low interest. It is difficult to imagine anyone highly interested in a campaign having little concern about the outcome.

Table 12.6 illustrates this hypothesis. If this hypothesis is correct, concern and interest are both measures of involvement, but interest is a better indicator than concern; people with medium involvement can show high concern, but only those people with high involvement can show high interest. Notice that this grouping leaves one cell of the table empty. Gamma seeks to measure this type of relationship. Gamma is 1.0 for Table 12.6 because there is a perfect relationship between interest and concern (with only high-concern types showing interest).

TABLE 12.6 Scale Relationship Between Interest and Concern

Concern Over Outcome	Interest in Election	
	Low	High
Low	300	0
High	400	300
Total		(1,000)
$\tau\text{-}b = .429$	$d_{rc} = .429$	$d_{cr} = .429$ $\gamma = 1.00$

The logic of gamma is based on the notion of **concordant** and **discordant** pairs in a cross-tabulation of two variables. Two respondents are considered to be a concordant pair if the person with a higher score on one variable also has a higher score on the other variable; two respondents are considered to be a discordant pair if the person with the higher score on one variable has the lower score on the other variable. The formula is

$$\gamma = (C - D) / (C + D)$$

where C is the number of concordant pairs and D is the number of discordant pairs. The numerator is the excess of concordant over discordant pairs; the denominator is the total number of pairs of respondents who respond differently to the two questions. Thus, gamma is the excess of concordant over discordant pairs of respondents, relative to the total number of respondents who respond differently to the two questions.

To illustrate how to calculate gamma, let's begin with a table with two rows and columns (Table 12.6). Compare one person in the top left cell with one person in the bottom right cell. The person who scored higher on one variable also scored higher on the other variable, so these two people constitute a concordant pair. The total number of concordant pairs, C, is then the product of the number of people in the top left cell and the number in the bottom right cell, or $300 \times 300 = 90,000$ in Table 12.6. Next, compare one person in the top right cell with one person in the bottom left cell. The person who scored higher on one variable scored lower on the other variable, so these two people constitute a discordant pair. The total number of discordant pairs, D, is then the product of the number of people in the top right cell and the number in the bottom left cell, or $0 \times 400 = 0$ in Table 12.6. Gamma for Table 12.6

is therefore $(90{,}000 - 0)/(90{,}000 + 0) = 90{,}000/90{,}000 = 1.0$. As this example illustrates, gamma will equal 1.0 in all two-by-two tables with one zero cell.

In larger tables, the calculation is a generalization of that given here. Two sums of products are generated. First, each cell of the table is multiplied by the total frequency of all cells below and to the right of that cell, and those products are summed to get the value of C. Second, each cell of the table is multiplied by the total frequency of all cells below and to the left of that cell, and those products are summed to get the value of D. After those two sums of products are computed, gamma is computed according to the formula given above.

When studying the relation between two ordinal variables, gamma measures how often knowing the relative ordering of a respondent on one variable allows the researcher to predict the respondent's relative ordering on the second variable. Numerically, it is the number of correct predictions (the number of pairs of respondents with the same order on the two variables) minus the number of incorrect predictions, divided by the total number of predictions. In this sense, gamma indicates the amount that prediction error was reduced by knowing the person's score on the independent variable.

Gamma is never smaller than tau and tends to produce much higher values. An extreme contrast is shown in Table 12.6, where gamma is 1.0 and tau-b is only .43. A more typical comparison is shown in Table 12.5, where gamma is .45 and tau-b is only .26. The larger values of gamma make it attractive to researchers who want to report relationships that appear to be strong. Some researchers (e.g., Costner, 1965) argue that gamma is a measure of predictive association for ordinal data and that therefore they prefer gamma to tau. Because of the prediction rule used by gamma, however, and because of the special circumstances under which gamma can have a value of 1.00, we do not recommend its use except when a researcher believes that two variables may reflect the same underlying dimension, as described above (Weisberg, 1974).

A Measure of the
Correspondence of Rank Orderings

One additional ordinal measure deserves mention. Some ordinal variables are **rank orders,** such as the rank order of people from richest to poorest or from most conservative to most liberal. Spearman's rho (r_s) is used to measure the association between two variables that constitute

TABLE 12.7 Calculation of Spearman's Rho

Person	Income	Ideology	Difference	Difference Squared
A	1	1	0	0
B	3	2	1	1
C	2	4	-2	4
D	4	3	1	1
E	5	5	0	0
Sum			0	6

N = number of people = 5

$$r_s = 1 - \frac{6\,(sum\ of\ squared\ differences)}{N(N^2 - 1)} = 1 - \frac{6\,(6)}{5\,(5^2 - 1)}$$

$$= 1 - \frac{36}{120} = .70$$

rank orders. Table 12.7 illustrates an example. In the Income column, 1 stands for the highest income and 5 for the lowest. In the Ideology column, 1 stands for most conservative and 5 for least conservative. The method for calculating Spearman's rho is shown at the bottom of the table. Because rho is large and positive (.70), the data show a strong tendency for people with more income to be more conservative. Spearman's rho can only be used when all respondents are rank-ordered on both variables. When, instead, the data consist of ordered categories of people, such as categories of conservatives, moderates, and liberals, Kendall's tau is more useful.

_____

Choice of Measure

When a study does not have rank-order variables, which of the measures of association should be used—tau, d, or gamma? Researchers would generally be correct in using tau. They might use d instead, but tau is used more generally. Use gamma only if your model of a perfect relationship is a scale. The most important thing is to understand the table; statistics should aid in that understanding, rather than substitute for it. Once you understand the table, you may want to use a measure of association to summarize the amount of relationship in the table.

These ordinal measures do not agree on what constitutes a perfect relationship. What is perfect according to one is not necessarily perfect according to another. These measures do agree, however, on what constitutes no relationship. If one ordinal measure for a particular table is zero, the others will also be zero. Also, these measures all have the same sign for any particular table. Thus, the choice between them will have only small consequences for your interpretation.

Use of Ordinal Statistics

The statistics described above should only be used with ordinal variables. Be careful when employing them: Many variables have categories that cannot be ordered in a meaningful fashion and are therefore not ordinal. For example, say that voting behavior in a presidential election is divided into the following categories: *voted Democratic, voted Republican,* and *did not vote.* Did-not-vote prevents this from being an ordered set of categories—it is not meaningful to suggest that voting behavior ranges from voting Democratic to not voting, with voting Republican somewhere in the middle—so it would not be appropriate to apply ordinal statistics. To apply ordinal statistics in this case, people who reported that they did not vote could be omitted, and the statistics could be computed by using only respondents who voted for either the Democratic or Republican candidate. Then, ordinal statistics would be meaningful. More generally, missing data must always be excluded before computing any measure of association.

So far, we have stressed using ordinal measures for ordinal variables. All ordinal measures of association assume that as one variable increases, the other will consistently increase or consistently decrease. This is called a **monotonic relationship** between two variables. Difficulties arise if the second variable increases for a while and then decreases, or vice versa. Table 12.8 illustrates a relation in which the independent variable—education—is not monotonically related to the dependent variable. Tau-*b* and gamma for this table are near zero. We can perfectly predict, however, the value of the dependent variable from the value of the independent variable. These ordinal measures of association suggest that the variables are not related to one another, which is not true.

Therefore, researchers should not necessarily apply ordinal-level measures to ordinal variables. They should apply ordinal measures of association only when examination of a cross-tab table reveals that the

TABLE 12.8 Predictive Relationship Between Education and Class

| | Education | | |
Class	Grade School	High School	College
Working	100%	0%	0%
Middle	0	0	100
Upper	0	100	0
Total	100%	100%	100%
N (total 2,164)	(474)	(786)	(904)
	$\tau\text{-}b = .060$	$d_{rc} = .060$	$\gamma = .060$
	$\lambda_{rc} = 1.000$		$\tau\text{-}c = .058$

SOURCE: Hypothetical.

relation between the variables is monotonic. If a researcher wanted to examine the relationship between age and turnout, he or she would probably not expect to find a monotonic relationship. Instead, turnout probably increases with age until about retirement age, when it may begin to decrease with age. In this case, ordinal-level measures are inappropriate because although the categories of the variables are ordered, the expected relationship is not monotonic.

Nominal Measures

If one or both of the variables in a cross-tab table have more than two categories that cannot be ordered, then there is no choice but to treat the variable as nominal and to apply nominal-level measures of association.

A Predictive Measure

The most useful nominal measure of association is lambda (λ). Lambda is asymmetric; it has different values, depending on whether the row or column variable is the independent variable. It conforms to the predictive model of a relationship, but it derives a very direct empirical interpretation from the predictive measure described above. The value of lambda is the proportion by which error in predicting the value of the dependent variable is reduced by knowing the value of the independent variable; that is, lambda tells you how much better your prediction of the dependent variable is if you know the value of the independent variable. Measures of association that have this property are called **proportional reduction in error (PRE)** measures.

Table 12.9 displays an example of the use of lambda. Both raw frequencies and percentages are shown there. If we did not know the independent variable—race—how would we guess that person voted in 1992? Well, more people voted against Clinton (852) than voted for him (782), so we would be correct more often if we guessed against Clinton (combining Bush and Perot voters). How often would we be wrong? We would be wrong 782 times out of 1,634. The proportion of errors will be 782/1,634. If we knew a person was black, how would we guess he or she voted? For Clinton. How often would we be wrong? We would be wrong 15 times out of 193. If we knew a person was white, we would guess he or she voted against Clinton, and we would be wrong 604 times out of 1,441. Hence, if we knew the value of the independent variable, we would have been wrong 619 (15 + 604) times out of 1,634. The proportion of error if we knew the independent variable was 619/1,634. Lambda, the proportion that we reduced our original error, is equal to the original proportion (782/1,634) minus the proportion of error if we knew the value of the independent variable (619/1,634), all divided by the original proportion of error (782/1,634),

$$\frac{\dfrac{782}{1,634} - \dfrac{15 + 604}{1,634}}{\dfrac{782}{1,634}} = \frac{782 - 619}{782} = \frac{163}{782} = .208$$

Another way to think of lambda is that it measures the improvement in prediction because of knowing the independent variable. The number of errors we would make not knowing respondents' races is 782. If we knew their races, we would only make 619 errors (15 + 604). Hence, we would reduce the number of errors by 163. Because it is easier to interpret measures of association if they range from 0 to 1, we divide the improvement (163) by the maximum that we could have improved, 782. By doing so, we produce a measure of association that varies between 0 and 1.

	Black		White		Total	
Vote	Percentage	Frequency	Percentage	Frequency	Percentage	Frequency
For Clinton	92	178	42	604	48	782
Against Clinton	8	15	58	837	52	852
Total	100	193	100	1,441	100	1,634

TABLE 12.9 The Clinton Vote by Race in 1992

$N = 1,634$

$\tau\text{-}b = .324$ $d_{rc} = .501$ $\gamma = .882$ $\lambda_{rc} = .208$

SOURCE: 1992 American National Election Study.

Dichotomous Variables

Variables with only two categories may be considered to be either nominal or ordinal. The categories of gender cannot be ordered, but because there are only two, ordinal and nominal measures of association are equally appropriate. A table involving two dichotomous variables is shown in Table 12.9. The value of d_{rc} is easy to interpret here (92% – 42% = 50% difference). Gamma is very high because few blacks voted against Clinton; if no blacks had voted against him, gamma would be 1.0. However, gamma is not appropriate to the type of relationship we are examining. One could make an argument for using tau-b or d_{rc} here, but the interpretation would be significantly different from what it is for lambda. Remember that the signs of measures of association for nominal variables are not substantively meaningful; in Table 12.9, it would not make sense to call the relationship between race and vote either positive or negative.

Choice of Measures

One of the largest contrasts between predictive measures like lambda and covariation measures like d and tau is illustrated in Table 12.10. Lambda is zero because knowing the value of the independent variable does not improve one's ability to predict the dependent variable; most blacks and most whites voted for Democrats for Congress, so knowing a

TABLE 12.10 Congressional Vote by Race in 1992					
	Black		*White*		*Total*
Vote	*Percentage*	*Frequency*	*Percentage*	*Frequency*	*Percentage*	*Frequency*
Democrat	89	126	55	664	58	790
Republican	11	15	45	546	42	561
Total	100	141	100	1,210	100	1,351

$N = 1,351$

$\tau\text{-}b = .213$ $\qquad$ $d_{rc} = .343$ $\qquad$ $\gamma = .743$ $\qquad$ $\lambda_{rc} = .000$

SOURCE: 1992 American National Election Study.

person's race does not affect the prediction of his or her vote. Regardless of the category of the independent variable, we always guess that the person voted for a Democrat. The covariation measures d and tau, however, show that the two variables vary together moderately. Therefore, a researcher must be careful to specify what type of model relationship is expected. The statistics are often quite similar, but as Table 12.10 shows, they can also be quite different.

Significance Tests

How do researchers judge whether a relationship between two variables exists? One possibility is to simply observe the size of measures of association. If they are different from zero, one might conclude that the two variables are related to one another. This approach would ignore the fact, however, that even though two variables are unrelated, a measure of association could be slightly different from zero due to chance. Because most surveys are based on samples of populations, slight variations in sampling can produce measures of association that are not the same as those for the population as a whole.

To handle this problem, researchers calculate a sample interval around an estimate of a measure of association. This interval specifies the range of values within which the true value of the measure for the population is likely to fall. The size of the interval depends on the sample size and on the observed magnitude of the measure of association. Researchers are most concerned about inaccurately claiming a relationship between two variables when there is, in fact, no relationship in the population. The question, then, is whether an observed relationship is statistically significant.

The Chi-Square Test

There are significance tests for most of the measures described in this chapter. We use as an example the best-known statistical significance testing procedure: the chi-square (χ^2) test. It is used to test the hypothesis that there is no relationship between the variables in the population (for an example of statistical independence, see Table 12.3), and it tests whether the observed data justify rejecting this null hypothesis.

Consider again the relationship between education and subjective social class. In 1992, 49% of the people considered themselves to be members of the working class, and 51% considered themselves to be members of the middle class. If education does not affect class status, 49% of each education group would consider themselves to be members of the working class. There were 381 people who did not graduate from high school, so 186 of them would be expected to be working class. However, the observed figure is actually 127 (see Table 12.5). Chi-square contrasts the observed and expected values for each combination of education and class. It squares the differences between the expected and observed values, divides by the expected value [$(127 - 185.62)^2/185.62$ = 18.51 for working class who did not graduate from high school], and sums up the quotients for all the cells in the table. This calculation for Table 12.5 gives a chi-square value of 190, as shown in Table 12.11.

Could this value have occurred by chance? To answer this question, one must determine the degrees of freedom for the chi-square, which is defined as $(r-1) \times (c-1)$ where r = number of rows of the table and c = number of columns—(1 less than the number of rows of the table) × (1 less than the number of columns). Table 12.12 shows the chi-square value required for significance for different numbers of degrees of freedom, taking no more than a 10%, 5%, or 1% chance of concluding that a relationship is significant when, in fact, it is not.

For the present example, the degrees of freedom equals $(2 - 1) \times (3 - 1) = 1 \times 2 = 2$. With two degrees of freedom, a chi-square value of 6 or more will occur by chance fewer than 5 times out of 100. Because we found a chi-square value of 190, we can confidently reject the null hypothesis that there is no relationship between the two variables. The relationship is greater than would be expected on the basis of chance

Table 12.11 Calculation of Chi-Square for Table 12.5

Category	Observed	Expected	$\frac{(Observed\text{-}Expected)^2}{Expected}$
Grade school, working class	127	49% of 381 = 185.62	18.51
Grade school, middle class	254	51% of 381 = 95.38	17.58
High school, working class	274	49% of 778 = 379.02	29.10
High school, middle class	504	51% of 778 = 398.97	27.65
College, working class	701	49% of 1,103 = 537.36	49.83
College, middle class	402	51% of 1,103 = 565.64	47.34
Total	2,262	2,262.00	190.02

Degrees of freedom = (Number of rows – 1) × (Number of columns – 1)

$$= (2-1) \times (3-1) = 1 \times 2 = 2$$

$$\chi^2 = \sum \frac{(Observed\text{-}Expected)^2}{Expected} = 190.02$$

NOTE: $p = .00000$.

and sampling error. Notice that chi-square is essentially a test for a predictive relationship at the nominal level; it does not check whether respondents who are higher on one variable are higher on the other.

The level of significance required in a significance test is set arbitrarily. The .05 level was employed in the previous paragraph, taking at most a 5% chance that the value is significant when it is not. Although the .05 level is most common, you will sometimes see .1 used (a less stringent test) or .01 (a more stringent test). Because the specification of any of these levels is arbitrary, some researchers prefer to report the probability of obtaining the observed chi-square value if the true relationship is zero. This reporting allows the reader to judge whether that probability is so large as to preclude believing that the two variables are associated with one another.

Computer programs that calculate chi-squares typically also indicate probability. The lower the value, the more likely it is that the two variables

TABLE 12.12 Chi-Square Values Required for Significance*

Degrees of Freedom	Significance Level		
	0.10	0.05	0.01
1	2.706	3.841	6.635
2	4.605	5.991	9.210
3	6.251	7.815	11.345
4	7.779	9.488	13.277
5	9.236	11.070	15.086
6	10.645	12.592	16.812
7	12.017	14.067	18.475
8	13.362	15.507	20.090
9	14.684	16.919	21.666
10	15.987	18.307	23.209
11	17.275	19.675	24.725
12	18.549	21.026	26.217
13	19.812	22.362	27.688
14	21.064	23.685	29.141
15	22.307	24.996	30.578
16	23.542	26.296	32.000
17	24.769	27.587	33.409
18	25.989	28.869	34.805
19	27.204	30.144	36.191
20	28.412	31.410	37.566
30	40.256	43.773	50.892
40	51.805	55.758	63.691
50	63.167	67.505	76.154
60	74.397	79.082	88.379
70	85.527	90.531	100.425
80	96.578	101.879	112.329
90	107.565	113.145	124.116
100	118.498	124.342	135.807

SOURCE: Generated by the authors, using the chiinv function in Microsoft Excel.
NOTE: *The χ^2 value must be larger than the value shown in the table for significance at the chosen significance level.

are actually related. Thus, if the computer output shows a significance or *p* **value** of .00001, then the odds against obtaining the observed results by chance are very high. The larger the relationship, the smaller the probability value. As an example, the chi-square of 173 with 2,164 respondents has a probability of .00001, which indicates that it is highly significant. By contrast, a chi-square of 4.4 has a probability value of .11, which shows that it is nearly significant.

Unfortunately, some problems are common to most tests of statistical significance. For one thing, they are based on the assumption that a simple random sample was employed. When other types of samples are used, the assumptions of these significance tests are not met. Most researchers believe that violation of this assumption does not bias significance tests substantially, so it is rare to see other tests in the literature.

Substantive Criteria

Because significance tests depend, in part, on the size of the sample involved, with a large sample almost any relation will be statistically significant. Therefore, except for very small samples (100 or less), tests of significance do not help researchers in deciding which relationships are large and which are not. They only help researchers in deciding whether a relation is different from zero. It is always important, however, to assess the **substantive significance** of a relationship between two variables. An association of .09 may be statistically significant, but it is not very important because it indicates that the independent variable is not of much use in predicting the dependent variable's value. In some cases, a weak relationship can still be substantively important. For example, if a certain television advertisement increased sales of a soft drink by 1%, that can amount to a change of millions of dollars in sales. Therefore, by this standard, the relationship is quite substantial. Researchers should always try to judge the substantive significance of relationships, in addition to their statistical significance.[1]

In any case, do not just look through data for strong associations. That strategy would not account for the chance variation in a set of data. If a researcher computes enough measures of association, a few large ones will occur just by chance. Rather than seek large associations, choose which associations to examine on the basis of well-justified theories. If those associations turn out to be small, that is a substantively important negative finding.

Finally, it is important to remember that finding a relationship that is substantively important does not mean one variable caused the other.

Association does not prove causation. That two variables covary does not in itself show that a change in one produces a change in the other. The possibility always exists that some other variable or variables are causing both of the original variables to change. To speak more definitely about causation, a researcher must examine more than two variables at a time—the subject of the next chapter.

SUMMARY

Measures of association are often useful in summarizing large cross-tabulations. The measure of association used to summarize a table depends partly on the level of measurement of the variables and partly on the model of association the researcher has in mind. Tau, d, and gamma are frequently used to summarize relationships among ordinal variables. Lambda can be used to summarize the relationship among nominal variables. The chi-square test is the most commonly used test of significance to determine whether a relationship in sample data is likely to hold in the greater population of interest. In addition to testing the statistical significance of a relationship, however, it is important to assess its substantive importance.

Further Readings

Measures of Association

Costner, H. L. (1965). Criteria for measures of association. *American Sociological Review, 30,* 341-353.

Freeman, L. C. (1965). *Elementary applied statistics for students in behavioral science.* New York: John Wiley.

Liebetrau, A. M. (1983). *Measures of association.* Beverly Hills, CA: Sage.

Siegel, S. (1956). *Nonparametric statistics for the behavioral sciences.* New York: McGraw-Hill.

Weisberg, H. F. (1974). Models of statistical relationship. *American Political Science Review, 68,* 1638-1655.

Note

1. For further development of the arguments for and against using significance tests, see Morrison and Henkel (1970).

☑ EXERCISES

How would you interpret the following situations? (Watch for fallacies in the applications of the statistics.)

1. The association between race and interest in politics is –.30.

2. Tau assessing the relationship between religion and attitude on abortion is .15.

3. Lambda assessing the relationship between region and vote is .20.

4. Gamma assessing the relationship between attitudes on abortion and divorce is .85.

5. Tau assessing the relationship between age and attitudes toward divorce is .05.

13 ☐☑ ☑☐ Control Tables

☑ Two-variable cross-tab tables and bivariate measures of association do not provide enough information to explain attitudes, beliefs, or behavior. Those techniques are useful for determining whether two variables are related to one another, but finding a relationship does not prove that one variable causes another. Having found that two variables are related, the researcher must test various possible explanations for why they are related.

For example, in Chapter 11 we examined the relationship between race and turnout. Having found a weak relationship, with whites slightly more likely than blacks to vote, we might then try to explain it. Because no genetic difference between whites and blacks causes blacks to vote less than whites, it seems likely that race and voting behavior are related because of social or psychological processes. A researcher interested in explaining this relation would construct some possible explanations and attempt to test each of them.

One way to test causal explanations is to introduce a third variable into a bivariate analysis. For example, in the case of race and voter turnout, we might hypothesize that education is an important determinant of voting behavior and that blacks were less likely than whites to vote in 1992 because of differences in education. Alternatively, one might argue that the most important determinant of whether a person votes is his or her beliefs about whether the candidate choice will make a meaningful difference. Perhaps, one might speculate, blacks were less likely to vote than whites because of differences in their beliefs about the usefulness of voting. These and other possible explanations for the observed relation can be tested by controlling for third variables in examining a bivariate relation. **Controlling** is a method of holding a third variable constant while examining the relationship between two other variables. In this chapter, we explain how this is done.

It is important to distinguish at the outset between a few situations in which third variables are controlled. One situation is when the third variable logically occurs between the independent variable and the dependent variable. In this situation, the third variable is called an **intervening variable.** It helps in explaining how the original relationship works. In the example above, race can affect education but not vice versa, so education must be an intervening variable. If blacks and whites with the same levels of education voted at the same rates, then the intervening variable would show that race affected turnout only in the sense of race affecting education, which in turn affects turnout.

A second situation is when the relationship between the independent and dependent variables differs for different categories of the control variable. This is called an **interaction effect.** We illustrate it later in this chapter by showing that gender effects on voting turnout may be different at different levels of education.

A third important situation is when the third variable is an **antecedent** variable—it logically occurs before the independent variable. If the original relationship between the independent and dependent variables can be shown to be completely due to both being caused by the same control variable, then that original relationship is considered to be **spurious.** In the next section, we give a simple example of such a spurious relationship.

Identifying Spurious Relationships

Consider the bivariate relationship (Table 13.1) between the number of fire trucks sent to a fire and the amount of damage done by the fire (measured in dollars). A strong positive relationship exists between these

TABLE 13.1 Fire Damage by Number of Fire Trucks at the Scene

Damage	Number of Trucks			
	None	1-2	3-4	5+
$10,000 or less	98%	40%	12%	2%
$10,001 to $100,000	2	39	26	14
$100,001 to $1,000,000	0	21	48	65
More than $1,000,000	0	1	14	19
Total	100%	101%	100%	100%
N (total 943)	(125)	(217)	(341)	(260)
τ-b = .570 d_{rc} = .563 γ = .750 λ_{rc} = .288				
SOURCE: Hypothetical.				

two variables (tau-b = .57). The more fire trucks sent to a fire, the more damage is done. Having observed this relationship, we might now want to explain it. Because fire trucks are sent to fires before damage is assessed, time ordering is consistent with the hypothesis that the number of fire trucks sent causes the amount of damage done. Naturally, however, we know that fire trucks reduce damage, so this explanation seems unlikely to be valid. We must generate another possible explanation for the observed relation.

If we think about it for a moment, we realize that the severity of the fire is related to both the amount of damage and the number of fire trucks at the scene. A fire chief is likely to send more trucks to serious fires, and the more serious the fire, the more damage is likely to be done. We might therefore imagine that the severity of the fire causes both the number of trucks sent and the amount of damage done. If this hypothesis is true, we would expect to find no relationship between number of trucks and amount of damage if we were able to examine only fires of the same level of seriousness. To do so, social scientists construct what are called **control tables.**

A control table in this situation would display the relationship between the number of fire trucks and the damage for minor fires only, the relationship of those same variables for moderately serious fires only, and the relationship for major fires only. We would expect no relationship between number of fire trucks and damage for any of these three

TABLE 13.2 Fire Damage by Number of Fire Trucks at the Scene for
Minor Fires Only

| | Number of Trucks | | | |
Damage	None	1-2	3-4	5+
$10,000 or less	98%	97%	97%	0%
$10,001 to $100,000	2	3	3	0
$100,001 to $1,000,000	0	0	0	0
More than $1,000,000	0	0	0	0
Total	100%	100%	100%	0%
N (total 230)	(125)	(76)	(29)	(0)

$\tau\text{-}b = .017$ $d_{rc} = .005$ $\gamma = .097$ $\lambda_{rc} = .000$

SOURCE: Hypothetical.

TABLE 13.3 Fire Damage by Number of Fire Trucks at the Scene for
Moderate-Sized Fires Only

| | Number of Trucks | | | |
Damage	None	1-2	3-4	5+
$10,000 or less	0%	10%	10%	9%
$10,001 to $100,000	0	70	66	67
$100,001 to $1,000,000	0	20	24	22
More than $1,000,000	0	0	0	2
Total	0%	100%	100%	100%
N (total 304)	(0)	(117)	(133)	(54)

$\tau\text{-}b = .042$ $d_{rc} = .036$ $\gamma = .075$ $\lambda_{rc} = .000$

SOURCE: Hypothetical.

subtables. Tables 13.2 through 13.4 show what this might look like. Keep in mind that the data in Tables 13.2 through 13.4 are the same as in Table 13.1. The only thing that has been done is to divide the cases into three groups, depending on the third variable (the seriousness of the fire, measured by the number of alarms). If you add up the cases in Tables 13.2, 13.3, and 13.4, you will once again have Table 13.1.

TABLE 13.4 Fire Damage by Number of Fire Trucks at the Scene for Serious Fires Only

Damage	None	1-2	3-4	5+
$10,000 or less	0%	0%	0%	0%
$10,001 to $100,000	0	0	0	0
$100,001 to $1,000,000	0	75	74	78
More than $1,000,000	0	25	26	22
Total	0%	100%	100%	100%
N (total 409)	(0)	(24)	(179)	(206)

$\tau\text{-}b = -.046$ $d_{rc} = -.037$ $\gamma = -.102$ $\lambda_{rc} = .000$

SOURCE: Hypothetical.

For minor fires (Table 13.2), the relationship between number of fire trucks sent and damage has effectively disappeared. Regardless of the number of trucks sent, the damage was almost always in the $10,000 or less range. Also, all the correlation measures are zero, indicating no relationship is present in the table.

Table 13.3 shows that, for moderately serious fires, the relationship between number of trucks sent and amount of damage has also disappeared. The distribution of cases in damage categories is almost the same for all categories of the independent variable; hence, no relationship is present. The association between the two variables is effectively zero.

Table 13.4, for serious fires, is very similar to the previous table except that the cases have moved down to the higher-damage categories. But again no relation exists between the independent variable and the dependent variable because the distributions are essentially the same for the categories of the independent variable. Also, the measures of association are again all approximately zero, indicating no relationship.

Not surprisingly, no relationship exists between number of trucks and damage for any of these three tables. Notice that all the taus are near zero. Thus, we conclude that the original relationship between number of trucks and damage (without controls) is **spurious.** It can be accounted for entirely by controlling for the seriousness of the fire.

Interpreting Controls
_____

How do we interpret the various patterns of associations in control tables? If the associations are all zero after controlling, as in the above example, then the bivariate relationship is spurious. The independent variable did not cause the dependent variable; instead, the control variable affected them both and induced an association between them.

On the one hand, if the associations in the separate control tables are considerably reduced but are still above approximately .10, it is safe to conclude that some, but not all, of the bivariate relationship is spurious. On the other hand, if the bivariate relationship remains unchanged after controlling (if the measures of association are just about as high in the control tables as in the original), we would conclude that the control has no impact on the original relationship.

Still another possibility is that the relationship between the two variables is different for the different categories of the control variable. The relationship might (a) be stronger for some category or categories of the control variable, (b) disappear—be zero—for some, or (c) be in the opposite direction (the association changes its sign) for others. In these cases, we say the original relationship is **specified** by the control variable. In other words, the control variable determines what the relationship is. An example follows.

A common control variable in survey analysis is education; often, two variables seem related to one another but both prove to be caused by education. The fact that education is related to both variables creates a spurious relationship between them. Consider an example from the 1972 American National Election Study. In that year, a greater proportion of men than women voted; the difference was about 6%. That difference is statistically significant, although only barely. Additionally, it is consistent with evidence collected since women won the vote in the United States in the early 20th century: All studies to that time showed women voting less than men.

When faced with this association, it is natural to speculate about why it occurs. One possibility is that gender causes turnout, although this is hard to imagine because no obvious genetic differences between men and women would lead to higher voting rates among men. It is reasonable to expect, however, that people with more education vote more than people with less education, because there is a positive association be-

TABLE 13.5 Turnout Rates by Sex

| | Sex | |
	Male	Female
Voted	80%	69%
Did not vote	20	31
Total	100%	100%
N (total 1,954)	(883)	(1,071)
τ-b = .12 d_{rc} = .11 γ = .28 λ_{rc} = .00		

SOURCE: Hypothetical.

tween education and turnout. Furthermore, men in the United States in 1972 were more likely than women to have a college education; that is, an association existed between gender and education. Thus, because high education is associated with both high turnout and being male, the apparent relationship between gender and turnout might be due to their both being related to education. To see whether this is so, we might look only at men and women who possessed the same amount of education (so that there are no educational differences between them). First, we would look at men and women with high levels of education, then at men and women with medium levels of education, and then at those with low levels of education. We would expect to find no turnout differences between men and women in any of these tables.

Table 13.5 displays a hypothetical bivariate relationship between sex and turnout. According to these data, men vote 11% more than women. The value of tau-b is .12, which indicates some relationship between sex and turnout. Table 13.6 shows the same hypothetical data broken down into three groups based on education. Controlling for education eliminates the relationship between sex and turnout. Turnout rates of men and women are identical for the college educated, the high school educated, and the grade school educated. For each category, the percentage difference between men and women is zero. The association between sex and turnout within each education category is therefore zero. Because no relationship exists between sex and turnout once education is controlled, it is appropriate to conclude that the bivariate relationship is spurious.

TABLE 13.6 Turnout Rates by Sex for Different Educational Levels

	Grade School		High School		College	
	Male	Female	Male	Female	Male	Female
Voted	60%	60%	75%	75%	90%	90%
Did not vote	40	40	25	25	10	10
Total	100%	100%	100%	100%	100%	100%
N (total 1,954)	(150)	(571)	(300)	(350)	(433)	(150)

$\tau\text{-}b = .00$ $\text{t-}b = .00$ $\tau\text{-}b = .00$

$\gamma = .00$ $\gamma = .00$ $\gamma = .00$

$d_{rc} = .00$ $d_{rc} = .00$ $d_{rc} = .00$

$\lambda_{rc} = .00$ $\lambda_{rc} = .00$ $\lambda_{rc} = .00$

SOURCE: Hypothetical.

One might wonder how there could be a turnout difference of 11% in the full table but zero differences within each category of education. Those with low education tend to turn out less, and women are over-represented in the low-education category. Consequently, when one looks at the composite Table 13.5, it appears that women vote less than men. The apparent turnout differences really prove to be educational differences between men and women.

Let's turn now from hypothetical data to real data from the Center for Political Studies, 1972 American National Election Study. Real data are seldom as clear or straightforward as hypothetical data. Table 13.7 shows the uncontrolled relationship between sex and turnout for 1972. (We use 1972 data here because they best enable us to make some important statistical points; the 1992 version of these tables is given as an exercise in Question 3 at the end of this chapter.) The three following tables show the relationship controlled for education.

The turnout difference between men and women with low education is 17% (Table 13.8); the difference was only 6% for Table 13.7. The turnout difference between men and women with high school education (Table 13.9) more closely resembles the weak relationship in the original table; there are about 6% differences in Tables 13.7 and 13.9. The final control table for those in the high-education category (Table 13.10) clearly indicates that education specified the relationship between sex and turnout.

TABLE 13.7 Reported Turnout by Sex for 1972

	Male	Female
Voted	76%	70%
Did not vote	24	30
Total	100%	100%
N (total 2,283)	(975)	(1,308)

$\tau\text{-}b = .07$ $d_{rc} = .06$ $\gamma = .16$ $\lambda_{rc} = .00$

SOURCE: Center for Political Studies, 1972 American National Election Study.

TABLE 13.8 Reported Turnout by Sex for 1972, Grade School Education Only

	Male	Female
Voted	67%	50%
Did not vote	33	50
Total	100%	100%
N (total 440)	(199)	(241)

$\tau\text{-}b = .17$ $d_{rc} = .17$ $\gamma = .34$ $\lambda_{rc} = .00$

SOURCE: Center for Political Studies, 1972 American National Election Study.

TABLE 13.9 Reported Turnout by Sex for 1972, High School Education Only

	Male	Female
Voted	74%	68%
Did not vote	26	32
Total	100%	100%
N (total 1,145)	(413)	(732)

$\tau\text{-}b = .06$ $d_{rc} = .05$ $\gamma = .13$ $\lambda_{rc} = .00$

SOURCE: Center for Political Studies, 1972 American National Election Study.

TABLE 13.10 Reported Turnout by Sex for 1972, College Education Only

	Male	Female
Voted	85%	89%
Did not vote	15	11
Total	100%	100%
N (total 696)	(362)	(334)

$\tau\text{-}b = -.06$ $d_{rc} = -.04$ $\gamma = -.16$ $\lambda_{rc} = .00$

SOURCE: Center for Political Studies, 1972 American National Election Study.

The relationship is moderately positive for those with low education, weakly positive for those with medium education, and negative for those with high education. In 1972, women were less likely than men to vote, but this is true only for those people with less than a college education and mainly for those with only a grade school education. College education proved to be the equalizer: College-educated women tended to vote more than college-educated men. College education apparently compensates for sexual biases in political socialization in the United States. Although we still might not know all there is to know about this relationship, we certainly know more than we did from only the bivariate table.

Incidentally, women no longer vote less than men. The above analysis suggests that the lower turnout of women in 1972 was because of their lower educational level. As the educational level of men and women equalized, one would expect the turnout difference to disappear—and that has been the case. Women now go to college nearly as often as men do, so the association between education and gender has declined. As would be expected, the turnout advantage of men disappeared with the increased education of women. Indeed, Table 13.10 hints that college-educated women might turn out to vote at a higher rate than college-educated men; this hint suggests that women will eventually vote at higher rates than men—which is exactly what the Census Bureau reported for the first time in 1984.

In this example, we examined the effect of sex on turnout while controlling for education. If we were interested in studying the relation of education to turnout, we might instead have examined the bivariate relationship between education and turnout, controlling for sex. Examining only the men in Tables 13.8 through 13.10, we find that men with

TABLE 13.11	Reported Turnout by Sex and Education for 1972			
	Male		Female	
Education	Percentage	Frequency	Percentage	Frequency
Grade School	67	199	50	241
High School	74	413	68	732
College	85	362	89	334

SOURCE: Center for Political Studies, 1972 American National Election Study.

more education voted more in 1972 than those with less education. A similar effect holds for women; in fact, education had a greater effect on turnout for women than for men. Again, the relationship has been specified. Which control is employed depends on our theories and what is being studied—sex differences and conditions that govern them, or education differences and the conditions that govern them.

In some cases, an analyst might want to determine which of a set of independent variables has the greatest effect on a dependent variable. The control data in Tables 13.8 to 13.10 need only be reorganized to highlight whether sex or education had a greater effect on turnout. Table 13.11 and Figure 13.1 show the turnout rates for different combinations of sex and education. The number beside each percentage in Table 13.11 is the number of cases on which it is based according to Tables 13.8 to 13.10. Clearly, education differences had a greater effect on turnout in 1972 than did sex differences. Different combinations of sex and education groups have different effects, however, with sex having greater effects on turnout at lower education levels. This is an example of an **interaction,** in which the variables have separate effects on turnout and also have a combined effect.

Using Additional Controls

Analysis of social science data usually involves using more than a single control variable, either trying a variety of separate controls individually or employing several controls together. If a control for education had not affected the original relationship between sex and turnout, then we would have to think more about why men might turn out more than

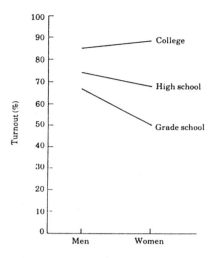

Figure 13.1. 1972 Reported Turnout by Sex and Education
SOURCE: Based on Center for Political Studies, 1972 American National Election Study.

women. For example, we might think that age is involved: Young mothers might turn out less than young fathers, but otherwise there would be no turnout differences between men and women. To test this, we might check whether men and women over age 30 turn out in equal proportions. We would be on the right track if they do (and we would then make further tests), but if not, we might look even harder for another possible third variable explaining the overall turnout differences. We might then hypothesize that women voted less than men because young girls are socialized to the attitude that politics is men's work. We could test this by examining men's and women's beliefs about political behavior.

Another consideration is that several variables might be involved in an explanation of why women vote less than men. Although we have shown examples of one control variable, it is possible to control for more than one variable at a time. For example, we could control the relationship between sex and turnout for both interest in politics and education. If we did so, we would have as many tables as there are pairs of values on the two control variables. The logic of this analysis could be extended to any number of simultaneous control variables, and the number of tables that must be constructed increases geometrically.

It is always difficult to decide which variables to control. Keep in mind several rules that help with that decision. First, control for only those variables related to both independent and dependent variables. Controlling for a variable cannot explain the original association unless it is associated with both. There is no need to try to control on a variable if there is no theoretical reason to expect it is related to either variable. Second, in testing whether a relationship is spurious, control for only variables that occur before both the independent and dependent variables. If the variable is temporally between the two instead of antecedent to both, it cannot explain the original relationship. Studying how such **intervening variables** operate can show how a causal relationship works but cannot render the causal relationship spurious. Third, use well-established theories as much as possible. Consider what variables theories suggest might be important. In particular, what variables might precede (and therefore be able to cause) the independent variable?

In this chapter, you have seen the reason why looking at two-variable relationships is only the beginning of data analysis. The apparent effect of one variable on another can change considerably when other variables are added to specify the causal process more completely.

SUMMARY

Sometimes, a relationship between two variables is spurious; both are caused by some third variable. One way to test for spuriousness is to control on a third variable, a potential cause, and see whether the relationship in the separate control tables is reduced. Before claiming that one variable causes another, it is important to control on third variables that might render that causal claim spurious.

Further Reading

Controls

Rosenberg, M. (1968). *The logic of survey analysis.* New York: Basic Books.

☑ EXERCISES

1. Tables 13.8 through 13.10 show the effect of sex on turnout rates, controlling for education. Use those tables (or Table 13.11) to construct control tables showing the effects of education on turnout, controlling for sex.

TABLE 13.12 Attitudes Toward Women's Role by Age

Role for Women	Age		
	Under 35	35-55	Over 55
Equal role	74%	70%	57%
Neutral	21	25	32
Traditional role	5	4	11
Total	100%	99%	100%
N = 2,370	(846)	(916)	(607)
τ-b = .133	d_{rc} = .112 γ = .236 λ_{rc} = .000		

SOURCE: 1992 American National Election Study.

2. The 1992 National Election Study measured attitudes on the proper role of women. Table 13.12 shows how age affects whether the person tends to favor a traditional role for women or an equal role for women. Education is a particularly useful control when the effects of age are being studied. The younger generation often seems to have different attitudes from the older generation, but

TABLE 13.13 Attitudes Toward Women's Role by Age, Controlling for Education

Women's Role	Grade School Only			High School Only			Some College		
	< 35	35-55	> 55	< 35	35-55	> 55	< 35	35-55	> 55
Equal role	65%	66%	46%	68%	62%	60%	80%	75%	60%
Neutral	22	19	35	28	33	30	16	22	34
Traditional role	13	15	19	4	5	10	4	3	6
Total	100%	100%	100%	100%	100%	100%	100%	100%	100%
N = 2,214	(78)	(82)	(182)	(288)	(281)	(188)	(405)	(494)	(216)
		τ-b = .155			τ-b = .074			τ-b = .138	
		d_{rc} = .152			d_{rc} = .064			d_{rc} = .110	
		γ = .262			γ = .128			γ = .266	
		λ_{rc} = .000			λ_{rc} = .000			λ_{rc} = .000	

SOURCE: 1992 American National Election Study.

TABLE 13.14 Turnout Rates by Gender, Controlling for Education, 1992					
	Did Not Graduate High School		High School Graduate		Some College
	Male	Female	Male	Female	Male	Female
Voted	50%	50%	71%	75%	88%	89%
Did not vote	50%	50%	29%	25%	12%	11%
Total	100%	100%	100%	100%	100%	100%
N (total 2,196)	(162)	(226)	(332)	(423)	(544)	(509)

SOURCE: 1992 American National Election Study.

this may be at least partly because they have more education than the older generation. An education control can reveal whether the supposed generation gap is really an education gap. Table 13.13 restates Table 13.12, controlling for education. Interpret the results. Is there a generation gap in attitudes on this topic, or is it an education gap?

3. The 1992 National Education Study data for turnout by gender with a control for education are shown in Table 13.14. Because education levels in the electorate have changed since the 1970s, results are shown for those without college education, those with some college, and those with college degrees. Interpret the results, with a focus on how they have changed since the 1972 data shown in this chapter.

14 ☑☐ Correlation
☑☐ and Regression

☑ In this chapter, we describe procedures for analysis of relationships among interval- and ratio-level variables. These procedures are the analogues of the techniques for analysis of ordinal and nominal variables discussed in previous chapters.

Simple Regression

Interval-level and ratio-level techniques are more powerful than ordinal-level and nominal-level techniques. They can measure how strongly related a pair of variables are and describe the effect that one variable has on the others. Such techniques can numerically measure the effect of a change in the independent variable on the dependent variable.

Linear Regression

Figure 14.1 illustrates a hypothetical relationship between education and income. Each point in this graph represents one survey respondent. Notice the exact linear relationship: All the points are on a single straight

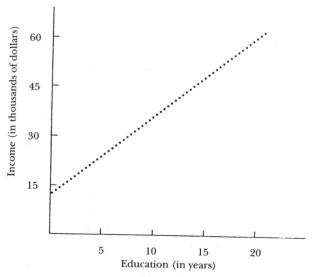

Figure 14.1. Hypothetical Linear Relationship Between Education and Income

line. It is a positive relationship; those with higher amounts of education make greater incomes.

How can the relationship between education and income in Figure 14.1 be summarized? First, we can determine how much of a change in income is associated with a specified change in education. According to the graph, an increase of 1 year in education corresponds to a $2,400 increase in income. For example, those with 13 years of education make $2,400 more than those with 12 years. In statistical parlance, the $2,400 figure is known as the **regression coefficient**—the change in the dependent variable associated with a one-unit change in the independent variable. It is the **slope** of the line—the increase in height corresponding to a one-unit move to the right in the figure.

We can specify the equation of the straight line. People with zero years of education have an annual income of $12,000, according to the figure. Therefore, the equation of the line is:

$$\text{income} = \$12,000 + \$2,400 \times (\text{years of education})$$

Thus, the income of those with 12 years of schooling is $12,000 + 12($2,400) = $12,000 + $28,800 = $40,800. Statisticians call the $12,000 figure the **intercept** of the line—the point at which the value of the dependent variable (income) corresponds to a value of zero for the independent variable (education).

We can summarize how well people's income can be predicted from their education. In Figure 14.1, perfect prediction is possible by using a linear prediction scheme. Statisticians use a **correlation coefficient** to summarize the accuracy of prediction. The correlation is perfect (equal to 1.0) for Figure 14.1 because the points are all along the straight line. It would be zero if education did not predict income at all, and it would be negative if greater education led to lower income. The statistic that is used to measure linear correlation is known as **Pearson's** r. Its square (r^2) indicates the proportion of the variance in the dependent variable explained by the linear prediction from an independent variable. The procedure for calculating Pearson's r is described later in this chapter.

Perfect relationships, such as that found in Figure 14.1, are never found in real data. Figure 14.2 illustrates a more realistic example: As education increases, people generally have a higher income. Even though the relationship is not perfectly linear, you can still seek the best-fitting linear prediction rule. This line has been drawn in Figure 14.2. The figure shows that an increase of 1 year in education is associated with an average increase of $2,400 in income, so the regression coefficient is the same as in Figure 14.1. The intercept is also $12,000, so the equation is identical to that in Figure 14.1. The correlation between education and income is lower, however, because the relationship is no longer perfectly linear. The relationship is still a positive one, but it is much weaker than that in Figure 14.1.

The Procedure for Regression

The best-fitting linear prediction rule estimates the income value for a person with a given level of education. For example, a person with 12 years of education is predicted to have an income of $40,800. The predictions will not be perfectly accurate. As seen in Figure 14.2, a deviation occurs between the actual values and the predicted values. The preferred prediction rule is one that minimizes these deviations so that the predictions are as close as possible to the actual values. Mathematically, one effective means for minimization is to minimize the sum of the squared deviations. This is known as the **least squares** criterion for the best-fitting linear relationship.

Notation. Let's call the dependent variable Y and the score of the person i on that variable y_i (read "y-sub-i"). The mean value of $\overline{Y}$ (Y, "Y-bar") is

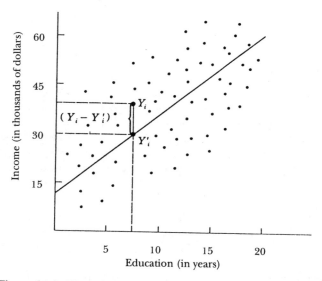

Figure 14.2. Hypothetical Imperfect Relationship Between Education and Income

obtained by summing the set of Y values and dividing by the number of individuals, N; that is,

$$\overline{Y} = \frac{y_1 + y_2 + \ldots + y_N}{N} = \frac{\displaystyle\sum_{i=1}^{N} y_i}{N}$$

where $\displaystyle\sum_{i=1}^{N} y_i$ is the sum of the N observations on Y. (This is read, "the sum of y-sub-i, where i goes from 1 to N").

All summations in this chapter are with respect to i, with i ranging from 1 to N (summing over the individuals), so we abbreviate this notation to just from $\displaystyle\sum_{i} y_i$ (or ΣY). In this system of notation, the mean is

$$\overline{Y} = \frac{\displaystyle\sum_{i} y_i}{N}$$

and the variance of Y is

$$s_Y^2 = \frac{\sum_i (y_i - \overline{Y})^2}{N}$$

Least Squares Criterion. Suppose we want to predict person i's score on the dependent variable (y_i) by using person i's score on some other variable (X). Let y_i' be the value we predict for y_i on the basis of the person's X score (x_i). If we do not predict person i's Y value exactly, there will be some error: ($y_i - y_i'$). We want this error to be as small as possible over the set of individuals. The least squares criterion minimizes the average squared error:

$$s^2_{Y'} = \frac{\sum_i (y_i - y'_i)^2}{N}$$

The equation for the straight line is:

$$y_i' = a + bx_i$$

where a is the intercept, the point on the Y axis at which the line crosses it when X equals zero, and b is the regression coefficient, the slope of the line. Algebra or calculus can be used to obtain formulas for the values of a and b that minimize $s^2_{Y'}$.

There are many ways to calculate the regression coefficient (b) and the constant (a). One formula for b is:

$$b = \frac{N \sum XY - \sum X \sum Y}{N \sum x^2 - (\sum x)^2}$$

When a person's X value equals the X mean, the best prediction for Y is the Y mean. So,

$$Y' = a + b\overline{X} = \overline{Y}$$

As a result, the estimate for the intercept is:

$$a = \overline{Y} - b\overline{X}$$

These formulas are illustrated in Table 14.1.

TABLE 14.1 Computation of Correlation and Regression Statistics

Person	Education (X)	X^2	Income (Y)	Y^2	XY
1	6	36	$11,400	129,960,000	68,400
2	6	36	$27,000	729,000,000	162,000
3	6	36	$40,800	1,664,640,000	244,800
4	12	144	$30,900	954,810,000	370,800
5	12	144	$41,700	1,738,890,000	500,400
6	12	144	$49,800	2,480,040,000	597,600
7	16	256	$41,400	1,713,960,000	662,400
8	16	256	$50,400	2,540,160,000	806,400
9	16	256	$59,400	3,528,360,000	950,400
10	20	400	$44,700	1,998,090,000	894,000
11	20	400	$60,600	3,672,360,000	1,212,000
12	20	400	$74,700	5,580,090,000	1,494,000
Sum	162	2,508	$532,800	26,730,360,000	7,963,200

$$r = \frac{12\,(7,963,200) - (162)\,(532,800)}{\sqrt{12\,(2,508) - 162^2}\sqrt{12\,(26,730,360,000) - 532,800^2}}$$

$$= \frac{9,244,800}{11,920,338} = .776$$

$$r^2 = .776^2 = .601$$

$$r = \frac{12\,(7,963,200) - (162)\,(532,800)}{12\,(2,508) - 162^2} = \frac{9,244,800}{3,852} = 2,400$$

$$X = \frac{162}{12} = 13.5$$

$$Y = \frac{\$532,800}{12} = \$44,400$$

$$a = \$44,400 - \$2,400\,(13.5) = \$12,000$$

$$Y' = \$12,000 + \$2,400X$$

These formulas are fairly complex, and most social scientists use a computer to perform these calculations. Although it is important to understand where the answers came from and how to interpret them, computers spare us the burden of performing the computations.

Degree of Linear Relationship. How well does the linear equation fit the data? The residual variance, $s^2_{Y'}$, gives one indication. Also, we can determine the degree to which we can predict the Y values better knowing X than without knowing X.

If we had no knowledge of a person's score on predictor variables, our best guess of his or her Y score would be the Y mean, $\overline{Y}$. The prediction error for person i would be $(y_i - \overline{Y})$, and the average squared error over the set of individuals would be

$$s^2_Y = \frac{\sum_i (y_i - \overline{Y})^2}{N}$$

which is simply the variance of Y. Had we made any guess other than the Y mean, the average squared error would have been larger, so the mean is our "best estimate" of Y without knowledge of X. If s^2_Y is the average squared error in predicting Y without knowledge of X and if $s^2_{Y'}$ is the average squared error in predicting with knowledge of X, then the proportional reduction in error is

$$r^2 = \frac{(s^2_Y - s^2_{Y'})}{s^2_Y}$$

where r is the correlation between X and Y.

Thus, the square of the correlation coefficient is the proportion of the variance of Y that can be accounted for by linear prediction from X. An r^2 of 1.00 indicates perfect prediction; an r^2 of zero indicates no linear relationship.

Correlation. In Chapter 12, we presented several measures of association that summarized the degree of relationship between two ordinal variables or between two nominal variables. The comparable measure of association between two interval-level (or ratio-level) variables is Pearson's r, the correlation coefficient. It follows the same conventions presented in Chapter 12 for interpreting measures of association:

1. The absolute value equals 1.0 if there is a perfect relationship between two variables—here if there is a perfect linear relationship as in Figure 14.1.

2. The value equals 0.0 if there is no relationship—here if the variables are statistically independent.

3. The larger the measure's absolute value, the greater the relationship.

4. A value greater than zero represents a positive relationship.

5. A value less than zero represents a negative relationship.

The formula for calculating the correlation coefficient r is

$$r = \frac{N \sum XY - \sum X \sum Y}{\sqrt{[N \sum X^2 - (\sum X)^2][N \sum Y^2 - (\sum Y)^2]}}$$

This formula is also illustrated in Table 14.1.

As shown in the previous section, the square of r indicates the proportion of the variance in Y that is accounted for by X. This provides a useful interpretation of Pearson r values. For example, if the correlation is above .7, more than half of the variance of the dependent variable is accounted for by the independent variable. If the correlation is below .3, less than 10% of the variance of the dependent variable is explained by the independent variable.

Regression Residuals. Recall that the regression was designed to minimize the sum of the squared deviations from the regression line. Table 14.2 shows the Y values predicted from the regression equation of Table 14.1 and the deviations between the actual and predicted Y values. These deviations, the $(Y - Y')$ column, are called **residuals.** Table 14.2 gives the $s^2_{Y'}$ value for these data. The r^2 interpretation in terms of the proportional reduction in error gives the same r^2 as in Table 14.1.

The residuals indicate what part of the dependent variable is not explained by linear prediction from the independent variable. If variation in the dependent variable is to be further understood, we must find other independent variables that are correlated with these residuals. For example, if we find that Persons 3, 6, 9, and 12 in Table 14.2 were older than the others and that Persons 1, 4, 7, and 10 were younger than the others, we would conclude that age is correlated with the residuals. Therefore, age should be included as an explanatory variable. Analysis of residuals is useful in deciding whether additional explanatory variables should be included in a model.

Summary. The regression coefficient, b, is the rate of change of the dependent variable (Y) with respect to the independent variable (X); the

TABLE 14.2 Calculation of Regression Residuals

Education		Income		Residual	
Person	(X)	(Y)	Y′	Y − Y′	(Y − Y′)²
1	6	$11,400	$26,400	−$15,000	225,000,000
2	6	$27,000	$26,400	$600	360,000
3	6	$40,800	$26,400	$14,400	207,360,000
4	12	$30,900	$40,800	−$9,900	98,010,000
5	12	$41,700	$40,800	$900	810,000
6	12	$49,800	$40,800	$9,000	81,000,000
7	16	$41,400	$50,400	−$9,000	81,000,000
8	16	$50,400	$50,400	$0	0
9	16	$59,400	$50,400	$9,000	81,000,000
10	20	$44,700	$60,000	−$15,300	234,090,000
11	20	$60,600	$60,000	$600	360,000
12	20	$74,700	$60,000	$14,700	216,090,000
Sum	162	$532,800	$532,800	$0	1,225,080,000

$$Y \text{ variance} = s^2{}_Y = \frac{12\,(26,730,360,000) - (532,800)^2}{12^2}$$

$$= 256,170,000$$

$$\text{Residual variance} = s^2{}_{Y'} = \frac{1,225,080,000}{12} = 102,090,000$$

$$r^2 = \frac{(256,170,000 - 102,090,000)}{256,170,000} = .601$$

correlation coefficient, r, measures how well the data fit the line described by a and b. The square of the correlation coefficient, r^2, can be interpreted as the proportion of the variance of Y that can be accounted for by X.

Interpretation of Regression

Some Cautions. Correlation and regression are based on a linear model, but sometimes there is a nonlinear relation between two variables. Imagine, for example, that people with high levels of education had

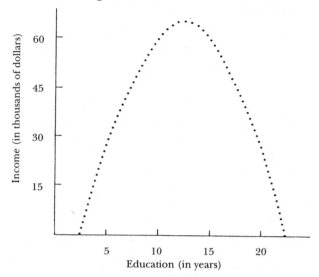

Figure 14.3. Hypothetical Curvilinear Relationship Between Education and Income

difficulty getting jobs because there were more such people looking for jobs than there were jobs suitable for them. The relationship between education and income might then look like the one shown in Figure 14.3. It is a strong predictive relationship, but it is not linear. Pearson's *r* value here would be very small because it measures *linear* correlation. The possibility of curvilinear relationships makes it important to look at the graph of the relationship between the variables, rather than to rely exclusively on the correlation coefficient.

Graphing the data can also help in detecting some undesirable conditions. For example, there might be a strong apparent correlation between the variables only because of one or two measurements. Figure 14.4 shows no correlation for the main cluster of people. However, two people have an unusually high education and unusually high income. This is enough to make the total correlation in Figure 14.4 large. A glance at a graph would be enough to indicate whether an apparently high correlation is caused by a few outliers, as in Figure 14.4.

Significance Tests. Researchers often want to know whether an observed correlation between two variables is totally explained by sampling error. This is equivalent to asking whether the correlation coefficient differs

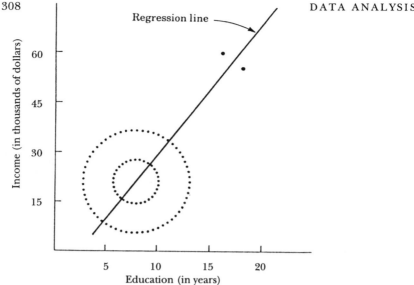

Figure 14.4. Effect of Outliers on Regression

significantly from zero. A correlation of zero would mean that the independent variable does not predict the dependent variable, so the researchers would want to test whether the independent variable has a statistically significant effect on the dependent variable. For example, if we have a simple random sample from a population and we assume that the variables have normal distributions (the bell-shaped form of Figure 10.1), then Table 14.3 can be used to test the significance of the correlation coefficient as a function of the number of respondents on which the correlation is based.[1]

To test whether a correlation is significantly different from zero in the present case, notice that the Nondirectional Test column in Table 14.3 shows the minimum correlation value required for significance (taking no more than a 5% chance of declaring a correlation significant when the population correlation is actually zero). For example, a correlation of .20 would be significant for a sample size of 100, although a correlation of .19 would not be.

In some situations, researchers have good reason to expect that a correlation is positive. For example, although we may be unsure that education has an effect on income, we expect that any effect of education on income is positive. In that instance, the Directional Test column in Table 14.3 is used to determine whether a correlation is significantly

TABLE 14.3 Pearson's r Value Required for Significance ($p = .05$)		
Number of Cases	Nondirectional Test	Directional Test
10	.632	.549
15	.514	.441
20	.444	.378
25	.396	.337
30	.361	.306
35	.334	.283
40	.312	.264
45	.294	.248
50	.279	.235
60	.254	.214
70	.235	.198
80	.220	.185
90	.207	.174
100	.197	.165
150	.160	.135
200	.139	.117
300	.113	.095
400	.098	.082
500	.088	.074
1,000	.062	.052
1,500	.051	.042
2,000	.044	.037
SOURCE: Generated by the authors, using Microsoft Excel.		

greater than zero. This test is less rigorous than the nondirectional or two-tailed test, as can be seen by the fact that .19 correlation is now significantly greater than zero for a sample size of 100. The directional or one-tailed test should be used only when you are sure of the sign of the correlation coefficient before looking at it.

Significance tests are not very useful for large samples, such as those used in most surveys. Recall that the square of the correlation coefficient indicates how much of the variance of the dependent variable has been explained statistically. Table 14.3 shows that, with large samples, a correlation may be statistically significant even though it does not account for much of the variance in the dependent variable. Even when a correlation of .20 is significant, only 4% of the variance is being explained! So, the researcher should not rely on significance tests, but rather should consider how much variance the independent variable explains. For example, the correlation between the arbitrary sequential number of each interview in the computer file and a person's presidential vote in the 1972 American National Election Study was .037, which will occur by chance with 1,582 cases only about 7 times out of 100. The correlation explains a trivial proportion of the variance on the vote (less than 0.2% of the variance), however, and has absolutely no substantive significance. By itself, statistical significance is not a good way to evaluate correlations in large surveys.

The significance tests given here hold exactly only when using simple random sampling, which is not the most common sampling procedure for surveys. In samples using clustering (e.g., most national surveys), the sampling error is almost always larger than for a simple random sample, so correlations larger than the values in Table 14.3 are required for significance.

When a correlation is significant according to Table 14.3, there is no more than a 5% chance that the true population correlation is actually zero. In other words, if a large number of correlations are examined, 5% of them will be significant by chance alone. Therefore, if a researcher generates 100 correlations and finds about 5 to be significant, those significant correlations may be due to chance. This is another reason not to judge the importance of a correlation on the basis of statistical significance alone.

Assumptions. The validity of the results of a regression analysis depends on a number of assumptions about the data. Violating some of these assumptions has little effect on the results, but other assumptions can be critical to an analysis. We describe the key assumptions below.

The most elementary assumption is that the variables must be interval or ratio. It is increasingly common, however, to see applications of interval/ratio statistics to ordinal data in the field of survey research. The critical question is, How great is the risk of faulty conclusions in analyzing ordinal variables with interval statistics? Some authorities claim that too much has been made of the distinction between numeric and ordinal measurement and that this situation does not pose much risk (e.g., Labovitz, 1979), but this point is controversial. There is even some chance of finding a negative correlation when the true correlation is positive (Grether, 1974), or vice versa, although it appears that the practice will not generally lead to faulty conclusions. We remain uneasy about the increased use of interval-level analysis on ordinal data, but we do use an example below in which the measured variable is ordinal, although the underlying variable can at least be viewed as continuous.

The relationship between the variables is assumed to be linear, rather than curvilinear. Another basic assumption is that the complete set of explanatory variables must be included in the regression equation. Of course, there is no way to prove that all relevant variables are included, but theory should be used as a guide in thinking through whether all important predictors have been included. This assumption means that the regression coefficients for a simple regression—with one predictor variable—may be incorrect if other variables that also cause the dependent variable are not included in the regression equation. This is called the **specification** assumption: A regression equation is properly specified only if all relevant predictors are included. This requirement leads researchers to use multiple regression, which we describe below.

The remaining assumptions get more technical. The independent variable must contain no measurement error, or else the estimates of the regression coefficients will be incorrect. In particular, the regression slope will be **attenuated**—closer to zero than it should be.

The regression equation states that the dependent variable Y is a linear function of the independent variable $(a + bX)$ plus an error term (e). The remaining regression assumptions concern that error term, which should have a mean of zero. This assumption is of little practical importance; violating it means that the estimate of the intercept term a is incorrect. The focus, however, is usually on the estimate of the slope term b, which is correct even if this assumption is violated.

For each value of the independent variable X, the variance in the error terms is supposed to be identical. If this assumption is violated, it is necessary to use a different form of regression analysis. To determine whether this equal variance condition, **homoscedasticity,** is met, examine scatter plots of the regression error term against the predictor variable.

In addition, the error terms are supposed to be independent from each other. This assumption is often violated when analyzing time series data. For example, if you were analyzing a time series that shows how a variable changed over time, the errors from one week would likely depend on the errors from the previous week, so this assumption would be violated. In such situations, it is necessary to use a different form of regression analysis to correct for this **autocorrelation** problem.

Also, the independent variable is assumed to be independent of the error term. When this is violated, the regression coefficients are incorrect. Generally, this problem is handled by adding more predictors to the regression equation because the error term becomes independent of the independent variables if all relevant predictors are included. Finally, one must assume that the error term has a normal distribution. This assumption is essential for significance testing but is not critical if the regression equation is being used for descriptive purposes only.[2]

Example. As an example of the use of the one-predictor regression analysis with survey data, we consider the 1992 American National Election Study question regarding the role of women. The question asked respondents to indicate their position on a 7-point scale, ranging from favoring an equal role for women (Category 1) to favoring a traditional role for women (Category 7). This variable could be considered to be ordinal, but we treat it as interval to illustrate regression analysis.

Because the question may reveal a generation gap, the effects of age on attitudes toward the role of women should be examined. The Pearson's r between age and the attitude question is .17. This correlation is very small, but it is statistically significant because it is based on 2,213 respondents. The regression equation is Attitude = 1.502 + .017 age. In other words, 1 year of age changes attitudes toward women .017 units on the 7-point scale. This effect may seem small, but it predicts a difference of .85 between 68-year-olds and 18-year-olds. Older people do have a more traditional image of women's role in society than do younger people, but the difference is slight. Age explains only 3% of the variance in attitudes toward women (r^2 = .0289). There is a generation gap, but it has a very slight impact on these attitudes.

Correlation Matrices

Often, the researcher is interested in the relationships among a whole set of variables. For example, to decide whether different questions on media usage all tap the same thing (Chapter 9), a researcher might examine all the pairwise correlations between questions asking how often respondents follow a political campaign on television and the radio

TABLE 14.4 Correlation Matrix

	Age	Education	Sex	Women's Role
Age	1.000	−.209***	.056**	.170***
Education		1.000	−.093***	−.187***
Sex			1.000	−.014
Women's Role				1.000

SOURCE: 1992 American National Election Study.
NOTE: $N = 2{,}213$
$*p < .05$; $**p < .01$; $***p < .001$.

and in magazines and newspapers. To do so, one would compute the Pearson's r between television and radio use, the Pearson's r between television and magazines, between television and newspapers, between radio and magazines, and so on.

The most efficient way to display this set of correlations is in a **correlation matrix** (Table 14.4). The variables are listed in order on the columns and the rows. The cell entries show the correlations between the row and column variables.

The correlation between watching television and listening to radio may be shown in either the cell for television as the row and radio as the column, or the cell for radio as the row and television as the column, or both. Usually, each correlation is just shown once, so the correlation matrix has the triangular pattern of Table 14.4. Notice that the diagonal cells have 1s in them because the correlation of a variable with itself is perfect.

Finally, we have used a common system to denote which correlations are significant. A single asterisk is used to show that a correlation is significant at the .05 level; there are no more than 5 chances out of 100 of getting correlations this large by chance alone if the true correlations are zero. Two asterisks are used to show significance at the .01 level, and three asterisks are used to show the correlation is significant at the .001 level.

Controls

Correlation does not prove causation. Two variables might be correlated, not because one causes the other, but because both are caused by

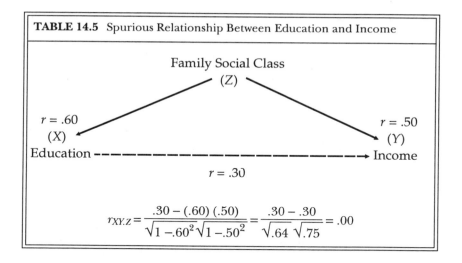

TABLE 14.5 Spurious Relationship Between Education and Income

Family Social Class
(Z)

$r = .60$
(X)
Education

$r = .50$
(Y)
Income

$r = .30$

$$r_{XY \cdot Z} = \frac{.30 - (.60)\,(.50)}{\sqrt{1 - .60^2}\,\sqrt{1 - .50^2}} = \frac{.30 - .30}{\sqrt{.64}\,\sqrt{.75}} = .00$$

the same third variable. For example, why are education and income correlated? Perhaps both are caused by the social class of the person's parents.[3] People who come from an upper-middle-class background may tend to have more education and greater incomes; people who come from working-class backgrounds may tend to have less education and a lower income. Table 14.5 indicates how family social class could cause the relationship between education and income. To determine whether family social class is the cause of the education-income relationship, we would look at the education-income relationship with the effects of family social class statistically removed.

Partial Correlation

How can the effects of a variable be removed from a relationship? The control table procedure in Chapter 13 does so by partitioning the sample into separate groups of respondents with the same value on this variable. The relationship is then examined separately within each group. The regression logic explained in the previous section permits a different approach for numeric data.

If regression is used to predict the person's education from the family's social class, the residuals indicate the variance in the person's education that could not be predicted by the family's social class. Similarly, for predicting the person's income from family social class, the residuals indicate the variance in the person's income that could not be explained by family social class. Having removed the effects of the control variable (family social class) from both variables, we recalculate the correlation between education and income. This correlation between residuals is known as a **partial correlation.**

If education is labeled X, income is labeled Y, and family social class is labeled Z, then the partial correlation coefficient of interest is the correlation of X with Y controlling for variable Z, denoted $r_{XY \cdot Z}$. Although it is equivalent to the correlation of the residuals, this partial is more commonly calculated from a formula involving the pairwise correlations:

$$r_{XY \cdot Z} = \frac{r_{XY} - r_{XZ} r_{YZ}}{\sqrt{1 - r_{XZ}^2}\sqrt{1 - r_{YZ}^2}}$$

In an analogous manner, **higher-order partials** remove the effects of two or more variables from a relationship—for example, between education and income controlling for family social class and age of the respondent.

Comparison With Control Tables

Controls are of three forms: experimental, physical, and statistical. **Experimental controls** are used when a control group is compared against the treatment group to judge the effect of an experimental manipulation. In survey research, respondents may differ on a third variable that can be **physically controlled** by using the control table logic of Chapter 13. The researcher divides the sample into groups based on their value on a third variable and then constructs separate cross-tabulations for each control group. Sometimes, however, some control groups have too few cases to produce reliable control tables. The **statistical control** procedure just described can be used instead: using partial correlations to correct the correlation between two variables for their relationships with control variables. Thus, when the data are interval or ratio, controlling by physically separating the cases into groups as in Chapter 13 is not necessary; partial correlations can be computed instead.

Partial correlations are especially useful in determining whether a two-variable relationship is spurious (see Chapter 13). The relationship between education and income would be judged to be spurious if it could be explained entirely in terms of the two variables having a common cause. In that case, the correlation between education and income would equal the product of the correlations of each of those variables with the third variable, as in Table 14.5. By the formula given above, the partial correlation between education and income controlling for the third variable is zero. Thus, if the original correlation between two variables is large but the partial between them controlling on a third variable is zero, the original relationship is shown to be spurious. If the third variable does not fully explain the two-variable relationship, then the partial correlation coefficient would indicate how related education and income are above and beyond their relationships with the third variable.

The partial correlation coefficient is less useful when a third variable "specifies" a two-variable relationship (Chapter 13). For example, suppose the correlation between education and income was positive for older people but negative for younger people (because young people with college education are still in school or just starting their careers). The partial correlation coefficient does not indicate whether a correlation is different in separate control groups. Instead, the partial correlation between education and income controlling on age would be near zero because it is a weighted average of the correlations for the different age groups.

Multiple Regression

The discussion of causal processes in Chapter 8 emphasized the possibility of several independent variables jointly causing a dependent variable. Perhaps income is a function of both education and age. An older person with a college education probably has more job experience and seniority than a younger person with a college education, so the older person is likely to have a higher income. Thus, a prediction rule is required that takes into account a person's education and age. Figure 14.5 illustrates this model.

The Procedure for Regression

We cannot merely calculate separate single regressions to determine the effect of education on income and the effect of age on income. After all, education and age are likely to be correlated, so part of the apparent effect of education would really be an age effect and vice versa. Instead, we must determine the effect of education on income with age held constant, and the effect of age on income with education held constant.

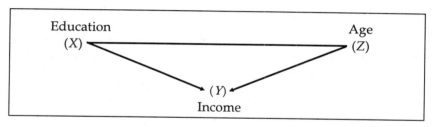

Figure 14.5 Income as a Function of Education and Age

This can be done by regressing residuals. To determine the effect of education on income with age held constant, first predict income from age, then predict education from age, and finally calculate a regression between the two sets of residuals. The resultant partial regression coefficient would give the effect of education on income controlling for age; a similar calculation gives the partial regression coefficient showing the effect of age on income controlling for education. The partial regression coefficients show the rate of change of the dependent variable with respect to each of the independent variables, controlling on the other independent variables.

Rather than computing the residuals and regressing them on one another, **multiple linear regression analysis** is usually used to obtain the partial regression coefficients. Its computations are different from those described in the previous paragraph, but they produce identical results. Multiple regression analysis seeks a linear prediction rule for the dependent variable Y from the independent variables (labeled X and Z), so that

$$Y' = a + b_{YX \cdot Z}X + b_{YZ \cdot X}Z$$

The a is an intercept for the regression, and the b's are partial slopes. In each case, the first subscript denotes the dependent variable, the second the independent, and control variables are listed after the dot.

As in simple regression, the a's and b's are chosen so that they predict the dependent variable, Y, with a minimum squared error; that is, the least squares procedure seeks to minimize the average squared error:

$$s^2 Y' = \frac{\sum_i (Y_i - Y'_i)^2}{N}$$

We do not derive the a and b here, nor do we show their formulas. These calculations are nearly always done on a computer.

As in two-variable regression, we can summarize the extent to which the dependent variable can be predicted from the independent variables with a correlation coefficient. The multiple correlation coefficient is called R, and R^2 gives the proportion of the variance in the dependent variable that can be explained by all the independent variables acting together according to a linear rule. In terms of proportional reduction in error:

$$R^2 = \frac{s_Y^2 - s_{Y'}^2}{s_Y^2}$$

Interpretation of Multiple Regression

Comparing Predictors. A common question in multiple regression analysis is which predictor is more important. This is often difficult to judge from the regression equation, in part, because the different predictors are sometimes measured in different units. In the present example, they are both measured in years, but that would obviously not be true if we were predicting income from education and parents' income. In addition, the different predictors have different amounts of variance. Even though education and age are both measured in years, differences in education (from 0 to 20 years) are much less than the differences in age (from 25 to 65). One year of age may seem to make less difference than 1 year of education, but 40 years of age could have a greater effect than 20 years of education.

A means of comparing the impact of variables measured in different units and with different variances is required. This is done by standardized regression coefficients, often known as **beta weights** (β). Each variable is given the same variance by subtracting the mean from the variable and dividing by its standard deviation. These standardized variables now have a mean of zero and a variance of 1. Once the variables all have the same variance, new regression coefficients are calculated; the resulting beta coefficients indicate the relative importance of the variables. The difference between standardized and unstandardized values depends on the variance of the variables:

$$\beta_{YX \cdot Z} = b_{YX \cdot Z} \frac{s_X}{s_Y}$$

Significance Tests. Tests of the significance of regression coefficients assume that simple random sampling was used and that the variables are normally distributed. The usual test (taking 5% chance of error) is whether the coefficient is at least twice its standard error. This is often expressed in terms of a "t statistic," which should generally be at least 2, or an "F statistic," which should generally be at least 4. More exact probability statements can be made by using special tables, but this rule of thumb is very close for regressions with at least 60 cases. If a coefficient is not significantly different from zero, then the variable can be safely dropped from the regression. The multiple correlation coefficient also has a significance test. If it is not significantly above zero, then the regression exercise has not helped explain the dependent variable.

Some Cautions. The regression approach explained here can encounter a variety of problems. Linear regression cannot detect the curvilinear form of the relationship between a pair of variables shown in Figure 14.3. It also does not detect the "interaction effects" of combinations of independent variables (see page 293), as when education has a greater impact on the income of younger people than of older people. It is possible to use more complex regression approaches, which can take even these factors into account. Doing so requires careful statement of theory in advance.

   Another potential problem is that two predictors can be so highly correlated that their separate effects cannot be distinguished. To use our example, the most extreme case would be if age and education were perfectly correlated so that older people always had more education than younger ones; the effects of age and education could not be separated. You will never find perfect correlations, but if two predictors are correlated at more than .70, their regression coefficients become so unstable that you cannot rely on estimates of them. This condition is known as **multicollinearity.**

Dichotomous Variables. Special problems are created by dichotomous variables. They can be used as predictors by scoring one Category 1 and the other Category 0. This coding produces a **dummy variable.** It is possible to handle nominal variables in a similar way. For example, if there are four categories to region (north, east, south, and west), then three dummy variables can be constructed: (1) north versus (0) rest; (1) east versus (0) rest; and (1) south versus (0) rest. (Why not west versus rest? Because the west is the only region with a score of zero in all the other variables, so its effect is actually the baseline.) These dummy variables

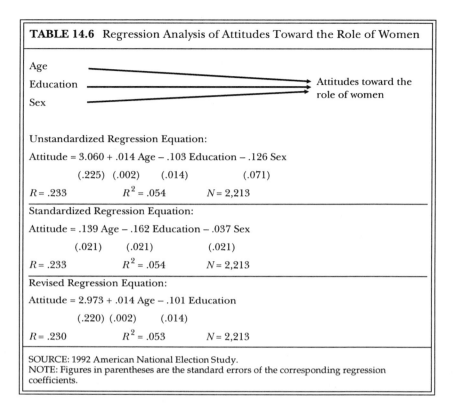

TABLE 14.6 Regression Analysis of Attitudes Toward the Role of Women

Age

Education ⟶ Attitudes toward the role of women

Sex

Unstandardized Regression Equation:

Attitude = 3.060 + .014 Age − .103 Education − .126 Sex

        (.225) (.002)   (.014)   (.071)

$R = .233$ $R^2 = .054$ $N = 2{,}213$

Standardized Regression Equation:

Attitude = .139 Age − .162 Education − .037 Sex

        (.021)   (.021)   (.021)

$R = .233$ $R^2 = .054$ $N = 2{,}213$

Revised Regression Equation:

Attitude = 2.973 + .014 Age − .101 Education

        (.220) (.002)   (.014)

$R = .230$ $R^2 = .053$ $N = 2{,}213$

SOURCE: 1992 American National Election Study.
NOTE: Figures in parentheses are the standard errors of the corresponding regression coefficients.

are included in the regression equation, along with the rest of the independent variables.

Unfortunately, a dichotomous variable cannot be a dependent variable in a multiple regression analysis. The problem is that although the regression approach will predict a large number of values, the dependent variable can only obtain the values of zero and 1. This limitation will inevitably detract from the quality of the regression. Therefore, avoid the usual regression approach with dichotomous dependent variables. Related procedures known as *logit analysis* and *probit analysis* have become popular for analyzing dichotomous dependent variables, but they are beyond the scope of this book.

Example. As an example, Table 14.6 is a summary of the analysis of the question regarding attitudes toward the role of women. High scores on the dependent variable indicate support for a traditional role for women. The independent variables are age, years of education, and sex (coded as dummy variable 0 for men and 1 for women). According to the correlations, older people, people with less education, and men are more likely to support a traditional role for women.

The effects of age and education are statistically significant when comparing the partial regression coefficients with their standard errors, because both are more than twice their standard errors. The respondent's gender does not have a separate significant effect on views toward the proper role of women. The beta weights in the standardized version of the equation reveal that education is somewhat more important than age. There is an education gap, as well as a generation gap.

Because sex effects are not significant, Table 14.6 also includes a recalculation of the regression using education and age alone as predictors. According to the prediction equation, 68-year-old people without any formal education would be expected to have an average score of 3.9 (near the center of the scale), whereas 28-year-olds with 20 years of education would be predicted to have an average score of 1.3 (toward the equal-role end). This analysis accounts for only about 6% of the variance in the dependent variable. Therefore, other variables must be brought into the analysis if we are to understand the determinants of attitudes toward the role of women.

Causal Modeling

The last complication in this introduction to multiple regression is the notion of the complex causal process, which we mentioned in Chapter 8. If the causal process has several elements, then a series of regressions is required. Simultaneous equation methods can handle such cases, and causal modeling and path analysis determine **path coefficients,** which show the relative importance of the various causal paths. We introduce the topic of causal modeling here, although a full description is beyond the scope of this book.

The most important distinction in causal modeling is between **recursive** models, such as that of Figure 14.6, in which the causation is all unidirectional, and **nonrecursive** models, such as the model in Figure 8.1, in which the possibility of reciprocal causation is allowed. The nonrecursive case is the more complicated, in that the analyst must make sure there at least as many equations to solve as there are unknown path coefficients to estimate—known formally as the **identification problem.**

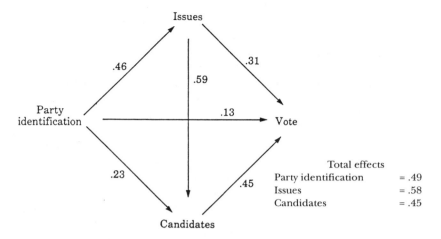

Figure 14.6. A Causal Model of Voting for 1972

SOURCE: Arthur H. Miller, Warren E. Miller, Alden S. Raine, and Thad A. Brown, "A Majority Party in Disarray," *American Political Science Review, 70,* 1976, fn 29. Reprinted with permission of the publisher.

In the simpler recursive case, the path coefficients are similar to standardized regression coefficients.

In regression analysis, we only had to differentiate between the dependent variable and the independent variable. In causal modeling, several variables may be explained in terms of several other variables. Therefore, we designate the variables that are being explained by other variables inside the model as **endogenous.** Variables that cause other variables but whose causes are not included in the model are **exogenous.**

In path analysis, it is essential to map out the entire hypothesized causal process, with arrows drawn for all plausible causal connections. All variables that affect the endogenous variables are to be included in the model, particularly if they cause more than one of the endogenous variables so that the errors in the regression equations for different endogenous variables are not correlated with one another. In nonrecursive models, it is particularly important to include sufficient exogenous variables so that it is possible to solve uniquely the regression equations for the endogenous variables.

An example of a recursive model is shown in Figure 14.6. Candidate orientation had the greatest direct effect on vote for 1972 in this model

(.45); however, because it affects the vote both directly and indirectly, issue position had the greatest total effect (.58).[4]

SUMMARY

Correlation coefficients can be computed to estimate the strength of relations between interval-level (or ratio-level) variables under a linear model. Simple regression shows the effect of one predictor on a dependent variable, whereas multiple regression shows the effects of several predictors with the others controlled statistically.

Further Readings

Regression Analysis

Achen, C. H. (1982). *Interpreting and using regression.* Beverly Hills, CA: Sage.

Berry, W. D. (1993). *Understanding regression assumptions.* Newbury Park, CA: Sage.

Berry, W. D., & Feldman, S. (1985). *Multiple regression in practice.* Beverly Hills, CA: Sage.

Lewis-Beck, M. S. (1980). *Applied regression.* Beverly Hills, CA: Sage.

Schroeder, L. D., Sjoquist, D. L., & Stephen, P. E. (1986). *Understanding regression analysis.* Beverly Hills, CA: Sage.

Tufte, E. R. (1974). *Data analysis for politics and policy.* Englewood Cliffs, NJ: Prentice Hall.

Causal Modeling

Asher, H. B. (1983). *Causal modeling* (2nd ed.). Beverly Hills, CA: Sage.

Blalock, H. M., Jr. (1964). *Causal inferences in nonexperimental research.* Chapel Hill: University of North Carolina Press.

Blalock, H. M., Jr. (Ed.). (1985). *Causal models in the social sciences* (2nd ed.). Hawthorne, NY: Aldine.

Advanced Statistics

Berry, W. D., & Lewis-Beck, M. S. (1986). *New tools for social scientists.* Beverly Hills, CA: Sage.

Hanushek, E. A., & Jackson, J. E. (1977). *Statistical methods for social scientists.* San Diego: Academic Press.

Notes

1. For two-variable relationships, the significance test for correlation coefficients given here is equivalent to testing the significance of the regression coefficient b.

2. Excellent discussions of the assumptions underlying regression analysis are provided by Lewis-Beck (1980, pp. 26-30) and Berry (1993).

3. Assume that we have an interval-level measure of parents' social class.

4. For an explanation of the measures used here, see A. Miller, Miller, Raine, and Brown (1976, p. 769).

☑ EXERCISES

1. A correlation of .30 means that the independent variable explains ____ % of the variance in the dependent variable.

2. A correlation of .10 is significant in a large survey. This means

   a. the relationship between the variables is important enough to study further.

   b. the true correlation is within .10 of the sample correlation.

   c. 10% of the variance is explained by the relationship.

   d. even if the relationship is too small to be very important, the relationship between the variables in the sample is more than sampling error can explain.

   e. none of the above.

3. The regression coefficient (b) in a single-predictor regression equation is found to equal .50. That means

   a. the independent variable explains 25% of the variance in the dependent variable.

   b. a one-unit change in the independent variable induces a half-unit change in the dependent variable when the effects of the other variables are controlled.

   c. the relationship is statistically significant.

   d. the correlation between the two variables is less than 1.0.

   e. none of the above.

4. Which variable is more important in the regression equation $Y' = 1,200 + 15$ (years of education) $- 9$ (years of age)?

P A R T

3

SURVEY GUIDELINES

15 ☑☐ Writing Survey
☐☑ Reports

☑ In this final part of the book, we consider some general guidelines for survey research: guidelines about how to write reports of survey analysis, guidelines about how to read and evaluate reports of polls, and guidelines about the ethics of survey research.

The final stage of survey research is writing a report. Reporting research results is important because it permits others to make use of the findings and can suggest the directions that future research should take. There is no single correct way to write a report; different authors use different approaches, all of which are valid. Different approaches for writing research reports are also appropriate for different audiences—for professors reading class term paper assignments, for readers of scholarly journals and books, and for clients who commission surveys. What is important is that the details of the survey procedure and results be clearly communicated to the readers. In this chapter, we suggest that when you prepare to write a research report, you think about the scope of the report, its organization, and its style.

Scope

Survey reports for commercial polls are usually exhaustive, providing a great deal of information to the client. By contrast, a relatively brief report (e.g., term paper, journal article, newspaper story) cannot address every question that can be asked in a field of study. It is best, in such situations, to limit the **scope** of your work; a more complete treatment of a narrow topic succeeds better than an incomplete treatment of a huge topic. Also, a concrete contribution to a field is more useful than a disjointed set of comments.

Choice of Topic

The scope of a report is partly established when the topic is chosen. Suppose you wanted to report the results of a survey of religious groups. First, you must choose between writing a relatively broad report and writing a relatively narrow one. A broad report might contrast different groups, such as Protestants and Catholics, in terms of their political attitudes. Such a report, however, would probably find relatively small differences and would not explain them. Instead, a narrower topic, such as the difference between Protestants and Catholics in terms of their voting behavior in presidential elections, might be indicated, first documenting a relationship and then assessing whether it is affected by a series of controls. This process amounts to testing whether the observed relationship can be explained by a series of alternative hypothesis. For example, voting differences between respondents of different religions can possibly be explained by differences in their educational and social backgrounds. This topic is likely to produce a more interesting report because the controls permit a detailed analysis of causes and effects.

Generally, an analysis of causes is more interesting than a simple descriptive report. One particularly unsatisfactory effort is a report of the attitudes held by a single group, such as one describing the political attitudes of women. Usually, studying the difference between women and men is the primary motivation for such a study. But focusing on a single group of people does not reveal whether their attitudes are distinctive. It may be that the political attitudes of men are identical to those of women. A report that contrasts the attitudes of women and men is better, especially if it then examines the reasons for these differences. A report that addresses different causal explanations is of even greater value.

In choosing a topic, make sure it is one that lends itself to statistical analysis. It is most important that there be some differences among people in terms of the variables of interest. For example, it is difficult to study attitudes toward political protest if almost all respondents share the same attitudes. Similarly, there must be differences in the independent variable if it is to explain differences in the dependent variable. Therefore, examine the marginal distribution of the variables before deciding what can be meaningfully studied.

Do not limit the group in question so severely that statistical controls are impossible. An in-depth analysis of the political attitudes of American Jews by using a regular national survey of 1,500 people would be difficult because the sample is likely to include too few Jews for meaningful analysis with controls. Again, check that a meaningful analysis is possible before committing yourself to a topic.

Research Results

Be careful not to overstate your conclusions. In previous chapters, we explained why it is difficult to document that a relationship between two variables represents the effect of one on the other. We also indicated that the effect of a variable can be gauged accurately only if all relevant predictors are included in the model. Because it is never certain that some predictors have not been omitted from an analysis, any statement about causality must be tentative. In addition, it is important to avoid the temptation to overgeneralize from the results of a survey. For example, you might find that people who attended school longer were more likely to vote in the last presidential election. It would be inappropriate to conclude from this finding that better educated people always vote more often. Different results might hold for different countries and in different years in the United States. It is therefore important to state conclusions in terms of the population and period being studied.

Finding that two variables are not related to one another does not necessarily mean that the choice of topic was poor and that the results are not worth reporting. Science progresses as much by disproving expected relationships as by discovering powerful relationships. Null findings should be reported candidly; there is no need to change the topic. It is also a mistake to examine a series of relationships and report only the strongest ones. The quality of a research report depends on its coherence, its theoretical importance, and the imaginativeness of the analysis, not on whether it documents strong relationships.

Organization

Different research reports have different schemes of organization. Commercial poll reports for clients usually give the results first, with methodological details described in an appendix. Newspaper stories on polls also give results first, with a brief description of the methods appearing toward the end.

Another scheme is very common in academic research. A typical academic report begins with a statement of the problem to be studied, along with an indication of why the problem is important. This is usually followed by a discussion of the results of previous studies in the area, the author's own theory, and the hypotheses that were tested in the research. In some fields, the hypotheses are listed and numbered, but a conversational style is more common in other fields, with the hypothesis developed as part of the presentation of the problem and the theory.

The next major section in most reports is a description of the methodology. This includes sampling details and sample size, interviewing method, questions used, and methods of analysis. The analysis of the data follows. Some authors restate their first hypothesis, discuss their test of it, then move to their second hypothesis, and so on. More common is a conversational approach in which the discussion flows logically, and hypotheses and results are brought up in a flowing, interwoven fashion.

After the analysis section usually come the discussion, conclusions, and summary. These sections review the importance of the results and indicate what future tests would be appropriate. This last point is important. Rarely does any research effort settle all the questions on a given topic. The report presents a summary of the research that has been conducted, and the author can put those findings in perspective by relating them to previous research on the topic. At the same time, it is important that weaknesses of the research be admitted, as it is better for the author to address such limitations than for the readers to notice unexplained limitations of the research. The author can indicate what other topics should be studied, what other ways of studying the topic would be useful, how the research design might be improved in the future, and so on. A final paragraph might restate the most important conclusions of the research effort.

Another requirement of a good research report is originality. Minimally, this entails avoiding plagiarism by putting quotation marks around material taken verbatim from other works, along with giving appropriate citations to sources of that material. Additionally, other people's ideas should not be reported as your own with only minor paraphrasing of their words. Research reports that parrot the ideas of published research are viewed as plagiarism unless full citations are given.

Style

Finally, it is useful to consider the style to be used in technical writing. Research reports usually include many tables and data displays. Most readers find it difficult to read a report that has sentence after sentence of numbers. The use of statistics does not provide an excuse for an unreadable writing style. If anything, the writing of research reports requires an especially engaging writing style because the author must keep the reader's interest while presenting many numbers. The report should be written in a readable style, without permitting the numbers and data displays to detract from the text.

A common error in research reports is trying to impress the reader with too many statistics. It is better to report only necessary and meaningful statistics than to include every one computed in the course of analysis. For example, there is no need to report percentages based on only a few cases; random change of a few responses would affect the result too much for it to be taken seriously. When reporting percentages, do not be unnecessarily precise. To report that 14.31% of the sample has a particular attitude is going overboard. Most survey analysts report only one digit after the decimal point (14.3%) and often just report whole percentages (14%). Do not include every percentage in the text. A few of the more important percentages might be worth mentioning in the text, but it is best to provide only a verbal discussion in the text and to report all numbers in tables. Similarly, when reporting correlations, avoid overprecision: A correlation of .5132 is better reported as .513 or .51.

Perhaps it goes without saying, but if you are unsure what exactly a statistic means, do not report it. A reader can usually tell when an author does not understand the correlations being reported and has included them only because the author believes that reporting correlations is good. A report using simple statistics that the author understands is more effective than a report presenting statistics that the author does not understand.

One term to use carefully in research reports is *significant*. Significance has a precise statistical meaning that must be appropriately documented with relevant statistics. If that meaning is not intended, then it is better to say *important* or *consequential*. Reserve the term *significant* for when formal significance tests have been used.

Writing research reports is actually an art. You must develop a readable style and discover how to display data in ways that are easy to understand. Well-planned percentage tables are a good idea, and clear figures and charts can effectively communicate trends and relationships. Do not put 100 tables in a research report, no matter how fond of them you are. A reader will not have the patience to read all of them. Instead of presenting many tables, perhaps one table summarizing the results in each of the separate tables would suffice. Or perhaps a few typical tables might be shown to make the same point as a dozen tables.

A tension often exists in preparing reports of commercial polls. Clients usually want to see simpler statistical presentations than researchers want to provide. Many clients are satisfied with simple statistics—single-variable distributions showing the percentage of people giving each response, along with the percentage distributions for selected subgroups of interest. Researchers, however, often recognize that correlations, regressions, and fancier statistical techniques would better answer the questions that the clients should be asking. Often, researchers report only simple analyses to a client, although they have actually performed more sophisticated analyses to make sure the conclusions are valid. In the end, of course, the client is the final arbiter, but the survey industry may have a duty to help educate clients that other information would be more useful to them.

It is becoming increasingly common to include graphic data displays in research reports. Such graphs are also commonly used in oral presentations of research results in the business world. Many personal computer statistics programs can prepare a variety of figures and charts, including three-dimensional graphs.

Perhaps the simplest way to develop a good style when writing research reports is to refer to the styles of journal articles that you liked and the styles of articles you found boring, and try to emulate the better written pieces. Good guidebooks to successful writing are also available. Research costs a lot of money, and analysis can take a long time; given the expense and effort, it is important to communicate the results in an effective manner. The suggestions given above will help you.

President	Partisanship			
	Republican	Independent	Democrat	Total
Approve	60%	50%	40%	48%
Disapprove	40	50	60	52
Total	100%	100%	100%	100%
Number of cases	(350)	(420)	(630)	(1,400)
$\tau\text{-}b = .153$	$d_{rc} = .135$	$\gamma = .266$	$\lambda_{rc} = .104$	$\tau\text{-}c = .174$

TABLE 15.1 Presidential Approval by Party

SUMMARY

The nature of a report on research involving a survey depends on its audience. In writing an academic report, limit the scope, organize the paper tightly, and do not overwhelm the reader with results.

Further Readings

Writing Style

Becker, H. S. (1986). *Writing for social scientists.* Chicago: University of Chicago Press.
Strunk, W., & White, E. B. (1979). *The elements of style* (3rd ed.). New York: Macmillan.

☑ EXERCISE

Use one or two pages to write up your analysis of Table 15.1. It is a cross-tabulation of respondents' party identification with whether or not they approve of the president's handling of his job. (Assume the president is a Republican.)

16 ☐☑ ☐☑ Evaluating Surveys

☑ Many criticisms have been leveled against surveys. All research techniques have potential problems, and survey research is no exception. Indeed, many people love to hate surveys. Politicians behind in the polls attack them, just as ancient kings turned against messengers who brought them bad news. Two major charges are made of surveys: that they are inaccurate and that they are destructive. We discuss these criticisms in this chapter.

The Accuracy of Polls

You probably have often read newspaper articles describing the results of recent public opinion polls. These polls address such questions as, How is the public evaluating the president's job performance? Who is likely to win the next election? How does the public feel about some current issue? and Is public morality changing or remaining stable?

How seriously should people take the results of surveys reported in the news media? Do they accurately describe attitudes, beliefs, and behavior of Americans? Critical readers of poll results should ask themselves these questions each time they read about a new survey. For some

334

The latest *New York Times*/CBS News poll is based on telephone interviews conducted from last Wednesday through Saturday with 1,190 adults around the United States, excluding Alaska and Hawaii.

The sample of telephone exchanges called was selected by a computer from a complete list of exchanges in the country. The exchanges were chosen to assure that each region of the country was represented in proportion to its population. For each exchange, the telephone numbers were formed by random digits, thus permitting access to both listed and unlisted numbers. Within each household, one adult was designated by a random procedure to be the respondent for the survey.

The results have been weighted to take account of household size and number of telephone lines into the residence and to adjust for variations in the sample related to region, race, sex, age and education.

In theory, in 19 cases out of 20 the results based on such samples will differ by no more than three percentage points in either direction from what would have been obtained by seeking out all American adults.

The potential margin of error for smaller subgroups is larger. For example, it is plus or minus five percentage points for Republicans, Democrats, or Independents taken as a group.

In addition to sampling error, the practical difficulties of conducting any survey of public opinion may introduce other sources of error into the poll. Variations in question wording or the order of questions, for example, can lead to somewhat different results.

Figure 16.1. How the Poll Was Conducted

SOURCE: *New York Times*, February 28, 1995, p. A11. Copyright © 1995 by The New York Times Company. Reprinted by permission.

polls, the answer to the second question is probably yes, whereas for other polls, the answer is probably no. In this section, we describe some problems a critical reader of polls should consider.

Reading Results of Polls

The best reports on polls are the ones that give the most information about how the study was performed. Compare, for example, the report of the gun poll discussed in Chapter 1 with the description of the method used for a poll from the *New York Times* (see Figure 16.1). The first says little about the sampling—only that the results are based on a "nationwide telephone poll of 1,251 adult Americans." The margin of error is not even mentioned. By contrast, the *New York Times* reports the sample size and margin of error, the dates of the interviews, an indication of how the telephone sample was taken (random-digit-dialing with stratification by region), and a description of the procedure for weighting to correct for demographic variation in samples. The *New York Times* clearly presents its poll as one to be taken seriously as hard news, whereas the Associated Press treats its gun poll as merely informative.

Reports of polls rarely provide complete information about the study design, sampling, questionnaire construction, data collection, coding, and data analysis. The less information you find about the details of a study, the more suspicious you should be of its results. Do not just read survey reports passively; ask yourself the questions described below.

Study Design. Who sponsored the study—someone with an ax to grind, or an objective organization? Trust the results more if the sponsor seems objective than if the sponsor might want the results for propaganda purposes. If the sponsor might have some bias, examine the report to see whether the procedures used to conduct the study might have biased the results.

When were the interviews taken? It is a mistake to assume that public attitudes are the same for the present as they were in the past. All sorts of events can change public attitudes, so it is important to determine whether the poll was taken before or after a news event focused public attention on the topic of the study. If the dates of the interviews are not given, assume that the study may be older than it looks and try to remember any news events that might be responsible for the findings of the study.

Sampling. Sampling is one of the most frequent sources of error in survey research. This is partly because of its complex and technical nature but may also be because of a poor sampling design or the sloppy execution of a well-prepared sampling design. Many errors at the sampling stage can be traced to a single problem: sampling without knowing the probability that any given individual will be selected from the population about which the researcher wants to generalize. For example, questioning people who walk down the street in front of a newspaper office does not yield a valid sample of all people living in a city. Each person in the city does not have an equal chance of being in the sample because some types of people may not walk through that part of town. Another example of the same problem is interviewing only Indiana University sophomores when the population of interest is all college students in the country.

The sample must reflect the entire population about which the researcher wants to generalize.

In reading the results of a poll, ask yourself how the sampling was performed. Was it a random sample? If the sampling appears to be a nonprobability sample, think through how the choice of people to interview might have affected the results.

How many interviews were conducted? Were there enough interviews to produce reliable results? Remember that the size of the population has little effect on the number of interviews needed; taking just 500 interviews across the United States provides results that are just as valid as those based on 500 interviews conducted in a city of 300,000 people.

What about the sampling error? Reputable researchers publicize their margins of error. If the margin of error is not reported, it might be because the sampling procedure was not a probability procedure and therefore did not permit its calculation. When enough money is spent on a poll to obtain a large sample with a margin of error of 3% or less, the sponsors are usually proud of their poll and publicize their low level of error. If they do not mention the sampling error, it may be much higher than 3%.

Was the appropriate population sampled? Sometimes, one group of people is sampled although the population of interest is a different group. Always think through whether the sample was of the appropriate group.

Questionnaire Construction. Unfortunately, respondents answer the questions they are asked, rather than the questions they should have been asked. In evaluating a survey, always check to see whether respondents were asked the right questions—questions that truly represent the objectives of the survey. Also, check how the questions were worded. If the wording is not given, that may mean the questions were slanted. If the wording is given, is it clear or ambiguous? Is the wording biased to favor one view over others? Would the "average" citizen have understood it? If the wording seems questionable, do not assume that the exact percentages given are accurate.

It is very difficult to eliminate errors in questionnaire construction. Even after repeated pretesting, when every question appears to be well written, investigators can still discover during the actual interviewing that a question is not eliciting the information they expected.

If a report says that attitudes have changed over time, were the same questions asked at both times? If polls conducted by two polling organizations are being compared, assume the wording differed unless you are told otherwise. Don't believe a report of attitude change if different wording of questions may have been used at different times.

Data Collection. Obtaining the actual interviews is the next stage in a survey and the next source of error. Often, despite a well-designed sampling procedure, the people responsible for executing it do not carry it out in full. For example, a careful sampling of respondents can be undermined if no attempt is made to contact designated respondents who are not at home when the first visit or call is made. The representative nature of the sample will be destroyed as the sample becomes biased in favor of people who are often at home. Check to see whether a response rate is reported, along with an indication of how many call-backs were made.

A relatively rare but nonetheless serious source of error is faked interviews. A similar problem occurs when the wrong person in a household is interviewed. This error usually happens because the interviewer hurries and does not exactly follow the instructions for respondent selection. Again, this behavior can introduce error into the survey.

Refusals are another source of error at this stage. People who refuse to be interviewed are probably less cooperative in general than those who agree to be interviewed. Additional biases may result from other differences between those who refuse to be interviewed and those who do not. It is necessary to know the refusal rate of a survey in order to determine how serious the refusal problem is for that survey. The results of a survey with a high refusal rate should not be generalized to the population of interest without extreme caution.

The interviewing process can introduce bias. Generally, you can expect little interviewing error on surveys conducted by professional interviewers because of their greater experience in dealing with difficult situations and in eliciting respondent cooperation. Professionals have less difficulty obtaining interviews, are usually well trained, and have the skills necessary to communicate to respondents that there are no correct answers to attitude questions. When you are deciding how much to rely on a particular survey, ask, Who did the interviewing? How were they trained? and How much experience have they had?

In evaluating a poll, ask yourself, Who did the polling—a fly-by-night, little-known operation, or a reputable polling organization? Most reputable polling organizations belong to the American Association of Public Opinion Research (AAPOR). When they join, members subscribe to a code of ethical conduct. If the polling operation is inexperienced, its people are less likely to conduct the poll correctly.

If the data were collected in a telephone poll, pay attention to when the interviewing took place. Media reports of polls should give the dates of interviewing. If the interviewing was done all on one day, then clearly interviewers had no opportunity for call-backs, so the sample is biased toward people who are most likely to be at home on that particular day of the week. A survey that was conducted over a weekend should similarly be regarded as suspect because some types of people are unlikely to be at home then. Minimally, surveying over a 4-day period that includes a weekend and some weekdays gives some opportunity to reach different types of people at home. Polls that are in the field for a week to a month are even better in this respect. Of course, the instantaneous impact of particular news events cannot be measured with such a design, but the validity of results is greater.

How were the interviews taken—by mail, by telephone, or face to face? Good polls can be taken by each of these means, but each has potential problems, especially with the response rate. What is the response rate? Beware of the response rates of mail surveys; they are notoriously low. Simply mailing out questionnaires to 1,000 people and tallying the replies that happen to come back is not good polling.

Coding. The next stage at which errors can arise is the coding process. On the one hand, coding is a relatively simple process for closed-ended questions and may therefore be boring to execute. As a result, it may be subject to the same kinds of errors that occur in any boring work. On the other hand, coding for open-ended questions calls for careful judgment about the meaning of respondents' answers. Coders often wonder what a respondent's inflection was when answering the question or wish that the respondent had been asked just one more probe question. In these cases, it is often difficult to classify responses. Two separate sets of coders sometimes code the same questions; this carefulness allows the reliability of the coders' decisions to be assessed. This technique is costly, but it allows investigators to determine the quality of the coding. If too many disagreements arise between coders, a new coding system must be devised.

The coding stage is fairly invisible to the reader of poll results. Still, when reading poll results, ask yourself whether the questions were open-ended. If so, does the coding scheme look clear-cut? Are the categories separate enough to make coding easy, or do they seem to overlap? Can you imagine what type of answers would be coded in each? Would any likely answers be difficult to code?

Data Analysis. Was causation adequately tested? Remember that causation is hard to demonstrate. Ideally, alternative explanations should be tested. If only one explanation is given, think through whether some other explanation could also account for a study's findings.

If the distribution of responses on a question is given, do the results look plausible? How are don't-knows and other missing-data categories handled? Was a filtering question used, or were all respondents asked the question? Can you tell what proportion of people gave real answers to the question? Can you tell the intensity of attitudes? Is there any reason to think that people on one side of the issue are more intense than those on the other side, even if they are less numerous?

Are percentages computed in the correct direction? Determine which is the dependent variable and which is the independent variable and be sure that percentages are within categories of the independent variable. If the percentages were calculated in the wrong direction, they may not prove what the author claims they prove.

Are appropriate subgroup comparisons made? If the attitudes of one group of people are being described, check to see whether they are actually different from those of the population as a whole. Reports sometimes focus on one subgroup (e.g., young people), but the results given for that subgroup may be the same as for the rest of the population.

Is the overall sample demographically representative of the population? If not, perhaps the data should have been weighted to correct for accidentally getting too many of one group in the sample. Is there any clue that the data were already weighted? Weighting can be completely legitimate, but sometimes it is used to cover serious sampling problems.

Conclusions. All in all, the best posture for reading reports of polls is suspicion. Don't believe the results just because the author wants you to; consider how good polls are supposed to be conducted and see whether the poll being reported measures up. If it does, the results can be taken seriously; if not, or if you cannot tell, treat the report as suggestive but not conclusive. It is possible to conduct a high-quality poll, but do not presume that every poll is of high quality.

In reading a report of a poll, remember the steps involved in conducting a good survey and think through whether you are being told enough to be sure those steps were followed. Many good polls are reported, but many bad polls are also reported, so do not automatically accept poll reports as scientific truth.

_____

Execution Errors in Surveys

Reports of surveys in the media generally give the study's margin of error. Rather than reassure readers, this information often makes them suspicious. Some readers view the sampling error as evidence the poll results are always wrong, whereas others do not believe it is possible to know how much error is in a survey. The truth is that the sampling error is just one type of error that occurs in surveys. When a news report identifies a 3% margin of error in a poll, all it is talking about is the error due to having interviewed a sample rather than the full population. The margin of error is reported because it can be calculated, but as you have seen, many other possible execution errors cannot be so easily quantified. Sampling error does not take into account the errors in research design, questionnaire construction, interviewing, or coding. As a result, the true level of error in a survey is always above the reported level.

Another way to think about errors in surveys is that sampling error is just the tip of the iceberg. Total survey error (Groves, 1989) also includes coverage error and nonresponse error (Chapter 3), measurement error in the questions and the questionnaire more generally (Chapter 4), respondent effects such as nonattitudes (Chapter 4), interviewer effects (Chapter 5), response effects associated with the choice of mode of data collection (Chapter 5), and sometimes reinterview effects (Chapter 7). A large survey conducted in a sloppy manner could report a small margin of error that would conceal a much larger total survey error.

It is useful to separate the errors in surveys into two categories: (a) random errors that do not bias a survey's conclusions and (b) systematic errors that are likely to bias a survey's conclusions. **Random errors** result from chance, as when a questionnaire is lost or when a coder accidentally writes 3 on a coding sheet instead of 2. Errors of this type can usually be assumed to cancel one another out and therefore do not affect the distribution of responses to questions in any significant way. If the survey has been executed in a particularly sloppy manner, however, random error could be so high as to threaten the results. A survey conducted at an unusually low cost may have skimped on error control and may not give reliable results. Random errors also diminish the apparent relationship of a variable with other variables, so it is important to avoid them as much as possible.

Systematic errors—for example, a high refusal rate among elderly respondents—are even more harmful to a survey's accuracy. Cultural and ethnic biases in a questionnaire are another source of systematic error, as when researchers use a questionnaire developed in the United States in another country without modifying the questions sufficiently to suit the differences in language and culture. When systematic biases occur in a study, all its conclusions must be suspect. There are no easy ways to detect systematic errors. It is often useful to think through the topic of the study to detect any unintentional systematic biases. Also, it is worth finding out who sponsored the study: Did the sponsor have a reason to want particular results? Look carefully for systematic errors.

It is often difficult to gauge how serious these errors are. Because technical details are rarely reported, it is usually impossible to be sure the sampling, interviewing, coding, and analysis were conducted appropriately. The reader is usually forced to trust, on the basis of the survey organization's reputation, that it performed these procedures professionally so that the random error was kept low and no intentional biasing of the results occurred.

With little information about the procedures used in conducting a poll, it is still possible to evaluate its quality by determining whether the results are consistent with relevant evidence from previous high-quality surveys. Do they fit with what is already known? How do the percentages compare with what other surveys have found about the same population? Do the demographic characteristics of the sample resemble what U.S. census surveys indicate they should be? Some of the most important errors in survey research have been discovered by a person who said, "That doesn't look right to me," and who investigated to find out why.

Propriety of Polls

Some critics charge that whatever potential benefits polls have, the costs to society of conducting them are much more significant. According to the critics, reporting the results of polls in the media has adverse effects on the political process. It is important to understand these charges against polls, as well as their benefits.

One charge sometimes made against polls is that they interfere with the political process. Some critics claim that polls interfere with elections by creating bandwagon effects. When the public learns that a particular candidate is ahead in the polls, this argument proposes, some undecided voters jump on the bandwagon and support that candidate. If poll results were not reported in the media, the critics claim, these undecided voters would be forced to study the candidates' views and to make their own decisions.

Consistent with this argument, evidence suggests that a candidate who looks good in polls and in early primaries has an easier time getting people to contribute money to the campaign and gets more attention from the news media. Many candidates have won, however, even though they were behind in the initial polls. In Britain, from the end of World War II through 1980, the party ahead in the polls when the election was called lost support by election day; this finding suggests more of an underdog effect than a bandwagon effect. Indeed, in the 1992 British general election, the Labour Party had the clear lead in the preelection polls but lost the election to the Conservatives. Also, George McGovern won the Democratic Party's nomination in 1972 after defeating the early poll favorites in the presidential primaries. George Bush won handily in 1988 even though Michael Dukakis had nearly a 20-point lead over him in early polls. All of this discussion suggests that candidates often can do well regardless of the polls. Thus, if surveys do have bandwagon effects, they can be counteracted.

Survey results can affect political behavior in other ways as well. For example, polls showing that one candidate is far ahead in a race may deter other potential candidates from mounting campaigns. By many accounts, Nelson Rockefeller chose not to run for president in 1960 and in some later years because he was behind in the polls, whereas an active campaign by him might have changed public attitudes sufficiently to get him nominated and elected.

Polls can also affect voter perceptions of whether it is worth their time to vote. When a race is portrayed as decided long before election day, some citizens may decide not to vote. Voter turnout in U.S. presidential elections has, in fact, declined since widespread publication of preelection polls became prevalent, although there is no way of proving that this is a causal relationship.

Another criticism of polls is a charge by Elisabeth Noelle-Neumann (1984) that polls lead to a "spiral of silence." She argues that people change their attitudes on political issues because they want to have attitudes that agree with the majority. Consider a survey reported in a newspaper that 65% of the nation opposes a national health insurance program. According to Noelle-Neumann, when the 35% of people who favor it read about the poll, they will feel out of step with others. As a result, some of them will change their attitude in order to conform to the majority. Two months later, a new poll in the same newspaper reports that 80% of the nation opposes national health insurance. Now, the remaining 20% of supporters feel even more out of step with the nation, and some of them change their attitudes. This spiraling effect leads, says Noelle-Neumann, to a suppression of minority opinion. If polls were not reported in the media, people might hold more heterogeneous views on political and social issues. Thus, polls may influence processes of public opinion formation and change.

A particularly serious problem occurs when a bad poll affects the course of a political campaign. In 1980, President Jimmy Carter and challenger Ronald Reagan did not agree on terms for a debate until late in the campaign. When the debate finally occurred, the ABC television network ran its own poll. People who thought Carter won were told to call one 900 phone number, and those who thought Reagan won were told to call another 900 phone number. This call-in poll found that Reagan won the debate according to two thirds of those phoning in, whereas a more conventional CBS News poll showed only a 44% to 36% margin for Reagan. The ABC poll was probably one of the worst polls in the history of political polling. Because people were charged 50¢ to phone 900 numbers, this polling procedure discriminated against people who would not or could not pay to register their feelings. Given the time-zone differences across the country, people on the West Coast had more time to phone in their views after the debate than people on the East Coast did—and Reagan had more supporters on the West Coast. Finally, the possibility of a party manipulating the poll by making multiple calls means that this poll may have been rigged. Regardless of these problems, the ABC poll was widely reported and may have affected public perceptions of who won the debate, which in turn could have affected the outcome of the election.

Another criticism of polls is that release of exit poll results during voting hours discourages some people from voting. In 1980, the television networks reported the results of exit polls on the early evening news. The results indicated that Ronald Reagan would win, even though there was still time to vote in most states. As a result of this announcement, Jimmy Carter conceded defeat while West Coast voting booths were still open. This prematurity caused some people in Western states to stay home instead of going to vote. Even if the presidential race was decided, this haste may have affected some close House and Senate races in the West. Several losing Democratic candidates claimed that most of the people who stayed home would have voted for them, so they might have won had this announcement not happened. In part, the fault was Carter's; he need not have conceded while voting was still going on. But it was also irresponsible for the media to report exit polls while people were still voting. The networks appeared to put their desire to be the first to report the election results ahead of the consideration that their behavior might affect the outcome of the election itself.

The 1980 early report led to public pressure on the media to withhold exit poll results until the polls close. Because of this pressure, the networks now withhold reports of the exit polls in a state until its polling places officially close. Often, however, it is easy to tell the results of the exit polls from the network coverage. For example, Dan Rather began the CBS coverage of the 1984 election day returns at 7:30 p.m. Eastern Standard Time, saying, "Good evening, everyone. Can Ronald Reagan make it a 50-state sweep?" He next summarized the electoral vote totals at that moment: 136 for Reagan, whereas Mondale had "zero, none, zip, nada." Then he added, "Walter Mondale has seen the light at the end of the tunnel—and it's out." Switching metaphors, Rather summarized the situation, "If today were a fish, Walter Mondale would throw it back in" (Corry, 1984). People who had not voted yet certainly could have guessed from this performance that network exit polls showed Reagan winning in a landslide, so their votes would not matter. CBS News used projections for states in which polls had closed to declare President Reagan reelected at 8:01 p.m., 2 hours before voting ended on the West Coast. Thus, ethical questions remain about the propriety of such tampering with the basis of democracy.

Although the release of exit polls is controversial in the United States, exit polls can be a useful democratic safeguard in nations where government tallies of votes are suspect. The public may view objective exit polls as more credible than official vote totals. An important case in point comes from the 1994 Mexican presidential election, in which exit polls were permitted as part of an attempt to move to a more credible electoral process (Mitofsky, 1994). These exit polls showed that the ruling party's candidate won the election. Because they were done by objective organizations for the news media, the exit poll projections had more credibility than the official vote count, and they helped give the election results the legitimacy that was lacking in earlier years, when the government was accused of rigging the vote count.

The problems from early release of polls in the United States lead to frequent calls for laws limiting the publication of poll results. Whenever an election result seems to have been affected by poll results, some legislators urge restrictions on publication. One common suggestion is to bar publication of poll results during the week or two prior to an election. Another is to outlaw broadcasting of poll results on election day before all the polls have closed. These suggestions, however, raise some serious questions about the right of the press to freedom of speech. Even if laws were adopted, they could lead to serious abuse if high-quality polls conducted by respected polling organizations were not published while candidates leaked their own lower-quality polls. Perhaps the real value of the continuing calls for official regulation is to make pollsters somewhat more responsible because they realize they could hurt themselves if they act too irresponsibly.

It is worth pointing out that problems with poll publication are not limited to political polls. Reports on other surveys can also have undesirable consequences. For example, publication of a poll documenting the extent of drug use on a college campus could adversely affect public perceptions (and alumni support) of that college. Suppression of such a poll would violate freedom of speech, but publication of the poll might not be necessary. A researcher does not have to seek publication of poll results in local newspapers to gain publicity, particularly if the real purpose of the survey is scientific.

Another problem is that media reports of poll results are often misleading. A survey can document current public attitudes on an issue, but the results may really be meaningless if the public has really reported nonattitudes. A poll might make it seem that a large proportion of the public supports a particular government action when, in fact, the public does not care one way or the other about it. The ethical question is how much attention the media should pay to polls on topics on which the public does not have well-established attitudes. Polls are often meaningless, and misleading publicity for such polls could have adverse effects on the government's decision making.

Susan Herbst (1993) provides an interesting viewpoint on the role of polls with regard to public opinion. She sees polls as symbolic, being used by participants in the political process for their advantage, as when interest groups give publicity to polls when the numbers support their positions. She argues that this use of polls should be considered a case of power and that polling gives more power to groups that can afford polls than to those that cannot afford them. In the end, though, her criticism of polls is that they narrow the range for public debate. Their results often suggest that citizens have made up their minds on an issue when, in fact, opinions are still malleable. Also, closed-ended questions treat only a small number of responses as legitimate, whereas public attitudes might be much more complex. Minimally, it is important that channels for the expression of public opinion (including such avenues as talk radio and electronic mail from the public to leaders) be maintained so that public opinion is not seen as synonymous with polls.

A final charge against the morality of polls is Benjamin Ginsberg's (1986) accusation that polls weaken the role of public opinion, rather than strengthen it. Because polling can be scientific, it now dominates other means of expressing opinions, such as protests, writing letters to public officials, and working through interest groups. Ginsberg argues, however, that polls provide government officials a greater chance to manipulate and shape attitudes than do those other forms of expressing opinions. As a result, Ginsberg concludes, polling has decreased the importance of public views in our democracy.

Ginsberg's arguments are provocative, but we wonder whether U.S. democracy would be better off without polls. Polls allow manipulation of public opinion, but they do answer conflicting claims about what majority opinion is. It is too easy for leaders to claim to speak for a majority when their position is actually a minority viewpoint, and polls help prevent that. We may not always be happy about what the public thinks about an issue, but it is appropriate to know what the real public opinion is—if there is a real opinion.

Importance of Polls

From this discussion, it should be clear that surveys can have a number of undesirable social consequences. Most people would probably argue that these risks involved in collecting survey data should only be taken if the benefits of these data are sufficiently large. And, indeed, some people argue that they are not. For example, critics argue that poll data on public opinion are unimportant because public opinion does not influence anything. Surveys may measure attitudes, these individuals say, but attitudes have no effects. This criticism seems clearly to be wrong, however, because an accumulating body of evidence shows that public opinion does influence what government does. Indeed, surveys are tools that allow social scientists to study the nature and extent of the relationship between public attitudes and government policy (Page & Shapiro, 1983).

A related criticism of polls is that they are not worth conducting because they only confirm common sense. On the contrary, academic surveys have been used to gain insights into voters' psychology, to build theories of voting behavior, to test such theories, to study public attitudes toward wars and presidents, and to gain information about such topics as fertility, religious views, race relations, and the urban community.

Public attitudes are much more complex than one might guess. For example, given that dissent against the Vietnam War was centered on college campuses, support for the war might have been expected to be least among the college educated—but the opposite was the case. Similarly, one might have expected those who thought the war was a mistake to favor withdrawal from Vietnam, but instead they were more likely to favor escalation. These findings are not illogical, but they were unexpected, and they were important because they suggested strategies to opponents of American involvement in the war for persuading others to oppose the war. Because public attitudes are complex and because survey findings often do not confirm common sense, polls certainly seem worth doing.

At the most general level, a democracy must be concerned with what the public thinks, and polls are a good way to measure public attitudes. One might argue that polls should not reign supreme because the public is not fully informed about every issue. Still, it is appropriate for government decision makers to know the shape of public opinion on an issue when they make policy decisions. One encouraging development in recent years has been a growth of polling in East European nations as the Communists lost power and the newly independent democracies became interested in monitoring public attitudes. The point is that public attitudes should be important to decision makers and that polls are a good means of measuring those attitudes. Thus, polls serve extremely important social functions and are beneficial to society, so it is worth guarding against abuse of polls so that everyone can enjoy their benefits.

The argument being made here is that surveys provide one of the truest forms of democracy. This argument is not original; indeed, it was stated with eloquence more than half a century ago by George Gallup as he was embarking on his career in polling. In a lecture at Princeton University on the eve of World War II, Gallup (1939, pp. 6, 14) argued that knowledge of the collective will of the public would increase the efficiency of democracy because "statesmen who know the true state of public opinion can then formulate plans with a sure knowledge of what the voting public is thinking." In the end, the question is how wise are the common people, and Gallup's response was that "the American people have a remarkably high degree of common sense." Individual people may not be fully informed, but democracy trusts the collective judgment. Gallup liked to quote Talleyrand's claim that "The only thing wiser than anybody is everybody." Democracy does not lack disadvantages, nor does polling, but faith in rule by the people requires a healthy respect for the opinions of the public, which can be well ascertained through survey research. Representative democracy tempers those opinions, with elected representatives making policy decisions by using their best judgment, but effective representation requires objective knowledge about what the public really thinks.

SUMMARY

Surveys have been criticized over the years on a variety of counts. It is important to understand the limitations of surveys, as well as their advantages. Surveys can be inaccurate, but at least there are clear guidelines on how to conduct high-quality surveys. In reading the results of a poll, think through its sampling and other factors that could have affected the results. Some errors are random, but systematic errors distort the results. The misuse of polls can distort the political process, which means it is particularly important for polls to be reported appropriately. The importance of surveys can be debated, but we contend that they provide useful information without overly distorting the political process.

Further Readings

Evaluating Polls

Asher, H. B. (1995). *Polling and the public* (3rd ed.). Washington, DC: Congressional Quarterly.

Bradburn, N. M., & Sudman, S. (1988). *Polls and surveys*. San Francisco: Jossey-Bass.

Crossen, C. (1994). *Tainted truth*. New York: Simon & Schuster.

Gallup, G. H. (1972). *The sophisticated poll watcher's guide*. Princeton, NJ: Princeton Opinion Press.

Roll, C. W., Jr., & Cantril, A. H. (1972). *Polls: Their use and misuse in politics*. New York: Basic Books.

☑ EXERCISES

1. In the news section of your local newspaper, find an article reporting on a poll. How complete is the description of the survey procedures? Is the sampling clearly described? Is it obvious what questions were asked? What additional details would you want in order to evaluate the poll?

2. In the features (e.g., entertainment, sports) sections of your local newspaper, find an article reporting on a poll. How does the level of reporting on survey procedures compare with that in the article you found for Question 1?

17 ☐☑ ☑☐ The Ethics of Polls

☑ Concern with the ethics of scientific research has grown in recent years. There is considerable potential for abuse in scientific research in general and in survey research in particular, so it is important to guard against that abuse. Safeguards need not hinder the research process; indeed, they protect researchers who might otherwise not think about the potential for abuse of their work.

Some guidelines have been established to help focus attention on issues of ethics. For example, the federal government imposes limits on the human subjects research it sponsors. Universities must comply with these federal rules because they receive federal funds. As a result, university-based research on human subjects must be approved in advance by a review committee. Ethical guidelines have also been established by several professional organizations, including the American Sociological Association (ASA) and the American Association for Public Opinion Research (AAPOR). The AAPOR Code of Professional Ethics and Practices (see Figure 17.1) is especially important because pollsters wanting to join that society must sign a statement subscribing to its code; most prominent survey organizations are represented in the AAPOR member-

We, the members of the American Association for Public Opinion Research, subscribe to the principles expressed in the following code. Our goals are to support sound and ethical practice in the conduct of public opinion research and in the use of such research for policy and decision making in the public and private sectors, as well as to improve public understanding of opinion research methods and the proper use of opinion research results.

We pledge ourselves to maintain high standards of scientific competence and integrity in conducting, analyzing, and reporting our work in our relations with survey respondents, with our clients, with those who eventually use the research for decision-making purposes, and with the general public. We further pledge ourselves to reject all tasks or assignments that would require activities inconsistent with the principles of this code.

THE CODE

I. *Principles of Professional Practice in the Conduct of Our Work*

A. We shall exercise due care in developing research designs and survey instruments, and in collecting, processing, and analyzing data, taking all reasonable steps to assure the reliability and validity of results.

    1. We shall recommend and employ only those tools and methods of analysis which, in our professional judgment, are well suited to the research problem at hand.

    2. We shall not select research tools and methods of analysis because of their capacity to yield misleading conclusions.

    3. We shall not knowingly make interpretations of research results, nor shall we tacitly permit interpretations that are inconsistent with the data available.

    4. We shall not knowingly imply that interpretations should be accorded greater confidence than the data actually warrant.

B. We shall describe our methods and findings accurately and in appropriate detail in all research reports, adhering to the standards for minimal disclosure specified in Section III.

C. If any of our work becomes the subject of a formal investigation of an alleged violation of this Code, undertaken with the approval of the AAPOR Executive Council, we shall provide additional information on the survey in such detail that a fellow survey practitioner would be able to conduct a professional evaluation of the survey.

Figure 17.1. AAPOR Code of Professional Ethics and Practices

SOURCE: *AAPOR Code of Professional Ethics and Practices.* © 1996, March, American Association for Public Opinion Research, Ann Arbor, Michigan. Reprinted with permission.

II. *Principles of Professional Responsibility
in Our Dealings With People*

A. The Public:

1. If we become aware of the appearance in public of serious distortions of our research, we shall publicly disclose what is required to correct these distortions, including, as appropriate, a statement to the public media, legislative body, regulatory agency, or other appropriate group, in or before which the distorted findings were presented.

B. Clients or Sponsors:

1. When undertaking work for a private client, we shall hold confidential all proprietary information obtained about the client and about the conduct and findings of the research undertaken for the client, except when the dissemination of the information is expressly authorized by the client, or when disclosure becomes necessary under terms of Section I-C or II-A of this Code.

2. We shall be mindful of the limitations of our techniques and capabilities and shall accept only those research assignments which we can reasonably expect to accomplish within these limitations.

C. The Profession:

1. We recognize our responsibility to contribute to the science of public opinion research and to disseminate as freely as possible the ideas and findings which emerge from our research.

2. We shall not cite our membership in the Association as evidence of professional competence, since the Association does not so certify any persons or organizations.

D. The Respondent:

1. We shall strive to avoid the use of practices or methods that may harm, humiliate, or seriously mislead survey respondents.

2. Unless the respondent waives confidentiality for specified uses, we shall hold as privileged and confidential all information that might identify a respondent with his or her responses. We shall also not disclose or use the names of respondents for nonresearch purposes unless the respondents grant us permission to do so.

Figure 17.1. *Continued*

III. *Standard for Minimal Disclosure*

Good professional practice imposes the obligation upon all public opinion researchers to include, in any report of research results, or to make available when that report is released, certain essential information about how the research was conducted. At a minimum, the following items should be disclosed:

1. Who sponsored the survey, and who conducted it.

2. The exact wording of questions asked, including the text of any preceding instruction or explanation to the interviewer or respondents that might reasonably be expected to affect the response.

3. A definition of the population under study, and a description of the sampling frame used to identify this population.

4. A description of the sample selection procedure, giving a clear indication of the method by which the respondents were selected by the researcher, or whether the respondents were entirely self-selected.

5. Size of samples and, if applicable, completion rates and information on eligibility criteria and screening procedures.

6. A discussion of the precision of the findings, including, if appropriate, estimates of sampling error, and a description of any weighting or estimating procedures used.

7. Which results are based on parts of the sample, rather than on the total sample.

8. Method, location, and dates of data collection.

March 1986

Figure 17.1. *Continued*

ship. In this chapter, we describe two broad ethical issues: the rights of respondents and professional practices.

Rights of Respondents

People who contribute their time to talk to interviewers have the right to expect that they will not be personally injured from participation in the project. The injury question is more severe in medical research than in survey research, and it is in the area of medical research that the need for regulation of research practices first became apparent. Ill people are often willing to participate in an experiment in the hope they will feel better, without realizing that the experimental drug or procedure could actually worsen their condition. In a few notorious cases, so-called medical research was performed without the consent of the subjects, such as the inmates of Nazi concentration camps and Japanese prisoner-of-war camps in World War II and the black Alabama prisoners in the 1950s who were not told that treatment of syphilis was being withheld. Reflection on such abuses has led some people to argue that participation in all research should be meaningfully voluntary, where *meaningful* means that the person understands the risks involved in the project before agreeing to participate.

Informed Consent

If participation in surveys is to be meaningfully voluntary, respondents must consent to be interviewed after being apprised of the topic of the research. Thus, survey respondents should give their informed consent before being interviewed (and parents or guardians should give informed consent before children are interviewed).

Survey researchers often believe that compliance with the informed consent rule hinders their research. There are two reasons for this belief. First, stressing the voluntary character of participation in a survey can lower the response rate. The more a researcher reminds people that they need not participate, the less likely they are to do so. The resulting lower response rate makes it more difficult to generalize the survey results to the population of interest. As a result, researchers typically want to underemphasize the voluntary character of participation, mentioning it only briefly while attempting to secure a potential respondent's cooperation. Interviewers generally handle this problem by giving a brief description of the project and by asking the person whether he or she is willing to be interviewed. If the respondent grunts anything that sounds like "OK," the interviewer quickly begins the interview before the respondent can think much more about it.

Informed consent is also problematic because telling respondents about the topic of the survey might lead them to answer questions differently than they would have had they not known the topic. For example, researchers conducting a study of American attitudes toward other countries might not want respondents to be alerted to that focus from the beginning. They might prefer to ask people many general questions to see how often the topic arises spontaneously. The interviewer may be instructed to say that the interview is to be about public affairs generally, without focusing the respondent's attention on world affairs. Stating the purposes of a study in general rather than specific terms is a common way to handle this trade-off of ethical and practical concerns.

Serious ethical problems can arise in research that conceals its purpose from respondents. Using surveys as a guise for observation is especially repugnant. For example, it would be unethical for researchers to claim to interview people about their political opinions when the real purpose is to make observations of people's houses or living arrangements. Similarly, it would be unethical to claim that a survey is intended to measure attitudes on one topic when the real focus of the research is on a different topic. People are suspicious enough of interviewers already these days, so deceiving respondents would only cause more problems for the polling industry. If mild deception seems to be essential, respondents should at least be told the true purpose of the interview when it is over, but it is better to avoid the deception totally.

One topic of frequent controversy is whether respondents have a right to know who is sponsoring a survey. Again, this information can influence whether or not a person is willing to participate in the survey. For example, Democrats might not be willing to participate in a survey sponsored by the Republican Party. If they do agree to participate, they might try to answer so as to skew the results of the survey. In such a situation, the sponsor would obviously be reluctant to have its identity disclosed at the beginning of the interview. Yet, one can reasonably argue that people have a right to know who is going to use their opinions before they decide whether to share those opinions.

Academic researchers generally favor disclosure of the sponsor as part of the introduction and the voluntary consent process, but other survey organizations often avoid such disclosure. The interviewer may be instructed to give the name of the research operation (usually an innocuous-sounding company, like Opinion Research Company), rather than name the financial sponsor if the respondent asks who is conducting the survey.

The ethical guidelines of government and professional organizations differ in how they handle the informed consent issue. Survey research is largely exempt from the federal government's guidelines for research on human subjects, but that exemption would not hold if the subjects were deceived as part of the research. The American Political Science Association has not issued any ethics rulings on informed consent of respondents, nor are such rulings included in the ASA's code of ethics. The AAPOR code states only that members must "strive to avoid the use of practices or methods that may . . . seriously mislead survey respondents," possibly because many polling organizations represented in the AAPOR membership do not want to limit what their interviewers can say to induce the cooperation of respondents.

This lack of emphasis on informed consent in ethical guidelines for survey research makes it especially important that surveys be conducted so as to minimize the potential risks to respondents. In particular, the confidentiality of the responses and treatment of sensitive topics are points of concern.

Confidentiality of Interviews

In many situations, respondents are willing to be interviewed only if they are guaranteed that they will not be quoted directly. One way to ensure this proviso is to keep the interviews totally **anonymous,** meaning that even the researcher does not know the names of the respondents. Such anonymity can be achieved in some surveys, as when an instructor distributes a questionnaire to a class and tells students not to put their names on the forms.

Unfortunately, anonymity often conflicts with other goals of the researcher. In mail surveys, for example, the response rate is typically low at first, so researchers want to prompt those who did not send back the questionnaires. Sending follow-up prompts, however, requires knowing who did and who did not send back the forms. Researchers generally handle this by putting an identifying number on each questionnaire so that they can tell which have not been returned, but that procedure destroys anonymity. Even in telephone and home interviews, researchers often want the names of respondents so that they can check back and be sure the interviews took place to avoid cheating by interviewers. Also, names are necessary if the researcher wants to do follow-up interviewing with the same respondents in the future.

Thus, researchers often do not want to provide complete anonymity to their respondents. Instead, researchers generally guarantee **confiden-tiality** by promising not to identify who made a particular statement even if the researcher knows who was interviewed. Most survey researchers are willing to ensure confidentiality because they want to use their surveys to describe the overall opinions of the public, rather than those of specific respondents.

Interviews are frequently kept confidential by removing identifying materials (names, addresses, telephone numbers) from interview schedules and just identifying them by a unique number. The research office will also maintain a secret file that records which respondents have which identification numbers so that the researcher can get back to the correct interview if it is necessary to check some information. Access to the confidential identification file is usually strictly limited, although its existence could still pose problems, as we describe below.

The rights of respondents to confidentiality extend to publication of the survey results. Respondents should be guaranteed that results will not be released in such a manner that they are **identifiable.** Most survey reports are intended to describe general tendencies, rather than particular respondents. The description of results, however, can sometimes accidentally identify the respondent. For example, a report on interviews with state legislators quoted a "five term majority-party legislator from a western suburb of Pittsburgh who is a lawyer with a degree from a prominent Massachusetts law school." By providing so much information, the respondent was identified as fully as if the lawmaker's name were given. Similarly, publication of survey data in such a way that an analyst can locate the attitudes of the one young black doctor in a northern suburb of Philadelphia who has three children violates the right to confidentiality.

Care should be taken to preclude such identification. In the case of the state legislative interviews, for example, the report could modify nonessential aspects of the person's background so as to camouflage identity. Data should not be published at so low a level of aggregation that individual respondents can be identified. The Census Bureau does not release its results on small areas that would permit such identifications, and surveys often do not include census tract numbers in their data files even if such information is known so as to make identification of individual respondents more difficult.

The ethical guidelines for survey research emphasize the importance of anonymity, confidentiality, and/or non-identifiability. The federal guidelines on human subjects research stress anonymity but exempt most surveys if the responses are recorded in such a manner that the respondents cannot be identified directly or indirectly. Both the ASA and the AAPOR require confidentiality unless the respondents waive it. Thus, signatories to the AAPOR code agree that

> Unless the respondent waives confidentiality for specified uses, we shall hold as privileged and confidential all information that might identify a

respondent with his or her responses. We shall also not disclose or use the names of respondents for nonresearch purposes unless the respondents grant us permission to do so. (p. 353, this volume)

Sensitive Topics

Some survey topics, such as sexual behavior, use of alcohol and drugs, and illegal conduct, are inherently sensitive. Respondents are not reluctant to discuss such topics; researchers have consistently found that people are astonishingly open about them. People apparently enjoy talking with someone who genuinely wants to listen to their ideas and experiences, and so respondents are willing to open up about most subjects when they meet an interviewer who is a trained listener. This tendency has permitted studies of several sensitive topics, such as interviews with people about their sexual behavior and interviews with jailed prisoners during the race riots of the 1960s.

Despite people's willingness to be interviewed on sensitive topics, a remaining issue of the ethics of asking questions may disquiet people. For example, questions about various forms of sexual behavior distress many traditional people. There is no way to avoid this problem completely because even what appears to be an innocent question may distress some respondents. However, the researcher should take care not to distress respondents unduly. Unless they are essential to the purposes of the research, risky questions should not be asked. Indeed, some potential questions raise so many ethical problems that they are better not asked even if that means some of the purposes of the research cannot be fully satisfied.

A more major problem with interviewing on sensitive topics is that respondents might be injured if their responses became public. Imagine that a newspaper publishes a survey detailing the extent of drug use on a campus, after which the local police subpoena the questionnaires to identify those respondents who admitted illegal drug use. The investigators might not want to release their interviews, but ignoring the subpoena would lead to legal action, possibly including imprisonment.

If information on sensitive topics must be gathered, the researcher should attempt to maintain the confidentiality of the interviews by removing identifying materials from the interview schedules. If an identification file is necessary, access to it should be limited, and that file should be destroyed after it is no longer essential. Even this strategy would not fully protect the respondent or the researcher because no legal protection for the interviewer-respondent relationship parallels the protections accorded to lawyer-client and doctor-patient relationships. Just as some journalists have gone to jail rather than identify their sources, so some survey researchers have hit legal problems when their interviews have been subpoenaed, and destruction of evidence is certainly not a complete defense in such cases. One political scientist has served time in jail because he refused to supply his interview data involving the Vietnam War.

Ethics Guidelines

It is useful to see how these problems have been handled in the various research guidelines and ethical codes. In the 1970s, the federal government's requirements for voluntary participation, informed consent, and minimization of risks in human subjects research included survey research. To comply, researchers had to defend any potential harm to respondents in their surveys on the basis of the value of the knowledge to be gained. Universities established human-subjects review panels (often known as "institutional review boards"), and these panels would examine survey questionnaires and procedures before a study could go into the field.

It soon became apparent that these requirements were delaying surveys from going into the field even though surveys generally posed no serious harm, so interviews were exempted from these rules in a 1980s revision of the federal guidelines. Exceptions are surveys on sensitive topics when confidentiality is not assured, surveys involving minors, and surveys involving prisoners. Whether this exemption for surveys is fully satisfactory on ethical grounds remains debatable. Intriguingly, surveys of public officials and candidates for offices are totally exempt from review regardless of the research topic. The federal government still requires approval of questionnaires before the interviews are conducted for surveys carried out under federal contract, which is an extreme form of prior clearance. As another example of strong control over survey content, institutional review boards can force researchers to modify questions they plan to ask of children.

The ASA guidelines emphasize that "research should avoid causing personal harm to subjects used in research." Those guidelines also illustrate the complexity of the dilemma involved in the confidentiality rule for sensitive topics:

> Even though research information is not a privileged communication under the law, the sociologist must, as far as possible, protect subjects and

informants. Any promises made to such persons must be honored. However, provided that he respects the assurances he has given his subjects, the sociologist has no obligation to withhold information of misconduct of individuals or organizations.

The AAPOR code seeks to avoid procedures that may harm or humiliate survey respondents, but that does not fully address the question of surveying on sensitive topics.

The Research Industry Coalition, an industry group in the marketing and opinion research fields, has endorsed statements labeling various practices unacceptable. Soliciting money and selling products or services under the guise of research is deemed unacceptable, as is revealing the identity of survey respondents without their permission.

Professional Practices

The history of science is littered with occasional instances of fraud. The faked fossil skull of Piltdown Man planted by a hoaxer in 1918 and the apparent forgery by British psychologist Cyril Burt of IQ data are but two well-known examples.

Although the perpetrators of these frauds were usually motivated by a desire for personal prestige, they often used their faked data to bolster their side of scientific arguments. For example, Burt claimed high correlations of intelligence scores for twins who grew up separately in order to argue that intelligence is inherited—an argument that often has been used to bolster the theory of genetic inferiority of some races and peoples. Given the possibility that scientific fraud can be used to advance particular arguments and theories, it is important that science be conducted with professionalism, with sufficient information reported about procedures employed in the study so that other investigators can conduct independent replications to confirm the results claimed.

Polls should be conducted with professionalism in accordance with serious concern for data quality, reliability, and validity. Even when a poll has been conducted in a completely professional manner, however, the reporting of the results may not be neutral. Analysis procedures should not be chosen so as to lead to a desired conclusion. Interpretations of the results should be consistent with the findings and should acknowledge the limits of confidence for the data.

Fortunately, the public seems to be aware that it is possible to lie with statistics; this awareness limits the ability to distort poll results. The burden of proof should be on the poll: If it does not report its procedures and does not test alternative explanations of its results, its credibility is in question. In the 1970s, concern about press reporting of polls began to mount, partly because some of the reports seemed inaccurate and partly because some polls seemed poor. The public clearly required more information in order to evaluate press reports of polls, and that need led to the polling industry adopting some disclosure rules.

Disclosure Rules

As emphasized in Chapter 16, when poll results are published, it is important that sufficient information be disclosed so that readers can decide for themselves how seriously to take the results. AAPOR has developed voluntary guidelines for the reporting of polls. These guidelines require that news reports of polls include such information as the name of the sponsoring organization, the dates of the interviewing, the sampling procedure along with sample size and margin of error, and the exact questions asked. These guidelines are policed by the National Council on Public Polls (NCPP). Conformity to these guidelines is voluntary and at best extends only to news reports of polls, but the NCPP does investigate charges against polls and has, on occasion, negated the validity of a poll.

Sponsored Research

A special set of ethical issues is involved in sponsored research. One important issue involves the right to publish from the survey. On the one hand, sponsors have the right to keep confidential any proprietary data they have collected by a private polling firm, and polling firms respect that right. On the other hand, openness should be a criterion for research in universities, so grantors should not be restricting publication on sponsored research in university settings. Prepublication clearance by the sponsor is considered to be a particularly unacceptable practice in academic research. Many universities and professional associations try to insist that surveys conducted for the government be unclassified.

Serious problems also occur when the sponsor tries to affect the research conclusions and when the sponsor tries to conceal its identity. The public has a right to know the identity of the sponsor of a study whose results have been published so that they may judge whether the sponsorship explicitly or implicitly affected the findings. If a private sponsor insists on anonymity, at the very least the nature of the sponsor should be described in general terms so that the reader can tell whether the research was sponsored by a business, a union, a political candidate, or some other type of sponsor.

Fraudulent Polls

Any research technique can be abused, and polls are no exception. A serious case of this arose in the 1996 presidential primary season when Bob Dole was accused of "push polls" before the Iowa precinct caucuses. Voters were phoned as if they were being polled on their views, but supporters of other candidates were asked if they would still support that candidate if they knew particular pieces of damaging information about him. What makes push polls particularly offensive is that the information told to the voters is sometimes false. The polling industry complained vigorously about this misuse of polling technology, fearing it would turn people off cooperating with legitimate surveys.

Limits to Surveys

A final ethical issue is whether the public has the right to know—or not know—some information that can be obtained only from surveys. In taking the census, the government claims it has a right to know the number of people living in an area, and most people accept that claim. Yet, the census also includes questions on many other topics, such as whether the person is a citizen of the country, the person's education, and the quality of the housing. It could reasonably be argued that such questions are beyond the proper concern of the government. The larger issues here are which matters the government has a right to know about and whether these matters extend beyond facts to public attitudes. Does society have a right not to know about certain matters? The fact that information can be collected does not mean that the public should know it, but which matters fall into each domain is a topic of disagreement.

SUMMARY

Ethical problems are involved in all research, including surveys. The survey researcher is not necessarily the best neutral adjudicator of these ethical problems, but inevitably the researcher must make ethical decisions. Minimally, it is important that the rights of the respondents and the rights of the public be consciously considered in planning a survey and in publishing its results. Some would argue that these rights are so important that external imposition of rules for survey conduct and reporting are necessary; others would argue that such rules would infringe on the rights of the researchers and the press. Like all ethical issues, these problems are likely to be debated without easy answers.

☑ EXERCISES

1. Have you ever been the respondent in a survey? If so, do you remember how the interviewer obtained your consent to participate? Were you given a choice, or was your participation assumed? Did you have a clear idea of who sponsored the survey? Did any of the questions bother you as inappropriate or nosy? Were you guaranteed that your answers would be kept confidential? Afterward, did you feel good about having participated in the interview, or did you feel taken advantage of in some way? If you have never been a respondent in a survey, ask your parents whether they have ever been interviewed and ask about their recollections of the experience.

2. Do you think legal limits should be imposed on surveys? For example, should surveys not be permitted on certain topics, or should certain intrusions on a person's privacy not be permitted? Or would you see limitations placed on survey research as an infringement on the right of free speech guaranteed by the First Amendment?

Answers to Exercises

Chapter 1

1. The headline given to this story by the *Columbus Dispatch* incorrectly summarizes the article. The article contains no data on whether guns help people feel safer. The poll shows that people who keep guns are no more likely to feel safe than those who do not keep guns, but this is different from showing whether guns help people feel safer. That would require interviewing people before they bought the guns and again afterward and then comparing to determine whether they feel safer after buying the guns, or at least it would require asking people who have guns whether they feel safer with the guns than if they didn't have any.

Chapter 2

Although there are no "correct" answers to these questions, it might be worth considering the answers given by an early study of this topic (Blumenthal, Kahn, Andrews, & Head, 1972). A survey of men was used, presumably because men are more likely than women to be violent. The sample included rural residents and urban residents, thus allowing comparisons between those groups. Questions were included on different types of violence so that the uniqueness of interracial violence could be studied. Violence was broadly defined to include lawful acts by police (e.g., shooting looters), as well as criminal acts by rioters (which were as diverse as burning a draft card and burning a person). The main differences found in attitudes centered on who was committing the violence—some people approving violence on the part of authorities, and other people approving violence that was intended to yield social change. That is, public attitudes were determined more by who committed the acts than by the degree of violence.

Chapter 3

1. b

2. Nothing; no conclusions should be based on only eight respondents.

3. c

4. b

5. d (This is the definition of sampling error.)

6. 3

Chapter 4

1. A person's education includes the number of years of school completed, the degrees the person earned, and the type of post-high-school education the person had. (This includes the possibility that some people went to vocational schools or business colleges. And it suggests the investigator might want to differentiate between different types of college education because people who went to private or small colleges might have different attitudes from those who went to public or large universities.) There is no single correct way to ask all of this, but it is important to get as much information as possible from the person for later use in the

analysis. (Notice that researchers can find information about the person's college themselves if they get its name, so there is no reason to ask the person its size, quality, or other information of that type.) Below is the wording of the questions used by the Center for Political Studies to measure education. This is only one of many ways to ask the question, but the question series illustrates the complexity of obtaining even factual data.

a.   How many grades of school did you finish?

a-1. (If less than 12) Do you have a high school equivalency diploma or certificate?

b.   Have you had any other schooling? (What was that?) (Any other?)

c.   (If attended college) Do you have a college degree?

c-1. (If yes) What degree(s) have you received? From which college(s)? Where (is that/are they) located?

c-2. (If no college degree) What was the last college you attended? Where is that located?

2. Again, there are many possible ways to phrase a question on this topic. Some major distinctions are between permitting abortion (a) under no circumstances, (b) only for medical reasons, or (c) under all circumstances. Below is one good wording that is used in the National Election Studies. What is most important is to avoid emotionally charged terms (e.g., "killing fetuses," "the woman should control her own body") so that the question wording does not bias the answers.

There has been some discussion about abortion during recent years. Which one of the opinions on this card best agrees with your view?

a. By law, abortion should never be permitted.

b. The law should permit abortion *only* in case of rape, incest, or when the woman's life is in danger.

c. The law should permit abortion for reasons *other than* rape, incest or danger to the woman's life, but only after the need for the abortion has been clearly established.

    d. By law, a woman should always be able to obtain an abortion as a matter of personal choice.

Chapter 5

1. The interviewer should probe to find out what is on the respondent's mind. Is R worried about the possibility of war, upset about U.S. attempts for accommodation with Russia, or what? The response could mean anything. Asking "How do you mean that?" can provide much clarification. Also, the question asked what the most important problems were. After R's initial answer (and probes for clarification), the interviewer should ask, "What do you think are some other important problems facing this country?" or, "Anything else?"

2. The interviewer should repeat the second question or probe in some other way to give the respondent another chance to say more. R's answer so far sounds very much like he or she is just giving the question a moment's thought before answering.

3. As for occupation, the interviewer should probe to find out exactly what the person does. "Engineer" could mean anything from janitor to spacecraft designer. Probes are essential for finding out precisely what a person's occupation is.

Chapter 6

There is no single correct answer, but your answer should take into account a large variety of possible replies to the question, as well as a variety of possible analyses of the question. One possible approach would be to use several short codes on traits of the person named plus a large general code. An example of a short code for sex is:

1. Male   7. Don't know

2. Female   8. Not a person (e.g., Mickey Mouse)

9. Question not asked

The large code would have some general code ranges (e.g., for Democrats, Republicans) and several detailed codes. For example:

000-099.	Democrat
001.	Bill Clinton
002.	Jesse Jackson
003.	Al Gore
004.	Patricia Schroeder
0 . . .	etc.
098.	"Any Democrat"
099.	Some Democrat other than named above
100-199.	Republican
101.	Dan Quayle
102.	Bob Dole
103.	Newt Gingrich
104.	Pat Buchanan
105.	Steve Forbes
106.	Christine Todd Whitman
1 . . .	etc.
198.	"Any Republican"
199.	Some Republican other than named above
200-299.	Nonpolitician (nationally known)
201.	H. Ross Perot
202.	General Colin Powell
203.	Rush Limbaugh
2. . .	etc.
290.	"Anybody but a politician"
291.	A nationally prominent businessperson
292.	A television figure
293.	A religious figure
299.	Other nonpolitician
300-399.	Personal acquaintance
301.	Me (Respondent)
302.	Respondent's spouse
303.	Member of R's family

304.	Friend or neighbor
305.	R's minister, priest, or rabbi
400-499.	Fictitious "person"
401.	Mickey Mouse
402.	Donald Duck
499.	Other fictitious "person"
900-999.	Miscellaneous answers and categories
900.	No one
990.	Someone in other than above categories
998.	Don't know
999.	Question not asked

Chapter 7

1. First, you cannot generalize about young people when the sample is of high school seniors. In particular, dropouts have been omitted from the study. At best, conclusions can be drawn about high school seniors. Also, answers about drug use may not be candid. Some students would not be willing to admit drug use, and many would be unwilling to admit they have not tried drugs. Finally, *drugs* is a very broad term that could include anything from marijuana to heroin (and some would say anything from aspirin to alcohol). The meaning of the question "Have you experimented with drugs?" is not clear.

2. The survey gave members of Congress a very abstract choice. It is very easy for them to claim they follow their constituents' wishes like good public servants. Their answers are not likely to be predictive of how they behave in the case of a real conflict. Presenting the legislators with an actual conflict would yield more meaningful answers.

3. It is probably difficult to code how ideological a given goal is. The intercoder reliability should be checked before believing this result.

Chapter 8

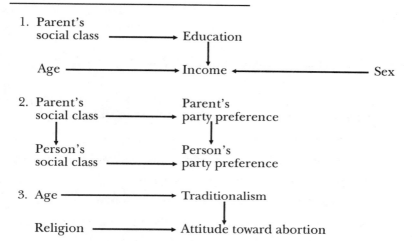

1. Parent's
   social class ⟶ Education
                      ↓
   Age ⟶ Income ⟵ Sex

2. Parent's   Parent's
   social class ⟶ party preference
        ↓   ↓
   Person's   Person's
   social class ⟶ party preference

3. Age ⟶ Traditionalism
                      ↓
   Religion ⟶ Attitude toward abortion

4. a. Interval (or ratio): This is a real number, the units are mean-ingful, and there is a meaningful zero point.

   b. Nominal: These are discrete categories, not in any systematic progression.

   c. Ordinal: These are ordered categories, without meaningful units.

5. One type of error would be convicting a person who is truly innocent (let's label this Type I), and the other would be finding a guilty person not guilty (Type II). Liberals tend to be more concerned with the former and conservatives with the latter. Requiring unanimous juries for conviction minimizes the likeli-hood of convicting innocent people, but there is always a trade-off, so it increases the chances of not convicting guilty defendants.

Chapter 9

1. 1,000

2. 25.0%

3. 40.0%

4. 35.0%

5. "Other party," "not ascertained," and "don't know what parties are."

6. Mode: Democratic; median: independent, assuming that Independents are between Republicans and Democrats.

7. $\overline{X} = 80 \quad s^2 = 100 \quad s = 10$

8. Recode old categories 0, 1, 5, and 6 into new category 2. Recode old categories 2, 3, 4 into new category 1.

9. New category 1 = 1 on both presidential and congressional vote, or

   = 2 on both presidential and congressional vote.

   New category 2 = 1 on presidential vote and 2 on congressional vote, or

   = 2 on presidential vote and 1 on congressional vote.

   New category 3 = 3 on either presidential or congressional vote.

10. Add up the three items so that 3 means three campaign activities, 2 means two campaign activities, 1 means one campaign activity, and 0 means none. Missing data is a problem here. One solution is to give a person a score of 9 for missing data if the person has a 9 on any of the three questions (thus, this is not strictly an additive process). Another possibility is to count the number of campaign activities the person performed and give the score 9 only if the person had missing data on all three questions.

11. Performed all three activities; attended meetings and did party work, but gave no contributions; attended meetings, but did no party work and gave no contributions; performed none of the three activities. No other pattern fits this scale perfectly.

Chapter 10

1. 30.85%

2. a. $z = (95 - 75)/10 = 20/10 = 2$, so .0228

   b. $75 \pm 1.96 \ (10) = 55.4$ to 94.6

3. a. $10/ \sqrt{101 - 1} = 10/ \sqrt{100} = 10/10 = 1.0$

   b. Yes. $z = (78.5 - 75)/1 = 3.5 > 2.58$

   c. $78.5 \pm 2.58 \ (1) = 75.92$ to 81.08

4. a. $10/ \sqrt{26 - 1} = 10/ \sqrt{25} = 10/5 = 2.0$

   b. No. $z = (78.5 - 75)/2 = 1.75 < 1.96$

   c. $78.5 \pm 1.96 \ (2) = 74.58$ to 82.42

5. a. $10/ \sqrt{26 - 1} = 10/ \sqrt{25} = 10/5 = 2.0$

   b. No. $t = (78.5 - 75)/2 = 1.75 < 2.060$, with 25 degrees of freedom

   c. $78.5 \pm 2.06 \ (2) = 74.38$ to 82.62

Chapter 11

1. Education

2. Position on relations with Russia

3. Yes. The percentages are within categories of the independent variable.

4. c

5. More militant

6. Small

7. The number of cases in each educational category

Chapter 12

1. Race is dichotomous (assuming that races other than white and black are set aside because there are too few cases for analysis), and the sign of a correlation between dichotomous variables is essentially meaningless. Therefore, the minus sign does not mean a negative relationship between a person's race and interest in politics. It may mean some relationship between race and interest in politics. The most useful statement, however, would be one that describes the relationship, as by saying which race has (or claims) the greater interest.

2. Religion is a nominal variable (Protestant, Catholic, Jewish, other, none), so a tau correlation should not be calculated. This correlation would make sense if the correlation were computed only on the basis of Protestants versus Catholics (or Christians vs. Jews, or some religion vs. no religion). Otherwise, lambda should be used to match the nominal character of religion.

3. Knowledge of the region in which a person lives yields a 20% reduction in error in guessing the person's vote. A statement of exactly how the regions differ would probably be of more value than this summary statistic.

4. There is a strong tendency for attitudes on abortion and divorce to scale. Yet, gammas can be much larger than taus, so there is no proof of high covariance between these variables.

5. This correlation is very small. Unless the sample is very large, it is not likely to be statistically significant. Even if it is, the correlation is not of major importance. One might believe this correlation if it fits with other known data, but age differences have only a minor effect on attitudes toward divorce, according to this result. One possibility to explore is whether age has a steady effect on the attitude. Perhaps the correlation is so small because young people are more tolerant of divorce than middle-aged people but middle-aged people are less tolerant of divorce than older people. A lambda correlation might test such a possibility.

Chapter 13

1. Reported Turnout in 1972 by Education, Controlling on Sex

	Males			Females		
	Grade School	High School	College	Grade School	High School	College
Voted	67%	74%	85%	50%	68%	89%
Did not vote	33%	26%	15%	50%	32%	11%
Total	100%	100%	100%	100%	100%	100%
N (total 2,281)	(199)	(413)	(362)	(241)	(732)	(334)

SOURCE: 1972 Center for Political Studies, American National Election Study.

2. Age differences occur in Table 13.12, with young and middle-aged people being more in favor of an equal role for women than are older people. Table 13.13 shows that these age differences remain among college- and grade-school-educated people but nearly vanish among the high-school-educated. Notice also that education has an effect on the views of young people, middle-aged people, and older people.

3. Gender did not affect voting turnout in 1992 even with education controlled. Those with more education voted at higher rates, and that was true for both men and women. Unlike in 1972, the differences between men and women in turnout rates were the same at each educational level.

Chapter 14

1. $r^2 = 9\%$

2. d. Statistical significance does not imply substantive significance.

3. e. It means that a one-unit change in the independent variable induces a half-unit change in the dependent variable (when the effects of other variables are *not* controlled).

4. It is impossible to tell from this information. Standardized regression coefficients (beta weights) are required to tell which variable is more important.

Chapter 15

Your answer should point out that, on balance, a majority of Americans do not approve of the president's performance but that the difference is slight and about the size of sampling error. Furthermore, the difference seems mainly to result from (a) greater support for the president among Republicans than among Democrats and (b) the fact that there are many more Democrats than Republicans.

Your answer should indicate that the effect of partisanship on approval of the president is slight. There is an effect, but it is not very large. You might want to quote the tau value, but you can probably make the point more effectively by indicating the 20% difference in support for the president between Republicans and Democrats.

You might also suggest some control variables that would help in testing this relationship. Region is one of the most likely control variables. For example, support for the president might be well above 40% for Southern Democrats although well below 40% for Northern Democrats. Thus, partisanship might have a much greater effect on approval of the president for Northerners than for Southerners.

References

Aldrich, J. H., Niemi, R. G., Rabinowitz, G., & Rohde, D. W. (1982). The measurement of public opinion about public policy: A report on some new question formats. *American Journal of Political Science, 26*, 391-414.

Anderson, B. A., Silver, B. D., & Abramson, P. R. (1988). The effects of the race of the interviewer on race-related attitudes of black Americans in the SRC/CPS national election studies. *Public Opinion Quarterly, 52*, 289-324.

Asher, H. B. (1992). *Presidential elections and American politics.* Pacific Grove, CA: Brooks/Cole.

Berry, W. D. (1993). *Understanding regression assumptions.* Newbury Park, CA: Sage.

Bishop, G. F. (1990). Issue involvement and response effects in public opinion surveys. *Public Opinion Quarterly, 54*, 209-218.

Blalock, H. M., Jr. (1964). *Causal inferences in nonexperimental research.* Chapel Hill: University of North Carolina Press.

Blumenthal, M. D., Kahn, R. L., Andrews, F. M., & Head, K. B. (1972). *Justifying violence.* Ann Arbor: University of Michigan, Institute for Social Research.

Bradburn, N. M., Sudman, S., & Associates. (1981). *Improving interview method and questionnaire design.* San Francisco: Jossey-Bass.

Brehm, J. (1993). *The phantom respondent.* Ann Arbor: University of Michigan Press.

Bunge, M. (1959). *Causality.* Cambridge, MA: Harvard University Press.

Clausen, A. (1968-69). Response validity: Vote report. *Public Opinion Quarterly, 32*, 588-606.

Converse, J. M. (1987). *Survey research in the United States.* Berkeley: University of California Press.

Converse, J. M., & Presser, S. (1986). *Survey questions.* Beverly Hills, CA: Sage.

Converse, J. M., & Schuman, H. (1974). *Conversations at random: Survey research as interviewers see it.* New York: John Wiley.

Converse, P. (1964). The nature of brief systems in mass publics. In D. E. Apter (Eds.), *Ideology and discontent.* New York: Free Press.

Converse, P. E., Dotson, J. D., Hoag, W. J., & McGee, W. H., III. (1980). *American social attitudes data sourcebook 1947-1978*. Cambridge, MA: Harvard University Press.

Corry, J. (1984, November 8). TV: The coverage on election night. *New York Times*, p. A24.

Costner, H. L. (1965). Criteria for measures of association. *American Sociological Review, 30*, 341-353.

Davis, J. A. (1993). *General social surveys 1972-92: Cumulative codebook*. Chicago: National Opinion Research Center.

Dillman, D. A. (1978). *Mail and telephone surveys: The total design method*. New York: John Wiley.

Finkel, S. E., Guterbock, T. M., & Borg, M. J. (1991). Race-of-interviewer effects in a preelection poll: Virginia 1989. *Public Opinion Quarterly, 55*, 313-330.

Fishkin, J. S. (1991). *Democracy and deliberation*. New Haven, CT: Yale University Press.

Fishkin, J. S. (1994, July/August). Britain experiments with the deliberative poll. *Public Perspective, 5*, 27-29.

Fowler, F. J., Jr. (1993). *Survey research methods* (2nd ed.). Newbury Park, CA: Sage.

Fowler, F. J., Jr., & Mangione, T. W. (1990). *Standardized survey interviewing: Minimizing interviewer-related error*. Newbury Park, CA: Sage.

Fox, J. A., & Tracy, P. E. (1986). *Randomized response*. Beverly Hills, CA: Sage.

Fox, R. J., Crask, M. R., & Kim, J. (1988). Mail survey response rate. *Public Opinion Quarterly, 52*, 467-491.

Frankovic, K., & Arendt, C. M. (n.d.). *Interactive polling and Americans' comfort level with technology*. Unpublished manuscript, CBS News, New York.

Gallup, G. (1939). *Public opinion in a democracy*. Princeton, NJ: Princeton University.

Gallup Poll Monthly. (1992, November). Gallup Poll Accuracy Record, p. 33.

Ginsberg, B. (1986). *The captive public*. New York: Basic Books.

Green, D., Kahneman, D., & Kunreuther, H. (1994). How the scope and method of public funding affect willingness to pay for public goods. *Public Opinion Quarterly, 58*, 49-67.

Grether, D. M. (1974). Correlations with ordinal data. *Journal of Econometrics, 2*, 241-246.

Groves, R. M. (1989). *Survey errors and survey costs*. New York: John Wiley.

Groves, R. M., & Kahn, R. L. (1979). *Surveys by telephone: A national comparison with personal interviews*. New York: Academic Press.

Guns don't help people feel safer. (1987, February 2). *Columbus Dispatch*, p. 1A.

Heeringa, S. G., Connor, J. H., Haeussler, J. S., Redmond, G. B., & Samunte, J. E. (1994). *1990 SRC national sample*. Ann Arbor: University of Michigan, Institute for Social Research.

Herbst, S. (1993). *Numbered voices*. Chicago: University of Chicago Press.

Kalton, G. (1983). *Introduction to survey sampling*. Beverly Hills, CA: Sage.

King, G., Keohane, R. O., & Verba, S. (1994). *Designing social inquiry*. Princeton, NJ: Princeton University Press.

Kish, L. (1965). *Survey sampling*. New York: John Wiley.

Krosnick, J. A., & Alwin, D. F. (1987). An evaluation of a cognitive theory of response order effects in survey measurement. *Public Opinion Quarterly, 51*, 201-219.

Krosnick, J. A., & Berent, M. K. (1993). Comparisons of party identification and policy preferences: The impact of survey question format. *American Journal of Political Science, 37*, 941-964.

Labovitz, S. (1979). The assignment of numbers to rank order categories. *American Sociological Review, 35*, 515-524.

Ladd, E. C. (1994, July/August). The Holocaust poll error. *Public Perspective, 5*, 3-5.

Laumann, E. O., Gagnon, J. H., Michael, R. T., & Michaels, S. (1994). *The social organization of sexuality: Sexual practices in the United States.* Chicago: University of Chicago Press.

Levitin, T. E., & Miller, W. E. (1979). Ideological interpretations of presidential elections. *American Political Science Review, 73,* 751-771.

Lewis-Beck, M. S. (1980). *Applied regression.* Beverly Hills, CA: Sage.

Lewontin, R. C. (1995, April 20). Sex, lies, and social science. *New York Review of Books, 42*(7), 24-29.

Lodge, M., Cross, D., Tursky, B., & Tanenhaus, J. (1975). The psychophysical scaling and validation of a political support scale. *American Journal of Political Science, 19,* 611-649.

Martin, E. (1983). Surveys as social indicators. In P. H. Rossi, J. D. Wright, & A. B. Anderson (Eds.), *Handbook of survey research* (pp. 677-743). New York: Academic Press.

Miller, A. H., Miller, W. E., Raine, A. S., & Brown, T. A. (1976). A majority party in disarray. *American Political Science Review, 70,* 753-778.

Miller, D. C. (1991). *Handbook of research design and social measurement* (5th ed.). Newbury Park, CA: Sage.

Miller, G. A. (1956). The magical number seven, plus or minus two. *Psychological Review, 63,* 81-97.

Miller, W. E., & National Election Studies. (1993). *American National Election Studies cumulative codebook: 1952-1992.* Ann Arbor, MI: National Election Studies.

Mitofsky, W. J. (1994, November/December). Electoral credibility was the issue. *Public Perspective, 5,* 17-18.

Moore, D. W. (1992). *The superpollsters.* New York: Four Walls Eight Windows.

Morrison, D. E., & Henkel, R. E. (Eds.). (1970). *The significance test controversy.* Chicago: Aldine-Atherton.

Nederhof, A. J. (1983). The effects of material incentives in mail surveys: Two studies. *Public Opinion Quarterly, 47,* 103-111.

Newsweek. (1995, February 15), p. 32.

New York Times. (1995, February 28). How the poll was conducted, p. A11.

Niemi, R. G., Mueller, J., & Smith, T. W. (1989). *Trends in public opinion: A compendium of survey data.* Westport, CT: Greenwood.

Nisbett, R. E., & Wilson, T. (1977). Telling more than we can know: Verbal reports on mental processes. *Psychological Review, 84,* 231-259.

Noelle-Neumann, E. (1984). *The spiral of silence.* Chicago: University of Chicago Press.

Page, B. I., & Shapiro, R. Y. (1983). Effects of public opinion on policy. *American Political Science Review, 77,* 175-190.

Riesman, D. (1958). *The academic mind.* Glencoe, IL: Free Press.

Schuman, H., Ludwig, J., & Krosnick, J. A. (1986). The perceived threat of nuclear war, salience, and open questions. *Public Opinion Quarterly, 50,* 519-536.

Schuman, H., & Presser, S. (1981). *Questions and answers in attitude surveys.* New York: Academic Press.

Smith, T. W. (1984). The subjectivity of ethnicity. In C. Turner & E. Martin (Eds.), *Surveying subjective phenomena* (Vol. 2, pp. 117-128). New York: Russell Sage.

Sniderman, P. M., Brody, R. A., & Tetlock, P. E. (1991). *Reasoning and choice.* Cambridge, UK: Cambridge University Press.

Squire, P. (1988). Why the 1936 *Literary Digest* poll failed. *Public Opinion Quarterly, 52,* 125-133.

Voss, D. S., Gelman, A., & King, G. (1995). Preelection survey methodology: Details from eight polling organizations, 1988 and 1992. *Public Opinion Quarterly, 59,* 98-132.

Warner, S. L. (1965). Randomized response: A survey technique for eliminating evasive answer bias. *Journal of the American Statistical Association, 60,* 63-69.

Warwick, D. P., & Liniger, C. A. (1975). *The sample survey.* New York: McGraw-Hill.

Weisberg, H. F. (1974). Models of statistical relationship. *American Political Science Review, 68,* 1638-1655.

Wilber, D. M. (1993, May/June). H. Ross Perot spurs a polling experiment (unintentionally). *Public Perspective, 4,* 28-29.

Yammarino, F. J., Skinner, S. J., & Childers, T. L. (1991). Understanding mail survey response behavior: A meta-analysis. *Public Opinion Quarterly, 55,* 613-639.

 Index of Notation
and Statistics

Level of Measurement	Statistic
Nominal (unordered categories)	
Central tendency	Mode, 201
Measure of association	λ (lambda)—predictive, 273-274
Significance test	χ (chi square), 277-280
Ordinal (ordered categories)	
Central tendency	Median, 201
Measures of association	d—predictive, 267-268
	γ (gamma)—scale, 268-270
	r_s—rank orders, 270-272
	τ (tau)—covariation, 266-267
Interval (numeric)	
Central tendency	$\bar{X}$, Mean, 199-201
Dispersion	s, Standard deviation, 204
	s_{diff}, Standard error of the difference, 239-242
	s_m, Standard error of the mean, 227-229
	s^2, Variance, 202-205
	$s_{\hat{y}}^2{}'$, Residual variance, 304
Measures of relationship	r, Correlation, 305
	a, Regression intercept, 300, 302
	b, Regression slope, 300, 302
	β (beta), Standardized regression coefficient, 318
	Partial correlation, 315
	R^2, Multiple correlation coefficient, 304, 318
Significance tests	Correlation, 307-310
	Difference in proportions, 251-253
	Mean, 230-239
	Proportion, 67-73, 74n
	Regression coefficient, 307-310, 319
	Difference-of-means test, 239-242

381

382

Other Statistics

Other Notation

 Index

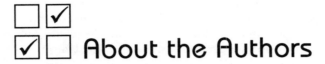

About the Authors

Herbert F. Weisberg, Professor of Political Science at Ohio State University, is Director of the Polimetrics Laboratory for Political and Social Research. He has coedited the *American Journal of Political Science* and is author of the Sage monograph *Central Tendency and Variation;* editor of *Democracy's Feast,* on the U.S. election of 1992; and coeditor of *Classics in Voting Behavior* and *Controversies of Voting Behavior.*

Jon A. Krosnick, Associate Professor of Psychology and Political Science at Ohio State University, is Codirector of the Summer Institute in Political Psychology. He is coauthor of the forthcoming book *Designing Good Questionnaires: Insights From Psychology.* He has published articles on questionnaire design, as well as on public opinion, political attitudes, and the influence of the mass media, in such journals as the *Journal of Personality and Social Psychology,* the *American Political Science Review,* and the *American Sociological Review.* He is editor of *Thinking About Politics* (a book on the cognitive consequences of political expertise) and coeditor of *Attitude Strength: Antecedents and Consequences.* He has taught courses on questionnaire design at Ohio State University, the University of Michigan, the University of Maryland, and the U.S. General Accounting Office.

Bruce D. Bowen is an Executive Consultant in the Internal Consulting Services group at Kaiser Permanente, the nation's largest independent prepaid group practice health maintenance organization (HMO). His duties include working with regional management to develop strategic objectives and business plans, and his work involves developing mathematical models of regional marketplaces that will be used for planning and strategy development in a rapidly changing health care environment. He has taught mathematical modeling, dimensional analysis, research methods, and social science statistics at the University of Michigan in Ann Arbor and at Arizona State University in Tempe, and he has been Manager of Corporate Research and Vice President of Research and Planning at Blue Cross of California. He is also the author of several articles on health care economics and coauthor of two books on survey research and data analysis and serves on the Risk Adjustment Committee of the American Academy of Actuaries.